Time Full of Trial

TIME FULL OF TRIAL

The Roanoke Island Freedmen's Colony, 1862–1867

PATRICIA C. CLICK

The University of North Carolina Press Chapel Hill and London

Designed by April Leidig-Higgins
Set in Monotype Bulmer by Keystone Typesetting, Inc.
Manufactured in the United States of America

The paper in this book meets the guidelines for permanence and durability of the Committee on Production Guidelines for Book Longevity of the Council on Library Resources.

Library of Congress Cataloging-in-Publication Data
Click, Patricia Catherine.
Time full of trial: the Roanoke Island freedman's colony, 1862–1867 / Patricia C. Click.
p. cm. Includes bibliographical references and index.
ISBN 0-8078-2602-2 (alk. paper)
ISBN 0-8078-4918-9 (pbk.: alk. paper)
1. Freedmen—North Carolina—Roanoke Island—History—19th century 2. Freedmen—North Carolina—Roanoke Island—Social conditions—19th century. 3. African Americans—Missions—North Carolina—Roanoke Island—History—19th century. 4. North Carolina—History—Civil War, 1861–1865—African Americans. 5. North Carolina—History—Civil War, 1861–1865—Social aspects. 6. United States—History—Civil War, 1861–1865—African Americans. 7. United States—History—Civil War, 1861–1865—Social aspects. 8. Roanoke Island (N.C.)—History—19th century. I. Title.
F262.R4 C58 2001 975.6′175—dc21 00-069951

05 04 03 02 01 5 4 3 2 1

To the memory of
the men, women, and children who labored
in the Roanoke Island freedmen's colony

We are beginning in the very wilderness, to lay the foundations of [a] new empire, but the results when carried out to their proper results no mortal mind can foresee. We sow in faith, and expect to reap in joy.

CAPT. HORACE JAMES,
Superintendent, Roanoke Island, 5 September 1863

It is with a heart full of gratitude to God that I seat myself to write you this morning. It brings to mind the scenes through which we have passed since the time when my quarterly report ought to have been written—a time full of trial and yet full of joy.

ELLA ROPER,
Missionary Teacher, Roanoke Island, 31 May 1864

These are truly missionaries, and indeed greater ones than many about whom history tells wonderful and famous things.

MAJ. GEN. CARL SCHURZ,
Roanoke Island, 5 April 1865

Contents

Illustrations and Maps

ILLUSTRATIONS

MAPS

Preface

THE STORY OF the Roanoke Island freedmen's colony is one of national significance, yet few people know anything about it. The colony first attracted my attention in the summer of 1981 when, just out of graduate school, I took a summer position as historian-in-residence for the town of Manteo, North Carolina. Manteo is located on Roanoke Island, a sandy, marshy island approximately three miles wide and twelve miles long that lies between the North Carolina mainland and the barrier islands known as the Outer Banks. Roanoke Island is best known as the site of the first English settlements in America, the last of which was known as Sir Walter Raleigh's "lost colony" because of its mysterious disappearance in the 1580s. In 1981 Manteo's energetic and visionary young mayor, John F. Wilson IV, was in the middle of preparing for the 1984 celebration of the 400th anniversary of Raleigh's colonization efforts. He had decided that more of the island's residents needed to become involved in the celebration, and that more than the first few years of the island's history needed to be celebrated. Thus I found myself, early in my summer tenure, sitting across a table from John in the Duchess of Dare Restaurant, the political and social hub of the town. Over a lunch of crabcakes, fries, and slaw, John mapped out his ambitious plans for sprucing up the town and commemorating the island's history. Then, with the combination of charm and directness that I soon realized was key to his many accomplishments, he presented my summer assignment: "I want you to write a history of the colony of former slaves that was established on the island during the Civil War—the Roanoke Island freedmen's colony."

At the time, I nearly went into a panic. What little I knew about the Roanoke Island freedmen's colony came from the general overview that David Stick presents in *The Outer Banks of North Carolina, 1584–1958* (1958). Still, the more I thought about it, the more I grew excited by the project. It was probably fortunate that I did not realize then just how much detective work would be involved in merely scratching out the outlines of the story, and just how challenging the project would ultimately become. For the next three months I devoted myself to uncovering as much as I could about the colony. In a search for some background information on Southern freedmen, I first turned to Willie Lee Rose's classic *Rehearsal for Reconstruction: The Port Royal Experiment* (1964). With both clarity and sensitivity, Rose examines the Reconstruction struggles on South Carolina's Sea Islands, highlighting the various roles of the military, the freedmen, and the Northern missionaries who had come to take charge of the Port Royal Experiment.[1]

Although in many respects the situations on the Sea Islands and Roanoke Island were quite different, Rose's discussion of the role of the various missionary societies involved in the Port Royal Experiment provided the first piece in my somewhat blurry puzzle. I figured that it was likely that some of the societies that had sponsored missionary work on the Sea Islands had also sponsored missionaries to the freedpeople in the Roanoke Island colony. My first major break came when I discovered that several had done so, and that the society that dominated the work on Roanoke Island, the evangelical American Missionary Association, had saved most of the letters that its missionaries wrote to the home office in New York. Further, I discovered that these letters were at the Amistad Research Center in New Orleans, that they had been indexed and microfilmed, and that the University of Virginia owned a copy of the microfilm. I also discovered that I could get my hands on several of the reports that had been written by the colony's superintendent, the Reverend Horace James. I was ecstatic.

I spent a good portion of the remainder of the summer going through the microfilm of American Missionary Association correspondence from North Carolina, reading every letter I could find from or about Roanoke Island. I tramped about the north end of the island in hopes of uncovering some sign of the existence of the freedmen's colony. I enjoyed many wonderful visits in the homes of some of the black islanders, many of them descendants of colonists, and interviewed many of the island's elderly residents in an attempt to uncover oral tradition about the colony. I soon discovered that most of the islanders knew about as much as I did about the colony—which at that time was very little.

I conducted an extensive literature search and discovered that although missionary work among former slaves had not received a lot of attention from scholars in the years since the publication of Rose's study of Port Royal, several historians had just completed studies of relief and educational work. In particular, Jacqueline Jones's *Soldiers of Light and Love: Northern Teachers and Geor-*

gia Blacks, 1865–1873 (1980) offered many insights that were pertinent to the missionary work in the Roanoke Island freedmen's colony. Jones put the work of the Northern teachers who came to Georgia to serve as missionaries among the freedmen in the context of Northern evangelical Christianity, moral reform, and abolition. I was not surprised to find that Jones had concluded that the missionary teachers in Georgia were motivated by evangelical Christianity, and that despite their rather patronizing attitude toward the former slaves, they were genuinely committed to improving the freedpeople's lives. By the time I read Jones's book, my examination of the Roanoke Island missionary teachers' letters had already convinced me that most of them had volunteered for their work on the island in response to deeply felt religious callings, and that they steadfastly believed that they could improve the lives of the freedpeople.[2]

As my summer work in Manteo grew to a close, I realized that the task of writing the history of the colony was much more than a summer's job. To do it justice would require a great amount of research in primary sources, especially in the vast holdings of the National Archives. I decided to write a paper for Manteo presenting a clear overview of the colony's history. The idea was to get people talking; in particular, I hoped that some of the colony's descendants who still lived on the island might uncover more information about the colony. I also knew that eventually I wanted to write a complete history of the colony.

I returned to Charlottesville to commence work on the interdisciplinary faculty of what was then called the Humanities Division of the School and Engineering and Applied Science at the University of Virginia. Like most new faculty, I soon became immersed in a number of research projects related to my pursuit of tenure. Still, though, the freedmen's colony continued to haunt me. Finally, in the spring semester of 1991, nearly ten years after my summer work for Manteo, a research sabbatical sponsored by the University's Sesquicentennial Associateship program provided the opportunity for me to get back to my study of the Roanoke Island freedmen's colony. I devoted that semester to transcribing the letters that the American Missionary Association missionaries had written from Roanoke Island, to outlining my future detective work, and to making some preliminary visits to several archives.

In the ensuing years, a heavy teaching load made it difficult to make much progress during the academic year, but I dedicated my summers to research trips and writing. I soon realized that my brief overview had mushroomed into a study involving the evangelical missionary teachers, the freedpeople, the military, and the white land owners. In fact, the more I researched the Roanoke Island freedmen's colony, the more I realized that it was the product of a complex and intriguing mixture of evangelical, traditional republican, and abolition sentiments that were tempered by the crucible of the military experience. In many respects the work in the freedmen's colony illustrated the limitations of the practical application of ideas that had been simmering in Northern abolitionist and evangelical circles for several decades. It was a local experiment with national implications.

By the time I sat down to write, I had decided that I wanted to share the results of my research with at least two audiences. On one hand, I wanted to bring the story of the Roanoke Island freedmen's colony alive for a broad audience, ranging from descendants of the colonists and Civil War enthusiasts to those with a general interest in North Carolina or United States history. On the other hand, I also wanted to write a book that would add to the growing body of scholarly work on freedmen's camps and the missionary work therein. My great fear was that in trying to reach both audiences, I would please neither; so I decided to devise an effective compromise: an accessible narrative history with extensive scholarly notes.[3]

I establish the historical context of the Roanoke Island freedmen's colony in the introduction, where I present background on the establishment of Southern contraband camps and give an overview of the Northern evangelical Protestantism that provided the impetus for much of the benevolent work among the freedpeople. The introduction also offers a general introduction to the freedmen work in North Carolina and a more specific introduction to the freedmen work on Roanoke Island. After this opening chapter, I do not interrupt the flow of the historical narrative with dissertation-like arguments about conflicting historical interpretations. For readers desiring more in the way of historiographical argument, I do, however, provide extensive endnotes in which I discuss sources, raise occasional questions about scholarly work, and suggest topics deserving future historical exploration. Readers will find that the endnotes also aptly illustrate the historical detective work that was involved in piecing together the story of the freedmen's colony from a variety of primary sources. The narrative history is supplemented with appendices containing primary source material related to the colony and colonists.

As I conducted my research, one ongoing source of frustration was the meager amount of primary source material that offered the point of view of the freedpeople. The best I can do in this preface is to confess that I truly regret the asymmetry of the nineteenth-century voices. I scoured the countryside in search of more material, and I did the best with what I was able to uncover. Nevertheless, given the nature of the existing sources, the book tends to focus more on the evangelical missionary work in the colony than on particular freedpeople.

Throughout the book I try to remain faithful to the language of the nineteenth-century participants. At first the settlement of former slaves or "contrabands" on Roanoke Island was a "camp" similar to others at Union outposts in Southern coastal regions. Then, in the spring of 1863, General John G. Foster instructed the Reverend Horace James to supervise the "colonization" of the island with former slaves. From that point, the military authorities, the missionaries, and the Northern press referred to the result as a "colony." Likewise, they wrote about the "village" that had been laid out in the colony. When talking about the former slaves who lived in the colony, the colonists, teachers, and military occasionally wrote about the "freed people" or "freedpeople," but more frequently used the term "freedmen" to refer to both men and women. When referring to themselves, the teachers preferred the appellation "missionary teachers." Although some historians of freedmen education have regularized the use of "schoolmarms" when referring to the female missionary teachers, that term was never used on Roanoke Island.

Horace James's office was in New Bern, which was spelled variously as NewBerne, New Berne, NewBern, or New Bern. Although I have chosen to use New Bern (the modern spelling for that city's name) when I refer to that city in the narrative, I do not alter the spellings in quoted material. When there seemed to be a consistent nineteenth-century spelling of a place or geographical area, I maintained that spelling. Thus, for example, I refer to Weir's Point rather than Weir Point. Throughout the book, when quoting from primary sources, I present the words exactly as they were written. I do not correct misspellings or capitalization problems, and I leave the punctuation as given. When the punctuation markings appear faint or obscure, I try to be faithful to what I assumed to be the writer's intentions. When I cannot decipher a word, I indicate this fact in brackets. Likewise, when the addition of a letter or word would clarify a sentence, I add such material in brackets. Since it is not easy to reproduce underlining in a printed book, the words that are underlined in the primary sources will appear as italics in the text. To abide by the University of North Carolina Press's editorial guidelines with respect to consistency of form of date notations, I employ the scholarly style (e.g., 31 March 1862 instead of March 31, 1862) in both the text and the endnotes. I do, however, present all dates in quoted material exactly as given in the original.

I frequently quote from primary sources because I believe that the story of the Roanoke Island freedmen's colony is often best told by those who had a close connection to it. While it is certainly true that such correspondence reveals as much about its authors' motives and biases as it reveals about the freedmen's colony, it is also true that an understanding of the former is necessary for a complete understanding of the latter. Part of the book's title is, in fact, taken directly from a missionary teacher's letter that effectively imparts both fact and feeling. In May 1864, when Roanoke Island missionary teacher Ella Roper sat down to write her quarterly report to the American Missionary Association's corresponding secretary, the Reverend George Whipple, she noted that she wrote "with a heart full of gratitude to God." The past quarter, she related, had been "a time full of trial and yet full of joy, because our 'Strong Deliverer' seemed so near."[4]

I based the title of the book on this excerpt from Roper's letters for two main reasons. First, the excerpt clearly conveys the evangelical sentiment of the American Missionary Association missionaries who dominated the Roanoke Island mission field during wartime. The missionaries steadfastly believed that God had called them to their labors in North Carolina; no matter the difficulties, the missionaries claimed joy in their work and repeatedly thanked God for allowing them the privilege of working among the freedpeople. I realize that cynics will assert that the missionaries were fooling themselves—that their actions must have grown out of economic motives, poor self esteem, or a desire to add adventure to their otherwise dull lives. Although I do not doubt that the missionaries' motives were complex, and they can certainly be faulted for both their naivete and their self-righteous insistence that the former slaves had to adopt the values of middle-class Northern white culture, I have chosen to take them at their word when it comes to their professions of missionary spirit. I believe that most of the missionaries really wished to improve the lives of the downtrodden. They thought that education would radically change the lives of the former slaves.

I also based my title on the excerpt from Ella Roper's letter because of the play on words inherent in "trial." Work in the Roanoke Island colony was a trial in two senses of the word. Roper meant to convey the challenges of life in the colony; it was a trying experience for the colonists, the teachers, and the military authorities. At the same time, in some respects the colony was a trial run for some significant ideas—free universal public education, small freeholding, wage labor—that could have drastically altered society and culture in late nineteenth-century North Carolina. As the following chapters will show, however, these ideas languished in the face of many obstacles—some of them natural, but many of human contrivance.

Acknowledgments

WHEN I INITIATED my study of the Roanoke Island freedmen's colony in 1981, I had no idea of the magnificent adventure that awaited me. Piecing together the story from a variety of primary sources ignited my curiosity, honed my detective skills, and led me to a number of archives. Along the way I met some wonderful people who graced my life with helpful advice and good cheer. I incurred many debts that I would like to acknowledge at this time.

Early in my research, Clifton H. Johnson, who at that time was director of the Amistad Research Center at Dillard University, encouraged my work and invited me to visit the center to take advantage of its collections, especially the American Missionary Association archives. By the time I visited the center, it had moved to Tulane University, and Fred Stielow was director. Fred and his staff went out of their way to aid me in my research and make me feel very much at home. More recently, Brenda B. Square, Director of Archives and Library, helped me obtain copies of materials from the center's collection for use as illustrations in this book.

At the National Archives, Mike Meier, Michael Pilgrim, and Bill Lind rendered great assistance during my numerous visits. Similarly, I owe thanks to the staff of the Southern Historical Collection at the University of North Carolina and the staff of the United States Army Military History Institute at Carlisle Barracks, especially Pam Cheney, who assisted me in the research room, and Michael J. Winey, who helped me locate photographs in the MOLLUS-Massachusetts Commandery photograph collection.

Throughout my research, the staff of the Outer Banks History Center, the regional library and manuscript repository in Manteo that is operated by North Carolina's Division of Archives and History, provided more assistance than can adequately be acknowledged in a few sentences. The center's director, Wynne Dough, proved instrumental in guiding me to valuable sources and introducing me to other historians whose research interests complemented my own. Meanwhile, Sarah Spink Downing, Brian Edwards, and Hellen Shore Wilson provided prompt and professional service as they guided me through the center's holdings.

In the Research Room at the National Archives I met Candra Flanagan, who at that time was a part-time employee at the Archives and full-time undergraduate student at the University of Maryland. She agreed to be my long-distance research assistant, which led to a collaboration that proved extremely fortuitous to the progress of my research. At one point, Candra suggested that I contact her professor, Leslie Rowland, director of the Freedmen and Southern Society Project at the University of Maryland. I did and was cordially invited to spend a day using the project's materials. When I arrived at the project's office and saw how cramped the quarters were, I realized that my visit there was quite a privilege. I am very grateful that I had the opportunity to use the project's materials and am especially appreciative of the time that Leslie, Steven Miller, and Susan O'Donovan spent talking with me about my work. Candra, meanwhile, graduated from the University of Maryland and enrolled in graduate school at the University of Virginia, where she continued to work as my research assistant, helping with various aspects of this book.

My attempts to gain a sense of the physical boundaries of the freedmen's colony were aided by a number of people at the Currituck County Court House and the Currituck County Governmental Center. In particular, Charlene Y. Dowdy, register of deeds, and her staff guided me through my initial deed searches, while Sheila R. Romm, clerk of superior court, aided my efforts to uncover evidence of litigation involving the colony's land. Similarly, Kim Cumber, archivist at the North Carolina Division of Archives and History, applied her awe-inspiring detective skills to aid me immeasurably in searches among archived records that were no longer available in Currituck and Dare Counties.

I could not have written this book without the great service I received from the staff of the University of Virginia's Alderman Library, especially the Interlibrary Loan Department and the Library Express on Grounds delivery service. On numerous occasions Lew Purifoy went out of his way to help me with requests. Likewise, the staff of the Periodicals and Microforms Department, especially Alice Parra and Irene Norvelle, also provided first-class assistance. Michael Plunkett, director of Special Collections, and his staff were helpful in my search for illustrations. Pauline Page, microphotographer in the Alderman Library Copy Center, did a marvelous job of photographing these illustrations, as well as those from my personal collection, so that they would be suitable for use in the book.

Nancy Knicely, librarian at the Family History Center of the Charlottesville

Church of Jesus Christ of the Latter-Day Saints, and volunteers Rodney Knicely and Martin Davis deserve special mention for the assistance they gave me as I used the center's extensive genealogical resources to discover what had happened to the missionary teachers after they left Roanoke Island.

At various times I received support that enabled me to labor unfettered, so to speak, by teaching obligations. The University of Virginia's Sesquicentennial Associateship program provided a semester of sabbatical leave that was crucial to the opening stages of my research. I am grateful to my colleagues in the Division of Technology, Culture, and Communication in the School of Engineering and Applied Science for filling in for me during that leave. Later, a summer grant from the Hewlitt Foundation provided critical support for research and writing. Likewise, a combined summer grant from the National Park Service, the Eastern National Monuments and Parks Association, and the North Carolina Division of Cultural Resources enabled me to devote a summer to research and writing. Robert Woody, coordinator of parks, Senator Marc Basnight, president pro tempore of the North Carolina Senate, and John Wilson IV, chairman of the Roanoke Island Commission, were particularly helpful in procuring and coordinating the latter grant. I am indebted to Outer Banks Conservationists, Inc., for nominating me for the grant, and to Melodie Leckey, Terry McDowell, and Bill Parker for their part in administering the grant.

I felt very blessed to have the ongoing support of Steve Reilly and David Wright as I moved through various stages of my work. Steve, whose dissertation on Horace James remains the only complete treatment of the man and his ideas, generously shared his notes and encouraged my efforts, even after he had put his own research behind him; it is impossible to estimate how much Steve contributed to this book. Meanwhile, David, who has been writing a book about the Pea Island Life Savers, shared notes and guided me to some sources that I had not yet uncovered. We also conducted countless phone and e-mail conversations that helped me hammer out my ideas about the freedmen's colony.

After the manuscript was drafted, a number of people read it and offered some very constructive criticisms. Dan Hallahan, professor of Special Education and chair of Curriculum, Instruction, and Special Education at the University of Virginia; Angel Ellis Khoury, author of *Manteo: A Roanoke Island Town* and former editor of the *Outer Banks Magazine*; Robert Oxley, professor and chair of Humanities and Social Sciences at Embry-Riddle Aeronautical University; and Steve Brumfield, manager of Manteo Booksellers, offered advice about the narrative and helped me to see things I needed to do to make the book more accessible to a general audience. Meanwhile, Ed Ayers, Hugh P. Kelly Professor of History at the University of Virginia; Robert Cross, professor emeritus of History at the University of Virginia; and David Wright, assistant professor of English and African-American Literature at Knox College, focused on my historical analysis. They helped me to see where my treatment was weak, pointed out historical scholarship that I had overlooked, and suggested things that I should consider adding to the book. I owe all of the readers a special debt, and in the case of Bob Cross, a double debt, since he read two versions of the manuscript.

I hesitate to name others who gave me help as I worked on this book, for fear that I will omit someone. I must, however, give special credit to Tim Radcliffe, media systems engineer in the School of Engineering and Applied Science at the University of Virginia, who created one of the book's maps. In addition, I owe thanks to my former research assistant Mary Bess Bolin, who read stacks of nineteenth-century newspapers and who also attempted to take information from nineteenth-century deeds and create a map of the freedmen's colony; my former research assistant Lauranett Lee, who had an amazing talent for locating obscure journal articles; Brendan Foley, a graduate student at the Massachusetts Institute of Technology, who helped me trace the postwar lives of a number of the missionary teachers; Herb Harrell, who shared his discoveries about the military history of Civil War Roanoke Island; Michael Wildasin, who provided lodging during my numerous research trips to the National Archives and also read drafts of the book's introduction several times; and Jack Sandberg and Sue Maloney, whose amazing shop, The Yellowhouse Gallery, was the source of all the illustrations in this book that are from my own collection. Thanks also to Burwell Buchanan, Tom Hutchinson, Richard Jacques, Deborah Joy, Loretta Lautzenheiser, Jocelyn Midgette, Vance Midgett, and Jerry Showalter. I would also like to acknowledge all those friends who never lost interest in hearing about my work, and my mother and my sister and her family, who always forgave me when I neglected them to work on "the book."

Besides the people from Roanoke Island who have already been mentioned, I am particularly indebted to Deloris Harrell, Roger Meekins, Louis Midgett, and Virginia Tillett. Across the sound, my summer neighbors on the Outer Banks, William and Ida Friday, Hope and Larry Mihalap, Emma Neal Morrison, Mary Lou Temple, and Rebecca Walker, were always generous with their enthusiasm for the work that consumed my summer days. Significantly, Bill Friday, former president of the University of North Carolina, encouraged me to submit the manuscript to the University of North Carolina Press; he also took time out of his busy schedule to call me occasionally in Virginia for updates—calls that never failed to brighten my day.

Finally, I will conclude by noting that I will be forever grateful to John Wilson for insisting that I tackle this project and for his continuing support throughout my years of work. There were times when I doubted whether it would be possible to uncover the story of the freedmen's colony, but John never did, and his enthusiasm was a continuing source of inspiration. I would like to acknowledge John's ongoing and widespread efforts to preserve the history and heritage of Roanoke Island by dedicating this book to the memory of all the men, women, and children who labored in the Roanoke Island freedmen's colony. John and I both agree that it is time for their struggles to be recognized.

Time Full of Trial

Introduction

IN DECEMBER 1863, several weeks after missionary teacher Elizabeth James arrived on Union-occupied Roanoke Island to commence her work among former slaves, she finally found time to write a letter recounting her experiences. "I can not tell you how busy I am," she related. "Those who are escaping from bondage are pressing in in all directions. From one to two hundred arrive every few days." James was not describing an isolated wartime event. Commencing with the beginning of the war, as soon as the Union army had established a foothold in an area, word spread among local slaves, who then streamed across Union lines hoping to obtain freedom.[1]

Although federal troops never occupied a vast amount of Southern territory, the Union presence was widespread. By May 1861, the federal government had secured its military installations in the District of Columbia and at Fortress Monroe in Virginia. Later that year, in November 1861, federal troops occupied Port Royal, South Carolina. Then in February and March of the following year, the Union military established footholds at various points along the coast of North Carolina. In April, the federal occupation spread to additional South Carolina Sea Islands, some of Georgia's barrier islands, and Fernandina and St. Augustine, Florida, as well as to New Orleans and the area of Louisiana lying between New Orleans and the Gulf of Mexico. By the middle of the summer of 1862, federal forces were also occupying Nashville and Memphis, Tennessee; Helena, Arkansas; Huntsville, Alabama; Corinth, Mississippi; and other points along major midwestern rivers and railways.[2]

Runaway slaves gathered in makeshift settlements on the periphery of Union encampments, taking refuge wherever they could find a spot, in abandoned buildings or hastily constructed makeshift shelters. Meanwhile, the federal occupation profoundly altered fugitive slave policy. At Fortress Monroe, General Benjamin Butler put the former slaves to work and offered them protection and food. More significantly, he offered them freedom, for he considered the refugees contraband of war and refused to return them to their former owners. Other military authorities followed suit, and the number of slave refugees, termed "contrabands," near Union encampments multiplied more rapidly than the local commanders had anticipated.[3]

By the fall of 1862, military officials were concerned about the "contraband problem." The contraband settlements were beginning to take on a more permanent cast. Local commanders feared that the proximity of the contraband settlements to the Union encampments would affect military discipline. They also realized that the crowded conditions in the contraband camps would create major sanitation problems that would have an impact on the Union camps. Officers were appointed to superintend the camps and put the contrabands to work in an organized manner. Within a short time, the various haphazard local policies in the field were superseded by a more unified policy within the War Department. Until the March 1865 creation of the Bureau of Refugees, Freedmen, and Abandoned Lands, contraband camps came under the direct purview of the Union army's Quartermaster's Department and were supervised by superintendents who were appointed by the general who commanded a particular area.[4]

Most of the contraband superintendents had been serving in the army as chaplains. Many had strong connections to the Northern contraband and freedmen's relief associations that were providing substantial aid to former slaves in various Southern locales. Consequently, most of the superintendents entered their jobs with the sincere desire that the camps would be more than safe refuges for the former slaves. They hoped that camp life would assist the former slaves as they made the transition to freedom. The superintendents, however, remained subordinate to regular army officers, and they were well aware that the camps existed first and foremost as a consequence of military exigencies. Some local military officials had great sympathy and respect for contrabands and contraband camps, while others only tolerated them because they knew that keeping the former slaves under Union protection prevented their use by the Confederacy. As the war progressed, the term "contraband" was frequently supplanted by "freedmen" in official military correspondence, but the treatment that some of the former slaves received at the hands of the military often suggested that these authorities still regarded the former slaves to be property ("contraband") rather than free persons.[5]

When the Civil War opened, there were approximately four million slaves in the South. Four years later, close to a half million of the former slaves were living in areas held by federal forces; many of them lived in the government-supervised contraband/freedmen camps. No one has attempted to chronicle all of the settlements, but research coming out of the Freedmen and Southern Society Project at the University of Maryland suggests that close to a hundred camps had been established by the war's end. They were situated wherever there was a strong Union military occupation in Southern territory—just outside of the District of Columbia, at various points along the Atlantic and Gulf coasts, at a number of locations in Kentucky and Tennessee, and up the Mississippi from New Orleans to Cairo, Illinois. Some camps lasted for a few months, while others evolved into settlements that continued into the postwar period.[6]

In the deep South, the former slaves were more likely to stay on or near the plantations where they had been enslaved; this was especially true in those areas where Union forces directly occupied the plantations. In the upper South and the border states, contrabands usually gathered in camps that were near Union outposts in occupied towns or villages. By 1864, military authorities had also established some camps in hopes of removing the refugees from the proximity of Union encampments or relieving crowded conditions in some occupied areas. Some of these camps were found in the vicinity of the District of Columbia and in various places in the Mississippi Valley and southern Louisiana. Although a few of the latter in Louisiana were called freedmen's home colonies or freedmen's labor colonies, they were, in practice, bleak temporary camps that aided the Union military in controlling the refugee situation and putting together gangs of black laborers. They were not meant to be permanent.[7]

Most slaves fled their homes with no inkling of the wretched and chaotic conditions that awaited them in their first days in the contraband camps. They just knew that however bad things got to be, they were never as bad as living in slavery. And so they continued to come, in large groups and small; day after day, the roads and paths in the countryside near Union encampments swelled with trains of weary but jubilant migrants in search of better lives. Some arrived in the camps with wagons, tools, animals, bundles of clothes, and small personal articles; while countless others brought nothing but the clothing on their backs. Likewise, they came with a variety of backgrounds and skills. Some had served as house servants, skilled laborers, and managers; while others escaped from backbreaking work as field hands and common laborers. More than half the refugees were children or old folks, dependent on family or friends.

As soon as it appeared that the military had a firm hold on an area and the contraband camp that was developing there was fairly secure, the former slaves' first impetus was to attempt to gather their scattered family members together and then to exercise their freedom by creating their own churches and schools. Many of the men and some of the women found jobs working for the military.

Often the men worked for the Quartermaster's Department as teamsters or common laborers, digging ditches or building fortifications, docks, and roads. Meanwhile, some of the women served as cooks, laundresses, and maids for officers and soldiers; and a few found jobs as nurses or attendants in the primitive army hospitals. The type of work varied with the camps' locations.

Frequently the work was not much different in kind from the sort of servile labor the former slaves had left when they fled from bondage, and often the jobs were dangerous—the sort that enlisted white soldiers did not relish. The significant difference from slavery was that the contrabands were supposed to be paid for their labor. Usually, however, they did not receive all of their wages in cash. The policy varied slightly from commander to commander, but often money for support of those who were unable to work was subtracted from the wages of those who were working. Similarly, clothing and government food rations counted against their earnings. Generally at least a fourth of the contrabands in a camp subsisted on rations, and that number increased after the early summer of 1863, when the Union army began recruiting the able-bodied black men to serve as soldiers, leaving the women, children, elderly, and unfit behind in the camps.[8]

There was no single model for the contraband camps; each camp evolved in its local context. The contraband camps on South Carolina's Sea Islands were typical of those in areas of the deep South where large plantations were common. In November 1861, soon after the establishment of the Union occupation in the area, General Thomas W. Sherman set up temporary camps at Beaufort (Port Royal Island) and Hilton Head (Hilton Head Island) for former slaves. Generally, these camps attracted blacks who were fleeing from the South Carolina mainland or other areas outside of Union lines, while contrabands who had been slaves on the island plantations remained where they had been. The two hundred or so plantations under Union control soon became the focus of a great amount of Northern benevolent activities and a grand experiment in free labor. More precisely, Northern reformers sought to replace slavery with a system of free labor involving the former slaves. The goal was a scheme that was both fair to the workers and profitable for Northern overseers.

The contraband camps, meanwhile, remained mere adjuncts to the plantations. The men in the camps found jobs working for the army's Quartermaster, Engineer, and Subsistence Departments. General Sherman paid the laborers and issued rations to those who could not work. Camp life, however, was not pleasant; most of the men did not stay in the camps very long, preferring instead to move in with friends or relatives on the plantations. By early 1862, a majority of the residents who were crowded together in the camps on the Sea Islands were women, children, and the elderly.[9]

A slightly different system of contraband camps developed in the Mississippi Valley, where local commanders had a great deal of latitude in setting everyday policy. In some places the able-bodied men found jobs with the military, and local military authorities provided housing and food for their dependents in the camps. In other places, government overseers put the men from the camps to work building military defenses, or harvesting cotton on farms that belonged to white resident owners who reimbursed the government for the labor, or on farms that had been abandoned. Conditions in many cases were not much better for these men than they had been under slavery. The men received little or nothing for their labors, coupled with promises of wages at the end of the war. Meanwhile, their families languished in camps that were little more than holding areas, and the small amount of personal property that some had possessed upon entering the camps was frequently seized by federal quartermasters for military use. General Ulysses S. Grant had also relocated some freedpeople who were within Union lines in the Mississippi Valley to "contraband retreats," temporary settlements that he had established for the families of men who were working for one of the military's departments. Most of these midwestern camps were also dismal gatherings of former slaves who were waiting for better times.[10]

An exception that illustrated what could be accomplished at a contraband retreat was the camp at Corinth, Mississippi, which was founded in the fall of 1862. Under the supervision of Chaplain James M. Alexander of the 66th Illinois Volunteers, the Corinth camp blossomed. The freedmen laid out streets and built houses, a school, a church, a commissary, and a hospital. By May 1863, Alexander had organized a nearly complete regiment of black troops from the camp. Meanwhile, the soldiers' families who remained in the camp cooperatively farmed four hundred acres of land, three hundred in cotton and one hundred in vegetables. In the summer of 1863, John Eaton, General Grant's superintendent of freedmen, estimated that the camp was making a monthly profit of $4,000 to $5,000. Despite its initial success, however, the camp was short-lived. In January 1864, in preparation for his winter campaign in the Mississippi Valley, General William T. Sherman recalled the troops that had been garrisoned at Corinth and ordered the residents of the contraband camp to be evacuated and moved northwest to the area around Memphis, Tennessee. By late January most of the camp's residents had completed the ninety-three-mile trip and were crowded into a foul improvised camp with seven hundred other contrabands in an orchard and cornfield two miles south of Memphis.[11]

After Corinth there were only a few attempts at large-scale cooperative farming experiments associated with freedmen's camps in the Mississippi Valley. One that proved to be successful, at least in the short run, was the Davis Bend plantation experiment. Initially General Grant had declared that he wanted the abandoned lands at Davis Bend, Mississippi, to become a "negro paradise." The area included the plantations of Confederate president Jefferson Davis and his brother Joseph, as well as many belonging to a number of other very wealthy Southerners. The contraband population consisted of former slaves from the plantations, as well as thousands who had fled to several wretched camps in the area. After a shaky start and a couple of reversals, the military authorities leased two thousand acres to seventy freedmen who managed, with the help of their families and despite an infestation of army worms, to make a profit on cotton in 1864. Plans for an expansion of the experiment were in place when the war ended. The seventy lessees were, however, but a fraction of the number of people—well over three thousand—who were crowded into the contraband camps in the Davis Bend area. Although the experiment at Davis Bend differed from what was being conducted on the Sea Islands, the relationship of the contraband camps to the plantations was similar. The camps existed alongside but peripheral to the plantations.[12]

A similar relationship between camps and farms existed in Union-occupied southeastern Virginia, where a slightly different model of cooperative farming prevailed. Former slaves started streaming into areas that were under federal control in May 1861 and did not stop until war's end. By May of 1863, military authorities had turned close to fifty abandoned properties near Hampton and Norfolk, including the plantation of former President John Tyler, into government farms. Men with families or groups of men who had been congregating at army posts or in temporary contraband camps were resettled and assigned plots on the farms. Most of these former slaves worked the farms, under the supervision of a white overseer, for a share—a third or half—of the crop; but a few rented small plots and farmed without close supervision. The result was not an effective solution to the contraband problem. While some of the former slaves ended up on well-run farms, many faced great obstacles, including food and fuel shortages, and even the possibility of being kidnapped. More importantly, around five thousand of the most destitute refugees—the women and children—remained in crowded camps, dependent on government aid.[13]

In many respects the contraband camps in and around the District of Columbia were similar to those that were established in Virginia's tidewater, yet there were also significant differences. The camps in the District of Columbia were established in a context that was shaped by the significant presence of the federal government and a tradition of free blacks laboring for the federal government. Prior to the opening of the war, the District had been home to approximately fifteen thousand blacks, of which around three thousand were slaves. Once the war opened, hundreds of slaves fled from Maryland and Virginia to the city in hopes of obtaining freedom. Initially the military authorities did not recognize the contraband status of the slaves from loyal Maryland, opting to return the fugitives; but many of the Maryland slaves found ways to circumvent that obstacle, and the stream of runaways continued unabated. Meanwhile, the federal government needed thousands of additional laborers, especially in the Quartermaster's and Engineer's Departments, to maintain the war effort, so there were plenty of jobs for the contrabands.[14]

The main problem that the newcomers faced was procuring housing. Many preferred finding lodging with friends in various shanty settlements around the city, but that was not always a realistic possibility. General Joseph K. F. Mansfield, commander of the Department of Washington, sent many of the new arrivals to a camp that had been organized at the Old Capitol Prison. The camp's superintendent found them jobs working for the military or private employers. When that location proved unsatisfactory, in part because some whites objected to housing the former slaves near white prisoners, the contrabands were moved to an area of tenements east of the Capitol known as Duff Green's Row. Representatives of several freedmen's relief associations provided aid to the residents and initiated some educational efforts as well. After Congress officially abolished slavery within the District in April 1862, the steady stream of former slaves pouring into the city turned into a torrent, leading to a great deal of crowding. An outbreak of smallpox at Duff Green's Row in July prompted the superintendent to relocate the former slaves housed there to some vacated army barracks and stables. The resulting contraband camp was known as Camp Barker.[15]

Conditions at Camp Barker were dreary, to say the least. Living quarters were cramped, and there was little privacy. The superintendent, Danforth B. Nichols, a Methodist minister, had scant relief to dispense to the contrabands, and his harsh manner made him few friends among the former slaves. The contrabands were, in fact, eager to secure jobs so that they could move their families out of the camp. Most of the men found it easy to procure jobs with the military, while many of the women found positions in households. The women who were unable to find work, especially women with small children, as well as the elderly and sick, were left behind. In December 1863, around 685 of the estimated 15,000 contrabands who had entered Camp Barker since it opened remained there. They were ordered to move across the Potomac to Freedmen's

Village, a camp that had been created in Arlington, Virginia, on the abandoned estate of Confederate general Robert E. Lee and his wife Mary Custis Lee.[16]

In contrast to Camp Barker, Freedmen's Village seemed a veritable paradise. Located near approximately 1,300 acres of government farms, the small cabins that were laid out on streets in the village each offered room enough for two families, plus there was land for gardens. In addition, there was a school, a chapel, a hospital, and workshops that offered the young men and women training in skilled trades. The government farms and Freedmen's Village had been created by Colonel Elias M. Greene, chief quartermaster of the Department of Washington, who was a tireless supporter and promoter of the project. He assumed that most of the residents would work for wages and leave the village once they had acquired enough training to support themselves. In reality, however, most of the able-bodied men had either enlisted in the Union army or found jobs in the District working for the government. By late September 1863, only 150 of the 900 residents were classified as healthy men; Freedmen's Village was primarily a haven for women and children, old folks, and the poor. Nevertheless, the freedpeople in the village attempted to sustain themselves, many through work on the nearby government farms. Those who could afford to do so paid monthly rents of one to three dollars for housing. Meanwhile, the needy poor in the village were supported by a contraband fund that was financed through taxes on black laborers in the District and northern Virginia. Instead of staying for a short time, as Colonel Greene had envisioned, many of the residents grew so comfortable in the village that they settled in for the long term.[17]

Even a cursory overview of contraband camps suggests that life in most of the camps was very unsettled, and dependence on government support was not unusual. Many of the residents were not able to work, and the ones who did work were not always paid fairly or regularly. Consequently, a majority of the contrabands throughout the South relied to some extent on government rations and the donations of the various freedmen's relief associations. By war's end, these organizations, the outgrowth of abolitionist sentiment in the North, had gathered and shipped hundreds of barrels of clothing, household supplies and hardware, medical supplies, Bibles, and books to be distributed in the Southern contraband camps. The freedmen superintendents coordinated the distribution of rations and donated materials and served generally as a bridge between the relief associations and the contrabands. The relief societies also sponsored much of the day-to-day educational and relief work in the camps—work that was conducted by a passionate group of Northern missionary teachers. Most of the teachers had strong abolitionist leanings. Many were deeply religious, infused with the evangelical Christianity that had played a significant role in Northern society since the Second Great Awakening. They were motivated by their belief that they had been called South to save both the bodies and the souls of the former slaves.

In the past twenty years, historians have shown a great deal of interest in Northern relief work in the Southern freedmen camps, resulting in some ground-breaking publications that establish a framework for understanding the missionary and educational work among the freedpeople. These historians suggest insights into the motivations of the missionary teachers and shed light on the successes and failures of their educational and benevolent aims. One thing that most of the studies have touched on was the role of Northern evangelicalism in establishing the moral environment that propelled thousands of men and women to come to the South as missionaries to the freedmen. With adherents among Baptists, Congregationalists, Disciples of Christ, Methodists, and Presbyterians, evangelicalism dominated the religious outlook in the North in the years leading up to the war. Historians have begun to realize that this group of well-educated and well-connected Christians had an influence on Northern culture and politics that extended well beyond their numbers.[18]

In contrast to their Calvinist ancestors, who focused on original sin, predestination, and atonement, Northern Protestant evangelicals emphasized the possibility that society and individuals could be perfected. Consequently, they were in the forefront of a number of antebellum social movements, including temperance and free schools, but especially abolition. Northern evangelical Christians were outspoken against slavery, and their antislavery arguments prompted many other Northerners to take up the abolitionist cause. Ever since the Second Great Awakening, Northern evangelicals had been especially active in proclaiming that the coming of Christ's millennial kingdom, which had been prophesied in the Book of Revelation, was at hand, and that it would occur in the United States. They believed that the sin of slaveholding was, however, preventing the coming of the millennium; slavery had to be eradicated before society could be perfected and Christ would return to earth. Invoking millennial imagery, they first worked at home to convince their neighbors and political leaders that it was not a question of fighting for either Union or emancipation: emancipation was a necessary first step toward the purified Union that was a prerequisite for the establishment of the millennium. Then, when given a chance, the Northern evangelicals went South to work among the former slaves to rectify the damage caused by slavery.[19]

The evangelical Christians were not, however, mere religious fanatics who were so swept up in millennial fever that they lost touch with the secular world. Overall they tended to be traditional republicans in outlook; they assumed that human beings made choices for which they should be held responsible and that hard work would lead to rewards, both material and spiritual. Generally, the evangelicals were, in fact, very successful in business and industry. Most advocated a laissez-faire philosophy with respect to the role of government in everyday life; they believed, for example, that extending government aid to the poor would discourage industry and prolong their poverty. At the same time, they believed that all human beings should have the right to the profits of their own labor, as well as the right to own personal and real property.[20]

While women were noticeably absent from their philosophical discussions, most Northern evangelicals did advocate equal political rights for all men, white and black. They did not, however, believe in the social equality of whites and blacks, nor did they assume that "equality before the law" would lead to social equality. In other words, they were not egalitarians; they thought that ultimately the former slaves would find their "natural" social position, which would likely be somewhere near the bottom of society. At times, in fact, their actions often manifested a racism that now seems curiously out of step with their antislavery sentiments, but which (however repulsive) makes some sense in light of the distinction they made between political and social equality.[21]

Studying the missionary work among freedmen in North Carolina provides a great opportunity to gain greater insight into what the Northern evangelicals wished to accomplish in their Southern missionary endeavors, partly because of the extensive untapped primary sources and also because of the role played by the superintendent of freedmen affairs, the Reverend Horace James, an evangelical Congregational minister from Worcester, Massachusetts. An abolitionist who advocated traditional republican values and supported many of the ideas championed by the Radical Republicans, James remained in close contact with other Northern Christian evangelicals, including the leaders of the American Missionary Association, one of the major organizations involved in relief work among the Southern freedmen. Although James was not an original thinker—most of his ideas mirrored those that were held by his fellow evangelicals—he was a prolific writer of letters, many of which included discussions of putting his beliefs into practice in the South.

In North Carolina Horace James found a widespread and frequently turbulent mission field. Once Union forces had taken control of several areas of coastal North Carolina, slaves began streaming into the occupied territory in hopes of finding sanctuary. By midsummer 1862, more than 10,000 contrabands were living in Union-occupied areas. By January 1864, the number had nearly doubled; 17,419 former slaves were living within Union lines in eastern North Carolina: 2,426 at Beaufort, 89 at Hatteras, 8,591 at New Bern, 860 at

Plymouth, 2,712 on Roanoke Island, and 2,741 at Washington. From that point until the end of the war, the population of North Carolina's contraband settlements stabilized at a number that approached 18,000.[22]

Although James would have preferred for the former slaves to have been spread out on government-sponsored farms, he had reluctantly concluded that contraband camps were necessary in North Carolina because the amount of land that the Union occupied was very small. The Union controlled "a broad area of navigable waters," but there was "scarcely room enough on land to spread our tents upon," he complained. If land had been available in the state for the former slaves, James noted, "it would have prevented huddling them together in the fortified towns and temporary camps. But there was left to us no alternative."[23]

During his tenure in North Carolina, Horace James supervised freedmen camps at Beaufort, New Bern, Plymouth, Roanoke Island, and Washington. Not all camps survived the war; wartime conditions led to some disruptive movements of contrabands from camp to camp, and the demise of some camps. During the Confederate attack on Plymouth in April 1864, for example, most of the freedmen in that camp were evacuated to Beaufort, New Bern, or Roanoke Island. Later that month, Washington was similarly threatened, and most of the freedmen there were evacuated to New Bern. By January 1865, a majority of the freedmen in North Carolina lived in three areas: 3,245 in Beaufort and vicinity, 10,782 in New Bern and vicinity, and 3,091 on Roanoke Island.[24]

James's headquarters were in New Bern, which also served as Union military headquarters for eastern North Carolina. Throughout the war, New Bern remained home to the state's largest population of freedpeople, whose numbers alone presented tremendous housing and sanitation problems to James's office. The majority of the population, 6,560, lived in town, and another 1,424 lived on its outskirts. The remainder lived in three contraband camps outside of town, but two of these camps were abandoned after a Confederate attack in January 1864. After that, the residents of all three camps were combined into one, the Trent River camp, which was about a mile and half south of town at the confluence of the Neuse and Trent Rivers. James and his men laid out a freedmen's village there. They created streets and divided the approximately thirty acres of land into lots that were, he recounted, "fifty by sixty, allowing a little garden spot to each house." Initially 2,798 freedmen lived in the village, which consisted of eight hundred cabins, mostly rough-hewn out of boards that had been split by hand.[25]

Conditions were primitive, and life was difficult for the early inhabitants of Trent River. The residents, however, persevered, and James wrote proudly of the conditions in the camp, whose name was later changed to James City in his honor. "If we must have camps, or African villages, in which temporarily to shelter and feed refugees from bondage," James declared, "this settlement, located healthfully on the banks of the Trent, is a model for imitation." The freedmen, James noted after the war, had turned what "was started as a temporary camp, in which to place colored fugitives and give them food and protection, while the country was disturbed by war," into a "self-supporting" settlement. Its inhabitants worked hard to obtain permanent title to the land they were renting. The community remained viable until 1893, when residents lost a court battle to obtain permanent land ownership, and many moved just south of the camp to a community that is still known as James City.[26]

Ironically, the Trent River/James City camp was never intended to be a permanent settlement. That distinction fell to the Roanoke Island camp, the first contraband camp to be established in North Carolina and the only one in the state that was given the official designation of "colony." That alone might be enough reason to justify a thorough study of the freedmen work on Roanoke Island, but there are other reasons related to the nature of the freedmen experiment that was conducted there. In contrast to South Carolina's Sea Islands, where the military commanded a vast area of land in the form of plantations, or Virginia's Hampton Roads area, where the government controlled a number of farms, the Roanoke Island settlement was not subsidiary to a larger agricultural experiment. At its establishment the authorities hoped that the Roanoke Island freedmen's colony would be a self-contained settlement supporting itself through a combination of domestic manufactures and small-scale agriculture. Likewise, in contrast to the "home colonies" and "labor colonies" in the Mississippi Valley, which were organized as holding centers and which, with the exception of a few camps such as the one at Corinth, were managed with little hope of permanence, the colony on Roanoke Island was established with an eye to the future. While it was a sanctuary for the families of freedmen soldiers, its organizers had grander hopes for what could be accomplished there.[27]

Although there had been a contraband camp on Roanoke Island since the battle in February 1862, in the spring of 1863, General John G. Foster instigated efforts to create a government-sanctioned settlement there. More specifically, Foster ordered Horace James "to establish a colony of negroes upon Roanoke Island." In James's mind, there was an important distinction between a camp and a colony: a camp provided a safe temporary haven for former slaves, while a colony offered the opportunity to mold a permanent community. Proposals to establish colonies of former slaves in places such as Africa, the Caribbean, or

Central America had been around since the early part of the nineteenth century. The American Colonization Society was founded in 1817 to promote such activity. What was new during the war period was the serious contemplation of colonization within the United States. In September 1862, for example, General Ulysses S. Grant had proposed that contrabands be transported from Union camps in the Mississippi Valley to Cairo, Illinois, where his command had made arrangements for them to work for civilians. Back in Virginia that same fall, General John A. Dix had sent inquiries to the governors of several Northern states asking that they take in some of the contrabands who had gathered at Fortress Monroe. Both proposals, however, had eventually fallen flat in the face of protest in the free states. Democrats had used the threat of a mass black emigration to whip up support in Northern elections, while Republicans feared that government backing of such proposals would diminish support for the war effort.[28]

Most likely James knew of the uproar created by some of the early proposals to remove the former slaves from the South. Similarly, he probably knew that the word "colony" had been applied in New Orleans and other areas to what were, in reality, squalid makeshift refugee camps. In June 1863, when James crafted a letter for publication in Northern newspapers soliciting support from friends for the creation of a colony on Roanoke Island for the "families of colored soldiers," he made it clear that his plans for the former slaves did not involve colonization in another state or country. He also emphasized that his colony would not be a mere holding place for the freedpeople. James noted that General Foster had selected Roanoke Island as the location of the colony because it was safe and had a variety of natural resources. James believed that the colonists would be able to support themselves through a variety of agricultural, fishing, and manufacturing ventures. Just as important, he looked forward to the time when the colonists would be independent and self-sufficient freeholders. James and his assistants laid out what amounted to a New England-style village on the north end of the island. He assigned the lots to freedmen families, who immediately began to erect homes and cultivate gardens. On several occasions, James indicated that he assumed that the freedmen soldiers would return to the island after the war and continue to live there with their families in the village. They would be proud freeholders in control of their own labors.[29]

It is impossible to know how much of James's discussion of his goals for the colony on Roanoke Island was intended merely for public consumption in the North. He worked diligently to rouse Northern support for the missionary work among the freedpeople; and Roanoke Island, with its historic connections, provided an excellent backdrop for his appeals. At the same time, it is hard to resist the conclusion that, at least for the first couple of years of his work, James got swept up in contemplating the possibility that the settlement on Roanoke Island could be much more than a mere camp. The utopian overtones to James's thoughts were motivated by a complex combination of evangelical and traditional republican beliefs. On several occasions, James, for example, emphasized the contrast between what the freedmen were attempting on Roanoke Island and what had been attempted there three centuries earlier in Sir Walter Raleigh's colony. In particular, he contrasted the socially progressive goals of the freedmen's colony with the materialistic goals of Raleigh's failed "lost colony." James was thinking beyond the war to the society that he hoped to see in a South that was purged of the "sin of slavery." He believed that Roanoke Island offered a chance for an important social experiment—a chance to create what he termed a "New Social Order" in which white and black citizens would live and work together. The Roanoke Island freedmen's colony would be a place to showcase his ideas about free labor, landholding, and self-sufficiency. More importantly, he thought that it would be a model for emulation throughout the South.[30]

James, as the story will show, was a complex individual who is not easily measured by a twentieth-century yardstick. Like many of his fellow evangelicals, he did not believe in social equality between the races. Yet he abhorred slavery and dedicated a number of years of his life to improving the lot of freedmen. Although he identified himself as a republican (with a small "r"), rather than a member of the Republican party, there were times when his ideas seemed to be as radical as those of any of the Radical Republicans in Congress. He was idealistic, but he did not hesitate to turn very quickly from methods that were not proving effective. He was suffused with enthusiasm and theoretical notions, but he thrived on details and lacked a sense of the big picture. His mind took delight in the contemplation of a "New Social Order," but he failed to anticipate what that would really mean in the destitute conditions of the postwar South.[31]

In the short run, however, work in the colony presented James and the Northern missionaries who labored there what they considered a grand opportunity to put into practice ideas about abolition and evangelicalism that had been simmering in the North for more than forty years. In company with James, most of the missionaries felt that they had been "called" to the Southern mission field—that they had a moral duty to serve the unfortunate and convert souls to evangelical Christianity. Roanoke Island provided a challenging real-life backdrop for their work. The missionaries came South firmly believing that education and religion could erase the damage suffered under slavery and prepare the freedpeople for citizenship. Although the missionary teachers were among the first to acknowledge that the former slaves would not succeed unless they had some land of their own and regular wage-paying jobs, they never lost this faith in the power of education and religion. The missionaries believed, in fact, that a significant part of their job was to change their students. The metaphor that they employed most frequently to describe their work—bringing the former slaves from darkness to the light—pertained equally to their scholarly and spiritual endeavors. The negative consequence of the missionaries' belief in the total rightness of what they were doing is that they failed to recognize that the freedpeople had any cultural heritage of their own. Instead, they sought to impose their own very prescribed ideas about religion and morality.

The freedmen were not, however, mere passive observers. Long before the arrival of the missionaries, contrabands had established a community on the island on the outskirts of the Union encampment. They had organized a school and had built churches. Throughout the history of the colony, the freedpeople came as families and worked hard to maintain family units. Once they had gathered their bearings, they set about to move from the dirty barracks that served as a reception area for new arrivals to the village that Horace James and his assistants had created. They cleared land and built homes. Many of the men took jobs working for the army's Quartermaster's Department, building docks and fortifications or carrying out arduous labor that the enlisted white soldiers on the island resisted. Meanwhile, many of the women found employment working for officers and soldiers. Once it was established that black men would be allowed to serve in the Union army, many of the men in the freedmen's colony enlisted so that they could go fight for their and their families' freedom. Although many of the freedpeople who remained in the colony grew dependent upon government assistance and looked up to the mission teachers, whose schools they packed, they did not give up their autonomy. They maintained their own churches and a few of their own schools, they joined together to complain about conditions in the colony, and they played a significant role in exposing military improprieties on the island.

Although the colony had been established by military orders, the local military authorities provided the greatest obstacles to the day-to-day existence of the colony. Many of the soldiers had no interest in improving the lives of the former slaves, and some openly mistreated them. Likewise, while the military authorities depended on the missionaries to provide a variety of services to the colony, the relationship was not one of reciprocity. The army provided transportation and rations, and the Quartermaster's Department helped to build and maintain the missionaries' schools and homes. The officers could also cut rations or order the missionaries out of buildings or away from the island if war conditions demanded it. Things did not improve with the transfer of freedmen's care to the Bureau of Refugees, Freedmen, and Abandoned Lands, whose officers were much more interested in removing the freedmen from the island in the postwar period than in helping to salvage the colony. A grand experiment in social reform was the last thing on their minds.

During its heyday, however, more than a few people thought that Roanoke Island might, at the very least, be the site of a successful colony. Apparently many in the North agreed, and the press eagerly followed the activities on the island, reporting on the colony's struggles and accomplishments. Some seemed especially fascinated that the freedmen's colony was located on the island that had been the home of the first English colony in America. In 1864, for example, Edward Everett Hale wrote an article for the American Antiquarian Society in which he discussed the early colonial experiment and noted with some interest that the "Government of the United States [had] selected the same island for the first colony planted under its own formal protection and direction." The second annual report of the New England Freedmen's Aid Society was even more exuberant. It declared the Roanoke colony "one of the most important and one of the best managed, experiments" that had "been undertaken in behalf of the negroes."[32]

Given its national prominence in the 1860s, the absence of a thorough, published treatment of the freedmen's colony is surprising. The time is truly ripe for an exploration of the Roanoke Island experiment. Evangelical doctrines played an important role in establishing the moral foundation for Reconstruction, and Northern evangelicals attempted to carry out these doctrines in their work among the freedpeople during wartime and the postwar period. In the Roanoke Island experiment, Northern evangelicalism intertwined with a traditional middle-class republicanism that advocated education, self-sufficiency, and freeholding, and encouraged the development of small-scale domestic manufacturing and a laissez-faire economy. A study of the Roanoke Island freedmen's colony presents an opportunity to come to a better understanding of the limitations of the practical application of some evangelical doctrines in a social experiment that predated, yet anticipated, Reconstruction. In some respects the freedmen's colony was, as historian Raymond Gavins has suggested, a "dress rehearsal for Reconstruction."[33]

The remaining chapters of this book present a fairly straightforward narrative history of the establishment and growth of the freedmen's colony on Roanoke

Island, from its initiation as a camp shortly after the Battle of Roanoke Island, in February 1862, to its development as a model colony, and finally, to its demise under the auspices of the Bureau of Refugees, Freedmen, and Abandoned Lands in March 1867. The book highlights the overlapping roles, and frequently conflicting expectations, of the military authorities, philanthropic organizations, missionary teachers, and former slaves who were major stakeholders in the freedmen's colony. Although most of the players in the drama that unfolded on the island from 1862 to 1867 were not aware that they were part of a dress rehearsal, their story aptly presaged many of the trials of Reconstruction. It is time to tell that story.

This Important Victory

BATTLE AND AFTERMATH

IN AUGUST 1870, when Peter Gallop took the census in northeastern North Carolina, very little remained of the freedmen's colony that had existed during the previous decade on Union-occupied Roanoke Island. The federal government had removed or sold the significant buildings; most of the colonists had moved to the mainland; and vegetation was beginning to cover the grand avenues and streets of the village. Perhaps Gallop smiled when he learned that an eight-year-old boy in the North Banks household of black residents Benjamin and Director Bowser had been named Burnside to honor the Union general who had defeated the Confederates on Roanoke Island shortly before his birth. It is also likely that he reflected on the changes the island had weathered in the decade just past—changes that occasionally propelled the island onto center stage in a drama with national significance.[1]

The drama had its roots in circumstances whose origins lay well beyond the island's shores and stretched back for a number of years. The immediate impetus for the island's involvement in the story, however, had arisen in the spring of 1861, in the aftermath of North Carolina's secession from the Union. Realizing the strategic value of the state's navigable rivers and sounds, Governor John W. Ellis and his successor, Governor Henry T. Clark, had called for the renovation and construction of defensive fortifications at a number of coastal outposts, including Roanoke Island. Thus, within weeks of the secession, the Confederacy had established a military presence on the island. By the next winter, there were three sand forts on the west side of the island, and small batteries on the east side and in the center of the island.[2]

Troop strength, however, fell pitifully short of what would have been a

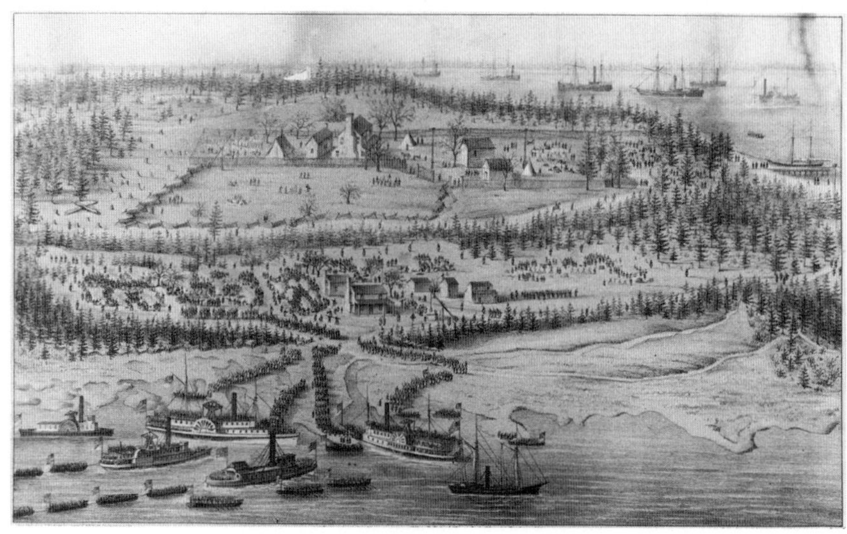

Less than a day after landing on Roanoke Island, Major General Ambrose E. Burnside's expedition quickly overwhelmed the paltry Confederate defenses. (Massachusetts Commandery, Military Order of the Loyal Legion of the United States and the U.S. Army Military History Institute)

sufficient defense. General Henry A. Wise, the Confederate officer in charge of holding the island, commanded a force that amounted to a little less than fifteen hundred men, who were, by his own account, "undrilled, unpaid, not sufficiently clothed and quartered, and miserably armed with old flint muskets in bad order"—in short, "a sad farce of ignorance and neglect combined." The Union occupation of Hatteras in late August 1861 further highlighted the vulnerability of Roanoke Island. When Wise begged his superiors for additional men to protect the island from an almost inevitable Federal attack, they argued that the troops were needed elsewhere. Consequently, the Confederate occupation remained tenuous, and on 8 February 1862, following an unprecedented amphibious landing, an arduous trek through marshlands, and a brief but bloody battle, the more the ten thousand Union troops under Major General Ambrose E. Burnside easily overwhelmed the paltry Confederate defenses and captured Roanoke Island.[3]

General Wise, who lost his own son in the battle, lamented the loss of a strategic post:

> It was the key to all the rear defences of Norfolk. It unlocked two sounds (Albemarle and Currituck); eight rivers (North, West, Pasquotank, Perquimans, Little, Chowan, Roanoke and Alligator); four canals (the Albe-

> marle and Chesapeake, Dismal Swamp, Northwest and Suffolk); and two railroads (the Petersburg and Norfolk and Seaboard and Roanoke). . . . It should have been defended at the expense of 20,000 men and of many millions of dollars.[4]

The *Congregationalist*, a weekly journal published in Boston, reported that newspapers in the South were "unanimous in admitting that their loss is very serious, and that this is far the most disastrous event of the war." Burnside also thought that the battle's outcome was significant. Some years later, he indicated his belief that the "results of this important victory were great, particularly in inspiring the confidence of the country in the efficiency of their armies in the field." Within several months of the capture of Roanoke Island, Union troops under Burnside swiftly captured Edenton, Winton, and New Bern, and then went on to take Carolina City, Morehead City, Newport, Beaufort, and Fort Macon. Moreover, Roanoke Island remained a Union stronghold for the duration of the war, and Union troops were stationed there until the spring of 1867.[5]

Although Union soldiers on the island after the battle professed ignorance of most things Southern, they were impressed by their proximity to the historic site of the first English settlement in America. Recalling his days on Roanoke Island as a soldier in the Twenty-fifth Regiment of Massachusetts Volunteers, Samuel Putnam later noted that the soldiers' "minds naturally went back to the discovery and first settlement of Roanoke Island in the days of Elizabeth of England, nearly three centuries before." Similarly, Alfred S. Roe of the Twenty-fourth Massachusetts later recalled that "there was a charm in standing where the brave pioneers of Sir Walter Raleigh may have been."[6]

According to William Derby of the Twenty-seventh Massachusetts, a fort said to have belonged to the ill-fated "lost colony" was located "near the north end" of the island, to the rear of the place where his company had bivouacked on 8 February. Derby noted that the fort's outlines were still "quite distinct." During the Union occupation, this fort, which was owned by island native Walter T. Dough, remained a popular spot among the soldiers and visitors. An article in the *National Anti-Slavery Standard* reported that the clear outline of "the moat of the old fort erected by Sir Walter Raleigh . . . in the form of a star" was "well worthy of the visit of the antiquarian." The fort eventually had to be placed under military guard because of vandalism.[7]

On the day of the battle of Roanoke Island, a writer for *Frank Leslie's Illustrated Newspaper* reported that the island was "a miserable place, being nothing but an inner sandbank, ornamented with stunted trees, scrubwood and tangled brushwood." Buffeted by storms and the constantly changing coastal

Major General Ambrose E. Burnside was very successful in eastern North Carolina. After the victory on Roanoke Island, Burnside's troops captured Edenton, Winton, New Bern, Carolina City, Morehead City, Newport, Beaufort, and Fort Macon. (Massachusetts Commandery, Military Order of the Loyal Legion of the United States and the U.S. Army Military History Institute)

General Burnside's headquarters on Roanoke Island were located on Pork Point. (*The Century War Book*, vol. 1, no. 15, p. 234, author's collection)

weather patterns, Roanoke Island did, however, provide a more stable environment for its nineteenth-century denizens than the beach areas fronting on the Atlantic to its east. In 1860, permanent residents numbered 590, including 395 whites, 24 free blacks, and 171 slaves. Most of the white islanders scraped out livings as fishermen, watermen, farmers, carpenters, workmen, or domestics. Several white residents were merchants or mechanics; and one, Samuel Tillett, served as keeper of a lighthouse. Most of the free blacks lived and worked as servants in white households. Only three of the eighty-seven dwellings occupied by free people on the island were headed by free blacks. The island's slave population resided in thirty slave houses on their masters' property.[8]

The evidence suggests that slavery on the island was not as harsh as it was in some parts of the mainland. A study of advertisements for runaway slaves in North Carolina in the antebellum period uncovered only one advertisement that originated at Roanoke Island. A few of the island's slaveholders had apparently even violated the state law and allowed their slaves to learn to read and write. Nevertheless, by early 1862, some of the island's slaves had found it desirable to escape to the Union lines at Hatteras Inlet. The *National Anti-Slavery Standard* carried an article in which a correspondent from North Carolina described one such family: Franklin and Nancy Tillett and their seventeen children. The article's author noted that the children bore the surnames of various former owners—five Tilletts, four Daniels, one Drinkwater, and seven Ashbys—rather than that of their father. The former slaves had built cabins and were beginning to create new lives for themselves as contrabands on Hatteras Island, where many of them worked for the Union officers. The writer conjectured that if the war ended with "an order directing their return to their owners," many of them would "commit suicide." The correspondent went on to relate that he had "heard them, when speculating in their cabins on this point, declare that they would never, never, never return to Roanoke and slavery."[9]

Union officers at Hatteras had welcomed the former slaves, whose knowledge of coastal currents and Roanoke Island fortifications proved helpful to the Union commanders preparing the attack on the island. According to Charles F. Johnson, a soldier who took part in the Roanoke Island battle, a contraband known as "Uncle Ben" spent the night before the attack "with General Burnside in the house that served as headquarters, giving information of the different works on the Island." This Ben was probably the "old Ben" Tillett described in the *National Anti-Slavery Standard* article as "a skillful inland sailor" who knew "all about the inlets and outlets, the winds and the currents, the moon and the tides, and would be a very useful man on the coast survey." Johnson reported that Ben not only provided information about "the battery defending the only pass to the enemy's rear, which he had helped to build," but he "was one of, if not the very first, to fire into it [the battery]."[10]

Another escapee, a young man named Thomas R. Robinson, offered to help Burnside's topographical engineer, Lieutenant W. S. Andrews, locate a good landing spot. Robinson guided Andrews to Ashby's Harbor, which Burnside chose as the point of landing. Twenty years later, Burnside's personal recollections of the landing gave full credit to the youthful former slave who provided him "most valuable information" and led him to Ashby's Harbor. Similarly, William Derby recounted the story of an unnamed former slave who shared valuable information about Confederate fortifications and served as a guide to the Union forces.[11]

The island's white residents, meanwhile, had never been strong secessionists. Independent and not inclined to be concerned with what their neighbors on the Carolina mainland were doing, many of them—even the slave owners—had traded with the North and offered assistance to the Union prior to the occupation. Bad feelings about the Confederate occupation, which had deprived islanders of much of their food stores and disrupted their lives, also contributed to their ambivalence toward the Union troops. Disconcerted by the shift in status of Roanoke Island after the battle, the natives were, however, unsure of what the new occupation would mean for them. One Union soldier noted that Samuel Jarvis, whose house was occupied and used as a Union hospital, seemed very bewildered by the turn of events. "I believe it was his firm conviction that we would, in the event of taking the Island, massacre the inhabitants generally," the soldier wrote.[12]

Actually Jarvis had little to fear. Before landing on the island, General Burnside had issued orders demanding that his troops observe "the laws of civilized warfare" and avoid "all unnecessary injuries to houses, barns, fences, and other property." Burnside did, however, authorize the troops to forage for food. Invading soldiers found hogs running loose, "so poor as to indicate the last stage of consumption," but they still captured them, as well as any loose hens, geese, turkeys, and cattle they could find. One soldier from the Twenty-seventh Massachusetts wrote home describing how some of his peers had killed a hog, then skinned and fried it in preparation for a festive meal. Likewise, the Union troops quickly confiscated sweet potatoes and other vegetables that were buried in pits in the fields. When a secessionist store owner on the south end of the island denied having any whiskey in stock, one Union soldier took over the store and commenced to give away goods at very low prices. One captured Confederate, Lieutenant J. W. Wright of the Eighth North Carolina, gleefully recorded a diary entry in which he noted that "the Yankees killed every cow and hog on the Island." Wright thought the islanders, who had betrayed the Confederacy by passing along knowledge to the Yankees and serving them as pilots, deserved the pillage.[13]

For the most part, however, the Union soldiers felt sorry for the natives, and some Union soldiers even shared supplies with the islanders. Captain Thomas H. Parker of the Fifty-first Pennsylvania indicated that the islanders had "suffered a great deal" under the Confederate occupation. According to Parker, the island residents had "scarcely anything to eat, all their provisions having been stolen from them." James Emmerton, a physician with the Twenty-third Massachusetts, remembered that the troops "found so much more poverty than potatoes." A foraging party from Emmerton's regiment returned to the camp empty-handed, apparently concluding that the islanders offered little that the soldiers could eat. The men of Company G of the Twenty-third were so moved by the sickness and hunger they found that they furnished rations and clothing to a family with ten children.[14]

General Burnside thought that the islanders were "ignorant and inoffensive" people who had endured much hardship under the Confederate occupation but had not supported the Confederate cause. Within the first few weeks of the battle, he ordered his assistants to administer the oath of allegiance to any of the white citizens on Roanoke who would take it. Some residents readily took the oath; most of the natives quickly, if begrudgingly, adapted to the Union presence on the island. Most islanders were also eager to return to fishing,

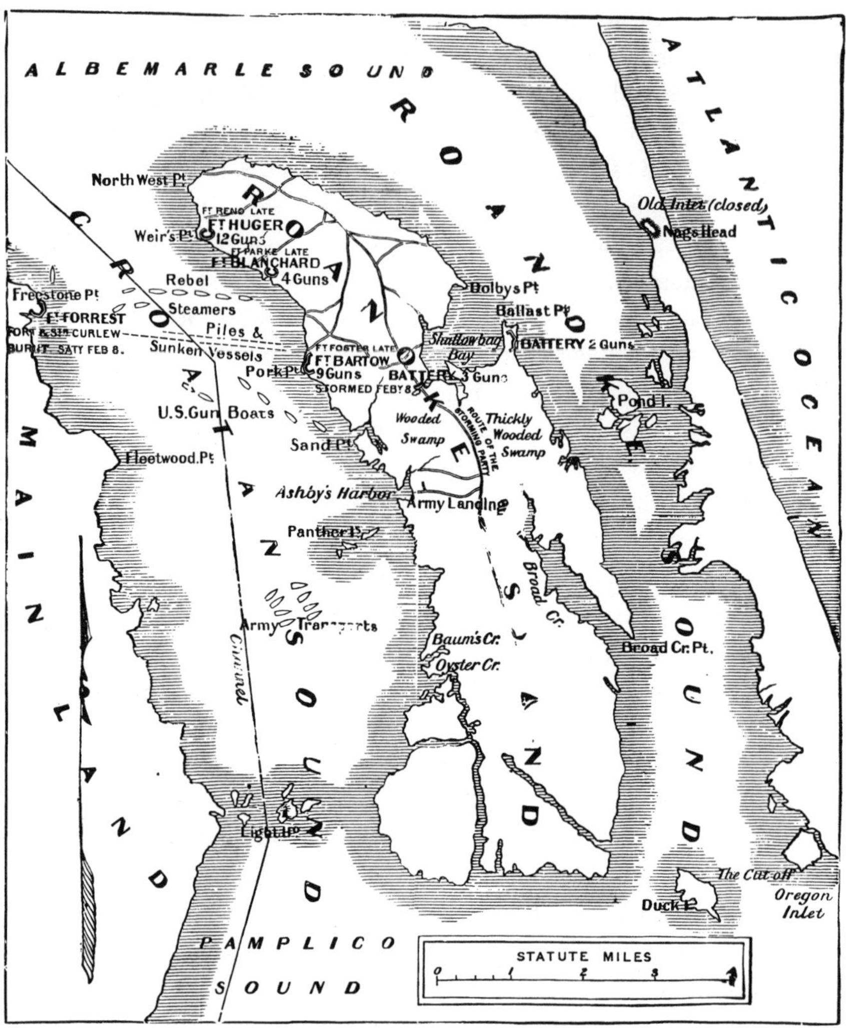

Map 1. This Civil War–era map of Roanoke Island shows the location of the Confederate forts. After the Battle of Roanoke Island, the forts were renamed in honor of the three generals who had led the troops to victory. Fort Huger became Fort Reno, Fort Blanchard became Fort Parke, and Fort Bartow became Fort Foster. (Mottelay and Campbell-Copeland, eds., *The Soldier in Our Civil War*, 1:205, Outer Banks History Center)

which the Confederate occupiers had prohibited for fear that the islanders would travel to Hatteras and share military secrets.[15]

Meanwhile, the Union victors put the captured Confederate forts on the west side of the island in order and renamed them after Brigadier Generals John G. Foster, Jesse L. Reno, and John G. Parke, the commanders who had led the three brigades in the successful battle on the island. The northernmost battery at Weir's Point, Fort Huger, became Fort Reno; the battery about a mile south of Weir's Point, Fort Blanchard, was renamed Fort Parke; and the southernmost battery at Pork Point, Fort Bartow, was newly christened Fort Foster. Fort Reno had a dock and served as the location of a market where, as one soldier recounted, natives sold "poultry, eggs, pies, [and] cookies" to the soldiers. Union headquarters and the primary landing were established further south, near Fort Foster at Pork Point. A small hospital was also located near headquarters. Battery Defiance in the center of the island became Battery Russell, while the battery on the eastern shore became Battery Monteil—both named in honor of Union officers who lost their lives during the contest on Roanoke Island.[16]

In addition to the Confederate forts, the Union army acquired barracks, officers' quarters, military hospitals, a number of incidental buildings, and supplies. During the battle, Fort Bartow bore the brunt of the naval attack; flames destroyed the barracks located in a clearing behind the fort. A member of the Twenty-third Massachusetts recalled that after the fighting, his regiment had marched along the parade ground in the camp between the "smoking embers of the barracks and the shell-torn officers quarters." Accounts from soldiers stationed on the island differed in their assessments of the capacity of the remaining captured barracks, with estimates ranging from four to twenty thousand. Most did agree that there were at least twenty-four to thirty large barracks in the camps, and that each barracks could house two companies.[17]

The soldiers set up camps in the barracks near the two northern forts. General Reno's second brigade (consisting of the Twenty-first Massachusetts, Ninth New Jersey, Fifty-first New York, and Fifty-first Pennsylvania) and General Parke's third brigade (consisting of the Eighth Connecticut, Eleventh Connecticut, Ninth New York, Fourth Rhode Island, and Fifth Rhode Island) encamped, as one soldier recounted, in the barracks "on the Northern point of the Island, in a fine, dry location sheltered on all sides by woods" in a site known as Camp Reno. Matthew J. Graham, a lieutenant of the Ninth New York, later recalled that the "commodious" barracks in this camp were "arranged in a column of companies and separated from each other by wide company streets."[18]

South of Camp Reno, General Foster's first brigade (consisting of the Tenth Connecticut, Twenty-third Massachusetts, Twenty-fourth Massachu-

Victorious Union troops established Camp Reno near the Confederate barracks behind Fort Huger. Later the barracks, shown in this engraving based on a sketch by R. Schell, served as the first home for freedpeople arriving on Roanoke Island. (Mottelay and Campbell-Copeland, eds., *The Soldier in Our Civil War*, 1:210–11, Outer Banks History Center)

setts, Twenty-fifth Massachusetts, and Twenty-seventh Massachusetts) settled into an encampment that was christened Camp Foster. The Union's main hospital was situated in this camp. One soldier of the Twenty-third Massachusetts later recounted that Camp Foster was located in the "newly taken barracks," while another recalled that Camp Foster included "some large wooden barracks supplied with fire-places, windows, and separate rooms for the officers." Lieutenant William J. Creasey of the Twenty-third Massachusetts noted that the fort nearest Camp Foster was Fort Huger, later renamed Fort Reno. The soldiers' recollections suggest that Camps Reno and Foster were probably both located in the same general barracks area, behind Fort Reno. After a short while the distinction between Camp Reno and Camp Foster disappeared; soldiers and others on the island called the entire camp area in the vicinity of the old Confederate barracks Camp Foster.[19]

Once all the Rebel prisoners had been rounded up, things calmed down and soldiers settled into camp life. Men who had been sworn enemies during the battle swapped stories and souvenirs. On 20 February, the prisoners were sent

After the Battle of Roanoke Island, Union troops took over the Confederate barracks in Camp Georgia, renaming the area Camp Foster. Later, freedpeople found shelter in the barracks. (*Illustrated London News*, 29 March 1862, author's collection)

to Elizabeth City to await exchange with Union prisoners. Alfred Roe noted that the prisoners "fairly went wild" when the regimental band of the Twenty-fourth Massachusetts struck up "Dixie" as they were loaded onto transports. Later that month, according to one soldier's diary, Washington's Birthday was celebrated "by salutes from the forts and a holiday in the camp." The *New York Times* reported that on 23 February, in "a pretty grove of evergreen" to the rear of the hospital at Camp Foster, a religious ceremony marked the dedication of Roanoke Cemetery, a resting place for the Union dead. Several chaplains of the Massachusetts regiments spoke, and the Twenty-fourth Massachusetts's regimental band provided music. In early March, most of the Union regiments left the island, with only the Fifty-first Pennsylvania and Fifth Rhode Island remaining as temporary garrisons. They were replaced by the Sixth New Hampshire and Eighty-ninth New York, who had been at Hatteras during the battle of Roanoke Island, and the Ninth New York, which had left the island after the battle to conduct military excursions in eastern North Carolina. The Ninth New York was also known as Hawkins's Zouaves in honor of the regiment's leader, Colonel Rush C. Hawkins, and because of their flamboyant battle attire, which was modeled after the brilliant uniforms of the French Algerian Zouaves. Colonel Hawkins was appointed post commandant.[20]

Settling in for what they thought would be a lengthy stay, the men of the

Colonel Rush C. Hawkins, regimental leader of the Ninth New York Volunteers, was the first Union post commandant on Roanoke Island. He is pictured here in his uniform, which was modeled after those of the French Algerian Zouaves. (Massachusetts Commandery, Military Order of the Loyal Legion of the United States and the U.S. Army Military History Institute)

occupying forces soon devised a number of recreational diversions. The Ninth New York established a reading room, debating club, post office, and several baseball clubs. Several companies erected gymnastic apparatus and held sparring and wrestling matches that, according to one witness, "would have delighted the eyes of a professional." The Ninth New York's crowning cultural achievement, however, was the creation of the Zouaves Minstrel and Dramatic Club, which presented plays and minstrels for audiences composed of soldiers and island natives. The club presented a play once a week, charging a regular admission fee. General Burnside, and later Colonel Hawkins, watched the plays from the comfort of a private box built for officers of rank. Although the group performed in a building that could seat five hundred people, the shows drew such large crowds that many people were turned away. One participant noted that the local response was especially spirited: "The natives of the island were not only pleased but incredulously astonished at the performances. . . . Few of the Roanokers knew what a theatre was, and scarcely any of them had ever seen a play." The Club cleared $364.00 during its first season of productions.[21]

The soldiers celebrated the first Fourth of July of the occupation by firing salutes from Forts Foster and Parke, followed by a reading of the Declaration of Independence and "all kinds of sport and amusement." Matthew Graham noted that "one specially notable feature" was a parade in which one company "gave a fine exhibition of light artillery drill with their wheelbarrow battery, which was warmly applauded by the enthusiastic spectators."[22]

In August 1862 an inspection of medical conditions at the Roanoke Island post indicated that the "sanitary condition of the camps and the men in quarters" was good, and that their food was of "good quality," but not well cooked. The post commandant had ordered the post surgeon, a Dr. Thomas, off the island, apparently because his addiction to opium rendered him "unfit to take care of the sick." The inspector noted that some "medical books and other property belonging to the hospital disappeared when Dr. Thomas left, and it is supposed that he took the articles with him." Otherwise, conditions were good at his hospital, which was near headquarters. The other post hospital, located at Camp Foster and staffed by a Dr. McClellan, was "in good order generally." The inspector noted that the distance between headquarters and Camp Foster—three miles—made it difficult for one medical officer to handle all the sick. Thus, he recommended that neither hospital be closed, but that the one on marshlands near headquarters "be moved to a more dry and elevated spot with advantage."[23]

The two hospitals remained open. James Emmerton of the Twenty-third Massachusetts temporarily assumed Thomas's old position of post physician.

He wrote that life on Roanoke Island was a bit monotonous but "not unpleasant." Although he occasionally sought relief from the "humid semi-tropical atmosphere of the island" by brief visits to the beach at Nags Head, where he enjoyed "the bracing sea breezes, rolling in unobstructed from opposite Africa," he was happy to be stationed on Roanoke Island. He thought the island was "a long step nearer civilization" than Hatteras.[24]

Military occupation on Roanoke Island was not, however, without difficulties. The most pressing problem for Union officers was what to do with the slaves streaming into the Union camp. At the time of the battle, more than two hundred blacks were working at the Confederate camp on the island. A few were free blacks who had been impressed into Confederate service to build Confederate fortifications on the island. Most, however, were slaves. Some of them had accompanied their masters, while others had been sent to the island to build fortifications after Walter Gwynn, the Brigadier General in charge of coastal defenses, had requested their service. After the battle, crowds of these black workers were, according to one Union soldier's account, "singing, dancing, and waiting on our men, or giving graphic accounts of the rebel boastings before the fight."[25]

Informed that they could remain on the island under Union protection or return to their owners on the mainland, most of the slaves working in the Confederate camp shocked their Union liberators by noting that they wished to return to their homes. When pressed for a reason, they stated that they did not want to leave their wives and children in slavery; they planned to go home to free them, presumably with the intent of returning to the island sanctuary. Matthew J. Graham noted that only twenty-seven of the two hundred slaves in the Confederate camp immediately passed into Union hands. Graham recorded that it did not take long, however, before "others, scattered about the island, were gathered together" with them in a small camp. Shortly after the battle, another group arrived in front of Union headquarters in a dinghy.[26]

Meanwhile, word that slaves who made it to the Union camp would be granted freedom spread rapidly to the rest of the island and various parts of northeastern North Carolina, and others soon sought refuge in the Union Camp. The Union soldiers "don't know what to do with them, but stand and watch them," declared Lieutenant William J. Creasey of the Twenty-third Massachusetts. William H. Johnson, a black soldier who served with the Eighth Connecticut, observed that by early March "quite a large number" of runaways had "congregated on the island." A writer for the *National Anti-Slavery Standard* estimated that seventy or eighty refugees had arrived by early March—many of them from Elizabeth City, Plymouth, and Edenton. He also reported that "hundreds" were "hiding in the woods" preparing to come. The Ninth New York, in fact, took in a number of fugitives who had been hiding in the Dismal Swamp, including one who had lived there since 1855. By early April the Roanoke camp numbered approximately 250. Although a smattering of destitute white families from the mainland took sanctuary on the island, most of the refugees were black. A few of these black refugees had been free before the war, but most had been slaves.[27]

Initially, the contrabands worked as laundresses, cooks, woodcutters, teamsters, and porters for the Union officers and soldiers; and they lived undisturbed on the periphery of the Union camp. As the former slaves poured onto the island, however, Union authorities grew very concerned about their living conditions, primarily because of fears that sanitation problems in the makeshift camp would have adverse effects on the Union encampment. There were also fears that the proximity of the contrabands to the Union soldiers would interfere with military discipline. The search for a long-term solution to the refugee problem ultimately led to the establishment of an officially sanctioned contraband camp. That camp, in turn, became the site of the Roanoke Island freedmen's colony.[28]

An African Village of Grand Proportions

THE BIRTH OF THE COLONY

VINCENT COLYER, an agent of the New York Christian Commission who had accompanied the Union troops to Roanoke Island, witnessed the early flowering of the community of former slaves. Within a short period of time after the battle of Roanoke Island, the scattered refugees had coalesced into a small settlement. Colyer recounted that the first thing they did together was to build a place for worship, a task that involved a great amount of creative improvisation. The former slaves framed their church from tall pines and pine branches, placing straight pines "parallel lengthwise for seats, with space enough for their knees," while fabricating the pulpit out of discarded boxes from the Quartermaster's Department. Despite the primitive conditions, the services impressed Colyer. "Many of their colored preachers exhort with great earnestness and power," he reported, which was all the more remarkable given that North Carolina law had prohibited black men from preaching since 1831. By the end of February 1862, the refugees had erected two churches on the island. At about the same time, Martha Culling, a former slave, opened the community's first school in a small building on Pork Point near Union headquarters and the landing.[1]

The refugees' first cooperative efforts suggest two things: that they valued religion and education, and that they planned to establish a durable community. In the latter endeavor, the former slaves faced numerous difficulties, the most significant related to the burgeoning of the camp's population. Throughout the life of the settlement, the numbers exceeded the community's ability to absorb them; in addition, there was a great amount of transience. Yet the people persisted in their efforts and expended great efforts to reconfigure and maintain family ties. During their first days of freedom, the former slaves claimed shelter wherever they could find it—mostly in the old Rebel barracks and other unused buildings on the north end of the island at Camp Foster. Given the significant role that Northern military officers and missionaries later assumed in the Roanoke colony, it is important to note that in its early stages, the former slaves were more or less acting on their own. The Union authorities watched the growing population but remained aloof from the day-to-day operation of the camp. Once the officers realized that the stream of refugees was not abating and that the crowding in the camp would most likely lead to wretched sanitary conditions and a variety of diseases that would ultimately affect soldiers on the island, they took a more active part in the organization and control of the refugees.

Early in the campaign in eastern North Carolina, General Burnside had realized that "it would be utterly impossible" to prevent slaves from crossing over Union lines. He established a four-point policy with respect to the runaways: he allowed them to enter; took their names, their masters' names, and their former places of residence; gave them jobs and charitable support; and refused to return them to former owners. On 20 February, Burnside ordered Sergeant Walter L. Thompson of Company I of the Ninth New York to take charge of the care and organization of contrabands in the eastern military district. At that time, Thompson was stationed on Roanoke Island with his regiment.[2]

Seeking to determine the status and disposition of the former slaves who were congregating on Roanoke Island, the military authorities initially looked north to the precedent that General Benjamin F. Butler had set at Fortress Monroe. In May 1861, Butler had established a policy for handling fugitive slaves when three black field hands were brought before him. After determining that these men were owned by a Rebel officer who planned to take them to North Carolina to work on Confederate fortifications, Butler confiscated the slaves and put them to work helping the masons who were constructing a new bakehouse within the fort. Butler justified his actions in a letter to General-in-Chief Winfield Scott, noting that confiscation of slave property would deprive the Confederacy of their labor, while at the same time the slaves could be put to work helping the Union. At the time, his Quartermaster's Department desperately needed laborers.

In demanding the confiscation of contrabands, Butler used Southern terminology—the idea of slaves as property—against Southern slaveholders. The entire activity was shrouded in ambivalence. Emancipationists applauded the action because they thought it would lead to emancipation, while conservatives approved Butler's plan because it seemed to maintain the idea of slaves as property. A contemporary writer pointed out that the person who would have revolted at the Reverend Henry Beecher's suggestion that freeing the slaves was a moral duty had no objections when Butler issued "an order commanding it to be done" as a "military necessity."[3]

Within several days of the initial confiscation, sixty-seven fugitive slaves—including women and children who were not aiding the Rebel cause—requested asylum at Fortress Monroe. Since his initial policy had covered only able-bodied slaves who were to be used against the Union, the new slave refugee situation prompted Butler to write another letter to Winfield Scott on 27 May. In this letter, Butler noted that he had decided to employ the able-bodied fugitives, issue rations to all, and charge the expense of taking care of the nonlaborers against the service of the laborers. Still referring to the slaves as property, Butler estimated that in good times the slaves within his lines would "be of the value of sixty thousand dollars."[4]

General Scott and Secretary of War Simon Cameron both approved Butler's policy. In a letter to Butler on 30 May 1861, Cameron acknowledged that Butler was supposed to enforce all federal laws, but he held that the need to suppress the armed rebellion of the Confederacy superceded an obligation to maintain the fugitive-slave law. Thus, he told Butler that he should not return fugitives to alleged masters. Butler began using the phrase "contraband of war" in official correspondence in late July 1861, and the label stuck. On 17 August 1861, Butler's local policy was echoed by the First Confiscation Act, which declared that all property, including slaves, used in support of the Confederate effort was "subject of prize and capture wherever found."[5]

On Roanoke Island, Post Commandant Rush Hawkins's contraband policy, issued on 12 March 1862, followed the general outline of Butler's policy. Significantly, Hawkins's plan also respected and helped reinforce the slaves' family and community ties. Hawkins ordered that each male contraband employed by the U.S. government or the army on the island should be paid ten dollars a month plus one ration and a soldier's allowance of clothing—more than contrabands were paid at either Fortress Monroe or New Bern. Each woman and each boy aged twelve to sixteen were to be paid four dollars a month plus one ration; in addition, each woman was to receive money equal to a soldier's allowance of clothing, while each boy aged twelve to sixteen would receive a soldier's allowance of clothing. Each child under twelve would receive one ration and remain with his or her parents.

Hawkins cautioned that while the regulations applied only to contrabands in public service, those contrabands who were hired by officers as servants should also be paid according to the terms of the regulations. He also commanded that the former slaves be treated "with great Care and humanity," and indicated his hope "that their helpless and dependent Condition" would "protect them against injustice and imposition." In mid-March Hawkins notified General Burnside that 130 contrabands were working for the government, and that most needed clothing. They had nearly finished construction of a storehouse, and would be put to work on a wharf and battery when proper tools arrived. The official policy authorized the deduction of a portion of their wages for the support of the sick or disabled in the camp who were unable to work.[6]

On 31 March 1862, as the first step toward a more organized handling of the contraband situation, General Burnside took the oversight of contrabands and other refugees out of the hands of regular military officers. Burnside appointed Vincent Colyer as superintendent of the poor in the Department of North Carolina. As part of his work with the Christian Commission, Colyer had distributed supplies to sick and wounded soldiers and assisted the regimental chaplain after the battle of Roanoke Island. He then followed the troops to New Bern, where he established his headquarters. Commenting on Burnside's motives with respect to the contraband policy, Colyer reported that the general was "by no means an abolitionist," but he "had too much sagacity to despise the services of the blacks" and "was too large hearted a man to love slavery."[7]

General Burnside ordered Colyer to see that the poor, whether black or white, were fed and sheltered. He also ordered him to employ up to five thousand black men in the building of forts in North Carolina. Until Colyer left his position in July 1862 he attempted to fill this order, but was never able to do so. His men, however, did work on three earth-work forts, including one named Fort Burnside on Roanoke Island. In addition, they built docks on the island. Colyer estimated that of the 10,000 freed blacks in his care in the spring of 1862, 2,500 were men and 7,500 were women and children; a thousand of the total were on Roanoke Island. In addition to fort construction, the male contrabands worked in a variety of jobs for the army's Quartermaster's Department as dock workers, carpenters, blacksmiths, coopers, and bridge builders and ship joiners, while others were knowledgeable spies, scouts, and guides. The women and children supported themselves by washing, ironing, and cooking for the Union soldiers.[8]

In the summer of 1862, the Reverend James Means, a hospital chaplain from Massachusetts who was serving soldiers in New Bern, replaced Vincent Colyer. Although his official title was changed slightly, to "Superintendent of Blacks in

In March 1862 General Ambrose Burnside appointed Vincent Colyer, a civilian who had been working in North Carolina as an agent of the New York Christian Commission, as superintendent of the poor in the Department of North Carolina. Colyer's Headquarters were in New Bern. (Mottelay and Campbell-Copeland, eds., *The Soldier in Our Civil War*, 1:206, Outer Banks History Center)

North Carolina," Means continued much of the work Colyer had initiated. In addition to distributing wages, rations, and clothing to the men who were working for the military, he also attempted to meet the spiritual and social needs of the contrabands. Since Means's office was in New Bern, Union officers supervised most of the day-to-day operations, such as the defense constructions, on Roanoke Island. The contrabands, meanwhile, continued to shape their own community, incorporating some aspects of white culture that they wished to emulate. For example, many of the former slaves, whose masters had "married them" without traditional religious or legal ceremonies, decided that they wanted to be married by a minister. So, in the late summer and fall of 1862, T. W. Conway, a Union chaplain stationed on the island, performed a number of marriage ceremonies. These included the one he conducted for Judy Dunton and John Sykes, who were married one evening after a prayer meeting in one of the contraband chapels.[9]

In January 1863, President Abraham Lincoln's Emancipation Proclamation gave even greater impetus for slaves to flock to Union camps throughout the

South. Roanoke Island was no exception. Increasingly, too, the situation in the camps seemed to call for a national policy. Thus, in March 1863, the War Department announced the formation of the American Freedmen's Inquiry Commission to look into "methods of protecting, improving or usefully employing" the freedpeople who were under Union control. The commission, composed of social reformer Robert Dale Owen (Indiana) and abolitionists Samuel Gridley Howe (Massachusetts) and James McKaye (New York), traveled to many of the contraband camps and questioned local authorities about the contraband situation. In June 1863 the commission released a preliminary report that recommended the creation of a freedmen's bureau, separate from the administration of the army, to oversee the freedpeople's transition from slavery to freedom. The commission noted that able-bodied men should be put to work as soldiers and military workers or as laborers on abandoned plantations, and family ties should be encouraged and respected. Although some humanitarian reformers believed that a long period of guardianship would be needed to protect the former slaves as they entered free society, the commission favored a more laissez-faire approach. They rejected permanent or semipermanent guardianship of the freedmen, calling for them to become self-supporting as soon as possible. In addition, the report urged the establishment of a school system staffed by people from the various freedmen's aid societies and supervised by a freedmen's bureau. The commission concluded that the government should continue to provide transportation, quarters, and rations for religious or secular teachers from authorized benevolent societies that were providing relief at various freedmen's camps.[10]

James Means served as Superintendent of Blacks in North Carolina until 6 April 1863, when he died as a result of complications from typhoid fever. In late April, Major General John G. Foster, commander of the Eighteenth Army Corps, appointed the Reverend Horace James, an army chaplain from Worcester, Massachusetts, to be "Superintendent of all the Blacks" in the Department of North Carolina. In May, even before the release of the report of the American Freedmen's Inquiry Commission, Foster ordered James to help establish an organized "colony of negroes on Roanoke Island."[11]

James, a direct descendant of New England Puritans, assumed his job with the confident enthusiasm of a man who had spent his life preparing for the task. Looking back, it does seem that the bearded man of scholarly demeanor, whose wire-rimmed spectacles framed eyes of piercing intensity, had been predestined for the job. Born in Medford, Massachusetts, on 6 May 1818 into a family of shipbuilders, James received his earliest spiritual training from his father Galen, an evangelical Congregationalist who had helped to found two churches in

After President Abraham Lincoln issued the Emancipation Proclamation, the number of freedpeople fleeing to freedmen camps increased. Sometimes, as this engraving illustrates, they were escorted by Union soldiers. Some of the freedpeople escaped with horses, wagons, or agricultural implements, while others brought only the clothes on their backs. (*Harper's Weekly*, 21 February 1863, Special Collections, University of Virginia Library)

Medford, and who later co-founded and edited the *Congregationalist*. Galen James was also involved in a number of social causes. He opposed slavery, was a strong advocate of temperance, and helped to establish a free coeducational high school in Medford, one of the first in Massachusetts.[12]

After common school, James spent two years at Phillips Academy in Andover, which reinforced his strong evangelical leanings. At Yale, James decided to study for the ministry, and following graduation, he attended and was graduated from Andover Theological Seminary. In 1843 he married Helen Leavitt and assumed the co-pastorship of the Original Congregational Church of Wrentham. Nine years of ministry there were followed by a pastorate at the Old South Church of Worcester. During these years he became an outspoken advocate of free public schools, temperance, and antislavery. At one point, he had, in fact, applied for a commission to be a chaplain of one of Massachusetts' all-black Union regiments, but all the positions were filled. He also maintained close ties with proponents of antislavery and abolition, including his wife's cousin, the influential abolitionist Joshua Leavitt.[13]

During the first week of October 1861, the men of the Twenty-fifth Massachusetts chose James for the elected position of regimental chaplain. One of the soldiers recorded that he thought the troops had "shown good judgment in selecting a chaplain of the orthodox faith, as no one visiting our camp for an hour could doubt their belief in the existence of the burning lake by the way they consign each other to that locality." James was mustered into service on 29 October 1861, in Worcester, and the troops soon learned that he was very serious about maintaining high moral standards, including intolerance of profanity and an advocacy of temperance. James served beside the men of the Twenty-fifth Massachusetts during the battle of Roanoke Island—at one point even manning a gun—and had spoken at the dedication of the cemetery in Camp Foster. He was in Plymouth with the regiment at the time of his appointment to the superintendency.[14]

Although James's headquarters were in New Bern, he always expressed a special fondness for Roanoke Island. He made a distinction between "sheltering" the former slaves in "temporary camps or settlements" in the vicinity of New Bern, Beaufort, and Washington, and "colonizing them" on Roanoke Island, "the only place in North Carolina" where the freedpeople's safety could be assured for the long term. James viewed the establishment of the colony as an opportunity to prove some of his ideas about freeholding and free labor in a permanent self-supporting community of former slaves. General Foster was a bit more ambivalent about the long-term prospects for the colony, but he also indicated that James would supervise the creation of a self-sufficient community on the island. In a report on his work issued later in his superintendency, James noted that General Foster's purpose in creating the colony on Roanoke Island was "to settle colored people on the unoccupied lands," to "give them agricultural implements and mechanical tools to begin with," "to train and educate them for a free and independent community," and "to arm and drill them for self defence."[15]

It was typical of Foster, James, and the Northern philanthropists who were later involved in the Roanoke colony that they failed to recognize that the freedpeople had already, on their own, established the rudiments of a community on Roanoke Island in the face of extraordinary obstacles. The colonists not only had to make up for insufficient tools and materials, but they also had to create a web of social and communal connections where none had existed. While freedpeople in each of the other Carolina camps were usually from the areas immediately surrounding the camps, and thus were likely to know each other, the freedpeople who congregated in the Roanoke colony were from a variety of geographical areas. Consequently, before they could even contemplate the creation of economic or political networks, they had to forge basic friendship networks.[16]

Ultimately, however, neither James, the Northern missionaries, nor the freedpeople themselves, had final control over the direction of the colony, which was first and foremost a product of military exigencies. Military decisions made hundreds of miles distant had dramatic impacts on the island experiment. The decision that had the most dramatic impact on the shape of the fledgling Roanoke Island colony grew out of a heated debate about the extent to which black men should be used as soldiers. Shortly after the firing on Fort Sumter, free blacks in the North had indicated their eagerness to serve the Union cause. The most progressive whites argued that all free blacks should be allowed to enlist and serve alongside white troops. Other whites agreed that blacks could be soldiers, but insisted that they be segregated from white troops and that their officers be white. Most Northerners, however, had doubts about the efficacy of the black soldier.

Well over a year after the start of the war, the Militia Act of 17 July 1862 authorized the use of black troops, especially in garrison duty, construction, and labor battalions. The Confiscation Act, passed that same day, declared that slaves of rebels who entered Union lines were free and authorized the President to organize and use blacks for the public welfare. By that time, many freedmen were already serving as laborers at various Union posts. The combination of President Lincoln's concerns about the reactions of the border states and his own ambivalence about the value of black soldiers, however, led him initially to refuse to use his power to raise black troops. By the fall of 1862, he was ready to risk their use provided they served in all-black regiments under white officers. Then, after the Emancipation Proclamation, Lincoln authorized the governors of New England to recruit black regiments. In May 1863, General Orders No. 143 standardized recruitment of black soldiers and centralized their control in the Bureau of Colored Troops under the adjutant general.[17]

In April 1863, Lincoln authorized Brigadier General Edward A. Wild, a physician and highly regarded military leader from Brookline, Massachusetts, to raise four regiments of black soldiers in North Carolina. Wild, who had suffered a crippling wound to his right hand at Seven Pines and had lost his left arm at South Mountain, had gained the attention of the War Department when he helped Governor John A. Andrew recruit blacks for the Fifty-fourth and Fifty-fifth Massachusetts Volunteers. An abolitionist, Wild had great faith in the value of black troops. Thus, despite Wild's injuries and a reputation for eccentricity and contentiousness, Secretary of War Edwin Stanton thought him the

Brigadier General Edward A. Wild recruited three infantry regiments and one heavy artillery regiment for an African brigade from North Carolina. He was also the first Union officer in charge of laying out the village in the Roanoke Island freedmen's colony. (Massachusetts Commandery, Military Order of the Loyal Legion of the United States and the U.S. Army Military History Institute)

right man to rally black troops in the tarheel state. Wild was willing to endure the ill will and occasional harassment that many Northerners directed toward the white commanders of black troops. Later in his career, Wild acknowledged that during the more than two years he had been associated with black troops, he "had nothing but prejudice, jealousy, misrepresentation, persecution and treachery to contend against."[18]

Wild eventually recruited three infantry regiments and a heavy artillery regiment for his African brigade, all in the face of mounting evidence that the soldiers were treated harshly by Confederate captors. In May 1863, for example, the Confederate Congress had authorized President Jefferson Davis to have captured black soldiers delivered to the civil authorities in the states in which they were captured, where the soldiers faced punishments that ranged from re-enslavement to death. Frequently, Confederate officers did not bother with the red tape; they executed captured black soldiers on the spot.[19]

On Roanoke Island and in New Bern, Wild's goal was to enlist all able-bodied black men between eighteen and forty-five years of age. According to Horace James, General Wild and several free blacks from the North began recruiting freedmen for North Carolina's first company of Colored Volunteers on Roanoke Island in mid-June 1863. James later wrote that he believed this company "was the first company of colored troops raised in North Carolina." Descriptive books for the three regiments that composed Wild's African brigade indicate that at least 139 freedmen were recruited on Roanoke Island for Wild's First, Second, and Third North Carolina Colored Volunteers, which in February 1864 were renamed the Thirty-fifth, Thirty-sixth, and Thirty-seventh U.S. Colored Troops (USCT). Since many of the soldiers whose families eventually settled in the Roanoke Island colony were recruited elsewhere, and some of the soldiers who were island natives enlisted elsewhere, it is difficult to say for certain how many of the soldiers in the African brigade had familial ties to the Roanoke Island colony. According to population statistics taken on the island in the autumn of 1864, approximately 650 men were absent, either as soldiers or civilians working for the Union army. In August 1864, one of the missionaries on the island reported that "every able bodied man" in the colony had enlisted.[20]

In June, while Wild was recruiting on the island, General Foster ordered Horace James to go north to collect money and materials to aid the colony on Roanoke Island. James wrote a compelling appeal for aid in a letter that he distributed to the Northern press. James aimed his letter at "all the friends of the NEW SOCIAL ORDER IN THE SOUTH," especially those who thought "the solution of the negro question" was "the turning point of the war." In the body of the letter, his first public articulation of the "colonization" policy, James defined the purpose of the colony on Roanoke Island, tying it to the recruitment of black soldiers. He noted that General Wild was in eastern North Carolina enlisting male freedmen for an "African brigade," which raised an important question: What, then, was to become of the soldiers' families, especially "the aged and infirm, the women and the children, the youth not old enough to enlist in the regiments?" The solution was clear: "The government or benevolent individuals and agencies cooperating with the government" must "locate them in places of safety, and teach them, in their ignorance, how to live and support themselves." The proposed remedy was to "colonize these freed people," James declared.[21]

James emphasized that the colonization of the contrabands did not involve "deportation out of the country" or "removing them north, where they are not wanted, and could not be happy" or "transporting them beyond the limits of their own State." Rather they would stay in North Carolina, where he planned on "giving them land, and implements wherewith to subdue and till it, thus stimulating their exertions by making them proprietors of the soil" and "self-supporting." James emphasized that Roanoke Island possessed many advantages. Its "insular position" made it fairly safe from attack. In addition, the island was "well wooded," and had "an abundance of good water, a tolerably productive soil, and a sufficient amount of cleared land for the commencement of operations." Further, it was "surrounded by waters abounding in delicious fish." James requested agricultural tools, building materials, and cash to purchase a steam saw and grist mill.[22]

As a result of his northern trip, James raised over $8,000, mostly from the various associations in Boston and New York that were interested in providing relief to the freedpeople. The New York National Freedman's Relief Association, for example, donated $500. Some, like the Oneida Company of New York, donated both clothing and money for the freedpeople on Roanoke Island. On 7 July, James wrote General Wild that he was sending some shovels, axes, nails, and hammers by the next boat and urged him to "put them right into use." Most of all, James made a great number of people aware of the venture commencing on Roanoke Island. For the next three years these Northerners would read about the progress of the colony in dispatches to a variety of journals, including the *Congregationalist*, the *American Missionary*, the *Freedman*, the *Freedmen's Advocate*, and the *National Freedman*.[23]

While James was in the North soliciting donations for the colony, General Foster ordered General Wild to take possession of unoccupied and unimproved lands on Roanoke Island and lay them out in lots for the thousand or so freedpeople on the island. In a July communication to Secretary of War Edwin M.

Stanton, Foster noted that he "intended to carry out the colonization scheme as a nucleus for the colored soldiers' families, and to make Roanoke Island the key-point." Later that month, in orders related to the organization of General Wild's brigade, Foster noted that the families of black soldiers would "accompany them to the settlement [on Roanoke Island] and then find the comforts of a home." Foster looked forward to the rapid expansion of the colony, anticipating that it would become home to hundreds of contrabands whose husbands and fathers were in the Union army.[24]

Although General Wild's primary goal was recruitment of the African brigade, by his own account he "gave much time and labor to the care and provision" of the soldiers' families on Roanoke Island. Joseph E. Williams, a free black from Pennsylvania who came south to help General Wild recruit black soldiers, wrote a letter to the *Christian Recorder* in which he reported that Wild had surveyed the island and "established a colony there for the support of the wives of the soldiers in his brigade, and also homes for the old and young and those who are not fit for service." Williams highlighted Wild's plans to build churches and schools, as well as his intentions to turn over captured Rebel schooners and sailboats for the colonists' use. "I was with him when he was exploring the island," Williams declared, "and I never saw a place that I ever liked better than Roanoke Island."[25]

Although no map of the colony has surfaced, its general location can be determined from contemporary descriptions of the colony, from deeds that were submitted by the native white islanders after the war when they petitioned for the restoration of over eleven hundred acres that the freedpeople had occupied, and from various postwar monthly land reports submitted by agents of the Bureau of Refugees, Freedmen, and Abandoned Lands to bureau headquarters. The monthly reports listed each parcel of land that had been occupied on the island, as well as its owner. The bulk of the property was on the northwest end of the island, running south from Weir's Point to Pork Point for approximately two miles, and stretching east for about a mile.[26]

In laying out the colonial village, General Wild was assisted by Sergeant George o. Sanderson, a Boston native serving with the Forty-third Massachusetts Regiment, who made the preliminary surveys and opened, as James later recounted, the first "broad avenue of the new African town." In his 1864 annual report, James noted that Sanderson situated the village "along the northern and western part of the island between head quarters and Ft. Reno." James very specifically described the work, emphasizing that "with compass, chart, and chain, and a gang of choppers" the village was carved out of an undeveloped wooded area of "pine, gum, holly, and cypress." He also reported that the woods began to "gleam at night with the fires which consumed the refuse vegetation, swept off in clearing the forests." Thus, James's report clearly indicates that the men laid out the village beyond the area that had been previously cleared for the former Confederate barracks.[27]

George Sanderson was assisted by H. E. Rockwell, who later penned a fairly explicit physical description of the colony for the *Freedmen's Advocate*. According to Rockwell, three straight avenues, each fifty feet wide and running northwest to southeast, were laid out twelve hundred feet apart and roughly parallel to the Croatan Sound. The avenues, which extended from about a half mile south of the northern point of the island to Pork Point, bore the names Lincoln, Roanoke, and Burnside. Twenty-six straight streets, each twenty-five feet wide and running southwest to northeast, crossed the avenues on the perpendicular every four hundred feet. The northern street was called E Street, followed by D, C, B, and A Streets and then the numbered streets from First to Twenty-first. Although Rockwell does not indicate why both letters and numbers were used as street demarcations, it seems likely that the lettered streets were pre-existing company streets in Camp Foster. The western avenue, Lincoln, began behind Fort Reno and ran in a straight line that varied from eight to fifteen hundred feet from the irregular shore of the Croatan Sound until it terminated at the marsh near Pork Point at Twentieth Street. The middle avenue, Roanoke, which was the most settled, extended a little beyond Twenty-first Street, just east of Union headquarters at Pork Point. The eastern avenue was Burnside; beyond it the island extended eastward for two to three miles, mostly occupied by island natives. According to a plan that Horace James submitted to the American Freedmen's Inquiry Commission in January 1864, the avenues ran from the northwest to the southeast at an angle roughly forty-two degrees west of magnetic north—generally the same orientation as that of the island itself.[28]

The crisscrossing streets and avenues created large rectangles that were four hundred feet by twelve hundred feet. James divided the rectangles into twelve lots, each two hundred feet by two hundred feet; each lot faced a street. The result, James explained, were lots that were slightly less than an acre apiece. "But the decimal measurement is much easier," James noted, "and we thus make square work." The lots were numbered—odd numbers on one side of a street and even on the other—and assigned to freed families for improvement. When discussing the size of the lots, James noted that General Foster never intended to give farms to the freedmen. Rather, the plots allowed for a small house and garden. The lots in the Roanoke village were, however, substantially larger than the plots of confiscated lands that were being distributed to freedpeople in Hampton, Virginia, and New Bern—a distinction that reflects the

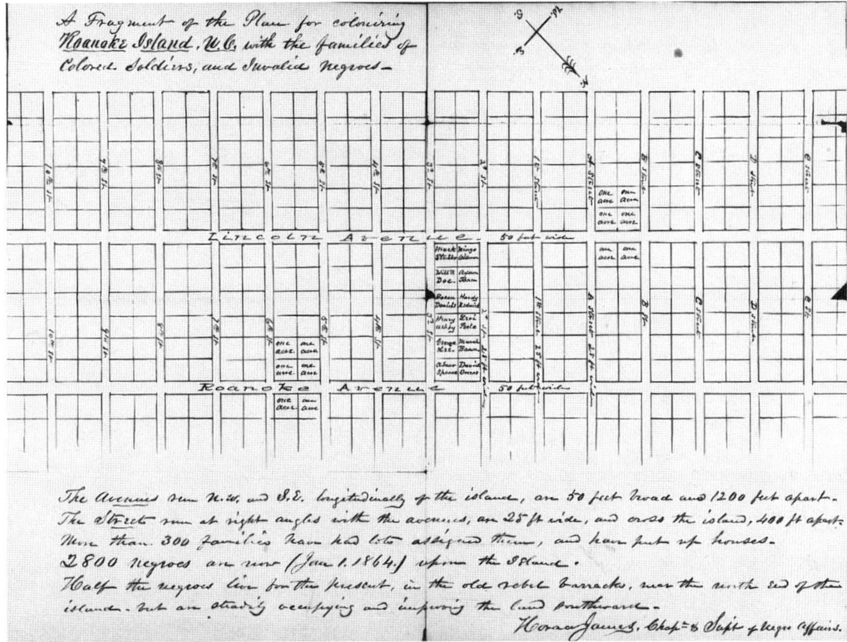

In January 1864 Horace James submitted a drawing of his plan for colonizing Roanoke Island to the American Freedmen's Inquiry Commission. James's note on the plan indicated that three hundred families had put up houses on assigned lots in the village. Although half of the twenty-eight hundred freedmen in the colony still lived in the old Rebel barracks, they were "steadily occupying and improving the land southward." (National Archives)

difference between Foster's and James's long-term hopes for the Roanoke colony and the anticipated short-term nature of the other settlements.[29]

The freedpeople—men, women, and children of all ages—eagerly cleared their lots and built their own houses. Many had been waiting on the island for over a year for the opportunity to have a place of their own. Orris and Winney Midgett, for example, had fled from Croatan to the island within months of the Union occupation. Once they had a chance to build in the village, Orris, despite failing health, pounced on it. Although Orris died before the war ended, Winney was still living in the house in the immediate postwar period. During the first year of home construction in the village, colonists used hand tools to fashion houses out of whatever wood that they could scavenge on the island. H. E. Rockwell recorded that the houses were built "of logs or poles, covered with a kind of board or shingle simply rived from the pine or cypress, making a tolerably comfortable house for fair weather." Horace James noted

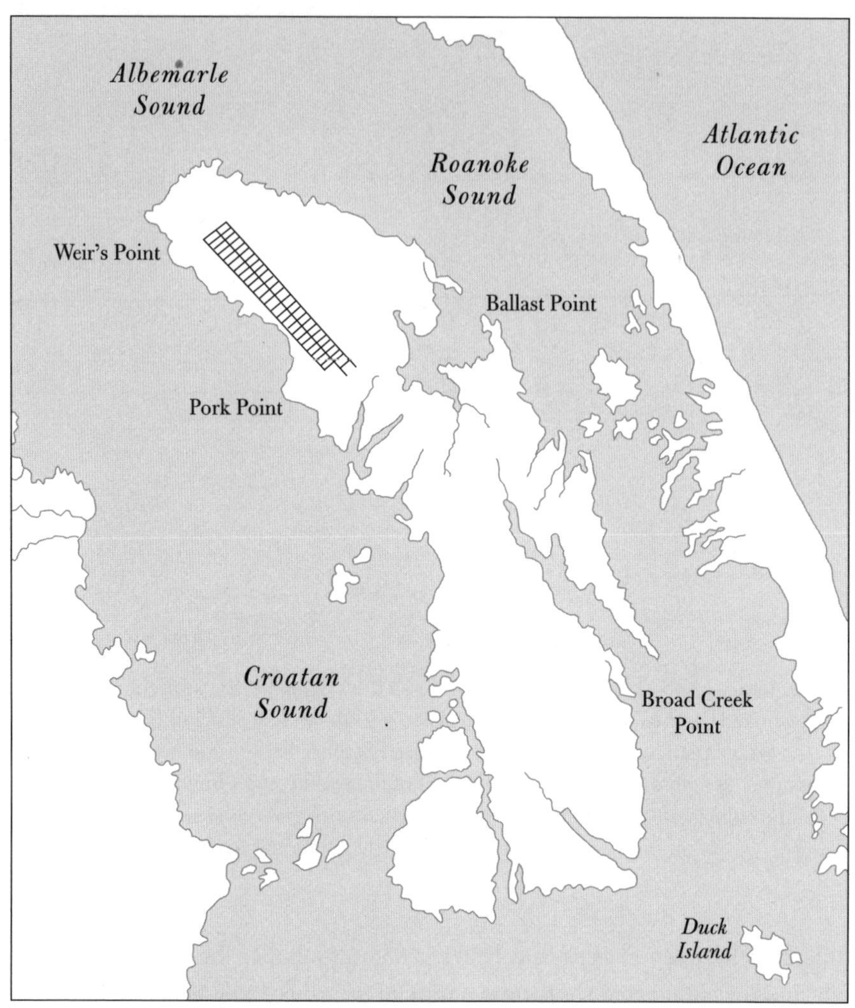

Map 2. The exact location of the Roanoke Island freedmen's colony remains a mystery, since all physical evidence has disappeared. Contemporary descriptions note that the colony stretched from the area east of Weir's Point to the area east of Pork Point. The westernmost avenue, Lincoln, terminated at 20th Street in marshland, while the other avenues, Roanoke and Burnside, stretched at least to 21st Street. (Drawn by Tim Radcliffe, from information supplied by author)

that these "split" houses featured "chimneys of the Southern style" constructed out of sticks and clay rather than brick.[30]

The resulting structure was drafty at best, as a soldier's description of a typical split house in the freedmen's settlement at New Bern underscores:

> Each house contains but one room, no rooms above. The boards used for building are made as follows. They cut down a pitch pine tree, then cut it in logs eight feet long, then with the ax and wedge, split into boards about ¾ inches in thickness, the grain being perfectly straight, but makes a very uneven surface. The wind blows through the crevices.[31]

Yet, the most significant characteristic of the houses was that they belonged to their builders, who were apparently elated by that prospect. In many cases, possession of a house in the village laid the foundation for future success in the colony, validating Horace James's assertion that freeholding went hand-in-hand with freedom. The story of one of the first men to move into the village, Mingo Obman, illustrates the point. Obman had escaped to the island in May 1863 with a few cents in his pockets. Joined by his wife shortly after her escape, the two moved into a small cabin that Obman had built at the corner of Lincoln Avenue and Second Street. When the Reverend Elinathan Davis, a Congregationalist minister from Fitchburg, Massachusetts, visited the island in December 1864, he found the couple in prosperous condition. They had "plenty of provisions for themselves and to give a meal to anybody who was hungry," as well as "a hundred dollars in cash, besides two hundred and fifty due him from the government," Davis reported. Obman noted, in fact, that he would "give a meal to a hungry rebel as soon as to others," but he would "want him to leave mighty quick after he'd got his victuals."[32]

Although General Foster ordered Wild and his black troops to Charleston on 31 July 1863, Wild left Sergeant Sanderson on the island to supervise the colony's development. Recruiting officers remained stationed on Roanoke Island and continued to enlist newly arriving freedpeople throughout the summer and fall. In mid-August, General Foster ordered Horace James to take complete control of the colonization on Roanoke Island, noting that Wild's order to take possession of unoccupied land on the island reverted to James. James returned to the island in early September 1863, spent two days inspecting the young colony, and then on 5 September wrote home to the *Congregationalist*. He noted that many of the former slaves were "living in close quarters, too much huddled together in barracks, formerly occupied by soldiers" in Camp Foster, but "the outlines of an African village of grand proportions" had been staked out on "a large tract of well-wooded land." James was delighted by "the energy and zeal" with which the freedpeople cleared their land and built their houses. "They are so animated by the prospect of a homestead of their own, and the little comforts of a freehold," James reported, "that they labor, every spare moment by night as well as by day, and are as happy as larks in their toil." Concluding that the freedpeople's efforts demonstrated their strong desire for personal property and real estate, James applauded their efforts and predicted great things for the colony. "We can already see the smiling cottages of virtuous and industrious people clustering along the straight streets which the woodman's axe has opened through these before unbroken forests, and which will be the future glory of this noted island," he declared.[33]

Writing to General Foster on the same day, James reported that the freedpeople were selecting lots and making improvements "with the greatest avidity"—that they were spending "every moment of their time" building "their first rude log houses" in the village. There were eleven or twelve hundred freedpeople "in a very comfortable condition" on the island. James underscored that if the government would pay the freedmen for the work they had performed for the military on the island, they would be able to purchase clothing "and make themselves very comfortable." Many of those who had worked for the government had not been paid for more than a year. James also complained that the colony lacked mules and horses, but concluded that "on the whole" the colony was "doing well."[34]

On 10 September, General John J. Peck, commander of the District of North Carolina, reaffirmed Foster's orders and officially transferred powers related to the "colonization of Roanoke Island with negroes" from General Wild to Horace James. "The authority of Chaplain James will be respected in all matters relating to the welfare of the colony," Peck declared. Peck also directed James to "take possession of all unoccupied lands on the Island, and lay them out and assign them, according to his own discretion, to the families of colored soldiers, to invalids, and other blacks in the employ of the Government, giving them full possession of the same until annulled by the Government, or by due process of United States law."[35]

Although the last clause of Peck's orders ultimately created insurmountable obstacles for the colony, in the opening months of the colonization efforts, James was not concerned about legalities. He immediately took possession of numerous pieces of property on the north end of the island. He recorded that under his direction the task of laying out the freedmen village was pursued "with vigor, though with little outside aid [from the military] for some time." He reported that he had not encroached upon any property that had been cleared or enclosed by the island natives. There were, however, some sour notes that should have put James on notice of upcoming difficulties. In September James noted that he had his eye on a "house owned by three brothers Meekins, (one of whom is in the rebel army,) and now occupied by negroes, that I propose to take and fit up for *teachers* and get them here at once." After James took possession of the property, one of the brothers, Isaac C. Meekins, protested that the property had been neither unoccupied nor abandoned, initiating a sometimes bitter correspondence that continued into the postwar period.[36]

General Foster gave unqualified support of the colonial efforts on Roanoke Island. A letter to General Peck on 11 September summarized some points that had been covered in a conversation between General Peck and General Foster. There would be an order "to turn over broken down Horses, Mules, Harness and Waggons" to the colony. Likewise, there would be an order to prepare houses for teachers and to procure a steam engine in Boston. The government would grant fishing and hunting privileges to colonists, and, if necessary, employ a schooner "to convey Manure to Roanoke Island." Presumably the latter effort was intended to benefit the freedpeople's gardens.[37]

General Peck visited the island in early October, and wrote that his "expectations in respect to the colony were more than realized." He noted that the superintendent was laying out the village and that he had instructed him "to make the avenues of ample width, with a view to increase the beauty and healthfulness of the Island." Peck confirmed that he had arranged for mules, horses, and wagons to be condemned and turned over to the settlement, and offered an optimistic assessment of its future. "The success of the enterprise I regard as certain," wrote Peck, who thought that the "African colony [could] be made self-supporting after the first year."[38]

In mid-October James sent General Foster a similarly glowing report of the colony, noting that it was "becoming increasingly popular among the negroes," with new arrivals each week. "The work of colonizing Roanoke Island goes on hourly," James reported. "I go up every week, and spend half my time upon the island." James did, however, reiterate his complaint about the government's failure to pay the freedmen who were working in the camp. Similarly, he lamented that he lacked the power to hire a gang of men to erect houses for the wives and children of freedmen soldiers. James reminded Foster that the government had promised to protect the freedmen families. Noting that the Medical Director of the District of North Carolina, Dr. D. W. Hand, wanted him to accommodate eight hundred to a thousand more freedpeople within the next six weeks, he stated that he could easily do so if "empowered to employ and pay the men" to work on construction in the colony. "I have not asked the government for a single nail, or foot of lumber, or axe or hammer or saw, for the

In May 1861 Major General Benjamin F. Butler established the precedent for sheltering contrabands at Fortress Monroe. In December 1864, as commander of the Department of Virginia and North Carolina, he established a groundbreaking policy for the recruitment of black troops and the care of their families in contraband camps. (Massachusetts Commandery, Military Order of the Loyal Legion of the United States and the U.S. Army Military History Institute)

island," James said. "Nor will I do it, if we can have the men paid what is due them, and a small gang, say 25, employed a few months for the general purposes of the colony—and one or two assistants to direct their labors."[39]

On 11 November 1863, General Butler succeeded General Foster as commander of the Department of Virginia and North Carolina. Four days later he ordered General Wild to direct the superintendents of contrabands at the camps in his department to issue subsistence rations to the families of black soldiers. Then, in early December, he announced a formal policy to deal with the recruitment of black troops and the care of their families in the contraband camps. The policy, stated in General Orders No. 46, superseded local policies such as those decreed on Roanoke Island by Rush Hawkins, and reflected Butler's personal belief in the value of black troops in combat—a view not universally shared by his Union colleagues. All able-bodied black men from ages eighteen to forty-five who could pass the medical exam were eligible for service and prohibited from other forms of government employment. Butler promised ten dollars to each recruit and reiterated his policy of providing subsistence rations to the families of enlisted men. Believing that true freedom entailed the liberty to labor and enjoy the fruits of that labor, Butler declared that able-bodied men who refused to work were to be arrested and put to work on government fortifications without the expectation of rations for their families.[40]

Butler's groundbreaking plans for the care of the black soldiers' dependents established a bureaucratic model that was later emulated in the Bureau of Refugees, Freedmen, and Abandoned Lands. Butler consolidated responsibilities for the freedpeople in Virginia and North Carolina into a Department of Negro Affairs, appointing his aide-de-camp, Colonel Joseph Burnham Kinsman, general superintendent. Horace James became superintendent of the third district, North Carolina, which included settlements at Beaufort, New Bern, Plymouth, Roanoke Island, and Wilmington. His official title was "Superintendent of Negro Affairs for the District of North Carolina." In this capacity, he was to serve as the liaison with the Northern charities that were offering assistance to the refugees. He was to see that the freedpeople received food, shelter, clothing, and medicine. He was also to help them find employment, raise crops, and market excess crops. To facilitate James's operations and give him more power over disbursements, in mid-December 1863 Butler recommended that James be appointed quartermaster, with the rank of captain. In that capacity he would have the power to receive and disburse funds, and thus be able to hire and pay freedmen who worked for the Quartermaster's Department.[41]

Thus, in the fall of 1863 the Roanoke colony seemed to be making good progress. The organizational changes appeared to be eliminating some of the difficulties connected with the maintenance of the colony. Most of the freedpeople were busy preparing for their first winter in their own houses. And meanwhile, Horace James was devising plans to turn the refugee settlement into a permanent village that would serve as a model of social enlightenment. "We are beginning in the very wilderness," he declared, "to lay the foundations of [a] new empire."[42]

A New Social Order

HORACE JAMES'S IDEAS FOR THE COLONY

BEFORE EVER SETTING a foot on Roanoke Island, in early February 1862 Horace James had written a letter from the Union encampment at Hatteras reflecting on the "historic interest" associated with the island. Contrasting Sir Walter Raleigh's failure to colonize Roanoke Island with the Pilgrims' success at Plymouth, Massachusetts, James concluded that the difference boiled down to the goals of the two colonies: material gain versus spiritual freedom. At the time that he wrote, James could not have predicted his future involvement with the freedmen's colony on Roanoke Island. His apparent prescience grew out of his ongoing interest in the contrast between Northern and Southern values.[1]

After James took charge of the freedmen's colony, in his annual report for 1864, he amplified his comparison of the Roanoke and Plymouth colonies. While maintaining his criticism of Raleigh's sixteenth-century Roanoke colony, James drew a parallel between the new Roanoke colony and Plymouth. James believed that the goals of the freedmen's colony, like those of the Pilgrims, were more noble than those of Raleigh's failed colony. He argued that "Sir Walter Raleigh's El Dorado, where gay cavaliers hoped to discover mines of gold, but only found starvation and an early grave," might still, "under the magic touch of freedom," realize "the expectations of its early settlers." James emphasized the significant role that free labor and republican institutions would play in the freedmen's colony, concluding that the island's "wave-kissed shores" might yet "be the abode of a prosperous and virtuous people, of varying blood, but of one destiny, differing it may be, in social position, but equal before the law, a happy commonwealth, in which Ephraim shall not envy Judah, and Judah shall no longer vex Ephraim."[2]

Prior to his appointment as superintendent of the freedmen in the eastern district of North Carolina, the Reverend Horace James was a chaplain in the Union Army. He also maintained close ties with the American Missionary Association. Although his headquarters were in New Bern, James had special plans for the colony on Roanoke Island. (Massachusetts Commandery, Military Order of the Loyal Legion of the United States and the U.S. Army Military History Institute)

Although James's headquarters were in New Bern, the Roanoke colony remained his pet. James managed the physical evolution of the Roanoke Island freedmen's village; but more significantly, he labored to shape the colony's social mission. During his tenure as superintendent, James resigned his position as chaplain in order to accept the office of captain and an official position as assistant quartermaster, but his outlook always remained that of an evangelical minister. In a letter to the *Congregationalist*, James suggested that his prospects for the colony extended well beyond the island's shores. He believed that once settled upon the cultivatable lands of Roanoke Island, the freedmen families would be ready to move westward and occupy even more land: "Having made such a beginning, in a place safe from hostile depredation, the intention is to push across the main land, and occupy in a similar way the fertile grain-growing counties of Tyrrell and Hyde, and so go onward and westward indefinitely, according to the needs of these people," he asserted. In another letter, James grandly proclaimed that the work on the island would lead to "results no mortal mind can foresee. We sow in faith, and expect to reap in joy." From James's point of view, establishment of the Roanoke colony marked the inauguration of a new era in the South.[3]

Part of James's enthusiasm stemmed from his steadfast belief in the rightness of what he was doing. James tackled his job with the zeal of one who believed that he was finally going to have a chance to put his philosophy, an amalgam of mid-nineteenth-century evangelical, abolitionist, and republican ideas, into practice. James's evangelical beliefs were shaped by the instruction he received at Yale from theologian Nathaniel William Taylor, Timothy Dwight Professor of Didactic Theology. In his required course on moral philosophy, Taylor taught that humans had free will, and thus could choose not to sin. "There can be no sin in choosing evil," Taylor asserted, "unless there be power to choose good." Taylor reasoned that human beings would choose sin if they thought it would bring more happiness than God; thus the evangelical who hoped to inspire people to change their ways needed to show that God would bring greater happiness. Taylor taught that God's grace could restore those who chose God over sin to a state of purity.[4]

The nineteenth-century word for this renewal was "regeneration," a word that appears frequently in James's writings. James believed that the South had fallen into a state of sin because of the widespread acceptance of slavery; he often referred to his hopes for the "regeneration" of the South. On various occasions James specifically noted that North Carolina was "destined not only to be overrun, but to be regenerated." James believed that individual Southerners could be regenerated; then, through them, Southern society could be perfected. "The first object of the Gospel is to secure personal holiness," James wrote. "It first regenerates the man; and then, through him, reforms society and perfects institutions."[5]

Initially James had hoped for gradual emancipation and had entered the war believing that the Northern goal should be the restoration of the Union. By 4 July 1862, he had changed his mind, asserting that the elimination of slavery should be the North's primary goal. In accomplishing this end, the North would be performing God's work, leading the South from its wicked ways and purifying the Union. In a Fourth of July speech to his regiment at New Bern, James underscored his new outlook, noting that the goal was not merely the maintenance of union, but "a union *purified*" that would "be an element of hope to the world." James declared that while slavery was an "unspeakable injury to the colored people," it imparted "still greater injury to their masters." As long as they chose to own slaves, slaveholders were sinners, and without repentance they would be denied salvation.[6]

Significantly, James and other evangelicals thought that Southern sin was a national sin. Slavery, the *American Missionary* editorialized, was "the COUNTRY'S SIN" despite its location in the South, because "the people of the North have consented to the deed; and therefore the sin is national." Northern evangelicals believed that the Southerners' renunciation of slavery was a necessary step in the South's regeneration, which would ultimately lead, as Horace James declared, to "A UNION RESTORED, ESTABLISHED, AND PURIFIED."[7]

In common with other antebellum evangelicals, James thought that spiritual progress was reflected in economic and technological progress, and that the nation's spiritual progress was leading toward a quite literal millennium—a thousand years of Christ's reign on earth, as prophesied in the Book of Revelations. "Behold civilization and Christianity advancing hand in hand with the ships of our commerce, the representatives of our nationality and the missionaries of our faith," declared James in a sermon. At the same time, James firmly believed that slavery prevented the nation's continued progress toward the millennium. Slavery led to technological stagnation and was, James asserted, "subversive of all business prosperity," preventing the sort of industrial growth that God intended. "In proportion to one's advance southward," he wrote to the *Congregationalist*, "things appear to be slack-twisted and shiftless. Everything from a mouse-trap to a meeting-house has a screw loose in it, and needs mending." The South was "a poisoned region . . . in need of disinfecting." James predicted that once the "shameful political apostasy" of slavery was "annihilated," the nation would move forward with "every wheel, spindle, and pinion again revolving" in a productive fashion. He looked forward to a time when the Southern states would "begin to stimulate *free labor*, establish *free schools*, call out the energies of all classes by elevating, rather than depressing them, and *level up* society to a standard of general intelligence and thrift."[8]

James never received additional pay for his work as superintendent of Negro Affairs in North Carolina, but monetary rewards were not his goal. James noted that he took on the job for more abstract reasons: "the love of Christ, the welfare of men, and the new social order in our land." From the spring of 1863 until near the end of the war, James's correspondence repeatedly touched on his belief that the regeneration of the South would require drastic changes in what he termed its "social order." After Abraham Lincoln issued his preliminary Emancipation Proclamation, James noted that Lincoln's statement marked the first step toward "a radical social revolution" that would involve "a destruction of the essential tyranny of Southern society, and the building up of democratic and free institutions in its place." James emphasized that the "South must be made republican and acknowledge the notion of equal rights." In a published letter to his Northern friends, James dramatically urged the creation of a "NEW SOCIAL ORDER IN THE SOUTH," noting that the North should "fight with our right hand, and civilize with our left, till the courage, the enterprise, and the ideas of the North have swept away the barbarism and treason of the South."[9]

James's advocacy of a "New Social Order" in the South was not a call for social or racial equality. He was not, as he clearly stated, "personally a believer in equality." More significantly, like a lot of his fellow evangelicals, James made a clear distinction between political equality and social equality. Thus he thought that the black man should be granted "equality, not of social condition, but equality before the law." Blacks, he believed, should be granted "the common rights of citizens." They should be able to own the products of their labor as well as real and personal property. At the same time, he thought that there was a natural stratification of society, and he implied that he believed that the black person's place in society was near the bottom. The black person's role "in the grand future," he noted, would "be a subordinate part," but also "a part noble, conspicuous, admirable and *human*."[10]

Although James never clearly defined what he meant by "New Social Order," it is apparent that he had in mind an economy of small farmers and manufacturers—an economy in which the laborers owned the product of their labor and where hard work would bring material and spiritual success. Horace James was influenced by ideas being articulated by the Radical Republicans: free labor, free soil, democracy, and industry. James, in fact, frequently stressed the concept of free labor. All citizens, black and white, would have the opportunity to work for wages and obtain economic independence, and all wage earners who worked hard enough would be able to become property owners. Writing favorably of some black men that he met digging graves at Camp Oliver in New Bern, for example, James rhetorically asked if, when the war was over, "such active, industrious, self-reliant young men as these" should not be able to "sit under *their own* vine and fig-tree."[11]

Early in his tenure on Roanoke Island, James noted that the freedpeople were "animated by the prospect of a homestead of their own, and the little comforts of a freehold." The terms "homestead" and "freehold" connoted very specific things in the United States in the mid-nineteenth century: self-respect, autonomy, and citizenship. James believed that land ownership was the former slaves' "strongest incentive to industry." Once they held real estate, they seemed "to attain at once to a kind of independence which they never had known before," James declared. "I know of nothing which can cause them to make progress so rapidly in the way of self-reliance and self-support."[12]

Some Radical Republicans believed that a landless class would necessarily be lawless, and thus supported a policy whereby the government would give Southern land to former slaves—a policy that would also, in the process, punish some of the former slaveholders whose lands would be confiscated. James, however, agreed with many Northerners of more moderate Republican persuasion that the government should not give land to the freedmen. Providing the freedmen land—in essence, giving something for nothing—violated the traditional middle-class republican values that James hoped to propagate. The freedpeople would, he asserted, "value more and take better care of that which costs them something." Obtaining title to the land, of course, presented big problems. Although the freedpeople on Roanoke Island initially settled on lots laid out on property that General Peck had ordered James to confiscate, James counted on being able to purchase the lands from the original owners and sell the lots to the former slaves. Later, in February 1864, he notified Butler that he was preparing estimates of the cash value of the island lands, and that he expected the white owners to sell.[13]

James thought that land ownership was the key to independence. James did not, however, believe that the freedpeople on Roanoke Island could support themselves on the product of their lots alone. Consequently, he encouraged the development of light industries and domestic manufacturing that were closely related to the island's natural resources in hopes that they would enable the freedmen's colony to be self-supporting. Although his plans did not include sophisticated technology, the ideas were progressive in a slave economy. James also hoped that the freedpeople's involvement in industrial work would lead to something a bit more abstract—the development of self-discipline and self control. Although James usually focused on the positive attributes of the freedpeople, at times he was also fairly patronizing in assuming that he knew what they needed in order to survive in the "New Social Order." In a letter cautioning Northern supporters not to expect the freedpeople to "become immediately independent of government aid and care," James noted that he believed that the freedpeople had to "pass through a tutelage before they [would] come into the promised land of perfect freedom and independence." Given the freedpeople's lack of training, they would not "leap at once into a state of free civilization," James asserted, "but they will learn rapidly, and with due patience on our part the work will be accomplished."[14]

In a letter written after the war, James explained how free labor served as training for citizenship. He noted that "Christians and philanthropists" wished to instruct the former slaves in work habits that would lift them "from subserviency and helplessness into a dignified independence and citizenship." The goal was "to prepare them to enjoy the rights and perform the duties of free men under the law in our great republic." James absolutely believed that Northerners had a responsibility to come to the South and contribute their talents to this social reform. "We may be sure that this is a work which *the South will not do*," James asserted. Accordingly, James advocated training in manufactures to instill "habits of industry" and raise former slaves "above the level of mere field hands," thus preparing the former slaves to participate in democratic government.[15]

Drawing upon the skills that the former slaves brought with them to the island, James encouraged basket making, shoemaking, barrel making, shingle splitting and shaving, and boat building. He organized shad fisheries and hired an assistant, Holland Streeter, a butcher from Lowell, Massachusetts, to oversee them. James thought that "the Roanoke fisheries alone would yield fortunes every year if pursued in a business-like manner." James also believed that the island would be "the seat of a profitable commerce, in cotton, corn, turpentine, resin, tar, timber, fish, oysters, wood, reeds, cranberries, and grapes." He looked forward to the "scientific cultivation" of the scuppernong grape, which "might be made to produce, on Roanoke alone, an income of $100,000 annually."[16]

James's requests for supplies indicated his emphasis on blending domestic manufactures with small subsistence agriculture. The needs at Roanoke Island, he reported, were "the same which any colony, designed to be agricultural and mechanical" would have at its commencement. He procured horses and mules through General Butler; many of these had been confiscated from Rebel supporters. James also sent some fairly explicit lists of needs to Northern newspapers. In one request, for example, he asked potential donors for a variety of tools and hardware:

> cross-cut saws and handsaws; crowbars, shovels, picks, and spades; hoes, axes, hammers, and nails; two or three sets of carpenter's tools, with extra augers, squares, and gimlets; butts, hinges, screws, and latches; an assortment of garden seeds; padlocks and door locks; oil-stones, and grindstones; bush scythes, water buckets, baking kettles and covers; tin plates, cups, spoons, pans and basins; knives and forks; files and rasps; coopering and soldering tools; glass and putty; fish-hooks, lines and leads, and twine for seines; a pair of platform scales, and counter scales, and a quantity of tin and sheet-iron and tools to work it.[17]

In another request, aimed at the supporters of the National Freedman's Relief Association, James asked for six crosscut saws, fifty grubbing hoes, six froes for riving shingles, an assortment of padlocks and hasps, and a grindstone with treadle. Noting that some of the women could card, spin, and weave, James sent notices to the *Congregationalist* requesting tools and spinning wheels. The Society of Friends of Philadelphia sent shoemaker's tools, which some of the freedpeople were capable of using. The National Freedman's Relief Association sent blacksmiths' and coopers' tools, as well as agricultural implements.[18]

James also showed great interest in making the freedpeople's homes a more permanent part of the settlement. He was convinced that sawed lumber would enable the colony's householders to replace their temporary split log cabins with more permanent, comfortable houses; lumber, he asserted, would "make us a city." In addition, James believed that the island's timber stores would prove sufficient for the development of a lumber industry on the island. The lumber could be sold to the government, and the proceeds would help support the colony. Thus, procuring a sawmill became one of James's most pressing goals. After his fund-raising trip to New England in the summer of 1863, funds for the purchase of a steam-powered saw and grist mill were set aside. That fall, James and General Butler corresponded on several occasions with respect to Butler's need for a formal requisition for the mill. James sent an official request for the mill to General Butler at Fortress Monroe in December 1863. Noting that the mill was a good idea, Butler approved the purchase and indicated that the government would likely pay part of the mill's cost. By that time, James had already ordered the schooner *S. B. Bailey* from New Bern to pick up the mill machinery in Boston, and was looking forward to its arrival that winter.[19]

Although James noted that the recruitment of the island's able-bodied black males into the army had altered the character of the colony, "converting it into an asylum for the wives and children of soldiers," he remained optimistic about the colony's ability to sustain itself. The first test of that ability arose during the winter of 1863–1864. In December 1863 General Wild led his African brigade of about seventeen hundred troops, including some of the enlistees from Roanoke Island, on a nineteen-day expedition and raid across the northeastern North Carolina mainland. As Wild's men moved through the countryside, they pilfered liberally from the Rebels and then destroyed what was left. One informant recorded that observers could "trace the track of the raid for ten miles by the turkey buzzards, feeding on the carrion made by the destruction of animal life." Although the white planters were terrorized by the idea of black soldiers, suppression of Rebel guerrillas was not the only reason for the raid, which was the first raid of any magnitude conducted by black troops in the Civil War. Rather, as one contemporary account noted, the primary objective of the raid was "to clear the country of slaves" and procure more recruits for Wild's brigade. Approximately twenty-five hundred slaves, mostly women and children, were freed. The young males were enlisted into the African brigade, while women, children, and the physically unfit were sent to Norfolk or Roanoke Island. At one point, Wild sent nine boatloads of these refugees to Roanoke Island, along with "their baggage, horses, and carts." On another occasion, he sent a steamer with a load of contrabands to Roanoke Island; in tow was a schooner that carried the contrabands' carts and horses.[20]

Once they disembarked on Roanoke Island, the former slaves walked three miles north from the landing at Pork Point to the chaotic temporary refugee encampment in the barracks at Camp Foster. In their first weeks on the island, they confronted many problems. The most immediate was finding shelter from the bitter winter weather. Reporting on his January 1864 medical inspection of the Roanoke Island camp, Dr. D. W. Hand painted a bleak picture. A thousand contrabands had arrived since 1 December 1863, bringing the total number of former slaves in the camp to approximately three thousand. Hand found over five hundred blacks living in huts made of brush and earth—seven to ten people in each hut. In addition, he found barracks and sheds "packed with human beings even in the daytime." Hand noted that many were so desperate to stay warm in the makeshift housing that they built indoor fires without adequate ventilation. The smoke could only escape "through the cracks in the roof." In barracks that had chimneys, conditions were not much better. Hand reported that "the chimneys were so bad the rooms were filled with smoke, and dozens of the women and children had sore eyes in consequence."[21]

Hand did not blame James for the difficulties; in fact, he noted that the management problems resulted from imposing too many other duties on James.

It was obvious that dealing with the volume of refugees would require gargantuan efforts. Hand noted that along with the women and children, at least five hundred able-bodied men languished in the buildings, waiting for their lots to be surveyed or for tools. Since Sergeant George Sanderson's time was devoted to drawing and issuing rations to the new arrivals, James had appointed someone else to lay out lots, but he appeared to be unsatisfactory in that job. Likewise, no one seemed to be in charge of sanitation. Hand was repulsed by the general filth and utter disregard for cleanliness in the camp. Attributing the high mortality rate to the cold and dampness, he concluded that the "newcomers seem to have no idea what to do when they get sick, or how to bury those who die." Hand also criticized the location of the colony's burial grounds "so near the main camp it will be a source of disease next summer." To compound these problems, there was only one inexperienced physician, who had to serve both soldiers and freedpeople, while hospital accommodations were inadequate. An outbreak of smallpox in January 1864 further indicated the deteriorating state of affairs. Meanwhile, someone was apparently selling some of the government supplies that were intended for the island's contrabands on a black market in eastern North Carolina. For a number of months, General Wild had been complaining that supplies from Roanoke Island were finding their way to the Rebels.[22]

Despite such ominous developments, Horace James was not yet ready to abandon hopes for the Roanoke colony. Around the time of Hand's January visit, James was on the island proudly conducting tours. In late January, for example, a Mr. Hillis, an agent of the Friends Aid Society of Philadelphia, and the Reverend William Hamilton, an agent of the American Missionary Association, visited Roanoke Island. James guided his guests through the newly laid out freedmen's village south of Camp Foster, apparently avoiding the disorder and filth of the most recent settlement of refugees in the old barracks. Shortly after the visit, in an article in the *American Missionary*, Hamilton described a scene that seemed a world apart from what Dr. Hand had encountered that same month in Camp Foster:

> Walking with chaplain James, we came suddenly to the main avenue. It is very imposing. Imagine yourself to emerge from a winding, dusty, forest road, on a wide street, cut through the wilderness a mile or more each way, straight as a bee-line. All along this grand vista, on each side, you see the smoke ascending from a hundred log-buildings. These are the dwellings of the emancipated negroes. They were industriously employed and seemed happy.

A few of the former slaves complained about their need for supplies, but all told the visitors that they would not be willing to return to their masters. "We are better here," they declared.[23]

James also played down the problems on Roanoke Island in an article to the *Congregationalist* that January, noting that the people who had arrived as a result of the march of General Wild's African brigade through northeastern North Carolina "suffered somewhat in the stress of weather which we experienced early in January, having come in so large numbers, before we had suitable accommodations for their shelter." Nevertheless, and despite six cases of smallpox, James optimistically concluded that the refugees were "comfortably provided for," and there was "room for more." James continued by reporting that the freedpeople were already beginning to plant their gardens. "It is difficult to believe it is midwinter," James stated, "for the people are calling for garden seeds and early peas to plant, and in some instances they are already planted." Similarly, after George Whipple, the corresponding secretary of the American Ministry Association, made a late-January visit to the island, his report of his stay did not mention any problems. In February, an article in the *National Anti-Slavery Standard* called the improvements on the island "remarkable." Even the swamps were "being wrested from the control of the reptiles," while the island was "being made to bloom by the industry of the blacks there gathered together."[24]

Less than a month later, in a letter to General Butler, James reported that it was "healthy" on the island, noting that "unless the weather be very inclement the people do not suffer." Similarly, writing to General Wild, he reported that the island was "gradually assuming more & more the aspect of a civilized community," and that "a large number" of the freedpeople would be able to "sustain themselves this season with the aid the govt allows the soldier's family." James hoped that by the time Wild paid a visit, he would see "the whole Island smiling with thrift, prosperity & happiness." In his letters to Butler and Wild, James was noticeably silent about some significant problems that had cropped up in the colony that first winter. Shad fishing, which James had viewed as a key to the island's self sufficiency, had not lived up to his expectations. Holland Streeter had difficulties procuring nets, and then the sound froze, impeding boat traffic and fishing. Similarly, James did not comment on the growing contrast between the thriving new village and the wretched barracks in Camp Foster. Instead of viewing the winter problems as a threatening portent of the colony's future, James dismissed them as growing pains. Another report from the island, sent to the New England Freedmen's Aid Society, was similarly optimistic. Noting that the weather and a "sudden influx of large numbers of

Freedmen" onto the island had led to "much solicitude during the past winter," the correspondent went on to assert that the time was "past when we need feel any anxiety for the comfort of the Freedmen there, or any doubt of the entire success of this experiment to colonize them on Roanoke."[25]

James, meanwhile, looked forward to the arrival of the sawmill, which he hoped to employ to improve conditions in all areas of the colony. He did not hide his irritation when delivery of the mill was delayed by the winter weather. "Such wretched delay is intolerable, and I should have been violently angry if it could do any good," he wrote. He had especially harsh words for William Perry, the engineer who acted as his agent in the purchase of the machinery. James complained that Perry did not "push matters vigorously." In addition, Perry was afraid to travel in the bad weather. When the schooner carrying the mill finally arrived on 17 February, it lay more than a mile west of the landing in the shallow and icy Croatan Sound. James reported to General Butler's aide-de-camp, Lieutenant Colonel J. Burnham Kinsman (who was also general superintendent of Negro Affairs), that the sound was "so covered with thick ice as to impede boats, close communications, and make fishing impossible."[26]

On 23 February, James noted that he had received word that "the scared engineer Perry" had finally arrived in New Bern and was leaving that evening for Roanoke Island. "I am disgusted at his want of pluck. I wouldn't give a fig for a *battallion* of such men," James grumbled. James also reported that he expected the mill and materials would be unloaded by that evening. Although the Sound was no longer frozen, shallow waters meant that the schooner had to remain anchored quite a distance from the shore. James noted that all the heavy machinery and sixty thousand bricks for the mill's foundation "had to be handled four times over and at a great disadvantage" by the "large number of hands"—freedmen in the Quartermaster's Department—who unloaded the materials. "It was the hardest work for us all that was done in the month," James later reported to Kinsman.[27]

The delays, however, did not dampen James's enthusiasm for the mill. He told Butler that the engine was "splendid," and "worth in the market today four thousand dollars more than it cost." James thought it "wonderful" that the island's freedpeople "could build so many hundreds of comfortable houses without our asking the government for a foot of lumber." Looking forward to the improvements in the village, he added, "A few months running of our circular saws will make our colony a picture of beauty." Money collected during James's Northern fund-raising trip covered all but $1,456.80 of the mill's cost, which was somewhere in the neighborhood of $8,000. James sent the bills for the machinery to General Butler with the expectation that the government

Horace James thought that the steam sawmill would be the centerpiece of industry in the Roanoke Island freedmen's colony. Although no drawings of the sawmill survived the war, it is likely that it looked like the one depicted in this engraving from an 1867 sketch by James E. Taylor. (*Frank Leslie's Illustrated Newspaper*, 10 August 1867, author's collection)

would pay the difference. Under William Perry's supervision, construction of the mill commenced at Pork Point, near Union headquarters. Freedmen working for the Quartermaster's Department provided the labor. By April workers had laid the brick foundation, a challenging task on sandy soil. In June James reported that the mill was "covered" and the "boilers set." The mill was finally ready for operation in early September.[28]

The completed mill was an impressive assemblage of machinery, consisting of a seventy-horsepower engine that powered several circular saws, a turning lathe, and a grist mill. Horace James thought that the mill was "the best piece of machinery in eastern North Carolina," and called it a "peaceful engineery of labor." A soldier stationed on Roanoke Island in the fall of 1864 described the mill as "a first class affair, like most anything belonging to the Government." He wondered, however, "why they had such a large and modern affair" on the island. The soldier was wrong in concluding that the mill belonged to the Government, but most likely it did not occur to him that some group other then the government could afford or wish to place such a mill on an out-of-the way island.[29]

To Horace James and his New England contemporaries in the experimental colony, the mill's function in the colony was obvious. James believed that the mill was the centerpiece of the colonial efforts, the key to self-sufficiency of the Roanoke colony. James fully expected that the mill's output would help validate his belief that the combination of free labor and technology was in all ways superior to the slave system. He estimated that most of the lumber produced at the mill was worth $25 per thousand feet, and some was worth $40 per thousand feet. He believed that in addition to supplying the immediate needs of the island, the mill would make it profitable to cut timber from the island's woods and sell the finished lumber to the government. James predicted that he would be able to "earn money enough, by lumber, shingles, wood and other articles of merchandise, to meet the expenses of the negro Department in this Dist." One army official had, in fact, estimated that the mill would be worth $100,000 to the District of North Carolina.[30]

There were precedents for such purchases, especially when the Union army could not meet the demands for building barracks. General Butler's encouragement of the mill's acquisition was, in fact, based on his desire to supply lumber to the Navy Department. In addition, Butler agreed with James that the revenue would help support the work of the Department of Negro Affairs on the island. James thought that the earnings would help him pay his assistants, support the Quartermaster Department's hiring of more freedmen, and finance further development on the island. Thus, from James's perspective, the mill was a crucial civilizing force, the fulcrum of the "New Social Order."[31]

By October 1864, the sawmill's maximum output was three thousand feet of boards per day. In addition, the gristmill could grind fifty bushels of corn each day. Unused lumber slabs and sawdust from the millwork fed the fires in the mill's steam engine. James also took a portion of the wood or grain that the freedmen were milling as payment for use of the mill. He estimated that the cost of running the mill—approximately $350 per month—would easily be met from the proceeds of the grist mill alone. James gloated about the success of the enterprise:

> It is a solid satisfaction to me to see this mill, sawing up lumber so beautifully, and grinding corn so rapidly. I sat and *enjoyed* it for some Hours! . . .
>
> Everybody is congratulating me that the mill is such a grand success and the croakers who have been belying this enterprise had better not show their heads hereabouts! I am already beginning to build schoolhouses and storehouses, and churches and private dwellings, and mean to make this island shine in a few weeks.[32]

In early November 1864, James reported that the mill was "working magnificently," and affairs in his department were "proceeding smoothly." William T. Briggs, the superintendent of freedmen education in North Carolina, thought the mill boded well for expansion of the educational endeavors among the former slaves on the island. "The music of the saw mill is now heard over the

Island," he declared in late November, "& this magnificent Educational field ought to be abundantly supplied with teachers & accommodations."[33]

James agreed wholeheartedly. While he believed that the sawmill was the way for "enterprise, thrift, and productiveness" to "enter the gates which have been opened by the demon of war," he also believed that formal education was necessary to equip the former slaves for participation in the "New Social Order." Writing to the Old South Sunday School Class of Worcester, Massachusetts back in May 1863, James had declared, "Next to the church I believe in the school-house, and next to the minister the school-teacher." James had in mind a very specific type of educational program—one that combined traditional reading, writing, and arithmetic skills with biblical studies and lessons in morality. It is likely that James also had in mind a very specific benevolent organization to promote such a program among the North Carolina freedpeople: the American Missionary Association (AMA). The AMA mirrored James's evangelical beliefs in both doctrine and work. In addition, James had personal ties to the leadership of the AMA, ties that grew even stronger during his tenure.[34]

In June 1863, shortly after he had become superintendent, James had notified the AMA's George Whipple that his Department of Negro Affairs was "prepared to give a limited no. of teachers military protection and soldier's rations with a house to live in & place in which to teach." In August he had written Whipple that he wanted the AMA to send his cousin, Elizabeth James, to Roanoke Island, for she was "just the person to rough it in a new country." The following month he informed Whipple that the "sanitary condition of Roanoke Island" was "good," and that he was ready for his cousin "and for one or two men" that Whipple might "see fit to send" to Roanoke Island. "Those who come," James advised, "had better bring sheets pillow cases (& *pillows* if they can) and towels—." The "prospects of the work on that island are excellent," James asserted, "and six months will do great things in developing our plans."[35]

Although Horace James encouraged and supervised missionaries from a variety of philanthropic organizations, he was especially interested in the labors of the AMA workers. On Roanoke Island, the AMA monopolized the charitable and educational efforts during the war period. The arrival of James's cousin, Elizabeth James, in October 1863 marked both the beginning of AMA involvement in the operations of the Roanoke Colony and the beginning of a new chapter in the colony's development.[36]

Tossed upon a Sea of Troubles

MISSIONARY WORK IN THE COLONY

IN 1865, when Horace James drafted his annual report on his work as superintendent of Negro Affairs in North Carolina, he noted that nothing could be relied upon in his district but the "certainty of change." Between the fighting and disease, he concluded, "the negroes (and poor whites as well) have been tossed upon a sea of troubles, and our care of them has assumed a new phase almost every month." Although the military authorities were responsible for the official supervision of the freedmen's camps in North Carolina, the real caregivers were the Northern missionaries who offered day-to-day assistance to the former slaves as they made their transition from slavery to freedom. The missionaries came South eager to establish schools and help the freedpeople prepare for integration into Southern society; much of their time, however, was devoted to helping the refugees cope with everyday problems. The difficulties that the missionaries encountered in their daily ministrations on Roanoke Island reflected the problems inherent in the situation and composition of the colony, as well as the strengths and limitations of the beliefs and values of the missionaries themselves.[1]

The premier benevolent organization on Roanoke Island, the American Missionary Association, arrived with a strong history of service to the destitute and a well-developed spiritual and social agenda. The AMA's origins went back to 1839, when the Reverend Simeon S. Jocelyn, Joshua Leavitt, and Lewis Tappan had formed the Amistad Committee to raise funds for the defense of the slaves who had mutinied on the Spanish ship *La Amistad*. Jocelyn, who chaired the Amistad Committee, had been minister of a black church in New Haven, Connecticut, a missionary to blacks in New York, and a member of the executive committee of the New York Antislavery Society. Leavitt was an outspoken advocate of abolition; and Tappan, a wealthy New Yorker whose credit-rating agency (the Mercantile Agency) later merged into the company known as Dun and Bradstreet, had also helped to establish the American Anti-Slavery Society. The slaves of *La Amistad* had been found guilty of piracy and murder and were imprisoned in the United States. With the support of the Amistad Committee, Roger S. Baldwin and John Quincy Adams successfully argued the slaves' case before the Supreme Court. The Amistad Committee later merged with the Union Missionary Society. Then, in 1846, the Union Missionary Society, the Committee for West Indian Missions, and the Western Evangelical Missionary Society merged to form the American Missionary Association. According to the AMA's constitution, the object of the organization was "to send the gospel to those portions of our own and other countries which are destitute of it, or which present open and urgent fields of effort." Early mission outposts were organized in Africa, Jamaica, Hawaii, Egypt, the Sandwich Islands, and Siam.[2]

The association limited its membership to those with "evangelical sentiments, who profess faith in our Lord Jesus Christ and who are not in the practice of any known immorality." The AMA defined "evangelical sentiments" as:

> a belief in the guilty and lost condition of all men without a Saviour; the Supreme Deity, Incarnation and Atoning Sacrifice of Jesus Christ, the only Saviour of the world; the necessity of regeneration by the Holy Spirit; repentance, faith, and holy obedience, in order to [achieve] salvation; the immortality of the soul; and the retributions of the judgment, in the eternal punishment of the wicked, and salvation of the righteous.[3]

A key part of the definition was the belief in the necessity of "regeneration by the Holy Spirit"—a belief that was also expressed very clearly in the sermons and writings of Horace James. Like many of their fellow evangelists, leaders in the AMA subscribed to ideas that had been advanced during the Second Great Awakening by revivalists such as Charles Grandison Finney. They believed in the efficacy of individual conversions. They emphasized that sin was voluntary; sin derived from a choice, not from human nature. The next logical step was to conclude that anyone could achieve salvation by choosing to follow God instead of the way of sin. They believed that sinners who were "born again" through a religious conversion experience were regenerated and sanctified. The regenerated, in turn, had a responsibility to work for God and convert others.[4]

Thus, instead of focusing on the control of sinners, these evangelical Christians hoped to convert *all* sinners and bring about a perfect society. The AMA was interested in many varieties of social reform, which, in addition to abolition, included temperance, prison improvements, and public education. Although the AMA attracted people from all social classes, its doctrine appealed especially to those who were successful in the competitive world of Northern capitalism—people who believed that individual efforts would lead to salvation in much the same way that individual initiative and hard work would lead to success in the business world. Prominent AMA supporters included a number of successful businessmen; in addition to Lewis Tappan, who underwrote much of the AMA's work, there were others such as William Jackson, a member of the Massachusetts legislature and principal agent in the construction of the Providence and Worcester Railroad. Although Baptists, Methodists, and Presbyterians belonged and contributed funds to the AMA, most of the members were Congregationalists.[5]

Chartered as a missionary association rather than an educational association, the AMA had indicated an early interest in benevolent work among the former slaves. The leadership of the AMA generally advocated the ideas that had been promoted by the so-called "Lane Rebels," the influential theology students who had moved to Oberlin Seminary after being forced out of Lane Seminary in Cincinnati because of their strong support of immediate abolition. Two of the AMA's corresponding secretaries, George Whipple and Michael E. Strieby, were, in fact, among the Lane Rebels. The AMA's 1850 resolution to disobey the Fugitive Slave Act marked the beginning of the association's emphasis on abolition. The AMA's monthly journal, the *American Missionary*, underscored that slavery was "a sin against God and man," and AMA missionaries were instructed to overthrow the evil institution. Both foreign and home missions were not "to give countenance to the abhorred system"; any person owning slaves was prohibited from membership and communion. The evangelical outlook did not allow for compromise with sin. The slaveholder could, however, be regenerated and renounce the sin of slavery. The slaveholder who chose God instead of sin—the slaveholder who chose emancipation—was welcome in the AMA.[6]

Although the AMA continued to support missionaries throughout the United States, beginning in the mid-1850s the association chose to concentrate on its work in the South. Thus, in July 1857, the *American Missionary* declared that the AMA was a "Southern aid Society," providing the gospel to the South, which needed "Christian missionary efforts, far exceeding any other portion of our country." Soon after the war commenced, the *American Missionary* proclaimed that slavery was the cause of the war, and its only remedy was, as an article boldly asserted, "IMMEDIATE AND UNIVERSAL EMANCIPATION." The leadership of the AMA criticized other mission boards for the tepid way they put forth the

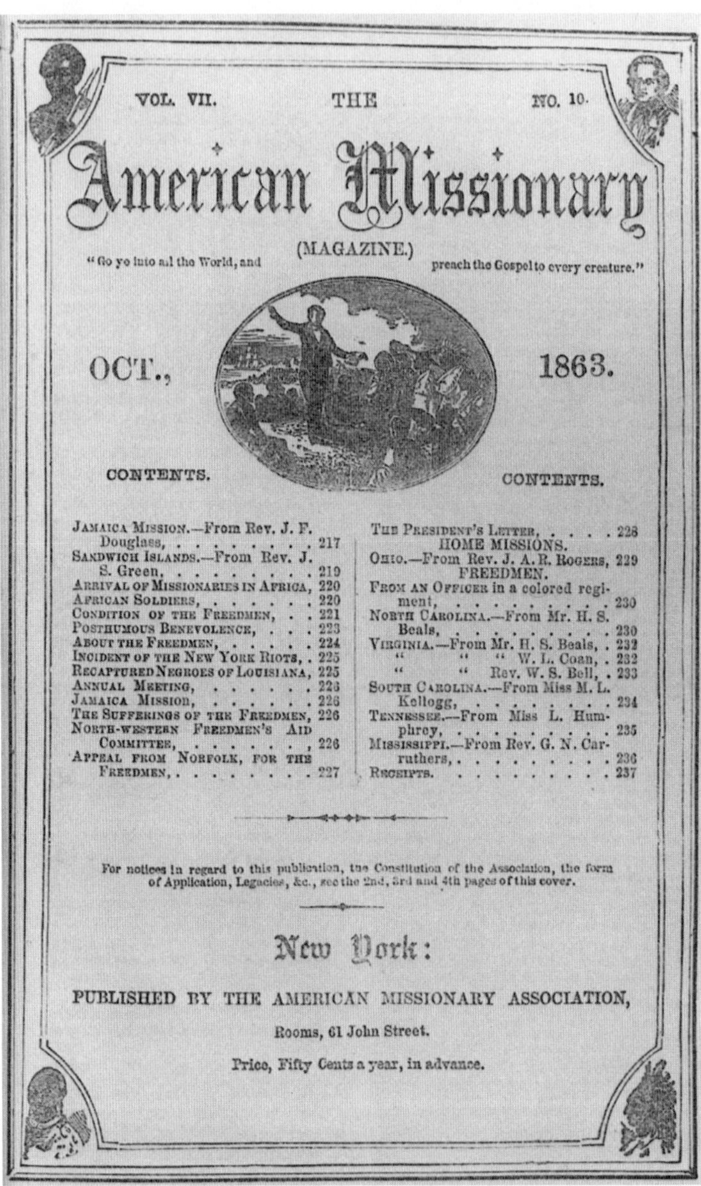

VOL. VII. THE NO. 10.

American Missionary

(MAGAZINE.)

"Go ye into all the World, and preach the Gospel to every creature."

OCT., 1863.

CONTENTS.

For notices in regard to this publication, the Constitution of the Association, the form of Application, Legacies, &c., see the 2nd, 3rd and 4th pages of this cover.

New York:

PUBLISHED BY THE AMERICAN MISSIONARY ASSOCIATION,

Rooms, 61 John Street.

Price, Fifty Cents a year, in advance.

This cover of the *American Missionary* illustrates the wide-ranging benevolent work of the American Missionary Association. (*American Missionary*, October 1863, Amistad Research Center, Tulane University) antislavery cause. The American Tract Society incurred particular censure for its failure to be "manly and christian" in carrying out the doctrine asserted in its constitution.[7]

By July 1861, the *American Missionary* was focusing on the need for missionary work among the former slaves. The journal's editor declared that the war would create "one of the grandest fields of missionary labor the world ever furnished." The following August, Lewis Tappan, in his capacity as AMA treasurer, wrote General Benjamin Butler inquiring about the possibility of the society supplying relief to the contrabands. Following Butler's reply welcoming the AMA's efforts, on 17 September the AMA commenced its missionary and educational effort among the freedpeople of the South with the sponsorship of a school in Virginia near Fortress Monroe. The following month, the *American Missionary* heralded the opening of a new mission field "among their colored brethren, who are under the protection of the military forces of the country."[8]

The rapid growth in the educational mission field among the freedpeople in the Hampton, Virginia, area prompted the AMA to send New York businessman Charles B. Wilder to Hampton in 1862 to superintend relief operations there. Soon the military authorities, who were searching for a way to handle the former slaves crowding into Union camps, officially recognized Wilder's position. In this way the AMA and Union army initiated a relationship that continued throughout the war. Later, after the Union decided to enlist blacks, the *American Missionary* declared that the decision gave "new interest to all operations for the improvement of the freed people" and compelled "measures for the protection of large masses of women and children" while the men were away serving in the Union army. One section of General Orders No. 46 that General Benjamin Butler issued in December 1863 outlined the relationship between the military and the charitable organizations supporting work among the freedpeople. Butler ordered his troops to assist the missionaries—to "treat all such persons with the utmost respect." He also mandated "that transportation be furnished them whenever it may be necessary in pursuit of their business." Between 1861 and 1869, the AMA supported 2,638 missionaries in the South.[9]

From the beginning of their work with the former slaves, the leaders of the AMA generally preferred to call the freedpeople "colored refugees." Their reasons for this choice give some insight into the AMA's attitude toward the former slaves:

> We prefer this designation of the people who are fleeing to our camps and fleets, to that of "Contrabands," "Freedmen," or "Vagrants," because the first implies property in man, the second describes the ex-slaves as actu-

ally free, when their condition is otherwise, and the third indicates a degradation and status which the Refugees do not deserve.

When the AMA officers wrote about the "great work of Southern REGENERATION," they maintained that the first and most necessary step was the eradication of the sin of slaveholding. Then, under the protective guidance of missionary teachers, the "refugees" would evolve into "freedmen" and assume their rightful position in the "New Social Order." Although AMA leaders remained a bit vague about what the rightful position would be, they implied that it would not be one of social equality with whites. In this respect their views mirrored those that were held by many Northern evangelicals of a republican persuasion, including Horace James. The AMA leaders were, however, eager to improve the minds and especially the habits of the former slaves. An educational program that featured a mixture of religious and secular teachings was central to the missionary work. Consequently, AMA work among the former slaves was an amalgamation of charity, religious instruction, and basic education, with some temperance thrown in for good measure. To the extent that it advocated universal education, the AMA's educational program was progressive. It was, however, also very conservative in that it was an attempt to impose traditional republican values such as self discipline, industry, and thrift, while also preventing the disorder that some Northern humanitarians feared would develop if the former slaves were thrown into society without adequate preparation.[10]

Those aspiring to become AMA missionaries had to show that they were people of "fervent piety" with strong "missionary spirit" and "a desire for the salvation of souls." The AMA advertised that its missionaries should be "only those who are moved to the work by Christian love." Other requirements included good health, energy for Christian missionary labors, culture and common sense, proper personal habits, teaching experience (especially as disciplinarians), and total abstinence. Since education in AMA classrooms was based on evangelical religion, successful candidates for missionary positions had to demonstrate that they were just as interested in converting their students to evangelical Christianity as they were in instructing them.[11]

In early 1863, following the Emancipation Proclamation, AMA leaders Lewis Tappan, Simeon Jocelyn, and George Whipple stepped up efforts to take advantage of mission opportunities in the South. In February the *American Missionary* reported that the AMA secretaries had received a large number of applications from people who wished to be missionaries, but they still needed for more ministers and teachers to apply. Increasingly, AMA leaders came to view the success of their mission work in "The New Field" as a prerequisite to military triumph. "Slavery is in its death-struggle," the *American Missionary* declared in a July 1863 article encouraging support of the Southern mission work. "We believe that God will not give complete success to our forces until the rights of the colored man are recognized and sustained." The leaders of the AMA were convinced that their work among the freedpeople was as important as what was occurring on the battlefield.[12]

The AMA was one of a handful of Northern benevolent societies that sent missionaries to work among the former slaves in North Carolina's contraband camps. Other prominent societies included the New York Branch of the National Freedman's Relief Association (NFRA) and the New England Freedmen's Aid Society of Boston (NEFAS). The primary difference between the AMA and other freedmen's associations was that the AMA sustained a strong evangelical religious focus in all phases of its work. The AMA forcefully promoted "the principles of the Gospel," as well as charity and education. Although the AMA sponsored most of Roanoke Island's teachers and schools during wartime, the NFRA and its successor, the New York Branch of the American Freedmen's Union Commission (NYAFUC), supported several missionaries on Roanoke Island after the fall and evacuation of Plymouth in April 1864, and a succession of missionaries for a year and a half after the end of the war. Abolitionist, but not evangelical, the NFRA focused more on practical ways to uplift the former slaves than on religious conversions. The NFRA's publications emphasized that the freedpeople should be encouraged to develop self-discipline, self-reliance, and self-support. According to the organization's first annual report, the NFRA sponsored missionaries with one goal in mind: to help the former slaves develop the competence "to sustain themselves as members of a civilized society." Thus, the NFRA supported instruction for the former slaves "in industrial and mechanical arts," the "rudiments of education," and "the principles of Christianity."[13]

Despite their different outlooks, the AMA, NFRA, and the NEFAS cooperated in supporting William T. Briggs, of Princeton, Massachusetts, as general superintendent of freedmen's schools in North Carolina. Horace James expressed amazement at the way the various societies worked together in the North Carolina field. "It is like soldiers of the regiments fighting side by side, though gathered from the east and from the west, from the north and from the south," he marveled. On Roanoke Island, the AMA missionaries and the NFRA missionaries collaborated informally in the mission work. Although the missionaries did not always agree about methods, the NFRA missionaries accepted the general direction of the benevolent work that had been established on the island by the

AMA missionaries. There really was not much time for consultation. The extent and ever-changing nature of the colony's pressing needs usually meant that the missionaries stayed busy with their individual labors.[14]

Much of what is known about the missionary work on Roanoke Island comes from the frequent letters and school reports that the missionaries, especially those sponsored by the AMA, sent to their home offices. In their letters, the missionaries requested clothing and household goods for the freedpeople. They also sent requisitions for personal items such as medicines, spectacles, kitchen utensils, cook stoves and box stoves, and food items that were difficult to acquire on the island. Mostly, however, the missionaries described conditions in the colony and reported on their work, illustrating their points with occasional anecdotes and frequent biblical allusions.

Most of the missionaries on Roanoke Island came from New England, from areas where abolitionist sentiment was fairly well developed. The first missionaries to arrive, the AMA-sponsored missionaries, were white, which reflected Horace James's belief that white teachers should prepare the way for black teachers by bringing influence and efficiency to the schools, "so as to accomplish the most in a short time." Unmarried women made up the bulk of the island's missionary corps, which was typical of both the missionary work among the freedpeople and teaching in New England at that time. The approximate average age of the missionaries was thirty-eight years, but their ages ranged from twenty-one to approximately seventy years. In general the women missionaries on the island were a bit older than those in other parts of North Carolina. It is possible that the association secretaries chose older teachers for duty there because conditions were a great deal rougher than at some of the other missionary outposts. Superintendent Briggs reported that some of the missionaries in North Carolina had "10—15—& even 20 years" experience in "select schools & academies & cheerfully dedicated this accumulated experience & the vigor of life to this work." That description fits a lot of the missionaries who served on Roanoke Island.[15]

Although it is difficult to generalize about the missionaries who volunteered to come to Roanoke Island, it is clear that they were motivated by a complex mixture of spiritual, ideological, and personal considerations. Given the AMA standards, it is not surprising that most AMA missionaries were evangelical Christians who firmly believed in the efficacy of religious conversion experiences for the salvation of souls and the transformation of society. They were also staunchly antislavery and interested in immediate abolition. The women were especially feisty, opinionated, and fearless; like their brothers, fathers, and uncles, they read antislavery literature and supported antislavery efforts. It is also safe to say that many of the teachers were prompted by the exhilaration of the missionary venture, which allowed them to travel beyond their proscribed domestic limits and exposed them to exciting perils.[16]

At the time of the Civil War, so many women were involved in missionary work that Henry W. Bellows, chairman of the U.S. Sanitary Commission, called the organization of women involved in wartime benevolent work "the uprising of the women of the land." Uprising or not, the army of female volunteers that descended upon the South during and after the Civil War adds an interesting twist to the stereotype of the "true woman" of the nineteenth century—the sweet soul who, by virtue of her self-proclaimed moral superiority to her male contemporaries, maintained the home and took pride in her domesticity, but did not venture forth very far into society. Instead of serving as a force of stability inside their Northern homes, the women missionaries aimed to bring stability to an entire society. Their work in the South was a logical extension of the roles they had assumed in their Northern homes. When nineteenth-century feminist Angelina Grimké noted that she believed that a woman could be "the acknowledged equal and coworker with man in this glorious work," she was expressing the beliefs of many inspired women who felt empowered by their evangelical religious experiences and wished to go South and convert others.[17]

The benevolent associations' acceptance of the women's services did not, however, translate into equal treatment. Although the associations promoted an enlightened outlook on slavery, they did not advocate absolute equality among the races or sexes. While the women earned salaries comparable to what they would have made as teachers in the North—an average of $15 per month—they were well aware that the men in similar positions earned more than they did. Nevertheless, the women in the Roanoke Island missionary corps generally accepted the nurturing role that the AMA officers expected of them. Although the women shouldered many responsibilities that involved managerial skills, none of the female AMA missionaries was promoted to an official managerial position on the island. While the NFRA showed signs of being a bit more open in its policy—one of the island's female NFRA teachers organized and ran the NFRA's store and also managed a farm—most of the female NFRA teachers were similarly shut out of official management positions. An AMA history of the missionary work among the freedmen published in 1874 offered a rhetorical question that summed up the AMA's attitude: "Who can minister to the hundreds of thousands of the aged, poor, ignorant, sick, but woman?" William T. Briggs called the women missionaries in North Carolina "angels of mercy."[18]

On Roanoke Island, the women were more vocal than the men in proclaiming that the mission work among former slaves represented the highest form of

Christian calling. They felt that being chosen to do such work was a great privilege. They were, as one declared, doing "the *Master's* work." It was a "joy" to open up the kingdom of heaven to the freedpeople. Perhaps the women needed to affirm—for themselves and others—that, having been "called" to participate in sanctified work, it was acceptable to flout the norms for feminine behavior while also serving in the role of nurturer. On the island, the missionaries endured all kinds of shortages, extreme weather conditions, and the mercurial whims of the local military authorities. Like their counterparts throughout the South, they effectively served in a variety of capacities, including teacher, minister, physician, storekeeper, and counselor. Nevertheless, while at times it seemed that their duties required superhuman energy and endurance, they were not saints. They were normal human beings who, while inspired by a fiery evangelism, were also tripped up by their everyday human shortcomings, especially petty jealousies.[19]

Before coming to Roanoke Island in October 1863, Horace James's cousin Elizabeth Havard James, who was from Medford, Massachusetts, had taught for seventeen years and had even been principal of a grammar school in nearby Milford. Early in her teaching career, a lingering illness had forced her to remain bedridden for four years. Although her physician had concluded that her illness was terminal, she recovered and, as she later recounted, "consecrated the residue" of her life to Christian service. In his recommendation to the AMA's corresponding secretary, Horace James described his cousin as "a clear headed warm hearted and very energetic girl, about 40 years old," who had much teaching experience, was "strongly Methodist in her religious faith," and "full of zeal." James also noted that his cousin was very eager to go to the South, "being one of the heartiest in her antislavery views, & sympathy for the slaves." In her letter of application to the AMA, Elizabeth James noted that she loved teaching, and that her teaching experience should fit her "for a large amount of usefulness in this department of the Lord's Vineyard." She pointed out that she had refused offers from five schools to go to the South and do missionary work. James also noted that although money was not her objective, she still depended upon her "own exertions" for her "daily bread."[20]

Neighbors and local clergy attested to Elizabeth's teaching skills and Christian sentiments. Judge Edwin Wright of East Boston wrote that she had secured the affection of her pupils and was "zealously careful of their moral, as of their scholarly culture." Similarly, the Reverend Elias Nason, minister of the Second Congregational Church in Medford, noted that she had "an excellent moral influence over her school." One of the members of the Milford School Committee emphasized that James had filled "a place designed for a male teacher in our system" when she served as principal. He underscored her "great energy and perseverance," as well as her "executive ability."[21]

On numerous occasions during her tenure on Roanoke Island, Elizabeth James reaffirmed that she thought it a duty and an honor to be involved in Christian mission work. "The world lieth in wickedness," James asserted, "& if I can, by power given from above, rouse any from this fatal sleep & bring them to the feet of Christ, my mission will be indeed accomplished." At another time James piously countered those who criticized the missionary efforts, noting that she was aware that there was "much bitterness of feeling toward us who especially care for the downtrodden ones." She believed, however, that "he who delivered Daniel in the Lion's den" would be able to deliver her "from an uncircumcised Philistine." Toward the end of her time on the island, after struggling through a bitter winter, James could still write that she rejoiced "every day of my life that it is my privilege to be a missionary."[22]

The sole male missionary on Roanoke Island commissioned by the AMA, Samuel Stickney Nickerson, arrived in December 1863. Nickerson, a twenty-eight-year-old Free Will Baptist minister from Tamworth, New Hampshire, also received some support from the American Free Will Baptist Association. Although he possessed no formal teaching experience before coming to Roanoke Island, that deficiency did not keep him from becoming principal of his own missionary school. Nickerson's background was, in fact, similar to that of most of the male missionaries, who were more likely to have prepared for the ministry than teaching. While on Roanoke Island, Nickerson juggled duties as minister and teacher. He maintained fairly close ties with the soldiers garrisoning the island and frequently conducted special services, including funerals and evening prayer services, for them. Nickerson also led a popular Sunday night prayer service for the freedpeople and missionaries.[23]

On 25 January 1864, James and Nickerson were joined by Ellen Eunice (Ella) Roper, a twenty-two-year-old graduate of Mount Holyoke Seminary from Templeton, Massachusetts. When Roper applied to the AMA, she indicated that she was well aware of what she would be giving up, but that she felt called by God to be a "self-denying teacher" in the South. "I know very well that the ease and comfort of home, the society of friends will be withdrawn," she declared, "but this is nothing to the consciousness of giving a cup of cold water to *one* of His little ones." Roper believed that women were especially needed in the Southern mission field. She thought that "a lady might have a more direct influence than a gentleman" on the contrabands, especially if she conducted prayer meetings for the women, and tried to get to know them outside of school. Once on Roanoke Island, she admitted to being "sometimes saddened by wants I cannot relieve by degradation and crime that make me shudder," but remained grateful for her calling. "I can truly say I am happy and do thank my Father in Heaven for the privilege of coming among them," she proclaimed. She also acknowledged that some people in the North would call the missionaries fanatics, but she believed that it was their "work to rouse enthusiasm and to increase it day by day."[24]

In early March 1864, the fourth AMA missionary arrived on Roanoke Island. The AMA transferred Mary Ann Burnap, a native of Fitchburg, Massachusetts, from New Bern. Burnap, described as a woman "somewhat beyond the years of youth," was twenty-five when she arrived on the island. Of all the missionaries on the island, she seemed the most fired up with evangelical fervor. Aspiring to be a handmaiden for Christ's work on earth, she punctuated her letters with Bible verses and effusive exclamations of God's love. "The clouds open, and the light of heaven comes down into our souls," she declared. "It seems some times as though Jesus was beside us, as when on earth." As part of her witnessing, Burnap consistently expressed an exuberant desire to convert most anyone she encountered, soldiers and freedpeople alike, to her brand of fervent evangelism. "Pray for the people of this island," she exhorted George Whipple. "I shall not be satisfied as long as there is *one* who has not a song of praise in the mouth for *my Saviour* and I expect the high walls of sin will fall," when "the music of heaven rings in these tall pines." Burnap enthusiastically jumped into every assignment; at one point Horace James noted that not even a nasty eye infection could interrupt "her accustomed sprightliness." Her students adored her, but her charismatic fits of ecstasy frequently got her into trouble with other teachers, especially the NFRA-sponsored missionaries, who were not inclined to emotional evangelical outbursts.[25]

In 1864, Samuel Nickerson returned to New Hampshire for part of the summer vacation, married Profinda Blaisdell Snell on 24 September in Tamworth, and brought her with him when he returned to the island in November. Although Profinda apparently had very little in the way of teaching experience, she assisted her husband in his school. She shared her husband's religious convictions, but was much more exuberant in declaring her passion for mission work. "Strangers wonder how we can be contented here and think it a sandy desolate place," she reflected after several months on the island, "but I guess they do not know the King of Kings dwells here and gives to those that ask that peace which passeth all understanding." Both Nickersons possessed exceptional oratorical skills, but Profinda's preaching was especially heart-rending. Elizabeth James noted that when Profinda spoke at Sabbath school or evening prayer meetings, it seemed "as if her tongue had been touched with a living coal from off the altar of the Lord." Northern friends had given her a melodeon, and despite daunting transportation difficulties, she managed to have it shipped to her home on Roanoke Island. Both Nickersons believed that music, especially hymns, provided an important educational experience for their students.[26]

James, Roper, the Nickersons, and Burnap constituted the nucleus of the wartime missionary teachers on Roanoke Island; periodically they were joined by other AMA teachers who stayed for short periods while traveling to or from mission sites at New Bern, Plymouth, and Wilmington. In addition, the NFRA also sponsored three black teachers on Roanoke Island during wartime. These teachers included Richard Boyle, Martha Culling (the former slave who had opened the first freedmen school on the island), and Robert Morrow. Little is known about Richard Boyle. His active support of the rights of the freedpeople on the island, especially in the spring of 1865 when rations were cut, suggests that he was a respected spokesman for the colonists. He was also one of two men who represented the island's freedpeople at the freedmen's convention that was held in Raleigh in October 1865. Similarly, while a report of North Carolina teachers noted that Martha Culling was "a bright, smart mulatto girl," very little is known about her origins or her nonschool activities in the colony. In contrast, Horace James specifically mentioned Robert Morrow in one of his reports. Morrow, who was born in Orange County, North Carolina, had been Confederate general James J. Pettigrew's body servant before he came into Union lines during the attack on New Bern. Despite strict North Carolina laws prohibiting the teaching of slaves, he had received what Horace James termed "a decent education," having been with Pettigrew at West Point and the University of North Carolina at Chapel Hill. In New Bern Morrow organized the Camp Totten Freedmen's School, where he was assisted by Mary Burnap. James described him as "an enthusiastic and excellent teacher." He thought so much of Morrow that after the Camp Totten school disbanded in February 1864, he asked him to be his assistant in his New Bern office. In May 1864 Morrow enlisted in Company B of the First North Carolina Heavy Artillery (later titled the Fourteenth U.S. Colored Heavy Artillery), but did not go into battle. Rather, James had him transferred to Roanoke Island to recruit black soldiers. He was also teaching in a school on the island in October 1864, when he died unexpectedly in his sleep one night.[27]

After the fall of Plymouth in April 1864, the National Freedman's Relief Association permanently transferred several of its missionaries from Plymouth to Roanoke Island. The group included Esther A. Williams, from Lowell, Massachusetts, and Sarah P. Freeman and her daughter Kate, from Maine. Williams was in her mid-fifties when she arrived on the island. Although Sarah Freeman's age does not appear in any of the missionary documents, descriptions of her suggest that she was quite a bit older than the other missionaries. In 1867, a writer described some missionaries that he had met in North Carolina, including "a very old woman [who] looks to be 70 and her daughter 45 or 50. . . ." It seems likely that the correspondent was describing the Freemans, since they seemed to have been the only mother-daughter team in the state. Freeman's age did not, however, prove to be a handicap; a visitor described her as "a woman of great energy, and well fitted for the place she fills at Roanoke." As would be expected from those with NFRA affiliations, the Freemans and Williams maintained an interest in industrial and vocational education for the former slaves.[28]

In the postwar period the NFRA sponsored at least fifteen additional missionaries, who stayed for various stints in the Roanoke Island colony. Later, after the NFRA joined with several other secular freedmen's aid associations to form the American Freedmen's Union Commission (AFUC), the New York branch of the AFUC took over sponsorship of the NFRA teachers. Most of the postwar missionaries had been stationed at other freedmen's camps, but a number, such as Peter Vogelsang, were new volunteers. Vogelsang had a particularly interesting wartime history, having served in the Fifty-fourth Massachusetts, the renowned black regiment initially commanded by Colonel Robert Gould Shaw. At the battle of Fort Wagner, Vogelsang was struck down by a bullet that lodged in his lungs, but he recovered and continued his duties as a noncommissioned quartermaster sergeant. At the end of the war, his commanding officer, Colonel Edward N. Hallowell, rewarded his leadership and battle skills by nominating him to become a commissioned officer with the rank of lieutenant, an extremely rare honor for black soldiers at that time. After the Fifty-fourth was mustered out in August 1865, Lieutenant Vogelsang returned to his Brooklyn home. Not one to rest on his laurels, Vogelsang soon signed up to be a missionary with the National Freedman's Relief Association, which sent him to the South once again, this time to operate a store for the freedpeople on Roanoke Island.[29]

Whether they arrived in 1863 or 1866, the Northern missionaries were hardly prepared for what they encountered on the island. Nevertheless, in the face of a harsh physical environment, frequent severe deprivations, and huge cultural differences, the missionaries attempted to carve out a home life comparable to what they had left in New England. Just as Horace James and his assistants had first attempted to impose order in the colony by creating a grid of avenues and streets, the missionaries first worked to establish order by preparing homes. Unlike their contemporaries in New Bern or Beaufort, who had no trouble finding adequate housing, the Roanoke Island missionaries had few options. Some found temporary shelter in officers' quarters, while others lived in small

At least twenty-seven missionaries, mostly women from New England, worked among the freedpeople on Roanoke Island. There were, however, some interesting exceptions, including Peter Vogelsang. Lieutenant Vogelsang, a free black from Brooklyn, New York, served in the Fifty-fourth Massachusetts, receiving a gunshot wound to his lungs in the charge on Fort Wagner. After the war, Vogelsang was mustered out of the service and then volunteered to go to the South as a missionary for the National Freedman's Relief Association. He helped operate a freedmen's store on Roanoke Island. (Massachusetts Commandery, Military Order of the Loyal Legion of the United States and the U.S. Army Military History Institute)

cabins that were not much better than the colonists' early splits shanties. The difficulties that they confronted in their efforts to establish homes presaged many of the obstacles that they later encountered in their missionary work on the island.

Elizabeth James initially settled in a log cabin, intending to build a house; but her plans were put on hold for want of nails—a problem that similarly hampered the freedpeople in their house-building efforts. After a short time in the cabin, on 28 January 1864 she moved into a house, known locally as Sunnyside, that her cousin Horace had discovered in one of his first trips to the island. Situated on the shore of the Croatan Sound about a mile and a half north of Headquarters, Sunnyside and the property on which it was situated remained a bone of contention between Horace James and island native Isaac C. Meekins, who strongly protested the Union occupation of his mother's home. James took the property, described as "a fine old house with outbuildings and many acres," for the use of the freedmen's colony, noting that he considered it abandoned. Elizabeth James described how "by dint of the most earnest effort" she had put the house "in perfect order within and without." She had also put "the garden, grounds, and outbuildings" in "good order," without any help from the army or the missionary association. After her arrival on the island, Ella Roper joined James at Sunnyside. In February Horace James reported that the women were "very comfortable and happy in their new home." Mary Burnap joined them at the Sunnyside house in March.[30]

Elizabeth James enjoyed her accommodations, but her pleasure proved to be short-lived. After the fall of Plymouth, Horace James asked his cousin to relinquish the house to Sarah and Kate Freeman, promising Elizabeth a new house as soon as one could be built. In May 1864, then, Elizabeth James moved to an uncomfortable cabin, which she termed a "little vermin filled shanty," in Camp Foster, the area around the old Confederate barracks that served as home to destitute contrabands when they first arrived on the island. Once again, she proceeded to clean and settle. James missed the house at Sunnyside, complaining that Camp Foster was "a fearful place," where "the debris of the people were left . . . while the energetic, thrifty, industrious ones" had built homes in the village laid out by General Wild and her cousin Horace. Elizabeth James also griped that Sarah Freeman had appropriated the bed she had obtained through the Post Surgeon, causing James to suffer "every night since." It was not until July 1865 that James moved to a comfortable house in the freedmen village. She was pleased that this house had a kitchen and two rooms, as well as a piazza and attic. She noted that while one of the rooms was small, it was "nevertheless a *room*, and I can dress without hitting the ceiling," a problem she had in her Camp Foster shanty.[31]

Sarah and Kate Freeman, meanwhile, moved into Sunnyside with Ella Roper and Mary Burnap. They were joined by Samuel and Profinda Nickerson, who lived at Sunnyside for a short period of time while they waited for men from the Quartermaster's Department to build them a house. Sunnyside also served as home for a number of NFRA teachers who stayed for short stints on the island. Similarly, Sunnyside was a pleasant stopover for missionaries who were on their way to New Bern, Plymouth, and Wilmington. Visiting Roanoke Island early in 1865, missionary teacher Lucy Chase wrote of walking along the shore of the Sound for about a mile and a half from the landing to Sunnyside. Chase noted that "four large North Carolina grape-vines spreading their branches upon level terraces beautify Mrs Freemans door-way." The missionaries walked a mile and a half or so from Sunnyside eastward into the freedmen village to hold their school sessions and minister to the needy.[32]

The Nickersons moved into their new house near the military headquarters at Pork Point on 10 December 1864, and soon discovered that construction techniques on the island left much to be desired. The house, which had been erected in twelve days, had been built from unseasoned lumber cut from the local woods. After the boards shrank, the structure was riddled with crevices that had to be patched. If she had lived in such a drafty shack in the North, she would have thought that she "belonged to the 'poor whites,' " Profinda Nickerson wrote. Compared to some of the freedpeople's shanties, however, the Nickersons' cabin appeared opulent. Samuel acknowledged that although the "dampness and openness of the house" made his wife sick, they had "*good* quarters"—much in the way of "home comforts" and several windows. Profinda especially enjoyed looking out the west window at "the glorious sunsets" over Croatan Sound. "I have thought as I watched them that we were nearer the celestial city and got glimpses of it," she declared. The proximity of the house to the landing meant that the Nickersons had what Samuel termed "considerable company," especially representatives from benevolent societies who were touring the Southern freedmen camps.[33]

The unofficial missionary headquarters, however, remained at Sunnyside, where the missionaries had created a quasi-family with "Mother" Freeman as the head. Like most families, the mission family had its share of squabbling; close quarters and disagreements about style led to ongoing bickering. Mary Burnap's charismatic fits of conversion enthusiasm seem to have provoked a good portion of the altercations, especially those between Burnap and the NFRA teachers. "I am pained every day by remarks by teachers from the other societies," Burnap wrote George Whipple. "They can see there is *something* that gives success to the christian, and it makes them feel *envious*." Without mentioning any teachers by name, because she did not want to "harm any ones character," she implied that the Freemans were the primary culprits. "If they wish me away from the island I can only say 'Blessed are ye when men shall revile you, and persecute you, and shall [spread] all manner of evil against you, *falsely*, for my sake,'" she declared. Although the AMA teachers continued to befriend her—Elizabeth James noted that Burnap was "a comfort to my heart every day," and Ella Roper referred to her as "my dear friend"—the relationship between Burnap and her NFRA detractors continued to deteriorate; she was transferred to Wilmington in early April 1865.[34]

Meanwhile, Elizabeth James, who preferred living by herself, had her own problems with Sarah Freeman. James did not hide her resentment of Freeman's intrusion into the colony's affairs, especially the elderly Freeman's usurpation of James's superiority. Both women wished to be in charge of the distribution of goods to the freedpeople; likewise, both hoped to direct an orphan asylum on the island. In various letters to the AMA home office, James complained that Freeman had not only taken her house and her bed, but had also appropriated her cooking stove and utensils. At one point her cousin Horace James posited that Elizabeth would prefer leaving the island to being "in the vicinity of Mrs. Freeman." William T. Briggs, whose position as superintendent put him in the middle of some of the quarrels, did not consider Elizabeth blameless. He thought she was "a little peculiar—a little nervous &c &c," and that it would take "a peculiar person to get along comfortably & pleasantly" with her. Briggs also observed that while the teachers in North Carolina were excellent, they were "not angels" and needed "to study the things that make for peace."[35]

Briggs knew that the missionaries had more than enough to occupy their time in the developing colony. Once they had prepared homes, the teachers devoted most of their energy and waking hours to their work. They had little leisure time. Although the missionaries occasionally wrote of social visits with colonists and white natives, and the Nickersons even dined with some of their students, generally the teachers only interacted with students in the context of their charitable work. Likewise, other than prayer meetings or Sunday schools, social interactions between the teachers and the Union soldiers on the island were limited; and judging by the rare discussions of such occasions in the teachers' letters, the teachers did not relish such gatherings. After a dinner in honor of Lincoln's 1864 election, for example, Ella Roper related that she had not enjoyed herself. Nevertheless, she was glad she had attended; it helped her "understand better the elements about me," she explained. Her disgust at the "excess of intoxication among our officers, from the post commander, down," prompted her to "lay a few facts before a member of a court martial of Norfolk," in hopes that the soldiers would "be treated as they deserve." She reported more positively on a Thanksgiving dinner with officers on board the *Henry James*, which was anchored off the western shore of the island, noting that the evening "passed off in a very quiet homelike manner," but she was relieved when she returned to her home. "The quiet of our ordinary life is more pleasant than ever," she reflected.[36]

By most standards of measure, the missionaries' life in the colony, however, could hardly be counted as "ordinary." What little pattern there was to the missionaries' work in the colony was disrupted daily as they wearily tried to keep up with the changing situations of the freedpeople. There was, as Sarah Freeman put it, no time for loneliness. Throughout the colony's history, the residents were in various stages of settlement, with different needs. Until they had established themselves, new arrivals often lived in Camp Foster amidst conditions that were worse than what they had left in slavery. Freedpeople in an intermediate stage were busy choosing their lots and building their house in the village south of Camp Foster. Those who had been in the colony for a while had their own homes, however primitive, and many raised chickens and had substantial gardens. Although most of the able-bodied men were away from the island working for or serving in the Union army, some of the men who remained in the colony worked for the army's Quartermaster's Department, mostly in construction. In the absence of their husbands, the women frequently were heads of families that averaged three or four children, although the numbers ranged widely from none to ten or twelve. The women attempted to sustain some semblance of family life, even as they exhausted themselves working for soldiers as cooks, laundresses, or maids. Finding wood to build homes, cutting wood for cooking (and for heating, during the cold months), and waiting in line for government rations occupied most free hours.[37]

After Elizabeth James arrived in October 1863, she immediately got caught up in caring for the sick and finding clothing and shelter for the refugees. Although she started a school, her school building was open to the elements, and she suspended classes once cold weather arrived. Instead, she spent her time visiting with the new arrivals, distributing clothing and shoes, and helping them adjust to their new life. "A crowd presses sometimes from before sunrise until nine at night, to buy, to beg, or to look on, & it exhausts my strength, but there is great need, & I volunteered to do this," James confessed. At another time, she reported that she was "so busy among the people" that she often forgot to eat.[38]

In December 1863, after several boatloads of former slaves set free by the Wild expedition arrived on the island, James recorded that she was very busy trying to help the constant stream of refugees to find shelter in Camp Foster, "where every nook and cranny is already crowded to excess." She reported that the former slaves landed at " 'headquarters,' about three miles south of the camp, and walk[ed] up bringing their children & parents, (the aged are not forgotten.)" Some brought a few worldly goods, but many escaped with nothing but the clothes they were wearing. "I see sights, *often*, *often*, that make my heart ache, & which I have no power to relieve," James lamented. Often her emotions got the best of her, as she admitted to George Whipple: "But feeling, as I cannot *help* doing, often stops the process of digestion & then my food sours & causes diarrhea."[39]

Most of the new arrivals were stuffed into several of the old Confederate barracks, which were not built for winter weather. James lamented that "the heavens, and the earth" were "visible through them in almost every direction." She described an extended family of twenty-two crowded into a single barracks room heated by an unvented stove from which smoke "poured into the room, so that is was impossible to see across it, & every individual shivering in rags." Noting that the refugees needed "friendly eyes to look after them and friendly hands to aid," James put forty-three of them in her schoolroom one night to get them out of the cold. Camp Foster grew so crowded and unpleasant that many of the new arrivals chose to create primitive shelters in the woods. James recalled one encounter when she mounted her horse and followed a woman three miles through the woods to a makeshift house built of pine boughs, where she and her family had stayed even through a heavy rain. The woman needed a blanket for her baby. By Christmas James had spent so much time "in the woods & bushes endeavoring to cheer these people" that her pair of thick leather boots were "torn through and through," prompting her to send the AMA an urgent request for another pair.[40]

The colonists turned eagerly to the lone white woman on horseback who trotted among them to offer comfort and advice that winter. "I go with my horse, they cluster about me," she wrote. "I hear the statements of a colored man, appointed by Mr James to learn their wants & how they may be best relieved, and then I talk to them a little, and tell them what they must do & what not to do, and my decisions are not only gratefully received, but blessings from every side are showered upon me." At another time she reflected that having

Contemporary reports indicated that extended families of weary but jubilant freedpeople—including children, invalids, and the elderly—gathered on Roanoke Island. The stream of former slaves into freedmen camps in eastern North Carolina continued throughout the war. (*Harper's Weekly*, 31 January 1863, Special Collections, University of Virginia Library)

had "an *opportunity* to do them good," she had gained the freedpeople's respect "in large measure." James's diplomacy proved the key to the people's acceptance of her help, for although they arrived in dire straits, they treasured their new-found independence. "There would be open rebellion should you *attempt* to direct them," James noted. Although she frequently complained that her duties exhausted her, it is obvious that she also enjoyed being in a position to offer advice to the new arrivals. Writing to George Whipple, Horace James indicated his immense satisfaction with his cousin's pioneering work on the island: "Miss James does grandly."[41]

In February Elizabeth James received some relief when Sergeant George Sanderson returned to superintend the day-to-day operations in the colony. By that time Holland Streeter had come to take charge of the shad fisheries, and A. R. Stover had arrived from Boston to take charge of buildings and roads. James recorded that things were "going prosperously" and that her labors had changed direction. The arrival of additional missionaries also helped spread the burden of the work, but the number of contrabands on the island was growing so rapidly that all the missionaries were essential merely to maintain the colony. Meanwhile, more refugees were on their way. In preparation for an anticipated attack on New Bern, in late February Major General Peck had directed General

I. N. Palmer, commander of the post at New Bern, to send all the contrabands who were living on the outskirts of that town, "exclusive of those in the service of the military department, to the colony at Roanoke Island." At the same time, Peck's assistant adjutant general had also advised General H. W. Wessells, commander of the sub-district of the Albemarle, that the "negroes on Roanoke Island should be prepared to resist a boat raid against the island in case of attack" there.[42]

In March, William T. Briggs reported that Elizabeth James, Ella Roper, and Mary Burnap were all busy "visiting families & doing missionary work preparatory to opening a school." The missionaries had barely gotten their schools in order, however, when they had to deal with another series of crises that had a dramatic impact on the colony. In late April, as the approach of the Confederate navy appeared to threaten Roanoke Island, the teachers were evacuated, first to New Bern and then to Beaufort. The military authorities allowed S. S. Nickerson to return to the island after an absence of five days, but compelled the women to remain in Beaufort for nearly a month. In mid-May, the women returned to the island to face hordes of new refugees from Plymouth who had been transported to Roanoke Island by the government after Plymouth fell to the Confederates. The primary impact of the fall of Plymouth on the freedmen's colony, like that of General Wild's expedition of December 1863, was that it wreaked havoc on the colony's stability. It threw hundreds of new refugees, mostly women and children who did not own much more than the clothes on their backs, into a colony that was just beginning to reach a state of equilibrium. "Our hearts were gladdened with a beginning, Day and Sunday schools organized, and preaching on the sabbath," Samuel Nickerson wrote, "when the attack and capture of Plymouth, by the rebels crowded the island with refugees from that place."[43]

Given the pressing needs of the refugees, the missionaries had to postpone reopening their schools. Instead, they spent much of their time that spring ministering to "the refugees from the fallen cities" and "relieving their suffering." One observer recorded that he had "seldom seen" people who were "more forlorn, sad, and sick looking" than the two boatloads of refugees, "in number about five hundred," from Plymouth. Sarah Freeman, who had worked in the Plymouth camp, recognized many of the new arrivals, whom she found in a "sad and destitute condition." The white refugees, mostly families of Union soldiers, took over two of the colony's churches and a former hospital that Nickerson had been using as a school, forcing him to find another building. The black refugees, many of them families of soldiers who were left to defend Plymouth, meanwhile crowded into Camp Foster—some in the old Confederate barracks and others with friends who had built cabins. Schools, as the teachers reported, remained in an unsettled state for several months. The colony's fishing operations, which had already suffered greatly from the impact of the winter's harsh weather, came to a standstill for several weeks, and barely recovered in the months that followed.[44]

The military's dumping of Plymouth refugees onto Roanoke Island exacerbated two ongoing problems that threatened the long-term success of the Roanoke colony: the wretched conditions in the Camp Foster barracks and shanties, and the growing number of dependent colonists. It was next to impossible for the colony to assimilate the large numbers of refugees in a smooth manner, resulting in a fairly permanent assembly of the most impoverished and hopeless freedpeople in Camp Foster. This only heightened the growing distinction between Camp Foster and the freedmen village. In April 1864, the annual report of the New England Freedmen's Aid Society articulated the distinction between the "Freedmen's Settlement proper, comprising now some three hundred cabins" and the dirty camp, north of the village, where the barracks were located. The report noted that the barracks had been "appropriated to the miscellaneous throng of Freedmen as they arrive in squads from time to time from various parts." These refugees had "not fairly begun to participate and cooperate in the more civilized mode of life *down town*" in the village "among the aristocracy" of the colony. The report went on to describe the living quarters in "rooms, partitioned off in barracks," which were "not so cleanly," and the personal appearance of the barracks' inhabitants, which was "much shabbier than that of their neighbors in the regular settlement."[45]

The population in the colony that spring was approaching three thousand. The distinction between the barracks area in Camp Foster and the village grew greater each day. About two-thirds of the colonists subsisted on government rations of meat, cornmeal, rice, hominy, and potatoes, each ration allotment being approximately two-third's that of an ordinary soldier. A teacher reported that James was considering a new way to distribute rations "among the *Northenders*" in the barracks. He planned to establish a cook-house to prepare rations and issue them to those living in Camp Foster, a move driven by economics but also intended to give further incentive for the freedpeople to move into their houses in the village. The former slaves would "be prompted to take to the regular settlement, as a step higher in life," the teacher stated.[46]

Despite the best efforts of the assistant superintendents to get the contrabands out of Camp Foster and into the village, however, they never caught up. Former slaves streamed onto the island faster than they could be assimilated. Disease and the military movements in eastern North Carolina threatened the stability of the Roanoke Island colony until the war's end. As the months passed, the refugees arriving on the island seemed to be even more destitute and forlorn than those who preceded them. The missionaries had no time to think about Horace James's "New Social Order" or to encourage the development of light industries. Instead, they devoted most of their time outside of school doggedly ministering to the refugees in Camp Foster who had not yet made their way to homes in the village.

Whether offering suggestions to improve sanitation and hygiene, or lecturing on proper behavior and morality, every encounter provided the missionaries an opportunity to impart their beliefs and values. The teachers assumed that there was a close relationship between disease and cleanliness; quite frequently their letters implied that they also saw a connection between cleanliness and moral rectitude. They gauged the freedpeople's progress in terms of the brightness of their clothes, noting, for example, that the students' clothes appeared to grow less dingy as the colony progressed. When the children's clothing was ragged beyond repair, the missionaries found new clothes among donations sent to the colony and dressed them up like little New Englanders. Profinda Nickerson's description of the joy that she took in such work was fairly typical: "Thursday was one of the happiest days of my life," she declared. "We commenced it by taking some children in and washing them all over, then dressing them through out."[47]

Crowding in the makeshift accommodations in the barracks led to some deplorable living conditions that threatened the survival of the entire colony. Although the settlement remained fairly healthy compared to other North Carolina locations, especially New Bern, where an outbreak of yellow fever killed hundreds of contrabands and threatened Horace James's life in the fall of 1864, communicable diseases and sickness related to the living conditions touched the lives of the freedpeople and the missionaries. Robert Morrow was the only missionary to die on Roanoke Island, but most of the missionaries suffered from a variety of ailments during their tenure there. During her first few months in residence, Elizabeth James endured chronic diarrhea so devastating that at one point she lay in bed "unable to move or be moved." At another time she suffered from "a bilious fever" that made her so weak she could not lift a hand. One summer Ella Roper was so ill with malarial fever that she did not have enough "strength of mind or body" to "write steadily," while Sarah Freeman's bout with the same disease left her "entirely prostrated, helpless, as an infant," and certain that her "work was done on earth."[48]

In the absence of the post physician, the missionaries provided medical assistance to each other and the freedpeople. The people called on her, James reported, "as though I had power to heal." In a short time she became an expert not only on which patent medicine worked best on particular illnesses, but also on proper dosages. Two of her favorites, which she frequently requested from the AMA, were Meikleham's Diarrhea Formula and Cholera Preventive and Hibbard's Wild Cherry Bitters. She found both remedies effective against her own ailments and a variety of the freedpeople's afflictions. Although she was an advocate of temperance and would never have taken a social drink of liquor, she did not hesitate to order up bottles of cherry rum and cherry brandy, which she extolled as "better medicine than any the doctors can give for the trouble so prevalent here." At various times, she also requested hot drops, quinine, morphine, and a variety of pills, as well as "a bottle of whiskey in which to steep dogwood and wild cherry bark," which she used to relieve chills "when all medicines fail." At one point in her work, she was aghast at the spread of "itch" in the camp. Although she admitted that she was "almost ashamed to mention" the malady, which soldiers had brought to the island, she wrote to the AMA secretary requesting an ointment of sulfur and cream of tartar to combat it.[49]

Against killer diseases, however, the missionaries' medical efforts proved to be puny and ineffective. Smallpox claimed at least six colonists' lives in the winter of 1864, and cholera and dysentery remained problems throughout the colony's existence. The missionaries could do little but comfort the bereaved and help prepare the dead for burial. Most of the victims remained nameless, but occasionally the missionaries devoted portions of their letters to particularly unsettling deaths. In September 1864, for example, Elizabeth James recorded the "sudden and violent" death of a "healthy, pretty girl of fifteen," who grew sick and died of Asiatic Cholera in a day's time. Such sad occasions also provided the missionaries with an opportunity to talk about salvation and to give lessons in the conduct of funerals and "proper" deportment during mourning. Ella Roper believed that teaching the freedpeople to "pay respect for the dead" would "do much to raise the moral tone" in the colony. Profinda Nickerson described the graveside lesson she gave her students. When one of her students died, the entire school "followed her remains to the grave" and then after her body was lowered into the ground, they sang a hymn, "Peacefully sleep beloved one."[50]

Concern for burial rituals extended to the very clothes that the dead wore to their graves. The missionaries wrote frequent letters to the corresponding secretary of the AMA or to other Northern benevolent associations and churches asking that donations for missionary work on Roanoke Island include burial shrouds. Their frequent requests for goods also included profoundly sincere pleas for bedding, blankets, household goods, and clothing for the impoverished former slaves. In September 1864, for example, Sarah Freeman asked for a supply of shoes. She noted that "most of the women" were barefooted and the children lacked shoes and stockings. She made a special plea on behalf of the freedmen who worked at the sawmill, noting that "many of the men are obliged to work in water, and unless they can have dry warm shoes to put on when they are through, they get sick directly." No doubt the conclusion to Freeman's letter summarized the thoughts of most of the island's missionary corps: "Oh, that some philanthropist from the North would come down and survey this field, and our wants, that I should not be obliged to write them."[51]

Once donations arrived, the missionaries then devoted a large amount of time to distributing the goods, a job that drained them physically and mentally. Sarah Freeman described the work that went into issuing supplies after the shipping crates and barrels were opened at the distribution office: "Worked all day, admitting eight or ten at once, and after attending to that number, dismissing them, and admitting more, till night overtook us, and then hundreds were obliged to go away without getting any thing." The next day she started all over: "Friday was again devoted to unpacking and assorting, preparatory to the work of distribution."[52]

The donated articles, in turn, brought the missionaries to the attention of more freedpeople, especially new arrivals. Mary Burnap had realized the power of donated goods when she was working in New Bern, her conclusions suggesting the efficacy of a sort of bribery that empowered her Christian witnessing. "Greater good might be done by holding a pair of shoes or a new frock in one hand, and the Bible in the other," she declared. "It is wonderful how much more influence you can have over those who do not believe, by doing something for their souls, and bodies, at the same time." Ella Roper went a bit further than Burnap, suggesting that the distribution of goods to the more impoverished contrabands would build trust and maintain order. "Having been imposed upon during a life of slavery and I deeply regret to say, sometimes in freedom, by those who should have their interests as their first care, they become suspicious; their confidence is easily shaken," Roper confided. "A liberal supply of goods, with the proper influences, around them [the freedpeople], will do much to keep them in a cheerful contented frame of mind."[53]

The issuance of donated materials was complicated by the missionaries' belief that it was better for the freedpeople to purchase goods than to be the recipients of charity. It was clear to the missionaries that working for a wage and then saving for desired items taught valuable lessons in self-discipline, self-reliance, and frugality. The receipts also helped to pay for additional items that were distributed without cost to those who could not afford to pay. As the *American*

Missionary noted, requiring some payment for donated goods would help the freedpeople develop "a laudable independence, and furnish means for supplying those who are more destitute." During the first winter on Roanoke Island, however, the goal of independence exceeded the people's ability to pay. In January 1864 Horace James reported that "a large quantity of agricultural and mechanical tools and implements" had been donated and issued to the colonists at Roanoke Island "at cost prices, they being expected to pay for them when able." Acknowledging that much of the money probably would not be collected, he concluded that the materials would probably "be reckoned as donated."[54]

Later that spring, however, Horace James happily reported that efforts to furnish some clothing "at reasonable prices" had been "steadily growing" during the past few months, leading to "a spirit of independence and self-reliance" among some of the freedpeople. In August 1864 Ella Roper indicated that the men working for the government were paid more regularly, and the soldiers' wives were receiving money from their husbands' pay, which led to an increasing number of freedpeople who would "proudly pay" for goods "in greenbacks or hard *silver*." Similarly, Elizabeth James reported that many felt "a desire to earn what ever they receive and are making earnest efforts to do so." Thus, while the missionaries were still forced to dole out donated goods to the destitute barracks dwellers, many of the established freedpeople were able to purchase a variety of items, including clothing, books, crockery, provisions, hardware, wooden ware, tin ware, and tools. After materials were sold, the cash received, except for a small handling fee (usually 10 percent), was sent to the parties who had forwarded the goods. They, in turn, re-invested the money in more items, which they sent to the missionaries for resale.[55]

In very little time, the missionaries had forged strong bonds with the freedpeople, and vice versa. Many of the former slaves overwhelmed the missionaries with their heartfelt outpourings of gratitude. Others brought whatever they could spare as love offerings. Mary R. Kimball described how the colonists in the village brought chickens, eggs, and potatoes to thank their teachers. In the summer, she reported, "they seem to vie with each other in bringing their offerings of melons and vegetables from their little gardens." The missionaries, for their part, frequently treated the freedpeople with what came close to possessiveness. "I feel as though they belonged to me," Elizabeth James declared, without giving a thought to the ramifications of what she had said. Similarly, Ella Roper's discussions of her work with the freedpeople suggest an association that was simultaneously familiar and condescending. The colonists seemed "like a family," she wrote, "so much do they depend upon me, for advice in their home affairs."[56]

Such ambivalence was clearly illustrated in the missionaries' relationship to the black children that they brought into their homes. Sarah Freeman took in five orphans, including a "bright little boy" that she referred to as "our Jim" and "our little Jimmy," to raise at Sunnyside. Shortly after he showed up, Freeman noted that she had "set Aunt Sarah at work with him with a tub of water, soap, fine comb, and scissors," and that she then needed to "find something to cover him with." Meanwhile, Jim, who was about six years old, followed on Freeman's heels, carrying out errands and odd jobs for her. Elizabeth James opened her home to a young girl named Jennie and a boy named Otter. James became especially attached to Jennie, who was not, technically speaking, an orphan. Jennie's father had joined the Union army and left her in the colony with her mother, who was too sick to take care of her. Although Jennie's status fell somewhere between that of a daughter and a servant, James referred to her as "my colored girl" or "my Jennie." Samuel and Profinda Nickerson similarly took in a young woman who quickly slipped into the role of servant, assisting Profinda with laundry and cooking. "She came naked," Samuel wrote, "and we have dressed her in old clothes sent out and given her a home with us." Such treatment was "all the remuneration she asks, and [she] seems happy in such a situation," Nickerson noted, apparently unaware that his sentiments were similar to those that were frequently mouthed by Southern slaveholders.[57]

In addition to visiting in the homes of the freedpeople, providing medical assistance, and soliciting and distributing donations, a day's work often included writing letters for desperate colonists. Every refugee had a story, and these stories frequently compelled the dog-tired missionaries to keep on writing even when they were exhausted. At the same time, such collaborations gave the missionaries further opportunities to offer advice to the freedpeople. Elizabeth James's letters to the AMA suggest that she spent much of her spare time writing such letters. In August 1864, for example, she gave up her vacation, which she had been anticipating "with so much interest," to stay on the island and help the colonists write letters to the men who were away from the island. The soldiers' regiments were stationed in North Carolina and around Petersburg. James noted that battles had been "hourly expected," and the soldiers' families were feeling "the deepest anxiety." So, even though the almost unbearable summer heat beat down on the colony, and James felt "faint & languid sometimes," she did not "feel justified in leaving" the colonists when they needed her. "They need not only one who will write their letters," she reported, "but one who will sympathize with them, express somewhat their feelings."[58]

James took advantage of these occasions to instruct the women on morality and "proper" behavior. She despaired that the women often assumed that because their husbands had gone to war, they could freely marry again. "I have endeavored to correct this feeling, and a great change has been wrought," James wrote, but still some assumed that their marriages were temporary. Although James's sympathy for the colonists was genuine, her lectures on marriage were probably a bit off the mark. Part of her problem was perceptual; in the summer of 1864 James was still living in her makeshift shanty in Camp Foster. Her neighbors in the Camp area who called upon her for help and advice—the people she was most likely to encounter in her daily exertions—were among the most destitute cases in the colony. At one point she had noted that she was living among the "wildest, and wickedest of the most degraded," and that the students in her school were "children of field hands coarse, dirty, in an extreme degree." Conditions prevented these refugees who had been thrown together in Camp Foster from settling down into the sort of stable households that were common in the colony's village.[59]

In addition, significant cultural differences influenced James's reproaches. Because state laws forbade it, the refugees who had been married while slaves were not legally bound by magisterial marriage certificates. James and the other missionaries did not believe that the paralegal marriages were valid, and quickly jumped to the conclusion that the colonists could not possibly be committed to such "temporary" marriages. More importantly, however, James's misunderstanding related to language. The former slaves were much more literal than the evangelical missionaries. When James asked women with large families "Where is your husband?" they, as she noted, "almost invariably" responded, "I have none." A little more prodding, and she uncovered that the men had "Gone *away*." Yet more prodding revealed that they had gone away "To war." Instead of realizing that the women meant that they literally had no husbands with them on the island, James automatically assumed that the women "supposed they *had* no partner & were at liberty to marry again."[60]

The very fact that the women wanted to write letters to their husbands said much about their marital ties. Other evidence from the island and anecdotes that Elizabeth James herself presented in various letters indicated that, in truth, the colonists respected their marriages and valued their families above all else. For example, in one of the letters in which James fretted about the lack of permanence in the colonists' marriages, she also recounted a touching story of a young woman who was aching to rejoin her family in Virginia. On a Saturday morning, just when James was at the point where she declared that she absolutely could not write another letter for a colonist until she had taken care of her own correspondence, the young woman tapped on her door and asked James to write a letter to her brother. The woman had been raised by her parents, who were house servants, and she had served in the privileged position of chamber maid. When she was nineteen, however, her master needed money and abruptly sold her away "from all she had ever known and loved" to "a brutal man." After four hellish years, the Union army had rescued her and brought her to the island. In the camp, she ran into a man who had just come from Norfolk, where he had seen her brother. She was desperate to write a letter to send her brother by the man, who was returning to Norfolk that evening.[61]

Ever since the first days of freedom on the island, when men who had been working as slaves on Confederate fortifications indicated their desire to leave the island to fetch their families, the history of the colony was punctuated by stories of extended families coming to the island as groups and striving to live together in the coarse conditions of Camp Foster, of families reuniting after many years of separation, of families who worked together in the village to construct homes, of soldiers volunteering to fight for their families, and of children who took over for absent soldier fathers. In light of the dislocations that the colonists had endured under slavery and were enduring during the war, it is all the more amazing that the freedpeople attempted to carve out a fairly traditional existence in the camp. They looked to the men, whether in the army or on the island working for the Quartermaster's Department, to provide the primary sustenance for the families. Frequently three generations lived in the same house, and, in addition, they took in orphans.[62]

When given the opportunity, married colonists emphasized that they believed that their marriages were valid. Those who had been free prior to the war underscored that they had been legally married by justices of the peace or magistrates before fleeing to Roanoke Island. Frank James and his wife Indianna were typical; they had been married by a justice of the peace in 1856 in Plymouth, where Frank worked as a waterman. Similarly, William H. Overton and his wife Rachel had been married by a magistrate in Perquimons County in 1861. James and Overton both enlisted in the Thirty-sixth USCT, and their wives and families stayed behind in the colony until the couples were reunited after the war.[63]

In documents filed after the war, former slaves pointed proudly to marriages that had endured since their days in slavery, noting that they had been joined "by the consent of their former owners" or "in the usual way that slaves then married," at the home of their owners. Martha and Jeffrey Johnson, who served in the Thirty-fifth USCT, were typical. They had been married "in the usual way that slaves were married," on their owner's farm. Martha Johnson was living in the Roanoke Island camp in December 1863 when she received word that her husband had died at Follys Island. John Tyler, who served in the Thirty-fifth

Black soldiers in the Thirty-fifth, Thirty-sixth, and Thirty-seventh U.S. Colored Troops left families in the freedmen's colony on Roanoke Island. Many, such as the troops of the Thirty-fifth USCT who are pictured here in the Battle of Olustee, fought bravely for their families' freedom. (*Harper's New Monthly Magazine*, November 1866, Special Collections, University of Virginia Library)

USCT, and his wife Sallie had been owned by two different slaveholders. They had been married sometime before the war "by the consent of their former owners," and the ceremony was performed by a minister. Thomas Sanders and his wife had been married by a black minister in Washington, North Carolina, in October 1861. They brought their infant child with them to Roanoke Island, where Thomas enlisted in the Thirty-sixth USCT in December 1863. Sanders died of complications from wounds suffered near Petersburg in 1864. Although not legally married, Albert Banks, of the Thirty-sixth USCT, and his wife "were considered man and wife . . . and were always living together as such" before they came to the island.[64]

Many of the soldiers had enlisted because of their families; they believed that fighting was the best way to help their families remain free. Out in the field, the soldiers remained in touch with their families through letters—letters that the missionaries frequently had to read to the wives and children—and they occasionally wrote letters to the military authorities complaining about conditions that their families were enduring in the colony. Evidence also suggests that some black soldiers left their posts, sometimes without official leave, to come to the island and check on their families. In August 1864, for example, when William Benson walked away from the Thirty-seventh USCT near Petersburg and returned to the island to check on his family, he was declared a deserter. Leon Bembury, of the Thirty-sixth USCT, played by the rules and was granted a twenty-day furlough to Roanoke Island to "see his family."[65]

Elizabeth James never comprehended the basis of her differences with the colonists on the marriage issue. In truth, however, questions about marriage were only different in kind from many concerns—time management, self discipline, and delayed gratification, among others—that embodied the gulf between the world of the missionaries and the world of the former slaves. That the missionaries spent much of their time ministering to the most difficult cases in the colony only served to heighten their belief that the freedpeople truly needed their guidance in matters of deportment.

No doubt the missionaries genuinely cared for most of the freedpeople. The problem was that the missionaries assumed that teaching them to adopt the habits of middle-class white Northerners was the only way to prepare them for freedom. They wanted the colonists to emulate them in dress, manner, and beliefs. The missionaries' certainty that they knew what was best for the former slaves found its clearest expression in their plans for schools on the island. They maintained that a Yankee education that included generous religious training and promoted traditional republican virtues would enable the freedpeople to overcome bad habits acquired through years of enslavement and become productive citizens. To fully understand the missionary work in the Roanoke Island colony, it is therefore necessary to turn to the missionaries' work as teachers.[66]

Letting In the Light

EDUCATION IN THE COLONY

IN EARLY APRIL 1865, while waiting at the Roanoke Island landing to board a vessel for New Bern, Major General Carl Schurz looked up to see the approach of "a little procession of negro women and girls, singing loudly." Schurz, on his way south to assume a new command under Major General William T. Sherman, recorded "a leave-taking scene of extraordinary cordiality," as students tendered their farewells to missionary teacher Mary Burnap, who was being transferred to Wilmington. Schurz was moved by the "demonstration of love and attachment" for the young woman who "behaved like a great loving mother who was parting from her children." On board the ship, he met Burnap, who told him of the students' "eagerness to learn," and their "loyal devotion," as well as "the difficulties and dangers which beset the women teachers."[1]

Schurz's account bore witness to much that characterized the relationships between missionaries and their pupils on Roanoke Island. By all accounts, the students were eager and loyal and the teachers were committed; yet their time together was frequently interrupted by things beyond their control. Just as the stream of contrabands onto the island, especially after the fall of Plymouth, had threatened the notion of a completely organized, self-supporting colony, the constant upheaval wreaked havoc with school plans. In the fall of 1864, Samuel Nickerson reported that the "longest *uninterrupted* term" in the island's schools had been seven weeks.[2]

Although the missionaries served in a variety of capacities, their most intimate connections with the freedpeople developed in the context of their classrooms. Benjamin Butler's General Orders No. 46 had, in fact, indicated that the army recognized that the missionaries' primary purpose in coming south was "for the charitable purpose of giving to the negroes secular and religious instructions. . . ." Butler ordered officers and soldiers to treat the teachers "with the utmost respect" and to aid the teachers "by all proper means" as they went about their work. He also noted that the military would provide transportation to the missionaries "whenever it may be necessary in pursuit of their business."[3]

Education superintendent William T. Briggs worked with the secretaries of the benevolent associations to recruit teachers for North Carolina, stressing that they should be "of great promise" and "prepared to endure hardness as good soldiers." He told the AMA's corresponding secretary, George Whipple, that he intended to maintain teachers "of the first order," and that he wanted only teachers with experience. "It costs something to send them here—it is not so easy to make a change as north," Briggs stated. "We had much rather have a *few* good teachers than *many* poor ones."[4]

In his capacity as superintendent of Negro Affairs for the District of North Carolina, Horace James consulted with the local military authorities on Roanoke Island to procure unoccupied buildings and convert them to classrooms. Armed with both determination and imagination, the missionaries set about to transform unused barracks, ration houses, and sheds into New England classrooms. Since the military had the authority to command that school buildings be relinquished for military exigencies, the teachers remained at the mercy of the local officers—a subordination that frequently created difficulties for the teachers and their students. Nevertheless, the teachers persevered. "Matters get to flow smoothly along, even under the regime of red tape—after one becomes 'used to it,'" Ella Roper conceded. The missionaries established day schools for children and all others who could attend during daylight hours; they organized evening schools for the men and women who had to work during the regular school sessions; and they organized Sabbath schools in the morning and evening for freedpeople and soldiers. Schools were scattered throughout the colony—in old buildings near the Camp Foster barracks and at Pork Point near Headquarters, and in newer buildings in the village.[5]

The pioneer missionary teacher, Elizabeth James, had organized her first school shortly after she arrived, but had to give it up because the building was not adequate protection from the weather. Although her everyday missionary duties overwhelmed her, in February 1864 she finally had time to organize the Lincoln School at the corner of Roanoke Avenue and A Street in Camp Foster. The Lincoln School initially attracted sixty students of varying ages. James also conducted an evening school for adults in her home. She reported that attendance at the evening session was "not large, usually from twelve to fifteen," but the students were the "leading men and their wives." They had "an intense desire to learn" and were "making earnest effort." After James moved out of Camp Foster in 1865, she organized another day school close to her new house in the freedmen's village.[6]

In February 1864 Ella Roper also opened a school, which she named the Whipple School, to honor George Whipple. According to Roper, the school was established "in a rude building erected by the colored people for a church" on Sixth Street near Roanoke Avenue. She noted that it was "comfortable in good weather" but "crowded to its utmost capacity." She did not exaggerate; she had two hundred pupils. Mary Burnap joined Roper as assistant at the Whipple School in March 1864.[7]

Samuel Nickerson opened his first day school in March 1864. He named this school, which met in a former Rebel barracks near military headquarters, the Cypress Chapel School. Martha Culling closed her school, which she had been meeting in a house, and assisted Nickerson at the Cypress Chapel School for several months that spring. Although conditions in the building frustrated Nickerson, he attempted to make the best of the situation: "We should call it a poor place for a school North—too open to be warmed by artificial heat, yet it is the best the island affords, and a great deal better than none." The seats were "empty ammunition boxes," which, he noted, "made quite fair seats" and "possessed the peculiar advantage of being easily arranged for the teacher's liking." In April 1864, Nickerson had barely had time to settle into the old barracks when the army appropriated his school building and turned it into a temporary shelter for some of the white refugees who had fled to Roanoke Island from Plymouth. In response, the intrepid Nickerson collected some of his former students and moved to a building known as the New Meetinghouse, another of the churches that had been built by the colonists, and named the new school the New Cypress Chapel School. Nickerson did not hide his irritation with the forced move to what he characterized as "a splits shantee of the poorest description."[8]

Meanwhile, the forced evacuation of the women of the missionary corps to Beaufort lasted until mid-May. Upon her return to Roanoke Island, Elizabeth James reopened the Lincoln School near her home in Camp Foster. Ella Roper opened a new school, which she called the Briggs School in honor of William T. Briggs, about a mile and a half from her Sunnyside home in the old Ration House in Camp Foster. In a letter to George Whipple she noted that she was "very happily situated" in that school, which she described as "a neat cheery white-washed room where I have gathered about seventy promising scholars." By the following January, the attendance at Roper's school had burgeoned to 130 students, who suffered from the primitive heating in the old

A. M. A. ARCHIVES
NO. 99903
FISK UNIV.

MONTHLY REPORT.

DISTRICT OF NORTH CAROLINA, March 1864

Monthly Report of a Colored School taught by Miss Roper and Burnap in Roanoke Id. for the month of March 1864.

Name or designation of the School, Whipple School.

Location of the School, Sixth St. near Roanoke Avenue.

When established, March 1st 1864.

Its first teacher, Miss E. Roper.

Its present teacher, or teachers, Miss E. Roper, Miss Mary Burnap.

Commissioned by what Society, Am. Miss. Society.

Date of commission, Jan. 20th 1864.

	Report for the month of March 1864
No. of days kept.	20
No. of sessions.	20
No. of different pupils.	217
Largest No. present at any session.	175
Average attendance for the month.	150
Smallest No. present at any session.	75
Whole No. of Males.	50
Whole No. of Females.	167
No. over 16 years of age.	
No. under 6 years of age.	
No. of pupils who read and spell.	120
No. who study mental arithmetic.	50
No. who pursue written arithmetic.	0
No who study geography.	4
No. who write.	0
Is singing taught in school.	It is.
No of mulattoes.	25
No. of pure blacks.	0
Do the mulattoes show any more capacity than the blacks?	They do not.
No. of whites.	0
No who attend to needlework.	0

Each teacher will make out a monthly report, sign, and return the same to Chaplain JAMES, Superintendent of Blacks, at Newbern, N. C., on or before the tenth of the succeeding month. All the blanks should be filled, giving approximate returns if exact ones cannot be obtained.

State the general progress of the school for the month, the chief obstacles encountered, any cases of insubordination that have occurred, and the method of disposing of them, with such suggestions as may have a bearing upon the welfare of the school.

In their monthly report for the Whipple School, March 1864, American Missionary Association teachers Ella Roper and Mary Burnap indicated that the school had met for twenty days. The school had attracted 217 different students, with an average attendance of 150. (Amistad Research Center, Tulane University)

Ration House. "We occasionally indulge in airy visions for ourselves of places where neither teacher nor pupil will tremble and grow tearful between the Smoke and cold," she admitted.[9]

Upon her return from the forced evacuation to Beaufort, Mary Burnap became Nickerson's associate at the New Cypress Chapel School, which had nearly two hundred students. Nickerson's wife, Profinda, assisted the two teachers. After their transfer from Plymouth, Kate Freeman and Esther Williams organized an NFRA-supported school. In addition, the elder Freeman and Martha Culling opened new schools in Sibley tents; each had thirty students. Thus, by June 1864 there were six schools in the Roanoke Island freedmen's colony; and several of these schools offered evening as well as day classes.[10]

Although Superintendent Briggs thought Roanoke Island was "a hard field" because of its scanty school accommodations, he predicted that the AMA would double its schools on Roanoke Island that fall. He had the backing of Horace James, who pledged to do something about the school building shortage, vowing that he would "at once put up school-houses at Roanoke; as many as we need." Briggs remained similarly enthusiastic about the prospects. "We shall strain every nerve to meet the great want on that Island," Briggs declared in December 1864. That same month, Briggs reported the opening of two new schools in the colony and previewed his plans to establish an additional school to meet the educational needs of the burgeoning population in Camp Foster. Meanwhile, Samuel Nickerson organized a popular evening school for adults, at one point attracting 115 students. Briggs continued his optimistic assessment in January 1865, when he forecast that the AMA would soon "furnish facilities for educating all who are disposed voluntarily to attend school." His plans for an additional school in the Camp Foster area materialized in February, when Mary Burnap established a school for a hundred students in the old ration house, also known as the Mental Commissary.[11]

Generally the schools were swamped by would-be scholars. Ella Roper noted that attendance was good and interest keen among all ages, "from the grandmother with spectacles to the child clinging to her side while puzzling out its 'A.B.C.'s.'" While "the earnest desire to learn" among both the elderly and the young brought great cheer to the missionaries, they also fretted that they were unable to handle more students. In June 1864 Samuel Nickerson reported that his Cypress Chapel School had "taken as many as the house will hold [128] without injuring the school." In January 1865 Ella Roper declared that "the avidity for learning" continued unabated, creating a dilemma for the sympathetic teachers. "One of the most painful things we have to encounter is the crowd besieging our schoolroom door for admission; no effort is too great for

Although the schoolroom depicted in this artist's rendering of a freedmen's school is probably much nicer than the schoolrooms in the mission schools on Roanoke Island, it does illustrate some features that were typical. The students' ages ranged widely, they were enthusiastic about learning, and the rooms were crowded. ("Teaching the Freedmen" from Trowbridge, *The South: a Tour of Its Battle-fields and Ruined Cities*, facing p. 338)

them," she reported. "They follow us everywhere till wearied with importunity we admit more than we can attend to, as no inst[itution], or as no full one ought to."[12]

In December 1865 an editorial in the *Christian Recorder*, the journal of the African Methodist Episcopal Church, denounced missionary teachers "who, while in the North make loud pretension to Abolition, when they get South partake so largely of that contemptible prejudice that they are ashamed to be seen in company with colored men." Although there is no evidence that the missionaries on Roanoke Island were overtly prejudiced toward the freedpeople there, their assumptions about the former slaves' character and intellectual capabilities did shape their teaching. The missionaries came South believing that the freedpeople's years in slavery had left them bereft of self-discipline and purpose—that their experience in slavery led them to lie and steal without compunction. Likewise, the missionaries believed that slavery induced laziness. The missionaries did not, however, think these traits were racially based or permanent. Instead, they believed, as the *American Missionary* put it, that the freedpeople's "low moral standard" was the "direct result of slavery." Slavery encouraged docility and sloth; the slaves could hardly be better than their immoral owners. Ella Roper reflected such ideas when she reported that "all grades of society" were present in the Roanoke Island colony, from the intelligent "down to the benighted ones, who reply with stupid looks of bewilderment" when questioned about their knowledge of God. "So faithfully has the master's character been reproduced in the servants!" she exclaimed.[13]

The missionaries also believed that years of servitude had robbed the freedpeople of a chance for intellectual development. They were convinced, however, that the former slaves were capable of great things if given the proper educational opportunities. The solution, as the *Freedmen's Journal* noted, was to "make another New England of the whole South," and the schoolroom was the place to start. From the missionaries' perspective, one of the major purposes of the freedmen schools was to inculcate Northern middle-class values and eradicate the former slaves' slovenly Southern ways. The missionaries' dual goals were to alter the position of the former slaves and restructure Southern society. The teachers truly believed that education would lift the freedpeople to their proper position in the "New Social Order" that was to replace the slave system. The Yankee school provided a ready and reliable model.[14]

Ella Roper maintained that the black refugees from Plymouth, who had "enjoyed the blessings of liberty, *employment* and education for some time," exemplified the unlimited potential of the freedpeople "when permitted to develope themselves as men and women." Elizabeth James thought that, once educated, some of the freedpeople would, in turn, teach others. "I think the way to elevate any race hitherto degraded is to educate some of their own number and bring them up to be teachers & leaders," Elizabeth James avowed.[15]

Inside the schools, the teachers attempted to foster an atmosphere that encouraged the students to make a connection between freedom, education, and productive citizenship. Popular mottoes such as "Give me liberty or give me death," "A day or an hour of virtuous liberty is worth a whole eternity of bondage," and "His people are free," adorned the schoolroom walls and celebrated the freedpeople's new status. Such maxims as "This school is for the Free," "Our chains are broken," and "What is worth doing at all is worth doing well" reinforced the importance of the activities that went on in class.[16]

Although the teachers frequently emphasized the variety of ages of their students or the general state of illiteracy, they did not alter their New England school model to accommodate the backgrounds or circumstances of their new students. They wrote of setting up classrooms that mimicked what they had grown accustomed to in the North. Likewise, they maintained the typical New England school calendar that consisted of fall, winter, and spring terms. In addition, when the teachers compared their school days on Roanoke Island with what they had left behind in New England, they usually noted that the organization of the school days was similar in the two places. Susan Odell, for example, noted that she was "teaching two sessions a day, the same as I did at the North, teaching the same hours." Since the older children were often needed at home for part of the day, the morning sessions were usually full, while the afternoon sessions were often sparsely attended. Generally each session lasted five hours, but it was shortened to four hours in hot weather. That sometimes led to problems, as Ella Roper noted in June 1865. Her session had been shortened to four and a half hours, but "the unanimous cry 'Can we have one more lesson today?' " made the day "seem all too short."[17]

Textbooks in mission schools included various readers by Parker and Watson, *The Freedmen's Reader*, *McGuffey's Reader*, Robinson's *Primary Progressive Arithmetic*, Davis' *Practical Arithmetic*, Fetter's *Primary Arithmetic*, Greenleaf's *Arithmetic*, Monteith's *Geography*, Small's *Geography*, Monteith's *United States History*, Goodrich's *Pictorial History of the United States*, Wilson's *Primary Speller*, and *Webster's Speller*. The teachers focused on the traditional three "Rs"—reading, writing, and arithmetic—but they also gave lessons in penmanship, spelling, geography, singing, and current events—the latter from the Northern perspective, as a matter of course. In addition, lessons in morality, focusing on virtues such as thrift, industriousness, punctuality, and sobriety, played a prominent role in the curriculum. The missionaries lectured against intemperate behavior, whether it was drinking, smoking, or sexual activity outside marriage, and emphasized honesty and frugality. As they had previously done in the North when teaching lower-class students, they stressed individual self-control and hard work, as well as the freedpeople's responsibility to earn their own livings. They encouraged their pupils to save their money, with the eventual goal of purchasing homesteads. Teachers' monthly reports emphasized that the progress of the black students in their studies equaled that of white children in the North.[18]

The five-hour morning session in Elizabeth James's Lincoln School commenced with the students repeating a passage from the Bible, followed by prayer and singing. The youngest students repeated their ABCs. Then came lots of drill work—repetition of the multiplication tables, spelling, and reading. James believed that recitations were valuable; even when a class had completed a reader, she made them go through it again repeatedly, for she thought there was "still something more to be learned from it, in the way of smoothness, modulating the voice, &c." She admitted that the "long continued sessions, together with earnest, incessant labor out of school" were "exhausting," but she thought the work very rewarding.[19]

School sessions were adjourned for the summer months of July, August, and September, as they were in New England. William Briggs encouraged his North Carolina teachers to go home for at least a two-month vacation. Only then, he noted, would they "come to their work fresh & vigorous, with a stock of strength laid up for eight or ten months of unremitting labor." The students in the Roanoke Island schools, however, implored the teachers to continue classes during the summer; they did not want to stop learning. Some of the freedpeople of the Methodist Episcopal Church felt so strongly about continuing school in the summer that they hired Richard Boyle to teach their children during the summer of 1864. Boyle's school attracted students who had studied in several of the island's regular schools, but many children were still left without classes for three months. The missionaries reported that these students were so eager that they continued to study on their own. "There was little need of the instructions so often given in our northern schools before the long vacation—to look at their books occasionally," Ella Roper observed. Elizabeth James's students were "grateful" that she chose to remain on the island for her vacation. Although school was out of session, they frequently came to her door, "book in hand, 'to get a little lesson.' " One of the most feared punishments a teacher could give a student was prohibiting him or her from attending school.[20]

Despite, or perhaps because of, their students' enthusiasm, maintaining the classroom decorum to which the teachers had grown accustomed in their New England schools provided many challenges and frustrations amid the changing conditions in the colony. Reports and letters to AMA headquarters suggest, in fact, that the teachers were preoccupied with maintaining order and discipline in the packed classrooms. Mary Burnap and Ella Roper reported in May 1864 that interruptions for repairs and storms had "unfavorable effects on general order" among the 171 students attending the Whipple School, but they had "no cases of insubordination" to report. They were pleased with their success "in stopping the great and common evil of loud talking." In July 1864 Samuel Nickerson reported that "talking is not heard in [Cypress Chapel] school and whispering is growing less daily"—no small accomplishment, considering that there were 128 pupils in the room. That same month, Ella Roper noted that she was pleased with the seriousness in her schoolroom. She reported that "no cases of insubordination" that required "more than a word to recall them to their duty" had occurred. After news of Robert E. Lee's surrender reached the island, Samuel Nickerson announced the news to his class and allowed three cheers. "It was done with an order and earnestness that would have pleased you," Profinda Nickerson reported in a letter to George Whipple. In June 1865, Roper noted that she had sent one from her school "for the evil influence he was exerting over others, but never *one* for disobedience." She believed that this record compared well with what would have transpired in Northern schools. "When could I remain so long in one school at the north," she asked, "and report so favorably?"[21]

The teachers made much of the contrast between the entering students and those who had absorbed some of the teachers' notions about proper behavior. They were not above congratulating themselves on their ability to make the students "apply" themselves to their schoolwork. Samuel Nickerson, for example, attributed the subdued behavior in his classroom to the influence of his teaching. Noting that his students' behavior in 1865 contrasted greatly with their behavior when he first started his school, Nickerson recorded that at first, the students "did not know that they must sit much less keep from *talking*." By October 1865, his students had learned to "take their seats with no whispering." Nickerson believed that the students' success was directly related to their self-discipline. "Those who apply themselves—and the number averages higher than in Northern schools," Nickerson asserted later that year, "make good progress in reading and spelling." Profinda Nickerson drew a similar conclusion about the three students in the classroom "from families usually called 'poor whites.'" They appeared to be "good specimens of filth, idleness, and ignorance," she reported, "but they seemed to engage in the duties of the school room with more energy and good will than we thought possible."[22]

The teachers' preoccupation with structure and order in their classrooms reflected their overall interest in maintaining order. They believed that discipline and control were tools that applied equally well to individuals and society. At the same time, they were also responding to demanding school situations that were unlike anything that they had encountered in the North. They had to manage, sometimes single-handedly, huge classes composed of students who were not used to sitting still in school and who were much more transient than their Northern counterparts. Frequently, the teachers were merely doing what they thought best to encourage learning. While their belief in the necessity of orderly classrooms required an exaggeration of the sort of discipline that they had applied in their classrooms at home, the motivations were similar. In many ways their assumption that students were students no matter their background was a compliment to the students in the mission schools.

In addition to disorder and insubordination, the teachers worried about attendance problems. In his annual report for 1865, William T. Briggs reported that "the two evils which have most annoyed the teachers & retarded the progress of the schools were tardiness and absence." Briggs touched on one of the ironies of the mission schools when he observed that a large number of the students "absent themselves & our teachers will soon have to do more missionary work & persuade them to come in." Although the freedpeople nearly always clamored for education and frequently exceeded the capacities of the island's mission schools, many attended sporadically, usually because of circumstances beyond their control.[23]

In what was one of the few departures from the New England School model, the teachers did not establish regulations with respect to attendance, primarily because they understood the obstacles that the students had to overcome merely to show up in class. First, they had to procure warm clothing and shoes. The missionary teachers frequently wrote letters to their Northern friends requesting basic garments that would enable their students to continue their education in cold weather. Once they had appropriate clothes, the students still faced significant hurdles. Since many of the family heads were away from the island, the adolescents were often responsible for cutting and gathering wood for home use, and they picked up occasional odd jobs to make some money. They also spent a day or two each week waiting in lines for government rations.[24]

Although the teachers did not indicate any difficulties maintaining order in their evening schools for adults, they did report erratic attendance, noting that the older students also had lots of calls on their time. Profinda Nickerson told the story of one of her persistent adult students who had to withdraw from his day classes because of work. Not willing to give up on education, he continued to do what he could to keep up with his schooling. "He studies nights and mornings, and the hour he has for dinner, he spends in the school room, reciting in his usual place in the class," Nickerson proudly reported.[25]

The teachers recounted many similar poignant stories of their encounters with grateful first-time students. Profinda Nickerson likened the black student to "a starving man holding out both hands and crying more give me more." She wrote of an elderly black minister who sat in the corner of her classroom, rarely taking his eyes from his book, a first reader. Although he had lost an eye, with his glasses he still had sight in one, "thanks to the blessed Master." One day she noticed drops of sweat falling onto his book, so she asked him if he were too warm. "No, no, Ise striving so hard over dis lesson," he replied. Even during recess, he continued to read his Bible. "You don't know how much good it does me," he declared. Similarly, Ella Roper described her work with an elderly man who attended her day school. "I received him gladly devoting all the time I could spare to him during the regular hours and after school commenced the

Bible with him, in course, explaining as he slowly picked his way," she noted. "The old man grew more and more earnest, till at last, one day, he dropped his book and with uplifted hands cried out 'Oh how you do let the light in!' "[26]

The old man was grateful for his newfound ability to read, the light of knowledge. He was also thankful for the spiritual illumination that was falling on him as a consequence, more specifically, of what he was reading, the Bible. The missionary teachers also talked about bringing their students into both types of light. Although they were not especially sophisticated with respect to metaphors, in "light" they had a simple symbol that merged all aspects of what they were attempting to do in their schools. While they were bringing the light of knowledge to people who had lived in the darkness of slavery, they were also bringing the light of their evangelical Christianity to people who had lived in the darkness of what the missionaries considered to be heathen religions. Ella Roper, for example, noted that the students in her school were "panting for the light—the light of knowledge" that they never expected until they "sat down at rest in the kingdom." Similarly, Mary Burnap reported that the teachers were "willing to live in danger" to bring the children "into the light, and liberty, of learning and religion."[27]

The AMA teachers did not distinguish between secular and religious knowledge; to them they were one and the same. Likewise, the missionaries marked very little distinction between public and private—between the academic and spiritual needs of their students. Although most of the freedpeople brought a set of spiritual beliefs with them to the island, the missionaries set out to convert them to evangelical Christianity. When it came to winning souls, the schoolroom was not off limits; if anything, the teachers saw it as the place to start. Just as they celebrated the memorization of states and capitals, or the movement to an upper level arithmetic text, the teachers rejoiced when the students adopted their Bible-focused religion. Thus, in addition to the standard textbooks, the Bible played a central role in the AMA mission schools. "They read in, spell from it, and recite day after day those precious words that are able to make them wise unto salvation, & I believe they are having some effect upon their hearts and lives," declared Elizabeth James.[28]

Most of all, they memorized. James believed that children should "be taught to do right in early life" and "to store the mind with the Word of God." In the first year that Jennie lived with her, the young girl memorized ten psalms, the first two chapters of Genesis, four chapters of Matthew, three chapters of John, two chapters of Acts, and more than a hundred other passages. James expected similar feats from her students, and spent many classroom hours leading them in recitations of Bible passages. She was delighted when her students asked about the meaning of particular passages. When one of her students inquired what it meant to "pay the uttermost farthing," she "endeavored to explain to her that we are not our own, that all our powers and services belonged to God, that we were only acceptable to him when, in the spirit of Christ we did our Father's will." The student seemed to understand. "I think she caught the idea," James recounted, "and I have since noted a careful earnestness in doing as she thinks Jesus would have her."[29]

Ella Roper reported that her students' favorite reader was the New Testament. She was teaching seventy students who could "all read a little," and some who could read well. In a letter requesting more Testaments, she reported that her students accepted them "more gladly than anything we can offer them." Many of the freedpeople on Roanoke Island, in fact, indicated that their primary reason for learning to read was to be able to study the Bible on their own. The teachers awarded Bibles to the students for major accomplishments, including the memorization and recitation of Bible verses.

The students also enjoyed memorizing and singing hymns. Susan Odell noted that the students' singing thrilled "one's heart" and seemed "to have a depth of meaning." Music lessons offered many opportunities for religious education. Samuel Nickerson thought that "singing was an important part of education, and especially so, when we realize what an amount of religious instruction can be given through it." Nickerson was grateful that Sergeant W. H. Relzen of the Sixteenth Connecticut Regiment, an experienced music teacher, volunteered to teach singing in Cypress Chapel School.[30]

In his report for 1864, William T. Briggs acknowledged that "seasons of peculiar religious interest" had been enjoyed in the schools on Roanoke Island. Mary Burnap, who called Roanoke Island "the Eden of North Carolina," recorded that many of her students in Cypress Grove School "would wait around the desk with fruit, and flowers, as love tokens, to have us speak to them of Jesus, and point them to the *Cross*." Her oldest student, a thirty-three-year-old man named Alexander Lane, "was so anxious, that he would drop his spelling book and take the Bible and say 'I feel so burdened that I cannot study,'" she recounted. He was so wrought up that "he could not walk straight." For a week he walked around "with his soul stirred within him," Burnap noted, "but he could not see the light." Then, he showed up at her Sunday school, and "with a burst of joy" he announced that he had seen Jesus. Burnap noted that Lane was "only one of many cases of conversion," in her school. "I never witnessed such a manifestation of the saviour's presence in a day school," she said. Similarly, Elizabeth James noted that "*many*" were "being converted." She recalled remaining after classes to hold prayer meetings with some of her students who had shown signs of conversion. "They pour[ed] out their hearts," leading her to rejoice that "they were indeed becoming 'the lambs of the flock.' "[31]

Teachers who lived at Sunnyside wrote moving letters describing baptisms in the Croatan Sound near their home. According to Mary Burnap, twenty-four "rejoicing in the love of Jesus, *in their* souls" were baptized "a few steps from the "Teachers' Home" in July 1864. The baptisms continued even in bad weather. Reporting a wintry baptism of twenty near the home, Ella Roper was hopeful that "a large proportion of the school who knelt around me daily in prayer last year" had been converted.[32]

In addition to the proselytizing that occurred in the classroom, most of the teachers taught Sunday schools for the freedpeople, often in their schoolrooms. Samuel Nickerson's very successful Sunday school at his Cyprus Chapel School drew teachers from the missionary and military corps, and attracted close to 170 students. In addition to a school held in her home on Sunday afternoon, Elizabeth James participated in two Sunday schools that were sponsored by freedmen churches. First she attended the session of the Methodist Episcopal Church, where she usually read the Bible and taught a large class in a school program that drew three hundred students. Nineteen teachers, including some of "the leading men in the church," as well as "some of the older boys and girls" from the AMA schools, led the classes. Activities included memorization of the New Testament and Psalms, singing, and listening to stories about Jesus. James was pleased to report that the students listened with "rapt attention" while she told them of Jesus' love. The students also prepared for a monthly Sabbath school concert, consisting of recitations from the Bible and hymns. James boasted that a large number of her Sunday school students could "say whole chapters and Psalms" and believed that, by having the passages locked "in their hearts," they would be "restrained from sin." Later in the day, she led a class in the Sunday school of the Baptist church.[33]

In between the Sunday schools, James sometimes took part in the services of a church attended by some of the white natives who remained on the island. The first time she attended that church, with several of the AMA teachers, she was surprised when the minister turned to the women and asked, "Will one of the stranger sisters lead us in prayer?" Although the others "shrank" back from the invitation, she volunteered and was invited to return the next Sunday, once again to share prayers. The following Sunday the minister requested that she give the sermon. Although she had not prepared for the task, she "spoke an hour & the people wept and trembled." The minister, too deaf to hear what she said, nevertheless grasped her hand and said, "Why *how the people listened*." The next Sunday, she thought she deserved a rest, but the old pastor had other ideas. Once again he asked her to speak, and once again she agreed, and as she noted, "the spirit of God bowed the hearts of the people, & again they wept." Although James's schedule stretched her to her limits, she felt that her calls upon the local whites "tended to soften and in many instances to do away the bitterness of feeling toward the north." She noted that they "have felt hurt that I have cared for the colored ones & passed *them* by." Perhaps more importantly from her perspective, they also provided another field for her evangelical labors. She reported that she had "conversed with most of them individually on the subject of their soul's salvation & many express a desire to do God's will."[34]

Sunday evenings in the colony were similarly filled with worship. The Nickersons conducted prayer meetings and religious services that were very popular with the soldiers. In January 1865, Ella Roper voiced cautious optimism that the provost marshal and the assistant adjutant general had been converted at one of Nickerson's prayer meetings. Although conversion involved more than the acceptance of a temperate lifestyle, the missionaries thought that abstention from alcohol and tobacco signaled the presence of God's spirit. Mary Burnap grew jubilant when describing how some of the soldiers had signed the temperance pledge, and "firmly took their oath that they would not drink, or smoke, from this time forth and *forever*."[35]

The Nickersons also held a Sunday evening meeting for the freedpeople. Profinda Nickerson reported that these meetings were "well attended," and that nearly every meeting led to new professions of faith. She rejoiced when nine of her day scholars who attended the Sunday evening prayer meeting "commenced a Christian life." She seemed to be especially proud that the students were learning a more decorous form of worship. The Sunday night meeting was "as quiet and orderly as any meeting in the North," she boasted. Ella Roper found the freedpeople's "deep interest in religion" encouraging, but was not as optimistic as Nickerson about their adoption of a more subdued worship style. Roper did not think the current generation would "ever abandon their rude forms of worship," but she hoped the next would "feel other influences."[36]

Elizabeth James believed that at least thirty-five of her day scholars had been converted at the Nickersons' Sunday night meetings. This number included her "little Jennie," the freed girl that she took into her home to raise. With great feeling, James described how Jennie poured out "an agony of petitions that the Lord would cleave her 'poor sinful heart' at one of the meetings, and yet came away with the burden resting upon her soul." On the way home James talked with Jennie about "the love and tenderness of Christ," and just before they reached the gate, "the light of heaven beamed into her soul." Later that night, before retiring, Jennie joined James in devotions, "one burst of joy, so *different* from before." James noted that although Jennie had been a "conscientious child," she was profoundly changed by the experience. "I long to see sinners converted to Christ and Christians living rightly before God, and He has graciously given me my hire," James declared.[37]

In the turbulent and difficult years of the postwar period, the AMA continued its sponsorship of Elizabeth James and the Nickersons, and they continued to offer up a blend of education and religion that was driven by their deeply held evangelical faith. Meanwhile, an island rumor led Ella Roper to believe that the Freedmen's Bureau was going to allow only one association, the NFRA, on the island, so she switched her affiliation to that organization in late September 1865. After the change had transpired, she explained to George Whipple that she would have preferred being under the care of the AMA, but she felt she had no choice. She wanted to remain on her "dearly loved island" and "continue with the scholars that have clustered about me." Thus the NFRA took over the sponsorship of the Briggs School, with an enrollment of sixty students. That fall the NFRA also sponsored Susan Odell's Hobson School (seventy nine students), Elizabeth P. Bennett's Hawkins School (sixty eight students), and Kate Freeman's Plymouth School (fifty students)—all three on Lincoln Avenue—as well as a number of short-lived schools. By late 1865, the balance of power on the island had shifted from the AMA to the NFRA. Although the NFRA teachers professed religious beliefs, their classroom teaching did not focus on the centrality of the conversion experience.[38]

Yet, while the NFRA focused on training in the practical arts, ultimately its postwar instruction also contained a heavy dose of New England virtues. It was, in fact, the NFRA rather than the AMA that came closest to implementing, at least on a small scale, some of Horace James's notions about small domestic manufacturing and self sufficiency. With the establishment of an Industrial School on the Meekins property near the Sunnyside home in November 1865, the NFRA had achieved an important part of its mission goals. Until the school closed in July 1866, the teachers, Esther A. Williams, E. A. Warner, Hannah W. Cole, and Lydia G. Stinson, offered instruction to over 130 women—aged from fourteen to fifty—in sewing, knitting, straw braiding, and quilting. Many of the students in the Industrial School had previously attended the regular missionary schools on the island. Most were mothers who had "the care and in many cases the maintenance of their families." In addition, most, according to Sarah Freeman, were those who had "no other means of clothing themselves or their families." Although attendance was irregular because the students had to "struggle hard for food enough to prevent starvation," the school averaged forty-eight students a month, with twenty attending regularly. From materials donated to be sold at the freedmen's store, Freeman selected pieces that were of little value. The students washed, ripped, and transformed them "into good serviceable garments." In the process, the students learned lessons in both sewing and frugality. During the school's short life, the students made 390 garments, repaired 44 more, sewed 14 straw hats, and pieced and constructed 5 large quilts. Since none of the students could afford to attend without some compensation, the teachers paid them for their work. "I keep an account of the work done and give them orders on the store for their work, keeping a record of the same," reported Esther Williams.[39]

It is difficult to estimate how many nonaffiliated schools, some taught by former slaves, were established on the island. In September 1865 Kate Freeman relayed her concern that pupils were being drawn away from association-sponsored schools in favor of "schools taught by colored teachers" on the island. She did not indicate why the freedpeople were drawn to the non-association schools. Perhaps that choice was merely a matter of convenience, but more likely it was related to a growing sense of community among the black residents in the immediate postwar period. It is also very likely that it reflected some of the colonists' mounting distrust of the white teachers in 1865. In the early months of 1865 the military authorities had caused an uproar on the island when they sent some of the young boys, without their parents' permission, to New Bern, where they were put to work. Ostensibly, the action was taken to alleviate the rationing problem on the island. Frightened parents hid their remaining sons for weeks, and did not allow them to go to school. They also feared that their daughters "would be seized and carried to cotton farms" to work. In early March the men in the colony met and drafted several letters, including one to the secretary of war in which they protested the treatment of their children. Although there is no evidence that the teachers knowingly cooperated in any scheme to send the boys away from the island, the men blamed the "White School-Teachers," who they believed had aided the military by telling the boys to leave class and meet at the ration house. Elizabeth James was heartbroken about the military's action and the effect on her school, but no amount of reasoning could convince terrified parents that their children would be safe. "More than once the parents rushed into the school room," Elizabeth James recounted, "and although assured there was no possible danger, respectfully, but with many tears took their children hurriedly home."[40]

Kate Freeman worried that the "continual change of pupils" throughout the immediate postwar period would affect the quality of the schools. Other teachers indicated that the usual classroom procedures were disrupted as old students returned to the mainland and were replaced with new, unseasoned pupils.

In late October, Elizabeth Bennett reported that at least a half of her old students had returned to their old homes—their places "filled by others as bright and as anxious to learn." Despite the changes, the NFRA continued to upgrade the schools, indicating long-term plans for their continuance in the postwar period. Bennett noted that Benjamin Pond, the NFRA's superintendent of education, had procured writing desks and several new windows for her school. "A blackboard is being made for me," she continued, "and I shall then have nothing to wish for."[41]

During and after the war, education in the mission schools drew fire from critics from both the South and North. Most Southern critics lobbed their criticisms at the ideas that they thought the teachers were perpetuating. Writing in the Raleigh *Sentinel*, a correspondent from Elizabeth City declared that the freedpeople were "cursed by the presence of a set of New England fanatics" who "pretend to teach them letters," but really filled their minds with revolutionary ideas. Similarly, a writer in the *Norfolk Virginian* described the teachers as "a lot of ignorant, narrow-minded, bigoted fanatics" who were sent "ostensibly for the purpose of propagating the gospel among the heathen," but really acted to rouse the masses.[42]

Others, including Booker T. Washington, believed that the teachers were trying to foist a traditional New England curriculum on students who had not been properly prepared for it. Washington complained that teachers "tried to use, with these simple people just freed from slavery and with no past, no inherited traditions of learning, the same methods of education which they have used in New England, with all its inherited traditions and desires." Certainly there was some truth in Washington's criticism, as there was in complaints that the missionary school curriculum did not do enough to help the freedpeople achieve access to political and economic power. The island's missionary schools might have equipped some people with the rudimentary ability to read contracts and protect themselves against injustice, but it was not adequate preparation for prospering in postwar North Carolina.[43]

A study of the teachers' letters suggests that they were less guilty of fanaticism than they were of idealism. They were optimistic about the former slaves' abilities and believed that the Northern educational program would be effective in erasing slavery-induced ignorance and preparing their students for their new lives. The AMA teachers' faith that a bit of education and a healthy dose of evangelical Christianity would lead to a reformed, productive society grew naturally out of the evangelical context in which the missionaries operated. At the same time, the NFRA teachers' belief that education was a practical solution to the problems facing the freedpeople grew out of their positive experiences with the public schools of New England. The missionary teachers also feared what would transpire if the former slaves were not educated; things would be disastrous for the freedpeople and the nation. Sarah Freeman clearly expressed this concern when she asserted, "The educating and elevating [of] this people must go forward, or they will become a curse to our nation, and their freedom a curse rather than a blessing to themselves." Although the missionary teachers never clearly articulated what they thought would befall the nation, they certainly hinted that the disaster had something to do with a breakdown in general order.[44]

Calculating the number of students who actually attended the missionary schools is difficult. Since the teachers tallied average daily attendance, but did not include class rolls in their monthly reports, it is difficult to ascertain how many of the students were regular attendees and how many attended sporadically. Computing the total attendance numbers for all missionary schools is also tricky, since not all of the schools provided regular reports. An optimistic estimate is that the schools served about 60 percent of the children in the colony at various times, and probably not more than 15 percent of the adults. Nevertheless, a substantial number of freedpeople were exposed to letters and numbers for the first time in their lives.[45]

The missionaries' assessment of their work focused on the accomplishments of individuals rather than the comprehensive education of the entire freedmen population. From this perspective, the missionaries remained convinced that their work on the island had made a positive contribution. Samuel Nickerson, for example, thought it had been the missionaries' "happy privilege to start many in intellectual culture, who we think will go on until they become intelligent citizens." Some students, he recounted, had mastered reading, spelling, and writing, and had learned arithmetic and geography. Others, like his student Charlotte Lewis, had completely altered their lives. In 1863, Lewis "was a slave worth a thousand dollars not knowing a letter." By 1866, she was one of his "best teachers" in "charge of twelve little girls all of whom can read the Testament quite well," Nickerson pointed out. "Though, we feel humiliated in seeing how many golden opportunities have been let slip, we can but see that God has blessed our work and more than answered our prayer," Nickerson confided. "Best of all," Nickerson declared with obvious satisfaction, the "most advanced scholars have become christians and are teachers in our Sunday School."[46]

The freedpeople had expressed their faith in the power of education when they established the first freedmen's school on Roanoke Island long before the missionaries arrived. After the missionaries organized schools, freedpeople of all ages eagerly crowded into the makeshift missionary classrooms, demonstrating an ardent desire to learn. Wartime upheavals and dislocations, however, took a huge toll on the direction and effectiveness of the instructional efforts in the colony. Education often took a back seat to military considerations or the plans and whims of the local military authorities. Cognizant that they were, after all, serving at the pleasure of the military, the teachers could do little but chafe at their circumstances and persist in their efforts to let in the "light." Meanwhile, the military's ongoing uneven treatment of the former slaves continued to impose almost insurmountable impediments to the colony's long-term existence. To comprehend the difficulties faced by the colony, it is therefore necessary to turn to an examination of the military's ambivalent treatment of the freedpeople.

Stamp Down or Troden under Feet

THE MILITARY'S TREATMENT OF THE ROANOKE ISLAND COLONISTS

IN THE SPRING OF 1862, after the Ninth New York had settled into occupation duties on Roanoke Island, the regiment's Zouave Minstrel and Dramatic Club found it difficult to procure hair for wigs for its minstrel chorus. Matthew Graham of the Ninth New York later described the ensuing events. Concluding that the freedmen were a ready source of the desirable tresses, the soldiers tried to talk them into cutting their hair and donating it to the club for its theatrical endeavors. A few of the former slaves cooperated, but apparently not enough to fill the club's needs, so the soldiers resorted to force. Graham recounted that the freedmen "who were the owners of the kind of head covering coveted" by the dramatic corps "were kidnapped, carried to a squad-room, [and] kept quiet by dire threats," until "a Zouave armed with a pair of shears" cut their hair and sent them "on their way as bald as babies."[1]

What from a modern perspective seems to have been cruel and thoughtless behavior did not strike the soldiers as inappropriate. In many ways the hair incident serves as a metaphor for the military's treatment of the freedpeople on Roanoke Island throughout the Union occupation. The occupation forces needed and frequently took advantage of the labor the freedmen provided in the Union encampment, but they only begrudgingly and infrequently provided support. Although commanding officers, including General Benjamin Butler and the Zouaves' own leader, Colonel Rush C. Hawkins, ordered soldiers to treat the former slaves with respect, the local officers and enlisted men filtered such orders through their own prejudices. Some soldiers, especially the New Englanders, voiced antislavery views, while those at the other extreme expressed their racism through acts of outright hostility toward the former slaves.

Most soldiers fell between the two extremes. They were not openly belligerent to contrabands, but their actions still frequently exhibited a subtle racism. That was the case in the soldiers' response to the first officer who had oversight of the former slaves on the island. Early in the occupation, Hawkins had ordered Sergeant Walter L. Thompson to organize and care for the island's contrabands. Matthew Graham recalled that the soldiers in the Ninth New York jokingly called the sergeant "Niggardier General Thompson." Thompson himself took a young freed boy, around seven or eight years old, to be his personal orderly, and set him up as a caricature of a Zouave soldier. According to Graham, the boy was "fitted out with a complete Zouave uniform, fez included," and Thompson had trained him "to follow at a distance of two or three paces, and to conform to every movement of his chief like a bugler to his commanding officer on drill or in action." Graham noted that the boy's performance "was a source of great amusement" to the soldiers stationed on the island.[2]

In the first two years of the war, the majority of the Northern soldiers indicated that they were fighting for maintenance of the Union, not abolition. Although many soldiers gradually came to believe that emancipation was intimately tied to the preservation of the Union, they still did not view the former slaves as their equals. Their only interest in the black refugees was their desire to employ them as servants. Initially, these soldiers viewed the freedmen camps as merely a military necessity—significant only as places to keep freedpeople who might otherwise provide labor for the Confederacy. After the Union Army started to recruit blacks, most soldiers begrudgingly recognized the need to provide food and safe shelter for the black soldiers' families, but they were still not interested in going beyond that. Such beliefs, which put the soldiers at odds with Horace James's initial goals for the experimental colony on Roanoke Island, proved to be a constant handicap to the missionary work on the island. Although the colony owed its very existence to the presence and assistance of the local military authorities, the colony did not figure very highly in the military's decision-making process. For the most part, the colony's prospects were determined by military decisions that had nothing to do with the colony itself.[3]

At the national level the Union commanders in charge of military occupation, the officers of the Treasury Department in charge of abandoned or confiscated lands, and the leaders of Northern benevolent societies in charge of missionary endeavors had more than their fair share of conflicts over jurisdiction and goals. Out in the field, the idiosyncrasies of particular officers and civilians working for the Department of Negro Affairs further colored relationships. Some of the soldiers and government employees on Roanoke Island sympathized with the missionary work or at least thought the missionaries were providing useful services, while many others thought the missionaries were meddlesome nuisances. The Quartermaster Department's Amasa W. Stevens, the superintendent of the Roanoke colony's sawmill, was a friend to the missionaries. Samuel Nickerson praised him for his assistance in building the Nickersons' house, "even to taking the trouble to borrow nails from the sutler to hasten it on." Nickerson attributed Stevens's actions to his strong support of the missionaries' goals, declaring that "he also manifests a soul in the work," an assessment that was confirmed the next year when Stevens signed a letter protesting the deteriorating conditions on the island. In contrast, Nickerson and just about every other missionary on the island criticized Holland Streeter, who had directed the shad fisheries and then succeeded George Sanderson as the assistant superintendent on the island from October 1864 through mid-1865. Streeter, who at fifty-four was too old for military service, had volunteered to come South and help the Union cause in whatever capacity he could. Although General Butler had recommended him highly to James for a position as assistant superintendent, many of the missionaries on the island believed Streeter was a crook who was not interested in improving the lives of the freedpeople.[4]

Ella Roper believed that most of the military authorities on the island had no respect for what the missionaries were attempting: "The military look on with no friendly eyes—this cannot be disguised—and matters have been much retarded in this way," she concluded. Roper believed, however, that "thanks to Him who turneth the hearts of kings" the orders from Headquarters were so compulsory that the local officers "*dare[d]* only *misconstrue* whenever it [could] be safely done." Nevertheless, while the colony's existence was assured, the local officers did not uniformly and consistently respect the property or rights of the teachers, and the teachers frequently had to adapt to bothersome situations. They discovered, as Roper wrote, "that beds are not *indispensable*—on ours being recalled this week to the Hospitals." Similarly, the soldiers came into the schools and confiscated stoves or stovepipe that the missionaries had obtained from their Northern sponsors, leading to smoke-filled schoolrooms and sometimes forcing the cancellation of classes.[5]

When the military authorities decided to reclaim buildings that teachers had labored to turn into schools, the teachers had no recourse but to oblige. Likewise, when the military authorities ordered evacuation, as they did in April 1864 after the fall of Plymouth, the missionaries had to drop everything and leave, not knowing what they would find *if* they were allowed to come back. Ella Roper and Mary Burnap indicated, for example, that they hoped "for the prosperity" of their Whipple School, whenever they were "permitted to return" to the island. Although the missionaries recognized that they were serving on the island at the pleasure of the military, they still chafed at their inferior position with respect to the local authorities.[6]

Most likely the failure of an experiment in self-government in the colony was also due to the colonists' lowly position with respect to the military authorities. In January 1864 Horace James, acting for the military authorities, appointed fifteen of the leading men in the colony to positions as councilors. Their job, as James noted, was to serve as liaison between the superintendent and the freedmen families. "We are thus attempting to give them lessons of self-government," James reported, "hoping that by another year they will be prepared to elect their own selectmen and discharge their own municipal duties." Although it seemed like a noble idea, it was difficult to implement for a variety of reasons. On one hand, conditions in the colony remained in a chaotic state; while on the other, the councilors did not have any experience as leaders. Horace James thought that the men were "too little raised in culture above the common people to command their respect, at least while the island is under military rule." He believed that additional education would solve this problem—a conclusion that, while reflecting his belief in the power of education, was also naive. The councilors had no real power to alter things related to the military occupation; they were dependent appointees without authority or community support.[7]

In the spring of 1864, by the time things settled down following the influx of refugees from Plymouth, the population of the Roanoke Colony had swelled to over three thousand. Although Horace James maintained his faith in the colony's future, a few outsiders were beginning to suggest that the colony should be moved. Charles Wilder, the superintendent of Negro Affairs in Hampton, Virginia, thought, for example, that the colony needed to be moved to a place with more fertile soil. That spring and summer the island's missionary teachers were also beginning to have their own misgivings about the colony's survival. Concerned about the subsistence of the colonists in the upcoming winter, Sarah Freeman lamented that "nine-tenths" of the colonists were "women and children." Many of the children were orphans. The missionaries hoped to ameliorate the orphan situation with the creation of an orphan asylum. "The homeless ones, the orphans, excite my own sympathies most," wrote Sarah Freeman. "I hope, before winter comes, we will have for them a home, an asylum, where they can be made comfortable, and instructed in those truths that shall make them free." Despite the missionaries' efforts, however, the military authorities never approved the construction of an orphan asylum on the island, and the number of homeless orphans remained an unresolved issue.[8]

Until the war ended, military movements in eastern North Carolina played havoc with the idea of a settled Roanoke colony and led to further evidence of the military's ambivalence toward the colony and its residents. On one hand, local military authorities continued to view the colony as a mere holding place for dependent freedpeople and whites who had been displaced by military movements. The military maintained an interest in providing food and shelter for soldiers' families because of the military's desire to recruit black troops. Thus, as Sarah Freeman noted, the stream of refugees "in a very forlorn and destitute condition" continued unabated. At the same time, when the military authorities thought it in their best interest to take advantage of the freedmen's services, they did not hesitate to exploit them, as soldiers or as civilians working on projects for the Quartermaster's Department. In fact, contemporary reports suggested that just about all of the men who had families in the colony served the Union government in one way or another.[9]

Horace James's annual report highlighted what the freedmen's service meant for the composition of the Roanoke Island freedmen's colony. By the time he wrote his report, the colony's population had climbed to 3,091. Of this number, 1,086 were females over fourteen years, 1,297 were children under fourteen years, and 491 were males between fourteen and seventeen years or over forty-five years. Only 217, or 7 percent, were males between seventeen and forty-five, and many of these men of military age were exempt from active military duty because of physical disabilities. One contemporary estimate suggested that fewer than twenty-five of the men left on the island "could pass the surgeon's examination for the military service." Thus, there were very few able-bodied men who could help with the day-to-day work of maintaining the colony.[10]

Freedmen who could not meet the requirements for enlisting in the army served in the island's home guard. In a March 1864 letter, Horace James reported to General Edward Wild that four companies composed of disabled Roanoke Island freedmen had been outfitted with guns, ammunition belts, and haversacks. General Butler had authorized the issuance of uniforms, which James thought would "go far toward meeting the want of clothing" among the islanders. After the fall of Plymouth, those living in Union camps along North Carolina's coast remained in constant fear of Confederate attack. In particular, the Confederate ram *Albemarle*, which had played an important role in bringing about the fall of Plymouth, continued to strike fear at Union camps. Even

The Confederate ram *Albemarle* threatened eastern North Carolina throughout the spring of 1864. Military authorities on Roanoke Island were so fearful of an attack that they armed a home guard of freedmen to help protect the Union camp. (*The Century War Book*, vol. 1, no. 15, p. 240, author's collection)

though the ram was moored in Plymouth, Union military authorities in the Sub-District headquarters on the island felt threatened and made extensive preparations for an anticipated Confederate attack. During that time, the anxiety level rose to such a point that military authorities on the island turned to the home guard for protection. Luther S. Dickey of the 103d Pennsylvania, which was stationed on the island, recounted that "the negro contrabands were furnished with arms and frequent orders were issued from headquarters cautioning the troops to be vigilant."[11]

Around the same time, Union preparations for the campaign against Richmond stepped up the demand for laborers in Virginia. Officers preferred former slaves, both because they did not trust Southern white laborers (even when Southerners claimed to be Unionists) enough to put them near the battle front, and because they thought that black civilians were better workers than white civilians. Often failing to meet their requirements through voluntary means, the military employers resorted to impressment of blacks in Virginia and North Carolina, sometimes treating the freedmen worse than they had been treated under slavery. In July 1864 Horace James wrote to General Butler complaining that "some dozens of colored teamsters" had been sent from New Bern to work on projects at Bermuda Hundred in such great haste that they had not even had time to say goodbye to their families. Further, it appeared that the Army had reneged on its promise to pay them. The Roanoke Island freedmen suffered a similar fate. On 20 August, General I. N. Palmer, commander of the District of North Carolina, notified the commanding officer on Roanoke Island that every freedman who was not absolutely needed for work on Roanoke Island should be sent to Virginia. Palmer promised that the men would be paid $16 per month plus rations, and that their families would be supported while they were gone. He also added that if the men could not be persuaded to go, they would have to be forced to do so. On 31 August, Lieutenant William R. King and Captain Frederick Martin undertook what amounted to forcible impressment on the island, sending the men to work on the Dutch Gap Canal, north of Petersburg, Virginia.[12]

In September, forty-five of the Roanoke Island freedmen sent a letter from Bermuda Hundred to General Butler complaining about their treatment. While the letter focused on the duplicitous events surrounding their impressment, it also underscored the military's ongoing mistreatment of the freedpeople on Roanoke Island and highlighted, once again, the freedmen's concern for the preservation of their families. The men related that prior to being sent to work on the canal, they had been working for four months on breastworks at Roanoke Island. On 31 August they were told to report to headquarters to be paid. When they reached headquarters, they were put under guard and "marched on board a steamer, at the point of a bayonet." First they were told that the paymaster was on board, then they were told they were going to Fortress Monroe, and finally they were told they were going to Dutch Gap to be paid, when in reality they were on the way to Dutch Gap to work on the canal. The men also complained that guards were sent all over the island, taking "young and old sick and well" and that "the soldiers broke into the coulored people's house's taken sick men out of bed." Further, "men that had sick wives, and men that had large family's of children and no wife or person to cut wood for them or take care of them, were taken, and not asked one question or word about going."

The men wrote that they had not been paid since February 1864, and their wives and families were suffering. "No one knows the injustice practised on the negro's at Roanoke," they lamented, "our garden's are plundere'd by the white soldiers. what we raise to surport ourselves with is stolen from us, and if we say any thing about it we are sent to the guard house." The men noted that when Horace James was not present on the island to oversee the colony, the assistant superintendent, George Sanderson, had "his own way" and allowed contraband rations and donated clothes to be sold to the white "secesh" citizens. The men indicated that they were especially upset that Sanderson was talking about sending two hundred women away from the island, "then our family's will be sent one way and we in another direction. . . ." They also reminded General Butler that most of the women were soldiers' wives whom General Wild had sent to the island for protection, and they questioned whether soldiers' wives

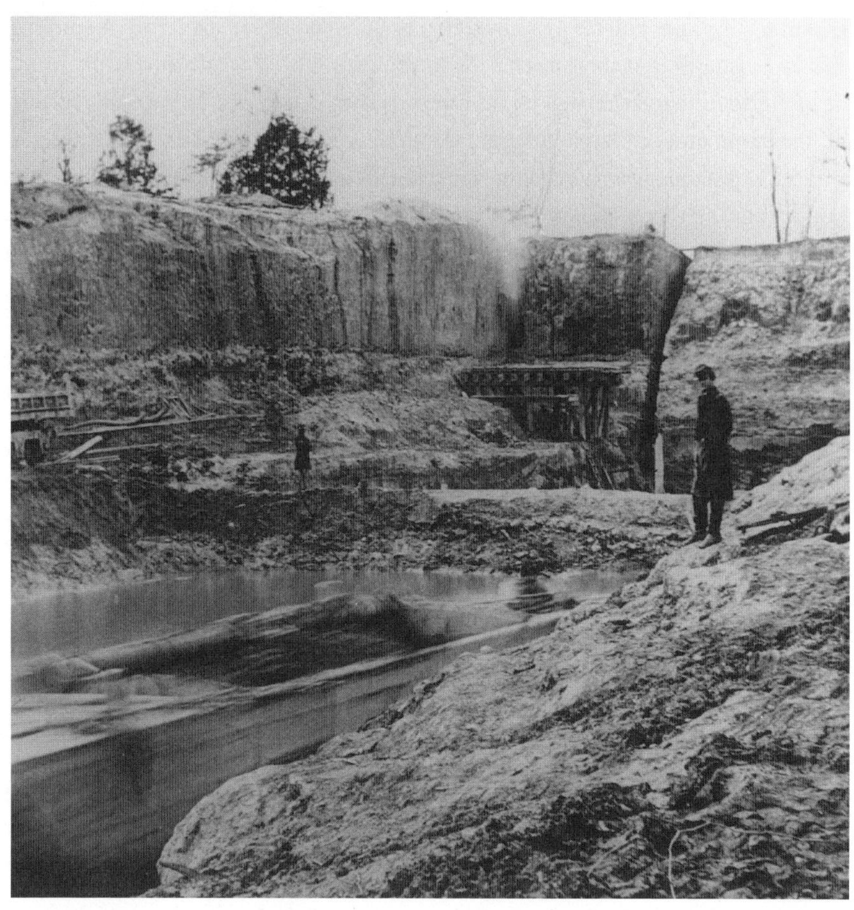

In August 1864, military officers forcibly impressed some of the men who had been working for the Quartermaster's Department on Roanoke Island and sent them to labor on the Dutch Gap Canal north of Petersburg, Virginia. In September some of the men wrote a letter to General Benjamin Butler complaining about the way that they and their families had been treated. (Massachusetts Commandery, Military Order of the Loyal Legion of the United States and the U.S. Army Military History Institute)

should be sent away "when their husbands are in the army fighting." Lieutenant King's endorsement on the men's letter stated that the men had been impressed because the army needed to obtain laborers as quickly as possible. King admitted that the men "were brought away by force," but added that "no one was authorized to tell them they were to be paid or practice any other deception complained of" in their petition.[13]

There is no indication that the officers responsible for the impressment were reprimanded; indeed, the military continued to impress black men for work duty whenever they were needed. In late September, Horace James did request that Assistant Superintendent George Sanderson be promoted to lieutenant and assigned to a position at the front, because he wanted "a person of more literary culture" as his assistant on Roanoke Island. It is, however, likely that it was a coincidence that James sent his request at about the same time the Roanoke Island freedmen wrote from Bermuda Hundred. James's letter was not critical of Sanderson; he noted that Sanderson had "ably conducted affairs as Superintendent at Roanoke Island" and that he was "well fitted in experience, energy of will, and personal bearing" for a position in the field.[14]

On numerous occasions the military failed to live up to promises made to the freedpeople, most frequently with respect to pay. After General Butler established a uniform pay policy throughout Virginia and North Carolina in his General Orders No. 46 in December 1863, many connected with the Roanoke Island colony assumed that the men working for the Quartermaster's Department would receive regular pay. They soon learned, however, that wages were not forthcoming and blamed Horace James, who, because of his position as assistant quartermaster, was in charge of the payroll. What the freedmen did not know, however was that James was also concerned about the freedmen's wages—a frequent topic in his letters to Colonel J. B. Kinsman, the general superintendent of Negro Affairs for North Carolina and Virginia. In late February 1864, James finally received a check for $1,257.56 to cover the payroll for January. He distributed the pay to the workers on Roanoke Island on 3 March, noting that it "was the first pay day the colored laborers have seen for a long time." He noted that the people had "waited so long for their dues, as almost to have lost faith in the intentions and honesty of the government," and that he "was heartily glad to redeem to them my promise of prompt pay in return for their labor, a thing which I was enabled to do through the approval of Gen. Butler." James also noted that Butler had not made promises to the former slaves "for effect upon the public mind, to be broken in practice."[15]

Maybe James was correct in declaring that it was not Butler's fault, but somewhere up the military chain of command someone was negligent with respect to paying the laborers working for the Quartermaster's Department on Roanoke Island. Perhaps it was merely a matter of priorities when money in the Union Army's coffers was tight. Perhaps someone assumed that providing the men with a place to stay and rations for their families was adequate pay, even though they had been promised more than that. Whatever the case, throughout the remainder of the year James continued to send letters to Colonel Kinsman requesting that the men on the island be paid. On 23 March, James wrote that he was readying a payroll for February, which if "ordered paid promptly . . . will be an immense relief to the people there." On 5 June he reminded Kinsman that he had not received funds for the March or April payrolls. James followed up that letter with one on 20 June in which he inquired if the money would soon be sent for March or April. On 7 July he wrote that money for the March or April payrolls still had not arrived. Although the control of the Department of Negro Affairs officially passed to the Treasury Department in August, General Butler told James to continue with his work—that it had been arranged with David Keaton, the supervising special agent of the Treasury Department, that James should retain control of the Roanoke Island colony. Thus, James continued to superintend the Roanoke colony and he continued to press Kinsman for funds. In November, James was still asking Kinsman for back pay for the laborers.[16]

The missionaries, who saw firsthand the consequences of the government's failure to pay the freedmen, commented on the injustice and its effects on the day-to-day lives of the colonists. Colonists who had worked for months without pay felt hopeless when they showed up at the freedmen's store and could not pay for the items they needed. In August 1864, Sarah Freeman observed that "a feeling of distrust and discouragement pervades the minds of the people generally." In mid-1865, Horace James reported that the unsettled accounts with freedmen laborers on Roanoke Island amounted to $18,570.07, an amount that if put "in circulation on Roanoke Island would make greenbacks tolerably plenty over its limited area of twelve miles by three or four." He concluded that the officers on the island kept the accounts "in a most unsatisfactory manner," which was "encouraged by the vacillating policy of the government toward the negroes"[17]

Later that year, Ella Roper recounted that "men have worked for many months—some two and even three years—for pay drawing *rations* but receiving no money." Moreover, as the freedmen who wrote the complaint from Bermuda Hundred had emphasized, the distribution of rations on the island was itself an area in which the freedpeople often felt cheated. General Butler's General Orders No. 46 had promised "suitable subsistence," to the families of black soldiers. Unlike Rush Hawkins's initial policy on Roanoke Island, which specifically spelled out the amount of subsistence for men, women, and children, Butler's policy at first left the interpretation up to the local superintendents of Negro affairs. At Fortress Monroe, the ration for dependent freedpeople was a little over half of a soldier's ration—in real value, about twenty cents compared to thirty-six cents. Similarly, Horace James reported that he "never issued full soldiers rations to negroes" in his district, because he thought the soldier's ration was "so liberal as to be more than can possibly be disposed of by the healthiest and heartiest man."[18]

In January 1864 the War Department had issued General Orders No. 30, which established a subsistence ration for each adult refugee or contraband who was not employed by the government and who had no means of support. This ration consisted of "ten ounces of pork or bacon, or one pound of fresh beef; one pound of corn-meal five times a week; one pound of flour or soft bread, or twelve ounces hard bread, twice a week; and to every 100 rations ten pounds of beans, pease, or hominy; eight pounds of sugar; two quarts of vinegar; eight ounces of adamantine or star candles; two pounds of soap; two pounds of salt; and fifteen pounds of potatoes, when practicable." Women and children were also allowed ten pounds of roasted rye coffee or fifteen ounces of tea per hundred rations. Children under fourteen were issued half rations. The New England Freedmen's Aid Society estimated that the government spent two dollars per month for each person who was rationed. Ration reports for Roanoke Island were kept irregularly and carelessly, so it is difficult to determine exact numbers for rations distributed during wartime. Contemporaries estimated that up to two-thirds of the residents of the colony received some sort of rations at least part of each year. Although Horace James and his assistant superintendents on the island encouraged the men to work and support their families without resorting to rations, the military's failure to pay the men for their labors severely limited their ability to achieve any sort of independence and kept many dependent on rations.[19]

On 3 March 1865, responsibility for freedmen affairs passed to the War Department's Bureau of Refugees, Freedmen, and Abandoned Lands, popularly known as the Freedmen's Bureau. Conditions remained fairly constant on the island, and personnel in charge of day-to-day operations remained the same. Horace James continued as superintendent of Negro Affairs in North Carolina and also became the acting assistant commissioner of the Freedmen's Bureau in North Carolina. Likewise, Holland Streeter continued as James's assistant superintendent on Roanoke Island, a position he had held since succeeding George Sanderson in the fall of 1864. There is, in fact, no indication that the freedpeople on the island took immediate notice of the transfer of power. The colonists were, however, becoming increasingly outspoken about the conduct of affairs on the island and their distrust of James and Streeter. Their anger over the failure of the military to meet its payroll, the haphazard distribution of rations, and other perceived injustices on Roanoke Island peaked in the spring and summer of 1865. The first outburst occurred after men in the colony "held a meeting to consult over the affairs" of their "present conditions" and their "rights." In a series of letters written in March 1865, the freedmen aired their grievances to President Lincoln and Secretary of War Edwin Stanton. Richard Boyle presented the petitions at the War Department in April 1865. With a simple eloquence, the letters poignantly described the treatment that the freedpeople had received on Roanoke Island.

Unaware of Horace James's frustrated attempts to meet the payroll on the island, the freedmen lashed out at the man who they thought had betrayed them. They asked the president if they were "to be Stamp down or troden under feet by our Superintendent," the very man they looked to for assistance. They appealed to the president as "the last resort and only help we have got, feeling that we are entily friendless" on the island. They indicated that they were willing to do anything they could to aid the president and the government, but were "not willing to work as we have done for Chaplain James and be Troden under foot and Get nothing for it." They noted that they were willing to work "for $10,00 per month and our rations," but some of the men had been working for three years and had not been paid. They had "Cut spiles and drove them and done any thing that they was told to do." Then, they stated, James told them to support themselves, and they did, but guards came and took them "by the point of the bayonet" and sent them to work at the battlefront where some of them died. The men complained that the officers who took them treated them meaner than their owners ever did, "just like we had been dum beast." Meanwhile, while they were "Trying to help the Government all we Can for our lives," Holland Streeter and his men were "Trying to Starve the woman & children to death" by cutting off their rations. Before the ten days between ration distributions had passed, they noted, the women had to go from one to another "to borrow a little meal to last until ration day." Many of the women were soldier's wives who "could hardly get any rations and some of them are almost starving."

The men also complained about the treatment of their male children, asking if James had right to send them to New Bern. They noted that James had issued a proclamation that boys over fourteen would not be issued rations. This order was hard on families that wanted their sons to go to school instead of labor, but recognizing the value of "learning," they struggled so that their children could stay in school. When Assistant Superintendent Streeter directed the teachers to tell the boys to leave school to pick up rations on a certain day, the freedmen suspected "the Game they was Going to play and a Greate many never sent they Children." The twenty or twenty-five who showed up for rations received them,

Many of the freedmen on Roanoke Island worked for the Union Army's Quartermaster's Department. Like the freedmen at Fortress Monroe, depicted in this engraving, the freedmen on the island were frequently put to work on projects that the white soldiers would not undertake. In March 1865 the men from the island sent letters to President Abraham Lincoln complaining about conditions on Roanoke Island, including the fact that they had not been paid in three years. (*Frank Leslie's Illustrated Newspaper*, 2 November 1861, author's collection)

but Streeter marched them to headquarters and put them on a boat for New Bern to work. The men noted that some of the soldiers' wives lost their only sons, the "one little boy to help them to cut & lug wood & Goe arrand for them." Some of the mothers went to James and "Grieved and beg for the little boys but he would not let them have them." Some of the boys "wasen oer 12 years olds."

Throughout the letters, the men complained about the soldiers' failure to respect them. They were especially irritated that white soldiers came into their churches and treated them "as though we were beast." Some of the soldiers even threw "Pop Crackers and Christmas devils" among the women, and then "put the pistols to our ministers breast because he Spoke to them about they behavour in the Church." Although the soldiers had threatened retribution if the freedmen notified higher authorities, the men finally reported the problem to James, who told them to identify the soldiers, but they were unable to do so.

The freedmen especially resented that the men in charge of freedmen affairs tried to fool them "just because they think that we are igorant," and they declared that they had "lost all Confidince in them."[20]

Again, the military's written documentation does not indicate any attempts to rectify conditions in the colony. Most likely the Secretary of War was not aware of what was taking place on the island. In particular, during the opening months of 1865, the 103d Pennsylvania, the regiment serving garrison duty on the island, was rejoined by its members who had been Confederate prisoners of war. Recalling the return of his missing comrades, Luther S. Dickey noted that the men "were allowed many liberties, and were practically exempt from duty." Further, Dickey stated, "The freedom given these ex-prisoners of war was not conducive to discipline, Roanoke Island afforded many opportunities for enjoyment, and Scuppernong wine was plentiful." In short, Dickey concluded, the soldiers "were having one continual holiday" that included dances and lots of drinking, facilitated by white islanders who eagerly took advantage of the "opportunity to dispense at a fair profit the Island's principal beverage," scuppernong wine. Meanwhile, that spring eight more companies arrived to be consolidated with the 103d Pennsylvania, and a similar number arrived to rejoin the 101st Pennsylvania. "Things are all in a mire," a soldier of the 103d reported in early May.[21]

Aware that the ex-prisoners of war were likely responsible for most of the depredations committed on the freedpeople's property, the commandant on the island, Colonel Theodore Lehmann of the 103d Pennsylvania, ordered that the men should remain "at quarters, night and day, unless given permission from headquarters to leave." The soldiers, however, paid no attention and continued to have their parties. One night the military patrol arrested over two dozen soldiers who were holding a dance, and then threw them into the guardhouse. By the time Lehmann showed up the next morning to talk to the men, they had tunneled their way to freedom. At an early reveille, Lehmann threatened to punish all the regiment if the guilty men did not come forward. Again, the soldiers ignored him, and as Luther Dickey recounted, "acted as though his denunciations and threats fell on deaf ears." Although Lehmann threatened further disciplinary action, the regiment's receipt of orders to New Bern to be mustered out of service impeded further attempts at punishing the soldiers. Just how serious Lehmann was about disciplining the soldiers will never be known. Dickey recalled that "subsequent to the war no one laughed more heartily over the Roanoke Island tunnel escape than did Col. Lehmann, when meeting the men who were participants in it." It appears that Lehmann was more than willing to allow his men their fun that spring, even at the expense of the freedpeople. Given the military's history of ambivalence toward the residents of the freedmen's colony, Lehmann's weak attempts to curb the soldiers' behavior is hardly surprising.[22]

Emphasizing that all they wanted was a chance to "Get a living like White men," the freedmen had concluded their petition to the president by declaring that they were "praying to God every day for the war to Stop So we wont be beholding to the Government for Something to Eat." The war's end did not, however, improve conditions on Roanoke Island. In fact, the situation steadily worsened under the auspices of the Freedmen's Bureau, despite the selection of a bureau head who was sympathetic to freedmen. On 12 May 1865, President Johnson followed Secretary of War Stanton's recommendation and appointed Major General Oliver Otis Howard to be commissioner of the bureau. A graduate of West Point, Howard was a career soldier who had spent most of his adult life as an officer in the army. He was also openly pious, having experienced a profoundly moving conversion at a Methodist camp meeting while on duty as a second lieutenant in Tampa, Florida, in 1855 and 1856. Refusing to drink alcoholic beverages or curse, his spirituality and self discipline set him apart from most of his fellow soldiers and earned him the nickname "the Christian Soldier." During the Civil War, he lost his right arm at the Battle of Fair Oaks, but then went on to win praise as the commander of the Army of the Tennessee. Although Howard had no experience as the head of a civil bureaucracy, contemporaries were unanimous in their praise of him as a good and just man who would act fairly as head of the Freedmen's Bureau.[23]

While Howard was settling into his office, the commander of the Department of North Carolina, General John M. Schofield, issued an order for yet another reduction of rations in contraband camps. Horace James indicated that on account of the orders, he had "ceased giving rations to any on account of their being members of soldiers families" and that he had "issued *only* to indigent, infirm and orphaned negros without reference" to their connections. Once again, the orders brought forth a stream of protest, including some complaints from soldiers on behalf of their families on Roanoke Island. Many of the soldiers were still away from the island, serving out their enlistment terms, and some of them had not been paid for eight to ten months. Frank James, a soldier in Company C of the Thirty-sixth USCT, wrote a simple letter to his commander, Brigadier General Alonzo G. Draper, that encapsulated the soldiers' feelings. In the letter, which was eventually forwarded to General Howard, James pointed out that when he enlisted, the government promised to take care of his family.

James believed that the government was breaking its promise. The soldiers' complaint was endorsed by Draper, who affirmed that the government had promised rations to the families of black soldiers.[24]

At about the same time, another group of men with connections to the Roanoke Island colony, soldiers of Company F of the Thirty-sixth USCT, stationed outside of Petersburg, Virginia, sent a similar letter to General Howard requesting an alleviation of their families' suffering. Writing on behalf of the regiment, Richard Etheridge and William Benson made many of the same points that had been offered in the March petitions. They noted that "the cause of much suffering" on the island was that James had not paid the freedpeople for their labor "for near a year," while at the same time he had cut the rations, "so the people have neither provisions or money to buy it with." The men reminded Howard that when they enlisted, they were promised that their wives and families would receive government rations. Yet, "three or four days out of every ten days" their families had nothing to eat, while Holland Streeter and others were stealing rations from the ration house and selling them. They demanded the removal of Streeter, "a througher Copper head a man who says that he is no part of a Abolitionist." Streeter offered their families no protection against the white soldiers who were breaking into their houses, stealing their chickens, and robbing their gardens.[25]

The missionaries on the island were also outraged by the new rations policy. On 3 June, Ella Roper wrote George Whipple denouncing Schofield's orders. She declared that the reduction in rations was "heart sickening." Post commandant Colonel Theodore Lehmann's doors were "besieged by starving helpless women and children," and "instead of the happy faces" that usually met her at school, she found "a silent group and among these grown up girls and little children sobbing bitterly" because they were hungry. "What is going to be done?" Roper lamented. "When and how will these wrongs be righted? Shall it be before these people starve?"[26]

Roper joined other teachers and friends of the freedpeople in drafting an appeal to General Howard on 5 June, urging "immediate action to prevent suffering which justice, humanity, and every principle of christianity forbids." This letter included the signatures of Chaplain William A. Greene of the Thirty-seventh USCT, who was supposed to be Streeter's assistant on the island, and Amasa W. Stevens, the superintendent of the sawmill. The appeal underscored that there were "not many families on the Island that have not furnished a father, husband or son, and in numerous instances, two or three members to swell the ranks of our army," and that these men had enlisted "with the as-

Black soldiers from the Thirty-sixth U.S. Colored Troops played a significant role in the Battle of Petersburg, which is pictured in this engraving from a sketch by E. F. Mullen. In the spring of 1865 the men from Company F of the Thirty-sixth U.S. Colored Troops sent a letter to O. O. Howard protesting the treatment of their families on Roanoke Island. (Mottelay and Campbell-Copeland, eds., *The Soldier in our Civil War*, 2:277, author's collection)

surance from the Government that their families should be cared for, and supported in their absence." Noting that the number drawing rations had dropped from twenty-seven hundred to fifteen hundred out of the population of thirty-five hundred, the men and women emphasized that living conditions in the colony were deteriorating. "If it is the design of the Government to return these families to their former masters to be supported and cared for by them," they stated, "this design has not been explained to them, and no facilities have been afforded them to leave the island, while the sweeping reduction of the rations brings hundreds suddenly face to face with starvation." On 6 June, Samuel Nickerson similarly criticized the government's plan to reduce rations before it was ready to provide for the freedpeople's return to the mainland.[27]

On 7 June, Francis George Shaw, president of the National Freedman's Relief Association, threw his weight behind the teachers with his own appeal to General Howard. Shaw advised Howard that letters from some of the NFRA's "most valued & reliable teachers" on Roanoke Island had informed him that "hundreds" were "suffering nearly to starvation [and] that death from famine stares many in the face." Shaw begged Howard to "send some confidential officer, whose sympathies are in favor of this work, to remedy the evils of which they complain." Responding to Shaw and the other complainants, Howard sent General Schofield a telegram about the situation on 8 June. Schofield then replied by telegram on 9 June that "the matter would be attended to." Schofield attended to the matter by having one of his assistants telegraph General Charles J. Paine, commander of the District of Beaufort, with a request that he send "a reliable officer to Roanoke at once to remedy this matter, make a full investigation, and forward a report to these Head Quarters." Paine, in turn, ordered Captain John McMurray of the Sixth USCT, who was acting assistant adjutant general in the District of Beaufort, to the island to conduct an investigation and make a full report. Paine also directed McMurray to instruct the commanding officer on the island that the term "citizens" in the order "forbidding the gratuitous issue of rations to citizens after May 31, 1865" did not include freedpeople, and that "no act required by humanity toward the people in his vicinity must be omitted."[28]

Captain McMurray arrived on the island on 9 June, finding over thirty-five hundred freedpeople and some white refugees in the Roanoke colony. McMurray proceeded to interview "the most reliable persons" he could find. Many of them complained about Holland Streeter's distribution of rations, asserting that he frequently took rations intended for the colonists and sold them, pocketing the money for himself. Chaplain Greene indicated that although he was an assistant superintendent on the island, Streeter had not allowed "him to take any part in the distribution of rations," and that he had only recently allowed him to "be in the ration house while rations were being issued. . . ." Greene pointed out that Streeter gave "little more than half" of the rations that he should have given to the freedpeople, and disposed of the remainder on and off the island. As an example, Greene noted that he had confirmed that one local resident, Roan White, had a bushel barrel of government pork in his possession, and was selling it in his grocery store. Greene accused Streeter of being a copperhead, pointed out that Streeter had frequently bragged that there was "not a particle of abolition about me," and testified that Streeter had also declared that he intended to "starve this people till God kills them."

The standard procedure for distributing rations on the island involved drawing them in bulk from the Post Command at Headquarters, then carrying them two miles north to the ration house with a horse-drawn wagon. McMurray quickly uncovered a number of discrepancies with respect to Streeter's method. One woman who lived near the ration house related that she "had seen several loads of rations come from the wharf, go past the ration house, and drive toward the far side of the Island." William Benson, a freedman who had worked for Streeter in the ration house, told McMurray that he became suspicious after he observed that the four or five bushel barrels of pork and two to three bushel barrels of sugar left after issuing rations "would always be gone before we would issue again." The wily Benson set a trap. On various occasions, after the last wagon had left the ration house at night, he went outside and covered the wagon tracks. The next morning he discovered "cart tracks coming from Mr. Streeter's house, stopping at the rations house & going off over the Island."

Another freedman, Mark Seymour, informed McMurray that he had frequently seen men carry sacks of meat and sugar from the ration house while Streeter was there. One of Streeter's helpers, a freedman named Pompey Britton, had admitted to Seymour that he had taken meat to a white islander named John Midget. Midget, in turn, had confirmed that he had purchased government pork on the island at fifteen cents a pound and had taken it to Elizabeth City where he sold it for seventy five cents a pound. James Willis, a former private in the Thirty-seventh USCT, related that he had seen Streeter's men take meat from the ration house, carry it to a wharf near Streeter's house, and put it on a boat. When Willis complained to Colonel Lehmann, Lehmann threatened to put him in the "Keep House." Willis asserted that at times the situation bordered on the ridiculous: "I have known of meat being taken from the Island and being captured by the yankees and brought back again. The story then was that the contrabands were selling their rations while at the same time they were not getting enough to eat."

McMurray concluded, "after making due allowances for the personal feelings of witnesses," that the colony's "affairs were not in a healthy condition." Although he had not learned "of any cases of starvation on the Island, or that there were likely to be any," he acknowledged that there were many problems related to the issuance of rations. While Streeter had argued that he had reduced rations because Horace James had instructed him to do so, McMurray believed that the evidence indicated that the problems emerged because Streeter "had not faithfully performed the duty assigned him"—that he had misappropriated rations. Thus, McMurray arrested Streeter and took him to New Bern, where he turned him over to authorities. Shortly after McMurray arrived on the island to conduct his investigation, Colonel John Holman, the white commander of the First USCT, arrived to replace Lehmann as post commander. McMurray directed Holman to appoint an officer to replace Streeter. Neither McMurray nor Holman mentioned the possibility that Chaplain William Greene, who was already an assistant superintendent, might assume Streeter's duties. Given the military's attitude toward the freedpeople, it is quite possible that the oversight was related to the fact that Greene was black.[29]

Upon assumption of command, John Holman launched his own inquiry into conditions on the island. In a letter to Captain Solon Carter, assistant adjutant general for the District of Beaufort, Holman reported that the island was "very barren and totally incapable of itself of supporting its inhabitants"; it was impossible for the large number of people there to find a way to "earn their subsistence." Consequently, the people on the island were "in a deplorable condition." He noted that rations had been made so small that "much suffering for the necessaries of life" had resulted. He also repeated what the people connected with the colony had charged in previous complaints—that the government had not paid the freedmen "one cent" for their work "upon the public works and in the mill," even though some had vouchers for more than two hundred dollars. "It is my opinion that these people have been very badly treated," Holman stated, "and that the dealings of their employers with them have not been altogether honest or else there has been gross mismanagement somewhere." Holman thought that "measures [should] be taken to remedy this evil as soon as possible," either by removing the people to a place where they could find employment or by providing paid employment on the island. He observed that the sawmill was "standing idle near the wharf seemingly because no man of responsibility or enterprise is connected with it." If put back in operation, it could provide "the means of living to many poor families" who were dependent upon the government. Holman finished his letter to Carter with a request for a thorough investigation "to determine by what authority these men were employed, whether there were ever any funds to pay them, and if so what became of the money."[30]

Writing to General Howard at the Freedmen's Bureau a day later, Holman enclosed a copy of his letter to Carter and reiterated his observations about conditions on the island. "Complaints that are evidently not without good foundation are coming to me constantly," Holman declared, "showing that these people have lost all confidence in the persons appointed to conduct their affairs, and that there is a great degree of corruption and dishonesty on the part of the latter." Holman indicated that he had temporarily appointed a lieutenant from his command to execute Streeter's duties, and he recommended "that some reliable man be sent" to the island to assume the position of assistant superintendent and conduct "investigations of the past treatment of the Freedmen with a view to correcting the evils that now exist." In an endorsement on the letter, Howard's inspector general, Joseph S. Fullerton, noted that Colonel Eliphalet Whittlesey, the new assistant commissioner of the Freedmen's Bureau in North Carolina, would "cause an investigation to be made of the affairs on Roanoke Island" and that he would "furnish such relief as he can."[31]

General Howard had appointed Whittlesey, a colonel breveted a brigadier general, to replace Horace James, who had not agreed to anything more than a temporary appointment as acting assistant commissioner of the Freedmen's Bureau in North Carolina. Howard and Whittlesey had forged a close relationship during the war, when Whittlesey served on Howard's staff, and thus worked well together in bureau work. Their friendship was not surprising given their backgrounds, and its basis provides insights into the work of the Freedmen's Bureau in North Carolina. The generals shared similar New England roots, and both were deeply religious. Although some of his army colleagues thought Howard's pious displays were self-serving and sanctimonious, Whittlesey appreciated Howard's spiritual depth. A Yale graduate who had also studied divinity at Andover, Whittlesey was an ordained Congregationalist minister. Like Horace James, he had been a student under Yale's influential Nathaniel William Taylor and had been active in a number of evangelical movements. He had also taught at Bowdoin College, Howard's alma mater, before the war.[32]

Whittlesey arrived in Raleigh on 22 June and set up his headquarters. On 1 July he issued his first circular, announcing that he was assuming "control of all subjects relating to Refugees and Freedmen in the State." On 15 July Whittlesey issued his second circular, announcing his appointments to the four districts that he had created in the state. Horace James, who had stayed in Raleigh to train Whittlesey, agreed to assume superintendency of the Eastern District, which was an expanded version of his old Department of Negro Affairs. Whittlesey also appointed James as financial agent for the state. Writing to the *Congregationalist*, James noted that he had stayed in North Carolina to "get the machinery of the Freedmen's Bureau well running," and that he thought he could be of most assistance by "remaining in charge of the Eastern District." Further, James admitted that he "could not honorably leave a work which I have so well in hand, every part of which is so familiar to me, until I had done all in my power to install in it my excellent and able successor."[33]

James and Whittlesey worked well together in North Carolina and remained close friends after their bureau labors ended. Their working alliance complemented that of Howard and Whittlesey. Just as Whittlesey frequently conferred with Howard as an equal rather than a subordinate, James freely offered ideas to Whittlesey as an equal rather than an underling. Since he had spent more time working with the freedpeople in North Carolina than either Howard or Whittlesey, and since he possessed some fairly well-developed thoughts about what the government should be doing in the South, James frequently wrote letters in which he extended programmatic advice to Whittlesey—advice that Whittlesey often readily accepted. Likewise, he had a great deal of influence over the long-term goals that Whittlesey set for the bureau in North Carolina.[34]

Although Howard had been less openly abolitionist than the other two men prior to and during the Civil War, he believed, as they did, that good men could win the war and then perfect society. All three realized that the Freedmen's Bureau was temporary. They looked forward to a South populated by black and white freeholders who owned their own labor and the products of their work. Likewise, the three men generally agreed on the means to achieve the social vision that was their end goal. They firmly believed, for example, that the freedpeople must attain true independence, and that giving the freedpeople handouts in the form of clothes or government rations would prevent the freedpeople from achieving self-sufficiency. James indicated that his reluctance to dole out rations to soldiers' wives grew out of his belief that these women needed to take charge of their lives and assert their independence. "To give them all full rations without regard to their circumstances is teaching them to be indolent, saucy, and unchaste," James asserted.[35]

After John Holman and the First USCT replaced Lehmann and the 103d Pennsylvania, spirits briefly rose among the colonists and missionaries. When the NFRA's secretary, the Reverend William G. Hawkins, visited the island in June, he was "gratified to find" Holman and the First USCT, "one of our best colored regiments," on the island. Hawkins indicated his admiration for Holman, "whose earnestness and true sympathy for our work, educationally and otherwise, we had frequent occasions of witnessing." Holman would "not encourage laziness," but would see that those who labored were paid, that "those unable to work" were aided, and "that the offenders against good order and virtue" were "promptly brought to judgment." Hawkins thought that Holman's "candid and kind" manner with teachers and agents and "his thorough sympathy with the cause and confidence in it," which grew out of his experiences leading a black regiment, "all promise new and better things for Roanoke." Hawkins speculated that the island might assume "a position of considerable importance" as a trade center for northeastern North Carolina, "both on account of its position and the resources by which it is surrounded."[36]

In the short term, at least, these optimistic assessments appeared to have been borne out in the communal celebration of the first postwar Fourth of July. Around sunrise that day the boom of thirty-six cannons shook the island's stillness. Private William H. Brown of the First USCT declared that the noise "appeared to arouse the very fish in the waters." After the noise died down, the regimental band played, "and every body seemed to be alive." Around nine o'clock the First USCT joined in a dress parade, marching to the front of military headquarters, "where the old flag was flung to the breeze amid the cheers of the assembled multitudes." By that time thirty-five hundred people had gathered, watching as the regiment halted in front of headquarters and stacked arms. Then Henry M. Turner, the African American chaplain of the First USCT, appeared with his wife by his side. Brown affirmed that Turner "delivered one of the finest orations, I can safely say, that was ever heard on this island." Turner opened with a discussion of the history of the United States, and then focused on slavery and its abolition. Turner stressed that "the extremities of color, white and black" had made the United States "the world's theatre," and "that as soon as God would knock down the wall of prejudice between the whites and blacks, sectional division would crumble into dust throughout the entire Globe." According to Private Brown, Turner's mastery of the subject moved many that morning—including some secessionists who "looked wild at its conclusion." There were, however, no outbursts or eruptions. After the speech, those who had gathered for the commemoration "returned to their homes, and the rest of the day went off quietly."[37]

Later in July, Holland Streeter went before a military commission to face three charges related to his corrupt activities on Roanoke Island: "misapplication and embezzlement of public property entrusted to his care," "fraud," and "cruel and abusive treatment of the colored people under his care, as Assistant Superintendent of Negro Affairs" from October 1864 until his arrest in June 1865. On 24 July the commission found him guilty of the first two charges. Although the commission acquitted him of the third charge, it did find him guilty of "cruel treatment to the colored women under his care as Ass't. Superintendent of Negro Affairs." The commission sentenced him to three months hard labor at Fort Macon and a fine of five hundred dollars.[38]

Horace James could hardly believe the sentence meted out to his former assistant. "It is most unjust, cruel, and monstrous," he complained in a letter to Eliphalet Whittlesey. "It is more than I can bear that a man whom I almost *know* to be innocent of crime (though he might have been injudicious) should be punished as a culprit." James sent a long appeal to the general in charge of the district, urging him to remit the sentence or at least reduce Streeter's punishment. James described Streeter as "an honest conscientious faithful man, diligently attempting to do his duty according to his understanding of it, and ability in it." He pointed out that Streeter had served on the common council of Lowell, Massachusetts, and had been an active member of a church and superintendent of a Sunday school in the city. Further, he had "held an important office of trust, which he resigned to come and aid the country in this department of endeavor." According to James, Streeter was merely following orders that had come down through James from General Schofield to reduce rations, and in doing so had "made himself very obnoxious to a portion of the colored people" under his care.

James did not put much faith in McMurray's investigation, which had relied on the "excited testimony of several negros" who had grudges against Streeter. After the removal of Streeter, interim authorities improperly distributed rations to 3,493 persons instead of 2,000, leading the freedpeople, noted James, "to believe that Mr. Streeter had really been defrauding them to this amount, made them bold, defiant and I may say saucy and led them openly and to his face to threaten revenge upon him when they saw him in arrest." James believed that the freedpeople had gotten together before the commission met and had agreed on a story that they could swear was true. James concluded his letter with a list of names of twenty men who "would warmly commend" Streeter. The list included General Butler, "who sent him out with letters to me [James] requesting that he be employed," several U.S. senators and representatives, and a number of officials from Lowell.[39]

On 30 July James wrote Whittlesey that the general in charge of Streeter's sentencing had indicated that he would "suspend the execution of the sentence" until he had sent James's letter to General Thomas H. Ruger, commander of the Department of North Carolina, "for his decision." James asked Whittlesey to intervene with Ruger on Streeter's behalf, and request a remittance of the sentence. "It is too bad that calumny and prejudice should be able to victimize a man in this manner," James declared. In August, when he learned that the punishment had been reduced to the fine, James was still chagrined. In another letter to Whittlesey, he announced that he was going to request that O. O. Howard cancel Streeter's fine because it "was perfectly unjust for him to pay it." James never conceded that Streeter might have been guilty of any dereliction of his duties, apparently finding it difficult to believe that someone he trusted could have acted improperly.[40]

The Streeter court-martial capped a series of events in the summer of 1865 that marked a turning point in Horace James's relationship with the Roanoke colony. In July, James had returned to New Bern after a short leave of absence. In his mail were copies of the letters that Richard Boyle had presented to the War Department in early April on behalf of the Roanoke Island freedpeople. Instead of championing the colonists' cause, James immediately penned a letter to J. S. Fullerton in which he charged that the colonists' descriptions of suffering on the island were "gross exaggerations." Employing copious underlining to help emphasize his points, James did not hide his exasperation. "The truth is *they have had too much* given them. And the times of wholesome *retrenchment* are the times of letter-writing, petitioning and professed abuse by their Superintendents." Significantly, for the first time since his association with the island, James strongly advocated breaking up the colony. The "*grand remedy* for Roanoke Island, now that the war is over and the thing is possible and safe," he asserted, "is to *put two thirds of its people upon plantations on the main land*, a result we mean to effect as soon as possible." Further evidence that James's enthusiasm for the Roanoke project was turning to disillusionment was revealed in his final sentence: "Those who come most in contact with the negros in the work of doing them good, *seldom win their gratitude*."[41]

In a letter forwarded with James's response, Assistant Commissioner Whittlesey concurred with James's assessment of the situation. He assured James that he had "done all that could be done by any man for the comfort of the people" on Roanoke Island. Believing that "a large number would leave, & find employment" if the government stopped supporting the "able-bodied men & boys there, living in idleness," Whittlesey noted that he was ordering a further reduction of rations. On the island, the poorest residents, those who for various reasons could not work, were once more the hardest hit by the ration policy. Many of these poor were wives of soldiers, who were still in the army because they had enlisted for three years. Hard times continued to widen the gap between the colonists crowded in makeshift housing in Camp Foster and those who had built houses on lots in the village. While visitors to the island continued to comment on the prosperity of the latter, as well as the developments at Sunnyside, where Sarah Freeman had organized a number of the women in farming the land under her control, those dealing with the people in Camp Foster saw only the severity of the colony's problems. The domestic manufacturing that James had espoused in his early discussions of the colony never amounted to much, and the shad fisheries, which had grossed only $1,404.27, rather than the "fortunes every year" that James had predicted, were a failure.[42]

By July 1865, Howard, Whittlesey, and James were beginning to move into a new phase in their policy toward the freedpeople on Roanoke Island. Concerned about deteriorating conditions on the island, they advocated cutting back the distribution of rations in hopes that this action would encourage some of the freedpeople to move back to the mainland and alleviate the overcrowding. To the colonists—many of them already suffering from the government's failure to pay their wages—the tough-minded ration policies appeared unnecessarily harsh. When they complained about James's treatment of them, they were reflecting their immediate concerns for their families' short-term well-being. Many expressed trepidation about returning to the mainland and working for their former owners; they thought that they had settled into a new life on the island that would be complete once the freedmen soldiers had returned home safely. At the same time, the wretched conditions among the colonists in the Camp Foster area raised doubts about James's abilities to improve the future.

Upon his arrival on the island in mid-July to take Streeter's place as assistant superintendent, Lieutenant S. H. Birdsall discovered a number of these problems, as well as the colonists' loss of confidence in the government. The population was hovering around thirty-five hundred, and the health of some of the colonists seemed to be on the decline. In late July, Birdsall wrote Whittlesey with a request for medical assistance and the authority to hire men to construct coffins. With "the sickly season just commencing," Birdsall felt that the absence of medical aid for the freedpeople put the colony in harm's way. The colonists had to depend on the assistant surgeon of the First USCT, and he could not answer more than a third of the freedpeople's requests. Further, Birdsall reported that "no less than five Freedmen" had been buried that day on the island, and his sick list was "increasing to an alarming extent." Whittlesey responded to Birdsall's request with a letter to Horace James asking him to send a surgeon to the island and also to give Birdsall authority to hire men and put them on the quartermaster's papers as laborers. James, in the meantime, had sent a doctor and a hospital steward, as well as fifty coffins, to the island from New Bern.[43]

In early August, Birdsall wrote James that even though the crops on the island looked good, the colonists would not be able to support their families of eight to ten children with what they could grow on their acre lots. Thus, he was encouraging the men in the colony to leave to find employment on the mainland. Recognizing the strength of the colonists' family bonds, Birdsall knew that if the men left, they would take their families with them. "But let it be borne in mind," he observed, "that these men love their families and that when a hundred men have gone a hundred families will soon follow." Although Birdsall's estimate of eight to ten children per family was an exaggeration—the number was closer to three or four children per family—he was correct in noting the enduring strength of the family ties in the colony. Even the military's haphazard and sometimes harsh treatment of the freedpeople had not altered these ties.[44]

Birdsall also correctly perceived that the people in the colony could not sustain themselves on their land, but he had not yet realized that the land itself was the issue. The military's treatment of the freedpeople played a major role in shaping the Roanoke Island freedmen's colony. Control of the land on which the colonists had settled was also crucial. While the actions of the military authorities kept the colonists in a dependent condition throughout the occupation, the conflict over land ownership would, in the long run, prove to be the colony's undoing.

No Foot of Land Do They Possess

THE DECLINE OF THE FREEDMEN'S COLONY

IN NOVEMBER 1865 Elizabeth James spent two weeks on the mainland in Elizabeth City looking for a suitable place to open an orphan asylum and for some way to ease the conditions on Roanoke Island. After her return, she penned a long letter to the AMA's corresponding secretary, George Whipple. It had been "very sickly" on the island that month, she reported, and she had spent her time attending to the freedpeople's needs instead of teaching. Many of the former slaves were returning to the mainland, and more would "soon be compelled to return" by the reduction in rations. Yet most of the colonists did not want to leave, "fearing lest their condition be as bad, or worse than before." Further, impressions from her trip had convinced her that not all former slave owners would want to hire freedmen, even if they could afford to do so. The future seemed bleak, for she knew that circumstances in the colony would only worsen in the upcoming winter. "They are to be driven by starvation from the Island," she declared. "Where shall they go? No foot of land do they possess, no cottage in the wilderness."[1]

Elizabeth James's lament highlighted the enormous problems that the Roanoke Island freedpeople faced in the immediate postwar period. They could not support themselves on the island or presume that the government would continue to grant rations, and, more importantly for the long run, they owned no land. From the freedpeople's perspective, however, the latter point was not as certain or clear as Elizabeth James expressed. Rumors that the government was going to grant land to all former slaves were rampant in the immediate postwar period. At the same time, many of the freedpeople on Roanoke Island assumed that they owned the lots that Horace James had assigned to them.[2]

Although Freedmen's Bureau officers on the island attempted to convince the colonists that they did not own their lots, many of the freedpeople persisted in regarding the lots as their own until late in 1866. When Dr. A. B. Chapin, surgeon in charge of the freedmen's hospital on the island, conducted a health inspection of the colony in June 1866, he discovered that the freedpeople were still unwavering in their assumption that they would soon be the recipients of government land. He notified his superior that "most of the freedmen believe the lands upon which they live are their own, or that the government will yet give them land." As late as October 1866, Stephen Moore, then the superintendent of the Freedmen's Bureau's Eastern District, reported that "the firm belief of the freedmen [on Roanoke Island] was and is that the lands were given them by the Government and that they have a perfect right to keep possession of it."[3]

Land ownership in the colony had, in fact, been shrouded in ambiguity from the very beginning of the colonial endeavor. In September 1863, when Major General John J. Peck commanded Horace James to "lay out and assign" the unoccupied Roanoke Island lands to freedmen, "giving them full possession of the same until annulled by the Government or by due process of United States law," the focus was on the establishment of the colony rather than its dissolution. No one worried about what the latter part of the orders would mean for the postwar life of the colony.[4]

Although there is no way to know exactly what Horace James and his assistants told the former slaves when they assigned them lots in the colonial village, the freedpeople later contended that the property had been given to them at that time. It is certainly true that on various occasions in public documents, James employed language that either explicitly stated or implied that the freedpeople owned their homesites. In one of his early reports to the *Congregationalist*, for example, James discussed the lots that had been "assigned to the various families." He noted that his friends in the North would be impressed by the freedpeople's enthusiasm for "the work of clearing up their little acre of land, by cutting the timber upon it, and preparing it for their rude log-house." The freedpeople yearned for their own land. "Let the unbeliever declare that the negro does not desire his freedom, and has no wish to secure the privilege of owning personal property, and real estate," James avowed.[5]

Similarly, in an April 1864 report to the New England Freedmen's Aid Society, James described how the former slaves on Roanoke Island eagerly "fenced their lots," built their own houses, and prepared gardens. "To be permitted to *own* a house and garden, and to be assured of protection by the authority of the United States," James declared, "is a privilege which they had never dared hope to enjoy. The instinct of property is stimulated in them, and being holders of real estate they seem to attain at once to a kind of independence which they never had known before." Likewise, in his first *Annual Report*, James described the former slaves as "absolute owners of the soil" who were building "upon their own lands cabins, however humble, in which they should enjoy the sacred priveleges of a *home* . . . more than they had ever dared to pray for." Although it is true that James's statements were couched in language that aimed to attract Northern support for the missionary efforts, his continuing actions to secure the lots for the freedpeople on Roanoke Island suggest that he really did envision a permanent settlement.[6]

James's initial efforts to obtain titles to land on Roanoke Island occurred when General Benjamin F. Butler was his commanding officer. Butler's interest in obtaining land for the freedpeople was a logical extension of his evolving political beliefs. By early 1863, he had indicated his acceptance of many of the ideas that the Radical Republicans were championing in Congress. In a speech in New York in April 1863, Butler had advocated that confiscated lands be distributed to those who had remained loyal. Early in his assumption of command of the Department of Virginia and North Carolina, General Butler encouraged James in his work on the island, including his attempts to secure property. On 3 February 1864, Butler instructed James to determine how much it would cost to purchase farms for the freedpeople on Roanoke Island. "Let the men understand that this is not a case for speculation," Butler warned, "because the government has some idea of seizing the whole property, if they cannot get it at a fair valuation." He also cautioned that it was "somewhat necessary that immediate action be taken in this matter in order to prevent collision between the whites and the blacks."[7]

On 20 February 1864, James indicated that he would soon be forwarding estimates of the "cash value" of the Roanoke Island lands to Butler. "I think there will be no objection on the part of the white inhabitants to selling out," James optimistically reported, "except the fact that the graves of their fathers are on their own farms." He dismissed this obstacle, however, noting that under Union ownership the graves "could be respected and adorned, as should those of our fallen soldiers be." He added that, in fact, he had already initiated a process to send the names of the Union soldiers who died on the island to their home states, with a request that the states erect suitable monuments as memorials on the island, and he expected that the memorials would "add to the beauty and historic interest" of the place.[8]

Much to his chagrin, James soon discovered that his prediction about the ease of purchasing real estate on the island was wrong. The white natives adamantly refused to sell their property. On 3 March James reported his findings to Butler. He noted that there were about eighty white families—approximately four hundred white people—on the island, and that "though not wealthy they are attached to their homes and to the birth and burial places of their fathers," prizing it more than they had before the war. "They never saw half the business done here that is now transacted," James fumed, "and despite their sneers at the negro and at what we are doing for him they are willing to live with him, and to share the prosperity he brings to the island." James concluded that since the islanders would not willingly sell their property, the government would have to make the sale "compulsory or a military necessity."

James then presented Butler some very specific details about the amount of land he wished to purchase on the island for the colony. He calculated that the colony's needs could be met if the government bought a tract six miles long by two miles wide, about 7,672 acres, at the pre-war rate of four dollars per acre, or $30,688. In practical terms, James was asking to purchase most of the island's inhabitable land. Offering some hints about his plans for the future of the Roanoke Island colony, James concluded his report with a list of reasons that the government should undertake the purchase. First, he noted, the island was the key to six "fine estuaries." Second, it was the center of a "splendid *trade*" in timber, tar, turpentine, and fish and would make a "grand depot for such stores." Finally, he thought that the island would furnish "a safe and convenient home for perhaps ten thousand wives and children of colored *soldiers* for whom the government could not provide so cheaply any where else in the vicinity of their home."[9]

On 14 March Butler enclosed James's report in a letter to Edwin M. Stanton, urging the secretary of war to make "some permanent provision upon Roanoke Island for the Negroes." Butler also warned Stanton of future problems if the government did not act quickly. "We are now putting so large a colony there that we shall have trouble with the owners of lands and hundred[s] of thousand[s] of dollars expense to extinguish the titles," Butler stressed. Butler realized that the government could not "buy land easily or without an Act of Congress," but he thought that trustees could buy it and "hold it in trust for the United States." Two days later, in a letter to General Wild, James further elaborated his plans to develop a permanent colony on the island. "I think the govt ought to purchase the Island," James stated, "so that we may occupy & improve the cleared lands which have heretofore been worked by the whites." After reiterating his arguments about the valuable resources on the island, James noted that the island would provide a postwar home for soldiers and their families. At the time of his letter, James apparently believed that organized units of freedmen soldiers would continue to police eastern North Carolina in the postwar period. "And when we remember that these negroes will be retained as a standing army after peace is declared," James noted, "it would seem to be desirable that the Island should be kept as a safe residence for soldiers' families after the war shall cease." Several days later, Stanton replied to Butler, noting that the plan would receive his "earnest consideration."[10]

In June, James once again solicited Butler's help in holding onto property on the island. He noted that "the interests of the colony (and of the country) at Roanoke Island" prompted him to write. In particular, he feared "that the growing importance of the island as a place of trade, a place for the manufacture of scuppernong wine. . . and a station on a line of travel through these sounds" would attract attention that might be "detrimental to the colored inhabitants of the island, and to the U.S. Government as well." In particular, he worried that "men of means and speculators in real estate" and the "old secession-tainted owners" were showing great interest in gaining control of island property, whose worth had increased substantially by virtue of the colonists' efforts. As an example of the sort of activity that James feared, he mentioned that a speculator named John McConkey had attempted to establish a claim on land near army headquarters. James implored Butler to "check-mate every selfish and narrow movement of this kind."[11]

Although Butler agreed that James's fears were valid, there is no evidence that he ever convinced Stanton to involve the War Department in any sort of scheme to purchase island property. Soon, the point was moot, anyway, for on 2 July 1864, Congress passed legislation that gave the Treasury Department jurisdiction, including leasing powers, over abandoned lands. Although Butler continued to sympathize with James's views, that summer he was unable to do more than retain control of the Roanoke Island colony for his Department of Negro Affairs, instead of letting it pass to the Treasury Department. Although not recognized as such at the time, retention of powers for the Department of Negro Affairs represented a major accomplishment for Butler. In other areas of the South, the War Department and the Treasury Department continued to clash over who controlled freedmen's camps; military authorities in charge of local occupations assumed that they should have control, while officers of the Treasury Department asserted that the legislation gave them control.[12]

Although Horace James had prepared to relinquish his position to Treasury Department agent David Heaton, he was pleased when Butler asked him to continue as superintendent of Negro Affairs for North Carolina. He had many projects to complete—including the Roanoke colony. He persevered in his efforts to purchase land for the freedpeople on Roanoke Island. In early 1865, James presented his strongest case for retaining land for the island's freedpeople in his annual report for 1864. Through a lengthy discussion of the colony's accomplishments, James intimated that the colony deserved to be permanent. Referring once again to the parallels between Raleigh's "lost colony" and the freedmen's colony on Roanoke Island, James proclaimed the superiority of the latter. Raleigh's colony, he noted, "became utterly extinct" and left "only some rude fortifications now overgrown with trees, by which to recognize this first attempt to settle America from our fatherland." In contrast, the freedmen's colony had "done better than Sir Walter's." Employing classic Republican rhetoric, James emphasized that the freedpeople had transformed undeveloped island land into a productive community. In particular, he noted that the colonists had already erected 591 houses, worth on average seventy-five dollars apiece—or thirty-seven times the old value of real estate on the island. A conservative estimate of the total property improvements, he concluded, exceeded $44,000, "a sum large enough to have purchased the whole island three years ago, with all the improvements of two hundred years, under the rule and culture of its white inhabitants."[13]

Noting that some people had predicted that the government "would fail to confirm to the Freedmen the rights and privileges they enjoy in these homesteads on Roanoke Island," James flatly declared, "I cannot believe it." He thought it "an element of our glory as a nation, that we can crush out a slaveholding rebellion with one hand and sustain a liberated people with the other." In his earlier correspondence with General Butler about purchasing land on Roanoke Island, James never clearly articulated whether he wanted the government to sell, rent, or give the land to the freedmen. His comments in the annual report, however, left fewer doubts about his intentions. The freedpeople, he asserted, deserved the land, at least for their lifetimes: "The person, be he white or black, who has taken an acre of piney woods, worth two dollars in the market, and increased its value thirty or forty fold by his own labor in a single year, certainly deserves well of his country, and should be permitted to enjoy, while he lives, the fruits of his industry."[14]

Strong statements in support of the government giving a lifetime land lease to freedmen might seem odd coming from a man who espoused a middle-class republican belief in self-reliance and self-support—a man who believed that the freedpeople would value what they purchased themselves more dearly than what was given them. A closer reading of his statements, however, indicates no inconsistencies with his basic ideology. James believed that the freedpeople had already paid for at least a lifetime lease of the land with the improvements that they had placed on the real property in the colony. Further, he was well aware that many of the freedmen had not been paid for work they had done for his Quartermaster's Department. Although James did not explicitly say what would happen to the land at the end of the freedpeople's lifetimes—and it is quite possible that he had not thought that far ahead—his actions subsequently implied that he thought the government would eventually sell the land to the freedpeople. On various occasions he urged the freedmen to save their wages to purchase land.

James seemed to waffle on the question of government confiscation of Rebel lands. Generally, he did not advocate confiscation of land without some compensation for the Southern owners. Similarly, he gave every indication that he believed that the freedmen should pay, with their saved wages or the improvements they had made on the land, for the property they occupied. At other times, however, he appeared to be reflecting the views of some of the Radical Republicans in Congress such as Thaddeus Stevens and Charles Sumner and many abolitionists, who thought it only just that the plantations of Rebel supporters should be confiscated and subdivided for freedmen. General William T. Sherman's Special Field Order No. 15, issued on 16 January 1865, which set aside a thirty-mile-wide stretch of coastal lands from Charleston, South Carolina, to the St. John's River in Florida for the exclusive settlement of freedmen, provided one model. Although some abolitionists disliked Field Order No. 15's separation of blacks from whites, noting its similarity to colonization, others applauded its intent, especially the provision that freedmen be given "possessory titles" to up to forty acres per family until Congress should "regulate the title." James never used language such as "possessory titles," but what he advocated for Roanoke Island appears to have been similar.[15]

James assumed that the March 1865 legislation creating the Bureau of Refugees, Freedmen, and Abandoned Lands in the War Department would provide the necessary impetus for the government to retain lands—at least temporarily—for the freedmen in eastern North Carolina. According to the rather vague provisions of the act, the Freedmen's Bureau, as it soon became widely known, was to have the "supervision and management of all abandoned lands, and the control of all subjects relating to refugees and freedmen," which seemed to suggest a continuation of the sort of work that James had been doing as superintendent of Negro Affairs. The abandoned lands, houses, and tenements that had been in the hands of the Treasury Department were to be turned over to the Freedmen's Bureau. Section Four of the enactment legislation stipulated that every male refugee or freedman would be assigned up to forty acres of the abandoned or confiscated land to rent, with the option to purchase within three years and receive "such title thereto as the United States can convey." Congress provided no funding for the Freedmen's Bureau, the assumption being that the rents from the lands would support the various operations of the Freedmen's Bureau.[16]

In April 1865 James applied for a brief leave of absence from his duties as superintendent of Negro Affairs, and then wrote President Andrew Johnson requesting a short meeting to discuss matters relating to the Freedmen's Bureau in North Carolina. While he was still waiting for responses to both requests, James penned a letter to the *Congregationalist* in which he indicated some of what he wished to discuss with the president. Drawing on his beliefs about the regeneration of the South, James indicated that the South was ready to be "saved" and that those in power could help show the white Southerners the right way to happiness. He hoped that the president would send a clear message to Southerners, encouraging them to "deal justly with the black man; make him free; give him the ballot; lay him off a farm, and give him clear title to as many acres as he can till. . . ."[17]

In late May James received his leave of absence and learned that the president had granted him an interview. The meeting with the president suffered, however, from remarkable ill timing. On 29 May 1865, between James's request for an interview and the meeting itself, Johnson issued an Amnesty Proclamation that illustrated that the president shared few of James's concerns about the freedmen's future. The Amnesty Proclamation allowed the "restoration of all rights of property, except as to slaves" to rebels who swore an oath of allegiance to the United States government and who could prove property ownership, except in cases where legal proceedings had been instituted for formal confiscation of lands. In a single act, the president struck significant blows to the basis of the nascent Freedmen's Bureau's leasing activity, as well as its funding. The Amnesty Proclamation had the potential to eliminate most of the property that the Freedmen's Bureau had to rent or sell to freedmen. Horace James did not record a description of his June meeting with the president, but Johnson's actions in the next few months further confirmed that he did not share James's goals for the Roanoke Island colony, especially those related to making provisions for the freedmen to become landholders.[18]

While in Washington, James also met with Freedmen's Bureau commissioner O. O. Howard. At their meeting, Howard and James agreed that the Freedmen's Bureau's goals in North Carolina should include universal education, a system of free labor, and permanent land ownership for the freedmen. Later that summer, Howard had no more luck than James in convincing President Johnson of the necessity of adopting the latter goal. When, for example, Howard suggested that Johnson should require Southern landowners to provide "a small homestead" for each of their former slaves, Howard noted that the president "was amused and gave no heed to this recommendation." As would soon become apparent, the president was more interested in returning lands to former owners than in providing reparations to the former slaves. Later that year and in 1866 Johnson also issued orders demanding that the freedmen who had taken lands under Sherman's Special Field Order No. 15 should be dispossessed of those lands.[19]

Oliver O. Howard spent his first few months on the job trying to clarify the vague areas of the Freedmen's Bureau's land policy. On 22 May, shortly after he assumed his position, and a week before the president's Amnesty Proclamation, Howard had issued Circular No. 3 in which he made it clear that the application for restoration of lands by those who had been disloyal to the government would "in no case be entertained by any military authority." Further, to prevent former owners from obtaining possession of their lands and forcing freedmen to leave before they had a chance to harvest the crops that they had cultivated on that property during the growing season, Howard provided for the freedmen to stay on the lands until harvest time. Howard ordered that abandoned lands "under cultivation by the freedmen be retained in their possession until the crops now growing shall be secured for their benefit, unless full and just compensation be made for their labor and its products, and for expenditures." Obviously, the president's proclamation of amnesty overrode Howard's orders with respect to refusing restoration applications from disloyal persons, as long as they could prove that they were no longer disloyal. The policy with respect to the freedmen's crops stood, at least temporarily, while Howard attempted to determine the extent of his authority over abandoned lands.[20]

In June, Howard requested the opinion of the attorney general with respect to his duties under Section Four of the statute authorizing the Freedmen's Bureau. Did he have a duty "to take charge and control of all abandoned lands, or all tracts of land that have been abandoned, or to which the United States may have acquired title by confiscation or sale or otherwise within the insurrectionary States"? Or was his "duty to take charge and have control of only such portions of the said lands as he may, under the direction of the president, set apart for the use of the loyal refugees and freedmen"? The attorney general, noting that he had no authority to offer an opinion except to the president or the head of an executive department, addressed his response to Secretary of War Stanton, who forwarded a copy to Howard. After declaring that few statutes were "disfigured by loose and indefinite phraseology to a greater extent than the

Major General Oliver O. Howard, who had earned the nickname "The Christian Soldier" during the war, was the first head of the Bureau of Refugees, Freedmen, and Abandoned Lands. Horace James met with Howard in the spring of 1865. They agreed that the goals of the Freedmen's Bureau in North Carolina should include universal education, a system of free labor, and permanent land ownership for the former slaves. (Massachusetts Commandery, Military Order of the Loyal Legion of the United States and the U.S. Army Military History Institute)

act of 1865 establishing this Bureau," the attorney general proceeded to dissect the law. He concluded that the commissioner's authority over the lands was "an incident of his power in regard to the persons mentioned in the act." In other words, Howard did not have, a priori, the authority to take charge of all abandoned lands; he had the right to control the abandoned lands only to the extent necessary to provide for the immediate needs of refugees and freedmen.[21]

In North Carolina the attorney general's opinion led, at least temporarily, to confusion both about which lands were under Freedmen's Bureau control and about which lands would remain under Freedmen's Bureau control. On 6 July Howard had his inspector general, Joseph S. Fullerton, inform Eliphalet Whittlesey that all abandoned or confiscated land in North Carolina that the assistant commissioner required for his Freedmen's Bureau work—whether in the hands of the Treasury Department or the Freedmen's Bureau—would be turned over to Whittlesey "upon proper requisition." Whittlesey had to document that his office needed abandoned lands for its work in the state. A few days later, on 11 July, Howard formalized the process by issuing an order requiring Freedmen's Bureau officers to submit regular monthly reports "of all lands in the possession or under the control of Assistant Commissioners or their agents that are held for the use or benefit of loyal refugees or freedmen" to his office.[22]

The true test of Howard's authority to control the use of abandoned lands came on July 28 in the form of his Circular No. 13, which aimed to provide property for the freedmen. Howard ordered Freedmen's Bureau officials to set aside all of the property that they controlled and divide it into lots for sale or rent to deserving freedmen at low rates. Howard did not obtain the president's approval before sending the circular to his assistants. In addition, he blatantly crossed Johnson by declaring that the provisions of the Amnesty Proclamation did not "extend to the surrender of abandoned or confiscated property" that had been set aside for the freedmen. Not surprisingly, the president strongly objected to Howard's Circular No. 13. At the same time, even some of the strongest advocates of freedmen's rights objected to the provisions of the circular. Writing to Horace James on 16 August, Whittlesey, for example, indicated that he did not know "that any portion of the farms we hold will be exactly disposed of in accordance with circular No. 13," but that he would use all of his "influence against such foolish proceedings," unless someone could convince him of the value of the plan.[23]

Whittlesey objected to Howard's plan for three reasons. First, he believed the "rents at 6 percent" would not pay the cost of their collection. His other two objections were related to the freedmen's lack of equipment. If the Freedmen's Bureau followed the plan outlined in the circular, Whittlesey noted, most of the freedmen lessees would have "nothing to work with, and we shall have no means to help them." Finally, Whittlesey thought that the freedmen, "taking good lands on such easy terms and with no teams, implements &c" would leave four-fifths of the land in waste and grow "not half a crop" on the other fifth. In a postscript to James, Whittlesey indicated that he was enclosing a copy of a different plan "for purchasing [and] furnishing homes by Freedmen"—a plan that he thought represented "a good move."[24]

Whittlesey was alluding to his own Circular No. 3, which he had just announced. In Whittlesey's first circular, which he had issued in early July, he had noted that the Freedmen's Bureau would "assist" the freedmen in North Carolina by letting them bargain with planters to obtain fair wages. In that same circular, he had also admonished the freedmen to save their money to purchase homes, support their own schools, and sustain their own churches. In Circular No. 3, Whittlesey developed his ideas with respect to how the freedmen could purchase real estate. Whittlesey reminded freedmen that they could "obtain farms with the money which they have earned by their labor." He also attempted to disabuse freedmen of the notion that the government was going to give them land. "It is reported that many freedmen refuse to enter into contracts for labor," Whittlesey wrote, "because they believe that farms will be given them by the U.S. Government. If any do this believe, they have no reason for their belief. The Government owns no lands in this State. It therefore can give away none." With classic Republican optimism about the possibilities inherent in a free-labor system, Whittlesey concluded: "Everyone therefore should work diligently, and carefully save his wages, till he may be able to buy land and possess his own home."[25]

Later that summer, responding to questions about his labor policies, Whittlesey stated that he had not established a standard wage, but expected the employer and laborer to agree on a fair one. "The employer has a right to decide what he will offer as wages; and the laborer has a right to decide what he will accept," he noted. Whittlesey fused his ideas about wage labor with his affirmation of the traditional male-headed family structure. He made it clear that the government would no longer provide for dependents—that was the husband's job. "A husband is bound to support his wife & children, and to take them with him wherever he labors, unless he makes a bargain for their quarters and support elsewhere," he declared. Whittlesey never indicated the motivation for his discussion of work and family, but it is likely that he was reflecting his fear of what several years in contraband camps had done to the freedpeople's work ethic. It is also possible that he was reacting to missionaries' reports that family ties among some of the freedpeople were weak.[26]

For many of the freedpeople on Roanoke Island, however, Whittlesey's ideas about family were neither new nor radical. Many of them had attempted to sustain family ties—sometimes over long distances and time—when they were slaves. Then, once in the island colony, they had attempted to reconstruct their family units and replace loose liaisons with formal marriages. Further, many of the men had attempted to shoulder the responsibility for their families once they reached Roanoke Island. The War Department's failure to pay the men for their labor on the island had, however, challenged the traditional male-dominated family structure in the colony. Thus, while Whittlesey's labor ethic did not demand a drastic shift in the way the freedpeople viewed families, it did, ironically, require them to trust that their Southern employers would treat them more fairly than their Union military employers had.[27]

Acting in his capacity as Freedmen's Bureau superintendent for the Eastern District of North Carolina, Horace James wrote to Whittlesey indicating that he agreed with him in denouncing the provisions of Circular No. 13 and in urging the freedmen to save to purchase their own lands. "Your views respecting the partition of land to the Freedmen agree with my own decidedly," he declared. "This law ought to be substantially modified early in the approaching session of Congress." James held that the freedmen should not be coddled—that making the rents or selling prices too low would encourage waste and discourage thrift. Further, he did not want to proffer aid to those who could support themselves. James's ideas were also based on his practical experience with the freedmen in the postwar South. Like Whittlesey, James believed that for the first year or so, the freedmen would have to work for someone else, and save their wages in hopes of eventually purchasing their own small farms. James and Whittlesey—and Howard, as well—assumed that the creation of a system of contract labor would automatically improve working conditions in the South. Neither Whittlesey nor James seemed to notice that many of the white landowners in North Carolina were so impoverished themselves that they could not afford to pay wages or participate in a crop-sharing system. Others could afford to hire men, but had no interest in paying fair wages to former slaves.[28]

Ironically, James had not seemed concerned about the freedmen's lack of operating capital and the potential for waste when he attempted to have the government grant the Roanoke Island freedmen the property that they had improved there. He never articulated why he thought that the freedmen would be able to afford seed and implements to cultivate their own land on Roanoke Island but would not be able to afford to cultivate rented property elsewhere in the state. He did, however, leave several clues that suggest more consistency in his reasoning than is readily apparent. On several occasions he had indicated that the small plots on Roanoke Island were not meant to be farms—that they were not going to be farmed in the strict sense of the word. He always assumed that the men and women would be employed in some sort of domestic manufacturing; they would not depend on their small plots for their livelihood. He envisioned a society in which free labor and freeholding would be intimately intertwined.[29]

James also had other reasons for not wanting all the land under Freedmen's Bureau control in North Carolina partitioned and set aside for freedmen. He wanted to encourage Northern businessmen to come to the South and invest in some of the property, but he knew that if the policies outlined in Circular No. 13 were followed, the Freedmen's Bureau would have had very little land left to rent out or sell. James thought that the "secret of practical reconstruction" was for Northern men who were well versed in free labor to lease or buy Southern lands and hire freedmen laborers. "Let Northern capital and Northern men go in and possess the land," he wrote in the appendix to his 1864 annual report. "Then shall the wilderness smile with plenty, and the desert shall bloom as the rose." James believed that Northern emigrants would transform the South by encouraging the adoption of middle-class republican values. In August 1865 James wrote a letter to the *Congregationalist* urging Northerners to come South "to purchase lands, open stores, start manufactories, or newspapers, or schools, or churches" for the betterment of the country. "This autumn should open a tide of emigration Southward sufficiently large to modify the whole structure of Southern society," he declared. James believed that bringing the "Northern sanctified mind into contact with the decayed, rotting institutions" of the South was "the way to save it."[30]

Thus, James had several reasons for wanting the Freedmen's Bureau to hold onto the lands under its control. In the middle of July, James indicated his increasing vexation at having to restore land to former owners. He wrote Whittlesey that he responded to all requests from old owners with a single reply: "I am simply the agent of the govt to control & manage this property until *ordered* to do something different with it. I have no discretion to use in deciding claims." Noting that some applications for restoration in the Eastern District that had been referred to Howard's office had been returned with requests for more information about the parties involved, James gleefully stated: "If so we shall have a fine opportunity to tell some wholesome truths." In another letter to Whittlesey several days later, James indicated that he wanted the return of houses and property to former Rebels stopped. "Of course," he asserted, "I do not give back a particle of property put in my hands til ordered to do so."[31]

James believed that the "rabid and leading secessionists" should have to pay for their disloyalty, and took delight when some restoration orders in the

Eastern District that had been issued improperly by General I. N. Palmer were rescinded. In September James wrote Whittlesey's assistant, Lieutenant Fred H. Beecher, that "the restoration of property should be very deliberate and tardy." He wanted Southerners "to be kept under tutilage some time longer. A general amnesty would be a great calamity." James also knew that every piece of restored property meant less rental revenue for the Freedmen's Bureau's coffers. In another communication with Beecher in September, James implored him not to "restore all the property so soon, as to stop our own income, for we shall sorely need some money to keep our machine running."[32]

On Roanoke Island, James turned once again to the steam sawmill for income to support Freedmen's Bureau work there. Although he had hoped to sell the mill to the NFRA in late July, the officers of that association decided against the purchase. James then decided to get the mill back in working order, "manned in a way to be run economically and efficiently," to make money for the Freedmen's Bureau. In a move that was apparently motivated by both personal and public considerations, he fired Amasa Stevens, the mill engineer who had joined the island's missionaries in protesting the reductions in rations on the island. Stevens, James complained to Whittlesey, had "more private axes to grind than public duties to perform." James replaced him with Lieutenant S. H. Birdsall, the assistant superintendent on the island. James thought that the mill's income would more than meet the expense of Birdsall's salary. By late September Birdsall reported that the mill had been repaired and was working. Lumber was ready for an industrial school and a new freedmen's store to be run by Sarah Freeman. Timber reserves on the island, however, were just about depleted, and James's hopes for profits from the sawmill rapidly dwindled. Late in November, James indicated that he was purchasing rafts of logs and bringing them to the island to be milled.[33]

Increasingly, James recognized the enormity of the difficulties confronting the approximately thirty-five hundred freedpeople crowded into the Roanoke Island colony. Howard and Whittlesey had indicated that they were going to continue the ration reductions that General Schofield had initiated earlier that summer, and James agreed that reductions were necessary to convince the colonists to return to the mainland and find employment. Neither Whittlesey nor James wished to encourage idleness, and James knew there were few wage-paying jobs on the island for the men and women. Although James wrote a letter in September to Beecher proposing that land occupied by freedmen in New Bern be set apart for those who had placed improvements on the lots there, he no longer proposed similar land arrangements for Roanoke Island. Having lost patience with freedmen who were complaining about the reductions of rations on the island, and with his pride wounded by the court-martial and conviction of Holland Streeter, he lost his zeal to maintain the Roanoke colony in the face of the overwhelming odds against it.[34]

James was also not sure whether he wanted to continue to work in North Carolina. Late that summer he wrote Whittlesey, complaining that he felt he was being pulled in many different directions. Friends in Washington, D.C., wanted him to head a Congregational church there. The AMA wanted him to be its New England secretary. And his aging parents wanted him to move near them and take over the editorship of the *Congregationalist*. "I feel like a bundle of hay between three or four jackasses," James declared in exasperation.[35]

James did, however, continue to defend the colony and colonists from its critics. Writing to the *Congregationalist* in early September, he emphasized that reports of "negro atrocities" on the island were exaggerated. "Great jealousy and terrible bitterness against the negroes exists among the white population of Roanoke Island," James explained. He pointed out that even though the blacks were "living in quietness on the north end of the island, full two miles from the wharf," rumors were circulating that it was "unsafe" for white people to land there. "The Southern chivalry found it particularly 'unsafe' to stay at this same point in February 1862," James huffed, apparently enjoying the opportunity to needle his detractors. He went on to note that the white natives who stayed on the island during the war had continually complained about the freedpeople. "When they were fortunate enough to find an acquaintance familiar with the mystery of pen and paper," James recounted with more than a touch of sarcasm, they wrote letters to the commanding general of the district, "setting forth their wrongs." In James's estimation, the old white settlers refused to see the truth: that the colony had been "an inestimable blessing to the island." It had "multiplied the value of real estate thirty-seven times during a single year" and had blessed the island with education, "which the whites might share equally with [t]he blacks, if they were not so afraid of the 'Yanks.' "[36]

Despite the colony's accomplishments, the chances that the freedmen families would become freeholders on Roanoke Island were decreasing rapidly as a consequence of Freedmen's Bureau policies. In September 1865, under strong pressure from the president, Howard rescinded Circular No. 13 and clarified his policy with respect to the restoration of cultivated lands. Its replacement, Circular No. 15, which in final form was drawn up at the White House, looked forward to the eventual restoration of all abandoned lands. As a temporary concession to freedmen, Circular No. 15 allowed assistant commissioners to set apart abandoned or confiscated lands "for the immediate use of loyal Refugees and Freedmen," as long as the assistant commissioners were "careful to select for this purpose those lands which most clearly fall under the control of this Freedmen's Bureau, which selection must be submitted to the Commissioner for his approval." The only lands that were completely exempted from restoration were those that had been legally confiscated.[37]

By the fall of 1865, it was clear that the president's goal of speedy restoration took precedence over a policy that could have radically altered landholding patterns in the South. In October Whittlesey asked James to send him a description of the lands in the Eastern District that fell under Freedmen's Bureau control, noting that he would forward the list to Howard. He warned James, however, that he did not expect Howard to act to retain the lands for the freedmen because the government did not have title to the lands, and presidential pardons could take them out of the Freedmen's Bureau's control. "I would not encourage men to build on land which they are not sure of holding," Whittlesey cautioned. By that time, James had almost completely reversed his ideas with respect to the freedmen being given land on Roanoke Island. Although he wished to make former slaveholders suffer, and therefore resented the policy of speedy land restoration, he also recognized that the restoration would force the freedpeople to leave the island and find homes in areas where they could support themselves.[38]

At the end of the war, the Freedmen's Bureau controlled approximately 1,800 acres on Roanoke Island. Freedmen's Bureau land reports indicated that 1,114 acres of this amount—owned by twenty-five different parties—had been occupied for the use of the freedmen. The local residents disagreed with the land reports somewhat; at least two of the white property owners later indicated that freedmen had not actually lived on their land, even though it had been held for that purpose. Although the military authorities were supposed to occupy only abandoned or confiscated land, many of the owners of the so-called abandoned property on Roanoke Island had never left the island during the occupation. Some, in fact, had stayed in their homes on their property, coexisting with the occupiers and the freedmen who were creating the village.[39]

White owners who petitioned for restoration of their property had to submit two things to the local Freedmen's Bureau agent: proof of land title, which often included a copy of the owner's deed; and either proof of a presidential pardon or evidence that the owner had sworn the required oath of allegiance to the United States government. A few owners presented copies of their property deeds as evidence of ownership, while others gave sworn affidavits. The local agent forwarded these materials to the assistant commissioner, who usually granted the request.

Early in July 1865, Isaac C. Meekins, owner of the Sunnyside property that

Horace James had taken for the missionary teachers, was the first white owner on Roanoke Island to request restoration of land. His application on behalf of the heirs of his late mother, Esther Meekins, also proved to be the most challenged of all the petitions submitted by the islanders, both because one of the Meekins brothers had served in the Confederate army, and because Horace James believed that the property was critical to the postwar missionary work on the island. The Meekins property was not only home to the teachers, but also the site of the two schools and a freedmen's store. In many respects, the lengthy fifteen-month correspondence between Isaac Meekins and the Freedmen's Bureau reflected, in microcosm, the tensions between many of the island's white natives and the Yankee occupiers. On one hand, Meekins, who thought his property had been wrongfully expropriated, clearly had no admiration for what the missionaries had been doing on the island. On the other, James and the missionary teachers, who thought that their good use of the property was justification enough for retaining control of it, believed that the Meekins brothers epitomized what was wrong in the South. At the very least, James hoped to delay the restoration of land to Meekins as long as possible.

In his initial petition, Meekins noted that the house and land he wanted restored to him was composed of the "old homestead given to my mother by her father when she was first married." His mother's will had directed that her property be sold to pay her debts, and since he was the one with whom she had contracted the largest debts, he took the house and land. Meekins insisted that he had always occupied the house prior to the war, and that he had not abandoned the property, but had vacated the house because the presence of defensive batteries on either side of the tract made it dangerous for him to stay. He had, he noted, left some blacks in the house to maintain it while he was away from the property, but they were removed by Horace James. (Apparently Meekins saw no irony in his decision to leave blacks on his property at a time when he felt that it was too dangerous to remain there himself.) His petition underscored his resentment of the teachers living in his mother's house. He complained that the missionaries not only paid no rent, they used or sold grapes growing on the property and cut "large quantities" of wood with "no compensation whatever" to him.[40]

Meekins's application infuriated Horace James, who had already experienced several run-ins with him related to the appropriation of this property. In early August, James informed Whittlesey that Meekins's petition contained "a great deal of effrontery" because one of the Meekins brothers had served in the Rebel army. In September, in another letter to Whittlesey, James elaborated on his recommendation against restoration of the Meekins property. James indicated that the property was jointly owned by three Meekins brothers: Isaac C., Francis A., and Ephraim. He emphasized that Ephraim, who resided on the property "after his mother's death and immediately before the war," had served "in the Confederate army through the whole war." James reminded Whittlesey that the Meekins house, which "was wrested by our forces from the hands of the enemy," had been assigned to James's department by order of General John G. Foster. The army's Quartermaster's Department had repaired the house before it was occupied by the teachers, who were still living there. "Whatever he may say," James declared, "Mr. Meekins never had an order permitting him to take possession of this property while it remained under my orders and control." James also pointed out that Meekins was wrong in accusing him of sending the blacks away from the property, for they still resided there. James informed Whittlesey that the Freedmen's Bureau would continue to need the Meekins house for some time.[41]

Meekins, meanwhile, persevered in his efforts to regain the property. Late in October, he wrote O. O. Howard, once again insisting that he had never abandoned his property, but had left temporarily for safety. Meekins added a few new details in this letter, and lobbed another barb at Horace James. Meekins related that after he left the property, soldiers had broken into the house and damaged the door and sashes, so he could not use the house. Then the Sixth New Hampshire had used the house for a hospital. After that regiment had departed, he had put some blacks on the property to retain it, but they were "turned out by one Horace James who seems to have things all his own way down here." Meekins complained that the timber on the property was cut to build, among other things, the freedmen colony's steam sawmill.[42]

Neither Horace James nor Eliphalet Whittlesey responded to the points raised in this new Meekins correspondence. Increasingly, James turned his energy toward New Bern's James City settlement, which had evolved into a self-supporting, permanent community, while Roanoke Island's colonial village, which James had designed with permanency in mind, floundered. Ever the practical reformer, James came to realize the urgency of moving the Roanoke colonists to the mainland. James also grew increasingly more interested in helping to establish a model system of free labor on some mainland plantations, a project that he took up in earnest in early 1866, after he resigned from his Freedmen's Bureau position. Without any fanfare, in the late fall of 1865 Horace James severed his ties to what was left of the Roanoke Island colony.[43]

Sarah Freeman did, however, enter into the dispute with Meekins, protesting the return of the property on which she and a number of other missionaries were living and working. In November, she wrote O. O. Howard a letter, relating that the NFRA wanted to purchase the property that belonged "to the heirs of Wid[ow] Meekins deceased." Freeman noted that the Industrial School, an additional schoolhouse, "a substantial Store" built by the NFRA, and the house where she lived were situated near each other on the property. The NFRA hoped to erect an orphan asylum on the property, "and thus to have all the buildings of the Association in one square of land containing about thirty acres," she stated. "There is no place more suitable for our buildings, and for the operations of the Association," she concluded. The stumbling block to the venture, however, remained the unwillingness of the Meekins brothers to sell the property. Freeman did not hide her feelings about the brothers. "They are unquestionably animated in their refusal to sell the land by a wish to get rid of the Institutions we have established," she complained. The president of the NFRA, Francis George Shaw, supported Freeman's letter with one of his own to Howard. He informed the commissioner that the NFRA would pay "a fair price" for title to the land and emphasized that the "enforced removal" of the NFRA "would be a serious injury to the colored population of the Island."[44]

In the spring of 1866, the Meekins property remained under Freedmen's Bureau control. At that time, Whittlesey decided that he wanted the Freedmen's Bureau to purchase it and establish a home for the indigent freedmen who remained on the island. He asked S. H. Birdsall's successor as Freedmen's Bureau's superintendent on the island, Lieutenant Alexander Goslin, to make inquiries. Goslin informed Whittlesey that it could not be bought, as Isaac Meekins refused "to accept any terms for it."[45]

In August 1866, Isaac Meekins renewed his battle to have the property restored. He noted that after his first attempt to regain the property, he had been informed that the property "would be retained till the necessity for its use should no longer exist." Then he asserted that in his "humble opinion" the "necessity has passed." Once again, he declared that "the house was not abandoned," but in this letter he added yet another argument. He indicated that during the first days of occupation, General Burnside had granted protection to him and the property. He enclosed Burnside's letter of protection, dated 12 February 1862, as well as a safeguard from Colonel Rush C. Hawkins, dated March 15, 1862, noting that he [Meekins] had taken an oath of allegiance "upon the arrival of the United States forces in February, 1862." Meekins also enclosed the oath of allegiance that he had sworn on 16 September 1865. He included a plea for Howard to consider the poor condition of the heirs of Esther Meekins "and restore to them, through me (the oldest of them) the house used as the Teachers' Home." In endorsements on Meekins's application, both Alexander Goslin and his successor, Captain Hugo Hillebrandt, recommended that the property be returned to Meekins. Goslin thought that the NFRA was planning to leave the island, so the property would no longer be needed. Hillebrandt added that restoration of property to former owners was the only way to break up the colony and induce freedmen to leave the island. Ultimately, practical considerations overrode all others.[46]

The Meekins "house and grounds" were officially restored to Isaac Meekins on 8 October 1866. In the meantime, Francis George Shaw addressed another letter to Howard requesting that the Freedmen's Bureau either purchase the Storehouse and the Industrial School, each worth $700, from the NFRA's successor, the New York Branch of the American Freedmen's Union Commission (NYAFUC), or allow the NYAFUC to sell the buildings and have them moved from the Meekins property. On 6 December Secretary of War Stanton approved the sale of both buildings. That was not, however, the end of Freedmen's Bureau correspondence related to the Meekins property.[47]

The other white property owners on the island did not exhibit as much alacrity as Isaac Meekins in their submissions of applications for land restoration. Although Samuel Nickerson observed there was an "agitation on the question of ownership of the land now on the island" in February 1866, documents in the Freedmen's Bureau records indicate that all of the other applications were initiated in the summer and fall of 1866, a year after Meekins's initial application, and well over a year after the war's end. Official restorations of this land to the owners followed shortly thereafter, from the fall of 1866 to spring of 1867. It is difficult to determine why the other owners waited to petition. Most likely they were aware of the difficulties that Meekins had encountered in applying for the return of his late mother's property, and perhaps that dispute led them to be cautious. It is also possible that they did not initiate formal application procedures until the local Freedmen's Bureau agents, hoping to compel the freedmen to leave the island, encouraged them to do so.[48]

When they did apply for restoration, generally the owners focused on the same thing: that their land had been "taken" from them for the freedmen who had been living on their property since the occupation, usually not paying rent. Samuel N. Midgett's petition of 20 October 1866, in which he requested the restoration of six acres, is fairly typical:

> My land was taken for the benefit of freedmen when they sought Roanoke Island as a place of refuge; was laid off into acre lots, streets opened, and, cutting the timber, they built several houses, which they continue to occupy till lately in large numbers. There are now several families residing upon this land, the heads of which families could procure work at almost

any place other than this Island, thereby being enabled to make a good living. . . . I respectfully ask that my land be restored to me. . . .[49]

The petitioners were especially peeved that the freedmen had depleted most of their wood. George W. Wescott complained that he was "entirely surrounded with freedmen," who would leave him "next to no wood" if they remained through the winter. Similarly, Nancy Gaylord stated that freedmen "cut most of the timber to build houses, thus leaving but little firewood. Of that remaining the freedmen continue to use." She indicated that until her land was restored, she would have her wood cut "without pay and receive no rent." Matilda Miller noted that the freedmen on her property continued "to burn my wood," even though they paid her no rent. Sarah E. Dough also noted that the freedmen paid no rent, but they used her wood "freely even going to parts of the land not adjoining their lots to procure it." Like Samuel Midgett, Sarah Dough thought the men should take their families to the mainland where there were jobs. Jesse E. Dough's application emphasized that his land was "entirely surrounded by freedmen," who would leave him "without wood for the winter all I can use now being but a few acres."[50]

Several of the landowners took pains to point out that they had not taken part in the war on either side. John Wescott, for example, noted that he never took "any active part in the rebellion," and had remained "always at home during the time." Wescott indicated that the six families of freedpeople living on his land were mostly his former slaves, who were "at liberty to remain as long as they desire." He wanted restoration so that he would be free to sell a part of his land. Other island natives emphasized that they had served the Union during the war. Lewis S. Mann noted that he had been a pilot of gunboats and transports during several months of the war. He also indicated that he had "nothing to say in the way of complaint" during the occupation. His house had been used as "headquarters of the commandants during eighteen months of the war," and freedmen also erected houses on the property. Martin Hubbard wrote that he, also, had been a pilot in the Union navy for two years. Many freedmen resided on his property, some paying rent.[51]

Walter T. Dough, owner of the property on which the purported fort of the "lost colony" was located, indicated that although his land was "never taken for the use of the freedmen," he wanted formal restoration since his name was included on the list of names of those whose lands had been used by the freedmen. Dough noted that he had remained on his property during the war, and had furnished wood to the Quartermaster's Department. Likewise, Esau Berry requested restoration even though no freedmen resided on his land,

Table 1. Roanoke Island Land Controlled by the Freedmen's Bureau

Owner	Estimated Acres	Deed in FB Papers
Abel Ashbee*	200	—
Samuel Baum	50	—
Mary Beasley	50	—
Esau (Eason) Berry*	50	—
Benjamin Daniel(s)	50	—
Abi Dough (heirs)	85	Yes
Jesse Dough	11	—
Sarah E. Dough	190	Yes
Walter T. Dough*	60	—
Jesse Etheridge	60	—
John B. Etheridge	50	—
John (LJ) Etheridge Jr.	50	Yes
Lizzie Etheridge	75	—
Lovey Etheridge	20	—
Tart Etheridge	50	—
Nancy Gaylord	50	Yes
Martin Hubbard	11	Yes
Samuel Jarvis*	200	—
Lewis S. Mann	50	—
Daniel Meekins	40	—
Esther Meekins (heirs)	100	—
Martha Midgett	30	—
Samuel N. Midgett	50	—
Matilda Miller	16	Yes
Carey (King) Walker	50	—
George W. Wescott	25	—
John Wescott	140	Yes

*This person's land was not occupied by freedmen.

Source: Various monthly land reports, Records of the Assistant Commissioner for North Carolina, RG 105, ser. 2470 and 2821, National Archives

because it had been entered on the Freedmen's Bureau records. Thomas A. Dough indicated that few freedmen were living on the land he wanted restored, but the Freedmen's Hospital was upon the property. He expected the government to except "this building together with all necessary out buildings" when making the restoration.[52]

Officers of the Freedmen's Bureau filed monthly land reports that included the names of owners and the number of acres in the property that the Freedmen's Bureau controlled. These reports, along with the owners' petitions for restoration and the special orders granting restoration, give a rough estimate of the quantity of land controlled by the Freedmen's Bureau on Roanoke Island. Information from the reports is summarized in the accompanying table. Several caveats should, however, be kept in mind when viewing the table. The Freedmen's Bureau's land reports are occasionally marred by some irritating inconsistencies; Freedmen's Bureau agents varied the spellings of names and sometimes even changed the names of the people who were listed as owners of particular pieces of property. Similarly, the acreage in the Freedmen's Bureau's reports did not always agree with the acreage in the owners' petitions. Finally, since visitors to the colony reported that some of the freedpeople built outside of the freedmen's village, it is likely that the land occupied by freedmen extended beyond the boundaries of the property listed in the table.[53]

Keeping these admonitions in mind, it is still possible to draw an important conclusion about the relationship of the native white landholders to the freedmen's colony. If Horace James's estimate that eighty white families resided on the island is correct, then from 25 percent to 30 percent of Roanoke Island's white families owned land that was in some way part of the freedmen's colony. Furthermore, most of these white landowners were related to the other landowners, their neighbors, through kinship or marriage—relationships that reinforced their strong ties to the island and each other. Horace James had not taken this affinity for place into consideration when he speculated in 1864 that the islanders would be willing to sell their property—the only homeland they knew—to the government for the establishment of a permanent freedmen's colony.

Looking back, it is easy to see that President Johnson's policy of amnesty and rapid restoration of lands to former owners sealed the colony's fate. The light industries and domestic manufacturing that were supposed to make the colony self-sufficient had never materialized. A succession of poor shad seasons yielded less than had been invested in nets, and hopes for scuppernong wine production were never met. Without jobs or some alternate support, the colonists could not afford to rent lands or maintain themselves on the island. Conditions in the colony, especially in the area of the Camp Foster barracks, were rapidly deteriorating. Even though Horace James complained about returning land to former slave owners, he realized that land restoration was the only thing that could compel the colonists to return to the mainland and find jobs. Thus, in his capacity as an officer of the Freedmen's Bureau, he helped initiate a process that his successors carried out to ultimately undermine the colony that he had worked so hard to establish. To appreciate the full impact of the land restoration, it is necessary to focus once more on the freedpeople, who were, ultimately, caught in a cruel "no-win" situation.

And the Partings Are Sad

THE FINAL DAYS OF THE FREEDMEN'S COLONY

THE MISSIONARIES' early letters from Roanoke Island had been suffused with their enthusiasm for opening a new field of mission work in a colony that they thought was very special. In contrast, their letters home in the postwar period suggest a cheerless resignation to the inevitability of the end of their work with the freedpeople on the island. That morose spirit is encapsulated in one of Elizabeth James's marginal notes to George Whipple: "The people are rapidly moving from the Island. It is a great labor, and the partings are sad."[1]

Monthly reports from officers stationed on the island in the postwar period repeatedly underscored the extent to which many of the colonists remained dependent on government support, especially rations. Although the people who had settled in the village continued to thrive, many of the freedpeople in Camp Foster, especially the newcomers, suffered grievously. In late July 1865, for example, after Holland Streeter was arrested, the acting superintendent distributed rations to nearly all of the approximately 3,500 colonists—this at a time when the colonists' garden plots should have been in their most productive state. In his semi-monthly report for January 1866, Captain F. A. Seely, James's successor in the Eastern District, reiterated what just about everyone connected with the district had been saying since the end of the war: the output of the colonists' small lots was "a mere nothing," and the freedmen were "almost entirely dependent upon the Government for subsistence." Freedmen's Bureau officers knew that the colonists would never be able to support themselves if they remained on the island.[2]

Thus, the established policy of the military after the summer of 1865 was to break up the Roanoke colony and send the freedpeople back to the mainland.

Even though many of the men were still away from the island fulfilling their three-year enlistment commitments to the army, the War Department no longer felt it necessary to maintain a sanctuary for the wives and families of soldiers. So, while the Freedmen's Bureau gave limited support to educational and sanitation efforts in the colony, and Freedmen's Bureau officers helped some of the men to contract to labor for white farmers on the mainland, the Freedmen's Bureau's primary goal on Roanoke Island was reduction of the freedpeople's dependence on government aid by removing them to the mainland where they would have more opportunities to support themselves.

A majority of the Freedmen's Bureau reports relating to Roanoke Island focused on the agents' endeavors to reduce the number of freedpeople on the island. Freedmen's Bureau officials encouraged resettlement by making life on the island difficult for the colonists; in particular, they further contracted rations and restored the colony's land to the white owners. The *James Guy* and the *Washington Irving*, locally piloted steamer ships, made regular runs to coastal towns in northeast North Carolina—areas that the freedpeople had called home when they were slaves. Those who could afford to pay for their families' passage did so, while Freedmen's Bureau officers arranged transportation for the destitute.[3]

Not surprisingly, during the time when colonists were leaving the island and restoration of property to white owners was ongoing, conditions in the freedmen's colony declined dramatically. Missionaries on the island, however, struggled to maintain a semblance of normality. Both O. O. Howard and Eliphalet Whittlesey had indicated that they would not supersede or interfere with the established efforts of the benevolent associations that were already engaged in educational work in the South. Both men had close ties to the AMA's senior corresponding secretary, George Whipple, and they were sympathetic to the missionary work. They also realized that the Freedmen's Bureau had no funds to finance educational work among the former slaves, so it was practical to encourage the work of the missionary associations. Whittlesey ordered his officers in the field to assist the missionary teachers; he also continued to provide school buildings and helped to renovate structures for new ones. Teachers did not qualify for rations as they had during the war, but money gathered from rents of abandoned property was used to turn former military buildings into schools and pay for books, furniture, and transportation for teachers.[4]

Although both the AMA and the NFRA kept their schools open on the island until mid-1866, some confusion resulted from the rumor that the Freedmen's Bureau was going to allow only one association to operate on the island. By late

1865, the number of NFRA-sponsored missionaries exceeded the number of AMA-sponsored missionaries on the island. During the ensuing year, the NFRA and its successor, the New York Branch of the American Freedmen's Union Commission, brought twenty additional missionaries, mostly from posts in other parts of North Carolina, to the island for brief stints. In addition, the New England Branch of the American Freedmen's Union Commission sponsored one missionary on the island. The NFRA opened several new schools, including the Industrial School for girls and women at Sunnyside. Counting the Industrial School, in mid-summer 1866 there were nine missionary-sponsored schools on the island. That number, however, did not last, for as the number of freedpeople plummeted, mission schools were closed and the missionary teachers departed for home or other mission fields.

By late October 1865, the number in the colony had dropped to a little over twenty-one hundred. Then, surprisingly, the population jumped back up to around three thousand in mid-December. The dramatic resurgence, which the Freedmen's Bureau officers had not anticipated, was due to several factors. Some of the growth came about because freedpeople from other freedmen camps came to the island for reunions with relatives. In addition, a number of the freedpeople returned to the colony after the fall harvest on the mainland because their labor was no longer needed. Taking advantage of the new free labor system, their employers, who in many cases had been their former owners, refused to support the freedmen and their families over the winter. In January 1866, the commandant on the island reported that the number of desperate freedpeople returning to the colony for shelter after they had been thrown off their former owner's farms following the harvest just about equaled the number who were leaving the island, thus accounting for the steady population in the colony despite emigration.[5]

Significantly, some of the growth could be also attributed to freedmen soldiers, men of the Thirty-fifth, Thirty-sixth, and Thirty-seventh USCT, returning to the island after fulfilling their enlistment obligations only to be met by bureau agents who wanted them off the island. One of the great ironies of the story of the Roanoke Island freedmen's colony is that while these men were away fighting as part of the Union army, this same Union army was neglecting their families. And then, upon their return to the island, these men who had acquitted themselves well in service to the Union in various battles, including Olustee, Petersburg, and New Market Heights, were treated poorly by the very army they had helped sustain. Of the 139 black men known to have enlisted on Roanoke Island—a small sample of the men who had families in the freedmen's colony, since many had enlisted elsewhere in North Carolina—31 died while in

ARMY OF THE UNITED STATES

CERTIFICATE

OF DISABILITY FOR DISCHARGE

Private David Berry, of Captain Oren A. Hendricks Company, (F) of the Thirty Sixth Regiment of the United States Colored Troops was enlisted by Lieut. Mc Clain of the Thirty Sixth Regiment of U S C Troops at Roanoke Island N.C. on the Tenth day of December, 1863, to serve Three years; he was born in Hertford Co in the State of North Carolina, is Twenty years of age, Five feet Ten inches high, Black complexion, Black eyes, Black hair, and by occupation when enlisted a Servant. During the last two months said soldier has been unfit for duty 60 days.* Private Berry received a Gunshot wound through his left shoulder in a skirmish with Guerillas at Jacksons Creek Va. on the 14th day of May 1864, and since that time has been unable to use his left arm

STATION: In the Field Va

DATE: May 10th 1865

Oren A. Hendricks
Capt. 31st U.S.C.T.
Commanding Company.

I CERTIFY that I have carefully examined the said David Berry, Private of Captain O. A. Hendricks Company, and find him incapable of performing the duties of a soldier because of† Partial Anchylosis of Shoulder joint, the result of a gun shot wound recd in a skirmish with guerillas at Jacksons Creek Va May 14 '64. He is unable in consequence of said wound, to lift his left arm more than a foot from his side, doubtless from paralysis of the nerve governing the movement of the deltoid muscle. Has done no duty since receipt of wound. Is entitled to a pension, unfit for Invalid Corps. Degree of disability two thirds.

J Clark [illegible] Surgeon.
36 U.S.C.T.

DISCHARGED, this 25th day of May, 1865, at Hd Qrs 36th U.S.C.T. Camp Lincoln Va

B. F. Pratt
Lieut Col 36 U.S.C.T.
Commanding the Reg't.

The *Soldier* desires to be *addressed* at

Town ______ County ______ State ______

* See Note 1 on the back of this. † See Note 2 on the back of this

[A. G. O. No. 100 & 101—First.] [DUPLICATES.]

At least 31 of the 139 black soldiers who enlisted on Roanoke Island died during the war; many freedmen who enlisted elsewhere before sending their families to Roanoke Island met a similar fate. Others suffered life-shattering disabilities. This certificate of discharge for Private David Berry indicates that he enlisted in the Thirty-sixth U.S. Colored Troops in December 1863 on Roanoke Island. In a skirmish near Jackson's Creek, Virginia, in May 1864, Berry received a gunshot wound that permanently impaired his ability to lift his left arm. (National Archives) service. Many others suffered injuries that caused pain and suffering throughout the remainder of their lives.[6]

Conditions in the colony continued to degenerate during the winter of 1865–1866, with the people who were living in the old barracks suffering the most. The disparity between their circumstances and those of the colonists who had built houses in the village grew greater, exacerbated by the reductions in rations and the ongoing arrivals of new, usually destitute, freedpeople. Elizabeth James complained that some of the colonists would "*steal* fearfully" from anyone. "I suppose they are hungry & they steal any thing they can lay their hands on anywhere," she explained. "They stole potatoes from the ground till they were dug & then broke open potato houses & stole from there." They would also steal hens and hogs, something she knew from personal experience, for they broke into her henhouse and took sixteen "splendid hens." After that violation, with typical missionary sentiment James declared, "I could have cried not only for my hens but over their sins." Samuel Nickerson said, quite simply, "They are poor."[7]

Steadily, even though some freedmen had returned to the island, others continued to leave in search of work for the upcoming season. "Every boat takes some of our scholars to the mainland," Samuel Nickerson observed in January. Most of the emigrants were returning to their home areas, and their former owners were "offering better" than he expected. Nevertheless, he realized that the freedpeople's situations would still be difficult—that "they understand, and we understand, that they go back to a semi-slavery for the present but hoping for better times in the future." He expressed his hope that by spring "half or more of the colony" would be where they could find employment.[8]

Although many of the freedpeople who had sought wartime shelter on Roanoke Island had traveled there on their own from nearby counties, some were there because the government had shipped them there. The latter included those who arrived after General Wild's raid, as well as those who landed after the fall of Plymouth. When they left the island, most of the freedpeople returned to their home areas. Popular destinations included Coinjock, Elizabeth City, Edenton, and Plymouth. In March 1866, the assistant superintendent on the island, Captain Alexander Goslin, notified Whittlesey that although most of those who were leaving were returning to adjoining counties, a few wished to go further inland to Washington, North Carolina. "I think it is best to comply with their wishes as far as possible in sending them into the country—they will be likely to be more contented," Goslin remarked. In response, Whittlesey affirmed that Goslin should consult with the freedpeople about their destinations, but that he should also "insist on their going."[9]

A few out-of-state employers recruited in the colony and were able to convince some of the men to leave the island and come to work for them. In April 1866, for example, Alexander Goslin certified transportation requests for forty-five freedmen to go to Tallahatchie County, Mississippi, to work for John D. Hawkins & Brothers. Others went north or to the Midwest to begin their new lives. In September 1866, O. O. Howard issued a transportation order for "Jim Banks, a dependent freedboy (under 12 yrs of age) to travel from Roanoke Island to Indianapolis, Indiana" in the care of Sarah P. Freeman, who had concluded her mission work on the island that summer. No doubt this "Jim Banks" was Little Jim, the orphan that the Freemans had taken into their Sunnyside home on the island.[10]

Those who willingly chose to leave for other states remained, however, the exceptions. Freedmen's Bureau officials encountered numerous difficulties in convincing some colonists to leave at all, even to return to the areas on the mainland that had been their homes before the war. In addition to believing that they owned their lots, the freedpeople feared what awaited them on the mainland, and quite a few had developed an attachment to Roanoke Island. F. A. Seely had grown increasingly irritated with the colonists' recalcitrance that first winter, reporting in February 1866 that many refused to leave despite "an increased demand for labor" outside the island. When the freedmen showed no interest in contracting with a man who visited the island in late March in hopes of hiring laborers, Seely could not hide his exasperation. Like the military officers who were stationed on the island, Seely did not understand why the colonists were reluctant to relocate. To him, it all boiled down to minimizing government assistance, and when the colonists refused to take work that was readily available, he had no sympathy for their circumstances on Roanoke Island. "If the offer was fairly made & generally understood, I should be inclined to stop rations at once," Seely declared.[11]

Even without Seely making good on his threat, only two hundred freedpeople out of a population of about fifteen hundred qualified for rations in May 1866. Life for the poorest colonists was grim. Sarah Freeman described how the teachers gave hungry colonists all the food that they could spare that spring, and then gave out "damaged food" that she had purchased to feed to the teachers' pigs. "This the people cooked and ate, to save life," she recounted. Meanwhile, Whittlesey continued to urge Alexander Goslin to pressure the freedpeople to leave the island. He concluded that the Freedmen's Bureau might have to establish a refuge for the destitute, the infirm, the elderly, and orphans left behind, but hoped that most of the colonists would be able to leave by the end of the summer. Although the colony's population had dropped to fourteen hundred by June 1866, Whittlesey was still unhappy with the pace of emigration. While noting that he did not want any freedpeople reduced to starvation, Whittlesey directed his assistant, Clinton A. Cilley, to have Captain Goslin "clear the island at once"—to determine how many families could be sent away from the island.[12]

In response, Goslin reported that the freedpeople offered various excuses for their unwillingness to leave. "Some wish to stay on account of their gardens, others that they can get no employment, & others that they will be illtreated on the main land." Exasperated, Goslin declared that the only way to clear the island was "to force them off." A sanitary inspector confirmed Goslin's findings, noting that he had learned that the men did not want to move their families because they feared "the oppression & injustice of their old masters" and they did not want to pay excessive rents for houses and gardens elsewhere "whilst, in Roanoke, they have houses & gardens of their own, rent free."[13]

It had not taken long for stories of mistreatment by former owners to reach the island. Although some of the anecdotes were exaggerated, some had a solid basis in fact, and the freedpeople realized that they could not automatically trust their old masters to be fair to them. Stories circulated in the colony throughout 1866 about the freedmen who had gone inland and worked for their former owners, only to be driven away after the fall 1865 harvest, when their labor was no longer needed. Although officers of the Freedmen's Bureau encouraged the freedmen to enter into labor contracts to prevent such abuses, many of the freedmen would not willingly enter into such agreements. Horace James concluded that the freedmen were not interested in making contracts because they did not trust their former owners to honor them—all the more reason, he thought, for Northern men to come South and establish a free labor-based farming system.[14]

While job security proved to be a lasting concern, the rarer, but more serious, problems stirred up the greatest apprehension. Stories, for example, about freedmen who had been physically harmed while attempting merely to go about their day-to-day business on the mainland floated back to the colony and reinforced the general trepidation about leaving the island. One colonist, Nelson Perkins, left the island, found work a few miles outside Elizabeth City, brought his family from the island to join him, and was "pursuing peacefully his avocation" when he was "shot down in cold blood" because while a soldier he had served on a picket line "not far from the place where he was at work." After his death, his family then returned to Roanoke Island. "Is there any wonder," Sarah Freeman inquired with respect to the colonists, that "they hesitate about leaving a place of safety?"[15]

When safety was not an issue, fairness was. Although some of the former owners offered honest deals and treated their former slaves with kindness, often the labor contracts arranged by the Freedmen's Bureau agents were more advantageous to the white planters than to the freedmen. Instead of furthering the development of independent black farmers, the Freedmen's Bureau perpetuated a system in which the black laborers were still dependent on white planters. In October 1866, in his annual report for the Eastern District of North Carolina, Stephen Moore described the various contract agreements that had become common in his region. The white farmers and freedmen were entering into both standing wage contracts and sharecropping contracts. When hired by the year for a standing wage, the freedman agreed that half of the wages would be kept until the contract was up. Moore noted that time "lost by idleness or absence without leave" was not compensated. Further, if the freedman left the "employer before the expiration of the contract without good and sufficient cause," he would forfeit the wages that had been held. The freedman also agreed "to work ten hours per day, and to be respectful in his deportment." Moore also outlined two types of sharecropping that were popular in the Eastern District. In one, the owner of the land supplied everything but the labor, and the freedman laborer received a third of the crop. In the other, the freedman furnished half the seed and feed for cattle and received half the crop.[16]

Both the standing wage contract and the sharecropping contract could be manipulated to the employer's advantage. The variety of restrictions in the standing wage contract frequently gave the employer an excuse to default on the wages, leaving the freedman with nothing after a year of work. Likewise, there were numerous reports that the white farmers found ways to cheat the sharecroppers. Sarah Freeman gathered information from a number of freedmen who went to the mainland to work, but returned to the island after discovering that their bosses were taking advantage of them. Kinohen Rennick, a carpenter who helped build the Industrial School and store for the Roanoke colony, left the island in February 1866. He found work and labored diligently to save money to support his family. Due $100, he received only $15. Similarly, John Mills left the island at the same time and found work making shingles. He had made an average of four thousand shingles per week, which should have netted him $16 per week. At his pay settlement in June, however, he received only $10, "and was obliged to work his passage to the island." Meanwhile, Alphonso Lenox, who had served in the army during the war, went to the mainland and contracted to work for fifty cents per day plus his keep on the six days he worked. He soon discovered, however, that he could not afford to pay for his supplies for the seventh day. It "cost him nearly as much to keep him over the

Sabbath as he could earn during the week," Freeman explained. The employers' supply stores frequently charged exorbitant prices, bilking the freedmen of the money that they had earned. "These facts speak for themselves," Freeman declared.[17]

Sarah Freeman understood why the freedpeople hesitated to leave the island, and her observations bespoke her great empathy for the freedpeople. In the long run, however, her sympathy did not make any difference. The colonists did not have many choices in the matter. Although Currituck County had levied a tax to support the destitute, regardless of color, the county could not, as Dr. A. B. Chapin noted, "take charge of the sick and indigent from other counties who have flocked to this Island expecting to be supported in idleness or at Government expense." As conditions in the colony continued to degenerate, the colonists' health became a prominent concern. In June 1866, Dr. Chapin reported that he was unable to obtain any rations other than hard bread for the Freedmen's Bureau's fifty-bed hospital, which fortunately had few patients. In July, he complained about the failure of the civil or military authorities to adopt "sanitary measures" in the colony. Once again, he decried the quality of the rations, which "would hardly sustain life" and were certainly unsuitable for the sick. He also accused Alexander Goslin's clerk, Charles B. Holman, "of selling gov't. property and pocketing the proceeds."[18]

Chapin's accusation once again highlighted the potential for impropriety among the lesser officers stationed on the island, a recurring problem among those in charge of distributing rations and supplies. Holman left the island abruptly without permission, suggesting that he had been guilty of something, but Goslin's reports for July gave no indication of any malfeasance. In contrast to Chapin, Goslin reported that his weekly inspections of the colony indicated that "the sanitary condition and health" of the settlement were good. "The streets and avenues are kept remarkably clean, and the houses are well ventilated and are also kept clean," he stated. In August, he reported that many of the freedpeople's houses had been whitewashed, that he had distributed ten barrels of lime and was requisitioning twenty more. Given the contrast between the upper and lower areas of the colony, it is possible that the disparity in the two reports grew out of the focus of the various inspections. If Goslin's inspections had been concentrated in the freedmen's village rather than the entire camp, he would have perceived much better conditions in the colony. If he had visited Sunnyside, he would have seen the men and women tending fields of vegetables and fishing for Sarah Freeman, and would probably have been impressed with their industry.[19]

It is also possible that Goslin was falsifying his reports, perhaps to cover for

Holman. In the late winter and spring of 1866, Goslin himself was strongly criticized by George Sanderson, who had been James's first assistant on the island. In testimony before a House subcommittee, Sanderson accused many of the North Carolina Freedmen's Bureau agents of corruption, and charged Goslin and another of his assistants with mismanagement of government supplies on Roanoke Island. It is difficult to determine Sanderson's motives; on numerous occasions when he was the assistant superintendent on the island the freedpeople had accused him of corrupt ration practices. Nevertheless, he proved to be a thorn in the side of Freedmen's Bureau men like F. A. Seely and Alexander Goslin, who did not empathize with the freedpeople and whose primary concern was the removal of large numbers of the colonists from the island. Seely responded to Sanderson's charges by accusing him of "exciting the negroes to disaffection in various ways," and of giving them advice that "was notorious and very injurious." Seely also ordered Goslin to arrest Sanderson and put him in close confinement if he showed up on the island. Goslin arrested Sanderson in February 1866, but there is no indication that his punishment was anything other than removal from the island.[20]

Goslin's successor, Captain Hugo Hillebrandt, arrived in midsummer 1866. In contrast to Goslin, Hillebrandt seemed to be genuinely concerned about the freedpeople's welfare. He did not paint as rosy a picture of conditions on the island as Goslin had reported, noting, for example, that he could find no houses that had been whitewashed. Indeed, conditions in the colony were rapidly deteriorating. The number of freedpeople qualifying for rations had fallen to sixty-three—thirty-seven adults and twenty-six children—and that number declined rapidly after 1 October, when rations were discontinued to all but the sick in hospitals and orphans. The poorest people in the colony desperately turned to robbery to survive. In August, burglars broke into the freedmen's store that Sarah Freeman operated for the NFRA and stole $350 worth of goods. Elizabeth James, always a regular correspondent with the AMA officers, wrote only sporadically that fall. In early December, she reported that all but seven of her eighty hens had been stolen; she had been robbed so many times that the quartermaster had given her a gun and taught her how to use it. "Similar depredations are committed anywhere and everywhere excepting where there is a large dog," she stated.[21]

As the winter of 1866–1867 approached and the number of arrivals—soldiers returning from duty, freedpeople from other camps who were reuniting with family members, and unhappy freedpeople returning to the colony after trips to the mainland—exceeded the number leaving the island, the population of freedpeople jumped back up to seventeen hundred. Stephen Moore, the officer in charge of the Eastern District, concluded that conditions on the island presented "every appearance of great destitution during the ensuing winter." Fearing the worst, Hugo Hillebrandt compiled a list of 679 freedpeople—286 adults and 393 children—who "were likely to become destitute during the ensuing Winter," and included their preferred destinations. Along with the district superintendent, he urged that "the land be restored to the original owners, so as to compel the freedmen to remove to other points, where they can procure employment." He also requested that the Freedmen's Bureau charter a schooner to move the poorer colonists to the mainland, since many could not afford "to pay the expenses of a boat." In response, the assistant commissioner of the North Carolina Freedmen's Bureau at that time, Brevet Major General John C. Robinson, arranged to transport large numbers of freedpeople off the island. In a report he submitted to Congress in November 1866, he stated that he had "reason to believe that great numbers of them will be induced to leave during the month."[22]

Throughout the fall, O. O. Howard, Stephen Moore, and Hugo Hillebrandt urged the freedmen to elect an agent to visit plantations in Texas and other states where the freedmen might find employment or take advantage of the Homestead Act. By December, however, the Freedmen's Bureau officers had given up their efforts to persuade the men to travel to Texas. Stephen Moore reported that the freedmen who wanted to do so could find jobs on the mainland near Roanoke Island, and they could not "be induced" to travel out of the state.[23]

By the end of 1866, the population was falling fairly rapidly. Assistant Commissioner Robinson's extensive efforts to transport the freedpeople were having the desired outcome. In addition, the land restorations that had taken place that fall and winter were also having an effect, as white owners reclaimed their property and attempted to evict freedmen settlers. In December, sixteen freedmen wrote to Whittlesey on behalf of themselves and "other old resident freedmen of Roanoke Island, N.C." complaining that those who had had their lands restored were refusing to allow the freedpeople to stay, even though they had offered to rent or purchase lots. The men pointed out that they had been born and raised on the island, and that the only way they knew to support themselves was by "fishing, fowling, and progging" (an island term for foraging). They emphasized that since they were not farmers, they would be able to earn "but a poor living" if they were forced to go to the mainland, "merely to gratify the whims of men who are not well-affected towards the government of the United States." The men petitioned for justice, requesting that "by paying reasonable rent" they should be allowed to stay on the island and eventually "lay their bones to mingle with the dust of their childhood's home." Although no response was recorded, many of the men were still on the island a year later, when they once again petitioned to stay.[24]

By mid-January 1867, the colony's population was down to 950, with only 17 people—7 sick in the hospital and 10 destitute—receiving government rations. The district superintendent, Stephen Moore, congratulated Hugo Hillebrandt for his success "in ridding the Island of 800 persons." Noting that it was time for the freedmen to hire themselves out for the upcoming farming season, Moore stepped up efforts to procure transportation for those who could not afford to pay for their own passages to the mainland. Moore followed Hillebrandt's recommendation that a small sailing vessel rather than a steamer be hired for the task, since a steamer might not be able to land in the coastal areas where the freedpeople desired to go. He thought that it might be possible to ship them all off the island by early March. It was late March, however, before his letter, which had circulated through various official channels, was returned with O. O. Howard's endorsement authorizing the charter of a small sailboat for thirty days.[25]

Meanwhile, determined not to encourage the colonists to remain on the island, the Freedmen's Bureau officers focused their energies on removing the colonists rather than helping them through the winter. In January the weather turned unusually bitter; the sound froze and a number of furious storms assaulted the island. Most of the people, according to Elizabeth James, were "without any possible means of obtaining food or clothing" on the island, and boats were unable to land with supplies. She had "no meat, nor meal, and but little flour," and was robbed twice more in January. Everything in her smokehouse was taken, along with her crockery, ironware, tin tea kettle, and tools. "The best of the people have left the I'd, the lazy and wicked ones remain," she confided to George Whipple. "I actually tremble not for my life but for my house now every night when I retire, they are *desperate*, and I know not what to expect next."[26]

James's only consolation was her young companion Jennie, but Jennie's father, having returned home from his stint in the army in mid-January, wished to take the child with him to the mainland. Although he greatly appreciated what James had done for Jennie, and wanted her education to continue, he did not want to leave the island without her. James was at her wit's end. "The child has been with me now two years day and night, in the house and out, sleeps near me, always goes out with me, has been my constant companion; and I have literally taught her not only while sitting in my house, but when I went out and came in; as I lay down, and rose up, and as I walked by the way," James wrote

George Whipple. "She is so accustomed to my feelings and doings," added James, "that she is of great use to me in my intercourse with the people, and is already beginning to impart religious instruction." Summoning up her best persuasive skills, James finally convinced Jennie's father to let Jennie live with her until the following summer.[27]

When some of her former students who had moved to the mainland invited her to move to their community in Tyrrell County and start a school, James pounced on the opportunity to continue her mission work there. So, on 14 February 1867, Elizabeth James said goodbye to Roanoke Island. In a brief reflection about her time on the island, she noted that she had endured "a complication of experience upon its evergreen shores." Nevertheless, she thought the work on the island had been worthwhile. "There have been many rejoicings there before the Lord and many souls have been born into his Kingdom; many, who, I believe will prove faithful and at last enter into the courts of the redeemed," she declared. She had "enjoyed much and suffered much," but departed "with less sorrow" than "she had anticipated," because she left few freedpeople behind her—they were "nearly all dispersed."[28]

By spring, affairs in the Roanoke Island colony were winding down fairly rapidly. The government had restored most of the land on which the colony had been situated to its former owners, and the colony's population had dropped to around five hundred. D. T. Bachelder and his daughter Ella, who had been teaching under the auspices of the New York Branch of the American Freedmen's Union Commission in one of the last mission schools on the island, asked to be relocated. The average enrollment at their school had dropped from a 130 to 50 and was still falling. Stephen Moore proposed that the Freedmen's Bureau officer on Roanoke Island "be entirely dispensed with" once the government property had been disposed. The island's lone Freedmen's Bureau officer, Hugo Hillebrandt, applied to have an office, two teachers' dwelling houses, three schoolhouses, two hospital buildings, a hospital dwelling house, and a bath house sold at a public sale. Hillebrandt observed that "the number of freedpeople has been so reduced, that there is no need of them." The freedmen's hospital, he added, had not been used since early February because the freedmen who remained on the island preferred being treated in their houses. Hillebrandt proposed that a schoolhouse and teachers' dwelling "be given to the freedmen remaining on the Island," because they were "not able to purchase the buildings to educate their children therein."[29]

In May, Brevet Major General Nelson A. Miles, the new assistant commissioner of the Freedmen's Bureau in North Carolina, issued the official orders to break up the Roanoke Island settlement. On 19 June, O. O. Howard indicated that he was requesting transportation home for some teachers in North Carolina who were still there teaching for the New England Branch of the American Freedmen's Union Commission. Included in the list was Mary R. Kimball, who wished to travel from Roanoke Island to Salem, Massachusetts. Presumably Kimball was the last missionary teacher to leave the island, since there is no further mention of any others. A few days after Howard's request, Hugo Hillebrandt notified the assistant commissioner's office that he was waiting for the printed advertisements of the government buildings to be forwarded. Although not particularly eloquent, Hillebrandt's simple statement said all there was to say about the status of the colony in June 1867: "I am here waiting and must say nothing to do, as in this place, there is no labor for me."[30]

Epilogue

REFLECTING ON her departure from Roanoke Island, Elizabeth James had noted that she "felt much sympathy for the white citizens," who rejoiced at the departure of the freedpeople. "Their island is, as they express it, 'ruined,'" she related, "the wood is cut off and nothing remains but the bright, glittering sand." According to oral tradition on the island, by the time the Yankees left, the devastation of the woods on the north end was so complete that residents on one side of the island could see laundry flapping on the other.[1]

Once the official occupation ended, the island's white natives, who had not been enthusiastic about either the Confederate or Union presence, swiftly set about to restore their accustomed way of life. Since the government had sold or moved most of the significant buildings, few physical reminders of the army's recent presence remained. And the islanders, who were used to foraging the trash they found washed up on local beaches, soon found many uses for what the Yanks had left behind. It is probably not mere coincidence that bricks, for example, started appearing in the foundations of some of the structures that were built on the island in the postwar period—bricks that had been part of the barracks chimneys and building pads, or part of the sixty thousand that composed the base of the steam sawmill. Between the harsh weather and the white islanders' determination to recapture their land, what remained of the freedpeople's primitive split shanties also soon disappeared. Meanwhile, the grand avenues and straight streets that had been carved out of the woods reverted to vegetation—overtaken by rapidly growing pines, turkey oaks, wax myrtles, and cypress. With time, even the outlines of the three major forts disappeared, as the west side of the island gradually eroded into the Croatan Sound.[2]

By the summer of 1867, most of the men, women, and children who had found asylum in the freedmen's colony had left the island. Those who were brought to the island after the fall of Plymouth had found passage to Bertie, Chowan, Martin, Perquimans, and Washington counties. Most of the others had returned to the nearby mainland where they had been slaves—areas in Camden, Currituck, Hyde, Pasquotank, and Tyrrell Counties. Although the postwar history of the freedpeople who returned to live on the mainland in northeastern North Carolina remains to be written, anecdotal evidence suggests that quite a few of them chose to work for their former owners as farm workers or sharecroppers. Some of the laborers were treated fairly, some were treated unfairly, and others were treated about as well as could be expected considering the impoverished condition of their employers. Although Horace James's vision of a society of black and white freeholders working side by side proved to be way off the mark, the freedpeople proved fairly resilient in fashioning their own communities once they returned to the mainland. They supported their own churches, and sometimes even their own schools. Free public education for blacks was not, however, readily available in rural northeastern North Carolina until the early part of the twentieth century.[3]

The Northerners who had helped to guide the direction of the Roanoke colony also went their separate ways after the war. The first post commandant on the island, the flamboyant Rush C. Hawkins, was mustered out with his regiment in May 1863. Although he saw no further service in the Union army, he was brevetted brigadier near the end of the war. He returned to New York and grew wealthy through real estate ventures. Well known for his interest in rare books, he authored several books on the subject, and his collection of printed materials from the fifteenth and sixteenth centuries rivaled a similar collection in the British Museum. After Hawkins was hit by a car and killed in New York City in 1920, most of his estate went to the Society for the Prevention of Cruelty to Animals.[4]

At the end of the war, Major General John G. Foster, the commander who issued the original order to colonize Roanoke Island, returned to service as an engineer in the regular army. Foster remained in the military until his death in 1874. Meanwhile, Brigadier General Edward A. Wild, the tempestuous general who first had charge of the organization of the freedmen's colony, was assigned to postwar duty as an officer of the Freedmen's Bureau in Georgia. After he was mustered out of the service in January 1866, he went into the mining business in the American West and South America. He died in Colombia in 1891.[5]

In the fall of 1865, Horace James resigned from his paid position with the Freedmen's Bureau. On 3 December, he entered into partnership with Eliphalet Whittlesey and another man to lease two plantations, Avon and Yankee Hall, in Pitt County, North Carolina, about twelve miles upriver from Washington. Like many other Northerners who were renting and operating plantations in 1866 and 1867, the men hoped to make a profit, and thus received their share of criticism for being carpetbaggers. In contrast to many of the postwar Northern entrepreneurs, however, James and Whittlesey hoped to carry out an "agricultural experiment," which would verify their ideas about free labor. Writing to the *Congregationalist*, James noted that he hoped to prove that blacks who would not work for their old masters or overseers who drove them "with the lash," would "cheerfully work for men who treat them like human beings, and pay them reasonable wages." Thus, on 1 January 1866, James and his wife moved to Avon Plantation, where he assumed the duties of resident manager. Whittlesey had, with O. O. Howard's approval, appointed James to be an unpaid citizen agent of the Freedmen's Bureau in Pitt County. Even though it was a fifty-mile journey to New Bern, James retained close ties with friends there, where he helped establish the First Congregational Church.[6]

For the first two months, everything seemed to be progressing splendidly on the two plantations, where James had also established popular day and Sunday schools for the laborers and their families. In early March, however, one of the black workers at Yankee Hall was caught stealing some clothes that had been given to James for distribution to the poor blacks. Instead of sending him to be tried in Washington or New Bern, James punished him by assigning him to dig ditches under an armed black guard. The prisoner escaped and was later shot and killed by Yankee Hall's white overseer, David Boyden. Illness prevented James from promptly filing a report with his immediate Freedmen's Bureau supervisor, F. A. Seely, but once he did, the matter seemed to be closed, as Eliphalet Whittlesey did not call for an official investigation of the fatal incident.[7]

Unfortunately, the case did not end there. In April, Generals James B. Steedman and Joseph S. Fullerton, whom President Johnson had appointed to "investigate" the Freedmen's Bureau, traveled through North Carolina looking for Freedmen's Bureau-related problems. Once they uncovered the Yankee Hall killing, they pounced on it as further evidence of the maladministration of the Freedmen's Bureau in North Carolina. They highlighted the incident in their final report, which many recognized as a blatant attempt to discredit the Freedmen's Bureau. More specifically, they accused Whittlesey of official malfeasance because of his monetary interest in the two plantations, and they blamed James for the shooting at Yankee Hall. Later that summer, Whittlesey, James, and a number of other officers were brought before courts-martial. Although the court did not go along with Steedman and Fullerton in condemning Whittlesey for having pecuniary interest in the two plantations, it did require General Howard to punish him for delaying an official investigation of the killing at Yankee Hall. Howard recalled his friend to Washington to work in the central Freedmen's Bureau office.[8]

Horace James was officially charged with misconduct in office because of his interest in the plantations and because he had authorized the shooting of an unarmed freedman. After hearing the evidence, however, the special military commission acquitted him of all charges. There was unanimous testimony that James cared for his employees. The judge advocate general's case report indicated that the trial had shown that the freedpeople on the two plantations were "well and humanely treated" and "promptly paid." The judge advocate general concluded that "nothing could be more clear" than that James was "most beneficial" to the freedpeople and "to the cause of free labor," and that his action "was in no respect in derogation" of his official duties.[9]

Vindicated, yet embittered by the proceedings and the amount of time it took to publicize the official report of the verdict, James returned to his work on the two plantations. The farms produced two hundred thousand pounds of cotton in 1866, and apparently did well enough for James to make contracts with the freedmen laborers for the following year. Failure of the cotton crop the autumn of 1867, however, led to the eventual termination of the Pitt County experiment in free labor; the Northerners gave up their lease on the plantations at the end of that year. Meanwhile, James's failing health—ongoing complications arising from his 1864 bout with yellow fever—and the birth of a daughter led him, that spring, to choose to move back to his beloved Massachusetts. James and his wife had buried eight children, including one who died in North Carolina, before having a healthy child, so he was very anxious about the survival of the new baby. He became pastor of the First Congregational Church in Lowell and associate editor of the *Congregationalist*.[10]

James's last two years in North Carolina had left him frustrated with Andrew Johnson's policies and disillusioned about the possibility that free labor would ever take complete root in the South. He no longer wrote passionately about establishing a "New Social Order," and he admitted that it might take "scores of years" for the South to be regenerated. In June 1867, when a friend asked him to pen an autobiographical sketch, he did not even mention his years of work with blacks in North Carolina. Dealing with the government had worn him out, and it never seemed to end. In July 1867 he received notification that Brevet Major General Robert Avery had accused him of misappropriating the steam sawmill at Roanoke Island. Ultimately, the charges were determined to be unfounded, but not before James had written a letter of explanation to Assistant Adjutant General E. D. Townsend. James noted that after consulting with Eliphalet Whittlesey, in the spring of 1866 he had sold the mill to M. C. Hubbard & Company for $5,000. That company had moved it "to the Neuse River some forty miles below NewBerne," where it was located at the time he wrote his letter. James emphasized that the mill belonged to a missionary association and had never been entered on the records as government property; furthermore, the proceeds of the sale went to destitute freedpeople. James then let loose a few lines of steamy prose. "I respectfully suggest therefore that the preferring of a charge and specification against me was wholly unnecessary," James countered, "and is a very poor requital of the services I have faithfully rendered to the Freedmen and to the Country through the whole war."[11]

In the next few years James turned to other mission fields. He helped to establish two overseas missionary organizations and assumed the pastorship of a church in Greenwich, Connecticut. Meanwhile, his health continued to decline. A lengthy trip to Southern Europe and the Holy Lands left him in a permanently weakened state. After his return to the states, he and his wife and daughter lived in Boylston, Massachusetts, in a modest cottage next to the home of his good friend John B. Gough, the noted temperance reformer. Although Horace James's critics had accused him of benefiting financially from his association with the Freedmen's Bureau, it is obvious that his own assessment—that he "entered the service poor and left it poor"—was more accurate. James died in Boylston on 9 June 1875, at the age of fifty-seven.[12]

Horace James's cousin Elizabeth James stayed on the mainland in Columbia in Tyrrell County for a year after she left Roanoke Island. Along with Lydia Stinson, she operated a day school and Sunday school, and held Sunday prayer meetings for a community of blacks and whites. From there she moved to Harrisonburg, Virginia, where she continued her mission work for the American Missionary Association in a school she named for George Whipple. She returned to Massachusetts in the late summer of 1870, and taught for many years in the Boston area. Elizabeth James died at the age of eighty in Taunton on 6 July 1900, as a result of a cerebral hemorrhage.[13]

After Ella Roper left Roanoke Island, she taught for several years at New Bern under the auspices of the NFRA. Then she renewed her affiliation with the AMA, which sent her to Macon, Georgia, in 1869. She stayed in Macon for about a year, operating the Lewis School. From there she moved to Wilmington, North Carolina, where she served as an AMA teacher until the spring of 1875. Roper returned to Massachusetts and taught in Worcester from 1876 through 1889. She died in Sterling, Massachusetts, in 1917.[14]

In the months before he left Roanoke Island, Samuel Nickerson thought that he and Profinda would probably continue their mission work elsewhere in North Carolina. The AMA, however, had other plans for them, sending them to Front Royal, Virginia. They operated the Front Royal School for nearly a year, and then, in the spring of 1867, the AMA transferred them to Harpers Ferry, West

Virginia, where they ran a school and also had their first child, a daughter. After their stint in West Virginia, they moved back to Vermont, where they had two more daughters. Profinda, who had suffered from health problems at various times on Roanoke Island, died on 27 March 1874, leaving Samuel with three young children. He remarried in May 1875, and the family moved to Colorado, where he continued his ministerial work and another daughter was born. After a lengthy career, Nickerson moved back to New England, where he died on 2 April 1930, in Lisbon, New Hampshire. He was ninety-four.[15]

Unlike the AMA missionaries, who continued to correspond with the AMA home office after their tours on Roanoke Island, the teachers sponsored by the other missionary societies on the island rapidly faded from public view. Perhaps some of them married, and no doubt some went to live with relatives. Others moved to new mission fields. Freedmen's Bureau records indicate that Sarah Freeman moved to Indianapolis, Indiana, but that is all that is known of her or her daughter Kate's whereabouts after 1866.[16]

Although most of the freedpeople who had lived in the freedmen's colony left Roanoke Island, a small group stayed and became the core of a lasting black community. This group was composed of blacks who had been born on the island and had moved into the colony after the battle, plus a few blacks from the mainland who had sought asylum in the colony during the war and chose not to return to their former homes. Most of the men had either worked for the Union army on the island or had served in the Union army as soldiers in the Thirty-fifth, Thirty-sixth, or Thirty-seventh USCT, having left their relatives in the sanctuary of the Roanoke Island freedmen's colony. After the war, some of the soldiers had served out the remainder of their service obligation on the Texas frontier near the border with Mexico—predecessors of the renowned "Buffalo Soldiers." They returned to the island in the fall and winter of 1866, only to find themselves up against an unfriendly military occupation that wanted them to move to the mainland. The former soldiers and their friends and relatives who had stayed on the island during the war stubbornly refused to leave. The island natives had very little knowledge of plantation labor and no interest in acquiring agricultural jobs on the mainland. Instead, they resumed their fishing, fowling, and small-scale farming on the island.[17]

Many of these men had already indicated that they were not adverse to raising their voices in protest of the military's treatment of their families in the freedmen's colony. This sort of awareness and social involvement continued in the postwar period. The freedmen who had petitioned the Freedmen's Bureau in December 1866 requesting that they be allowed to pay "reasonable rent" and remain upon lands that had been restored to white owners, were apparently given permission to stay, but they ran into further obstacles a year later. At that time they called a public meeting to air their grievances. At the meeting, held on 23 December 1867, sixty-seven men signed a petition to Colonel Charles Benzoni of the Freedmen's Bureau headquarters in Plymouth requesting that they once again be allowed to stay on the island until the shad season was over. The petitioners noted that they had received "orders to remove from the lands of I. C. Meekins and others," and that they would suffer greatly if they were "thrown out without shelter" in midwinter. They promised "to vacate every foot of said lands" in the spring. In a separate letter, they also noted that the military and the Freedmen's Bureau had told them that if they moved from the island, they could dismantle their houses and carry the lumber with them—"that the houses were our own property to do with as we saw fit." They complained that Isaac Meekins had, however, forbidden them to take down their houses or move them.[18]

A Freedmen's Bureau officer wrote to Isaac Meekins recommending that these freedmen be granted an extension until 1 June 1868. Whether the freedpeople vacated the property in question or stayed on it is not known, since the boundaries of the property were never clearly described. In September 1868, eleven of the petitioners jointly purchased a two-hundred-acre parcel of land on the west side of Roanoke Island from the heirs of Thomas A. Dough for $500. The description in the deed suggests that the property, which was south of the Isaac Meekins property and bordered by the Croatan Sound, might have been part of the land that the freedmen had mentioned in the December 1867 petition. In 1900, an official commission divided the property, which by then was known as the "California Tract," into eleven lots, equally distributed among the original claimants and their heirs and assigns, and the commission recorded its report in the Dare County deed books.[19]

In 1870, when the census was enumerated, there were approximately three hundred blacks living on the island, in sixty black households. In addition to the men who had purchased the tract in common, at least three other freedmen owned land on the island, bringing the total to fourteen—a remarkable achievement in the immediate postwar period. Forty-five of the sixty-seven men who had signed the 1867 petition, or 60 percent, were still living on the island, most with families. Furthermore, twenty-seven of the men who signed the petition, or 40 percent, were listed in the 1880 census, again most with families. Considering that some of the decrease from 1867 to 1880 could be attributed to deaths and some to faulty census enumeration, it is fair to say that the December 1867 petitioners and their families formed the nucleus of a stable postwar black community on the island. By 1900 over four hundred blacks lived on the island,

and there were at least a hundred black households. Approximately 65 percent of the black heads of household owned their own homes, most without any mortgage debt.[20]

Since detailed voting records for Dare County for the period just after the passage of the fifteenth amendment are not extant, it is impossible to know how many of the Roanoke Island freedmen participated in the electoral process in the postwar years. In September 1865, while still in a very chaotic and transitory state, the island's black community had sent two representatives to the Freedmen's Convention that met in Raleigh. One, Richard Boyle, was the black missionary teacher who had presented the islanders' petitions to the president in the spring of 1865. The other, Joshua Fleming, was not mentioned in any other documents related to the freedmen's colony. How these two men were selected to represent Roanoke Island is not known. Since the island freedmen had shown more propensity to handle issues in public assembly rather than through an organized system of self-government, it seems likely that they were chosen at a public meeting. Or perhaps they volunteered.[21]

J. W. Hood, minister of the A.M.E. Zion church of New Bern (Craven County), served as president of the 1865 Freedmen's Convention. He set the tone for the meeting by declaring that the watchword of the meeting was "equal rights before the law." Specifically, the freedmen wanted the right to testify in court, the right to serve on juries, and the right to vote. (There is no evidence that the Freedmen's Convention advocated legal rights for women, black or white.) The convention appointed a committee to relay its wishes to the state constitutional convention that was slated to meet in Raleigh the next week. All things considered, the meeting was rather moderate, even conciliatory, in tone; but the freedmen did make it known that their goal was definitely equal legal and political rights for black men in North Carolina.[22]

The island's black community did not send any representatives to the 1866 Freedmen's Convention, which also met in Raleigh. Meanwhile, the two men who represented Roanoke Island at the 1865 convention were not among the freedpeople who stayed to form a postwar African American community on the island. The actions of those who remained on the island in the latter part of the nineteenth century suggest that rather than focusing on the sort of political activity that the Freedmen's Convention represented, they concentrated on obtaining economic independence. Horace James believed that the two most important earmarks of the "New Social Order" were that the freedmen would own real property and the product of their own labor, two goals that were not completely met in the Roanoke Island freedmen's colony. It is worth noting, however, that the freedmen who ultimately succeeded in establishing a community on the island did so because they achieved both goals. By 1870, in addition to their attainments in landholding, many of the black men on the island had attained financial independence as self-employed fishermen, watermen, or farmers.[23]

In the 1870s, after the U.S. Life-Saving Service opened seven stations on the North Carolina coast, some of the island's black veterans found jobs as surfmen. Presumably, their military service helped them obtain these jobs, which ran from the beginning of September through the end of April, the most dangerous season for boaters along the coast, and provided a reliable source of income. Until 1880, the black men were usually assigned the lowest ranks in integrated or "checkerboard" life-saving crews. Although there seems to have been less prejudice against blacks on the Outer Banks than in other parts of North Carolina, some of the white surfmen did object to having to live in close quarters with black surfmen for eight months.

In 1880, Sumner Kimball, the general superintendent of the U.S. Life-Saving Service, appointed one of the black surfmen, Roanoke Island native Richard Etheridge, as keeper of the Pea Island Station. Etheridge was the soldier in the Thirty-sixth USCT who, along with William Benson, had written from the battle front in Petersburg to O. O. Howard complaining about conditions in the freedmen's colony in the spring of 1865. During the war, he had proved himself a leader; by war's end he had been promoted to the position of regimental commissary sergeant. After some transfers and a bit of recruiting by Etheridge himself, the crew of the Pea Island Station became the first all-black crew in the history of the U.S. Life-Saving Service. The six surfmen serving under Etheridge that first year included Lewis Wescott, William C. Davis, William Daniel, William C. Bowser, Henry Daniel, and George Riley Midgett. All apparently had familial connections to the freedmen's colony; four of them, and Etheridge as well, had signed the December 1867 petition requesting permission to stay on the island until the following spring.[24]

Although the Pea Island crew got off to a rough start—a suspicious fire destroyed the life-saving station the summer of the year that they commenced their duty there—they soon gained a reputation for being the fiercest and bravest crew on the Carolina coast. Perhaps their most dramatic rescue was of the people aboard the *E. S. Newman*, a three-masted schooner that wrecked just south of the Pea Island Station on 11 October 1896. A raging storm prevented the surfmen from building a platform on which to anchor the Lyle gun apparatus that they normally used to shoot a line to a struggling ship. Thinking quickly, Etheridge lashed two of the strongest surfmen together, gave them a line that was tied to the other surfmen on the shore, and watched as they swam through the treacherous sea to the schooner, picked up frantic ship-wrecked passengers, and returned them safely to the shore. As the first two men grew tired, they were replaced by other surfmen until the rescue was completed. The surfmen's efforts that day saved all nine on board, including a woman and child.[25]

Richard Etheridge's skills propelled him into a position of leadership in Roanoke Island's black community. Meanwhile, surfman George Riley Midgett became the first black justice of the peace in North Carolina, and one of the first black commissioners in Dare County. Several generations of descendants of the Roanoke Island freedmen served in the U.S. Life-Saving Service and its successor, the U.S. Coast Guard, creating a tradition that has persisted into the twenty-first century.[26]

The total population of Roanoke Island did not approach the total seen in the colony at its high point until the 1970s. By that time, the focus of the island's economy had shifted from small agriculture and fishing to tourism. Few people on the island—even the descendants of the colonists—knew much about the colony whose history, for the most part, lay buried in the documents of various missionary associations and in assorted record groups at the National Archives. The Dare County Regional Airport covered a large area that had been part of the colony, and residential developments dotted the remainder of the land on the north end of the island. Some local residents remembered stories of a black cemetery that was located just west of the entrance to the National Park Service's Fort Raleigh National Historic Site. Others had heard anecdotes about buildings or parts of buildings, said to be connected with the colony, that had been moved and renovated. Elderly black and white citizens interviewed for an oral history project in 1981 could give no significant details about the settlement. One woman recalled that her mother had told her stories of cooking for the Yankees after her escape to the island. Another interviewee reported that his great-grandfather had taken his grandmother and her brother from the Currituck mainland to the island to live in the colony with friends during the war. Unfortunately, none of those interviewed could provide any specifics about day-to-day life in the colony or its location.[27]

In the late 1980s several archaeologists conducted surveys of areas on the north end of the island and identified a few sites with probable Civil War connections. In 1991, North Carolina's Office of State Archaeology requested further evaluation of one of these sites, which was located partially in a tract of land slated to be developed into a residential subdivision, Heritage Point. The site was about 1,750 feet southeast of the island's Northwest Point, which juts into the Croatan Sound. During the war, the tract in question was owned by

Sarah E. Dough (widow of Thomas A. Dough), and was part of the property she applied to have restored after the war. Archaeologists from Coastal Carolina Research, Inc. (Tarboro, North Carolina) and Archaeological Research Consultants, Inc. (Raleigh, North Carolina) conducted their field research in April 1991. They concluded that the site appeared "to be the remains of a military camp from the Civil War occupation of Roanoke Island," most likely Camp Reno, the northernmost barracks area.[28]

This conclusion seems consistent with contemporary descriptions of the location of the camp and with Assistant Superintendent Hugo Hillebrandt's endorsement on Sarah Dough's application for restoration of her land. Hillebrandt recommended that her land be restored "under the condition that the buildings belonging to the U.S. Government shall remain on the land until disposed of." Sarah Dough also noted in her application letter, however, that freedpeople were living on her land, which raises some questions about the relationship of the freedmen's village to this property. Were the freedpeople on Dough's property the remnants of those who had lived in the barracks, in what became known as Camp Foster, or were they living in the northern fringe of the freedmen's village?[29]

During their fieldwork, the archaeologists recovered some artifacts, mostly glass and ceramic fragments, but their project report noted that the integrity of the site had been so seriously compromised by extensive relic hunting that it yielded scant information about the Civil War camp. The relic hunters had "removed items vital for the interpretation of the site, while destroying the context of the remaining artifacts." The pot hunting activity had "destroyed even the outlines of the features which were being looted." Thus, the archaeologists were not able to distinguish barracks areas or company streets. Likewise, it was impossible for them to determine if any of the freedpeople were housed in the military camp. After the archaeologists submitted their report, Rial Corporation/W. M. Meekins, Jr. commenced development of Heritage Point on the tract of land that included the site.[30]

In 1992, the Fish and Wildlife Service of the U.S. Department of the Interior proposed the building of a visitor center on a thirty-five-acre tract of land on the north end of the island just south of present-day Route 64 and approximately a half mile east of what is now called Weir Point. The property had been part of the land the Freedmen's Bureau restored to Tart Etheridge in 1867. Recognizing the potential historical connections, the Fish and Wildlife Service consulted with the State Historic Preservation Officer and then requested that an archaeological survey of that tract be taken. Once again, archaeologists from Coastal Carolina Research performed the research. During their field work in October

1992, the archaeologists uncovered four sites, including two with probable connections to the Civil War period. Unfortunately, relic hunters had also looted these sites, leaving very little behind but large and deep potholes. Based upon the artifacts that they were able to uncover, the archaeologists concluded that the two Civil War sites were likely associated with the military occupation or the freedmen's colony, noting that one of the sites might have been part of Camp Foster, the area of the freedmen's colony where the freedpeople lived in the old Rebel barracks.[31]

Again, this finding seems consistent with the extant historical evidence, which indicates that the colony's northern boundary was somewhere southeast of Fort Reno, which was located at Weir's (Weir) Point. As noted earlier in this book, the five northernmost streets in the colony's village were designated with letters, running southward from E to A, while the remaining streets were designated with numbers, running southward from 1 to 26. The lettered streets were probably the wide company streets, described by the soldiers, that had been laid out between the military barracks in the area that came to be known as Camp Foster. Since the streets were four hundred feet apart, this part of the colony would have extended southward at least seventeen hundred feet (including the widths of the streets)—even further if the land above E Street and below A Street were counted in the total. The Tart Etheridge property would have definitely been in this area of the colony. Whether it was inhabited by soldiers or freedpeople, or both, remains unclear.

Although the archaeological integrity of the Fish and Wildlife Service's property appears to have been destroyed by the looters, it is still possible that some artifacts that would help resolve questions about the freedmen's colony remain there. Coastal Carolina Research recommended that further extensive testing would be necessary to determine if the two possible Civil War sites would be eligible for inclusion in the National Register of Historic Places. To prevent disturbance of "deeply-buried isolated features or unmarked graves," the team advised that an archaeologist supervise the stripping of the land in preparation for the construction of the visitor center. The Fish and Wildlife Service has yet to build the proposed center.[32]

Along with relic hunting, environmental conditions and real estate developments on the north end of Roanoke Island make it increasingly less likely that much of the physical remains of the freedmen's colony will be unearthed. Although houses built on "acre" lots that had been laid out on the grid of streets and avenues that composed the freedmen's village were central to Horace James's plan for the colony, its legacy has proved to be much more subtle. The colony did not achieve permanent success, and at times, especially in the filthy, crowded barracks in Camp Foster, the former slaves endured conditions that were worse than what they had left on the mainland. The distribution of rations, ongoing until early 1867, clearly indicates that some of the colonists had a rough time of it. Domestic manufacturing, shad fishing, and small-scale agriculture never came close to meeting Horace James's expectations. Nevertheless, and despite many obstacles, including the absence of most of the able-bodied men, thousands of contrabands who arrived on the island with very little but the clothes on their backs made the transition to freedom. Many built and occupied houses that for the first time in their lives they could, at least for a while, call their own.

In hindsight, it is apparent that the "rehearsal for Reconstruction" that was carried out on Roanoke Island vividly anticipated some of the mistakes that were repeated in various locales during the Reconstruction era. Throughout the formal existence of the colony, the actions of the military authorities tended to promote a state of dependency among many of the colonists. While the army's Quartermaster's Department offered jobs to many former slaves who had never before had the opportunity to control their own labor, the army's failure to pay the workers mitigated most of the potential positive lessons of the free labor arrangements on the island. Colonists who became dependent on government rations remained powerless to achieve true self sufficiency. It is rather remarkable that some of the colonists—most especially those who built homes in the village—accomplished as much as they did. Once the war ended, President Johnson's amnesty proclamation erased any hopes of permanent ownership of the village homes and lots. Meanwhile, officers of the Freedmen's Bureau, who could have had a significant impact on the sort of labor arrangements that the freedmen negotiated with farmers on the mainland in the postwar period, seemed to have been much more interested in propelling the people off the island than effecting long-lasting social change.

In the long run, the missionaries' educational work in the colony was probably their most successful undertaking. Although the number of freedpeople who were able to attend school on a regular basis did not come close to being a majority of those who made the colony their home, many students were changed by their experiences in the missionary schools. Considering that just about all of the students in the colony's schools were former slaves who had been legally prohibited from learning to read or write, it is hard to escape the conclusion that the teachers made some contribution to literacy in northeastern North Carolina. The missionary teachers distributed hundreds of Bibles, which the people treasured. In addition, it is plausible to assume that the education offered in the island's missionary schools provided some people with the rudimentary ability to read contracts and protect themselves against injustice.[33]

A grounding in middle-class virtues and literacy (or semi-literacy) was not, however, sufficient preparation for prospering in rural North Carolina in the postwar period. It soon became clear that the experiment that had taken place on Roanoke Island was woefully inadequate in one important respect. Horace James had foreseen the predicament: the former slaves would never achieve true independence or status in an agrarian society until they possessed land. Lacking the financial resources to rent or purchase land, most of the freedpeople who had lived in the Roanoke Island freedmen's colony returned to the northeastern North Carolina mainland and were compelled to enter into labor or sharecropping arrangements with white farmers. Had the government been able to hold onto some land for the colonists, or make it easier for the colonists to rent or purchase land on the mainland, the situation of the freedpeople on the mainland in the latter decades of the nineteenth century would probably have been substantially different.[34]

Of course it is easy, from the perspective of the twenty-first century, to cast blame on a variety of easy targets—the Union army, the Freedmen's Bureau, President Andrew Johnson, and even the weather—for what went wrong in the Roanoke Island freedmen's colony. Perhaps the Northern evangelicals also deserve a share of the criticism. Had the evangelicals possessed a less ephemeral vision of what the freedpeople would need to succeed in the postwar South, their activities might have been more effective. "Work hard, save your money, and pray," might have been good advice, but it did not adequately address the practical problems that a newly freed but landless people would face in a racially conscious postwar South. And the Northern evangelicals did not even pretend to address social equality. They had always been much better at constructing theoretical arguments supporting the abolition of slavery and talking about their hopes for a regenerated, slave-free South than they were at envisioning what life for the former slaves would be after emancipation. Just as the military authorities had talked about a "contraband problem," the evangelicals rather consistently employed the singular when they wrote or talked about the "Negro's" future position in society. They had not contemplated the question outside of the abstract. The key question, how individual blacks would find their way in a white-dominated Southern society, escaped them. Although a few evangelicals stayed in the postwar South to work with the freedpeople, most moved on to other projects and other causes.[35]

Meanwhile, the island environment offered certain advantages to the small group of colonists who stayed on Roanoke Island. Most likely they were more successful than those who returned to the mainland at achieving financial independence in the immediate postwar period because many of the men supported their families through fishing and fowling—things they could do on their own without a lot of investment in equipment or land—instead of farming. Some of the former soldiers had saved some money from their time in service, and a number of them drew military pensions, but these factors are not enough to account for the widespread economic security of the island's postwar black community. No doubt the strength of the bonds within the black community and the relationships that the freedpeople developed with some of the sympathetic whites on the island also helped foster economic development. Tradition on the island holds that segregation was never as strict there as it was in other parts of northeastern North Carolina; blacks and whites struggled alike and sometimes even together to make ends meet. By the end of the nineteenth century, many of the industrious freedmen had bought real estate and erected their own homes on the island, had established their own businesses, and were supporting several churches, including one of the first A.M.E. Zion churches in North Carolina.[36]

The completely integrated utopian community envisioned by Horace James—"the abode of a prosperous and virtuous people, of varying blood, but of one destiny . . . a happy commonwealth"—never became reality on Roanoke Island, but some of the black men, women, and children who had fought for their freedom as Union soldiers, military laborers, or struggling colonists carved out a thriving community that became an integral part of island life. Descendants of some of the Roanoke Island colonists—island natives with names such as Berry, Bowser, Collins, Daniels, Etheridge, Meekins, Midgett, Scarborough, Simmons, and Tillett—continue to make vibrant contributions to the culture and livelihood of the island to this day.

APPENDIX A

Constitution of the American Missionary Association

Art. I. This society shall be called "The American Missionary Association."

Art. II. The object of this Society shall be to send the Gospel to those portions of our own and other countries which are destitute of it, or which present open and urgent fields of effort.

Art. III. Any person of evangelical sentiments,* who professes faith in the Lord Jesus Christ, who is not a slaveholder, or in the practice of other immoralities, and who contributes to the funds, may become a member of the Society; and by the payment of thirty dollars, a life-member; provided that children and youth, who have not professed their faith, may be constituted life-members without the privilege of voting.

Art. IV. This Society shall meet annually, in the month of September, October, or November, for the election of the officers and the transaction of other business, at such time and place as shall be designated by the Executive Committee.

Art. V. The annual meeting shall be constituted of the regular officers and members of the Society at the time of such meeting, and of delegates from churches, local missionary societies, and other co-operating bodies—each body being entitled to one representative.

Art. VI. The officers of the society shall be a President, Vice-President, a Recording Secretary, two Corresponding Secretaries, Treasurer, two Auditors, and an Executive Committee of twelve, of which the Corresponding Secretaries and Treasurer shall be ex-officio members.

Art. VII. To the Executive Committee shall belong the collecting and disbursing of funds; the appointing, counselling, sustaining, and dismissing (for just and sufficient reasons) missionaries and agents; the selecting of missionary fields; and, in general, the transaction of all such business as usually appertains to the executive committees of missionary and other benevolent societies; and its doings to be subject always to the revision of the annual meeting, which, by a reference mutually chosen, and whose decision shall be final, shall always entertain the complaints of any aggrieved agent or missionary.

The Executive Committee shall have authority to fill all vacancies occurring among the officers between the regular annual meetings; to apply, if they see fit, to any State Legislature for an act of incorporation; to fix the compensation, where any is given, of all officers, agents, missionaries, or others in the employment of the Society; to make provision, if any, for disabled missionaries, and for the widows and children of such as are deceased; and to call in all parts of the country, at their discretion, special and general conventions of the friends of missions, with a view to the diffusion of the missionary spirit, and the general and vigorous promotion of the missionary work.

Five members of the Committee shall constitute a quorum for transacting business.

Art. VIII. This Society, in collecting funds, in appointing officers, agents, and missionaries, and in selecting fields of labor, and conducting the missionary work, will endeavor particularly to discountenance slavery, by refusing to receive the known fruits of unrequited labor, or to welcome to its employment those who hold their fellow-beings as slaves.

Art. IX. Churches and other local missionary bodies, agreeing to the principles of the Society, and wishing to appoint and sustain missionaries of their own, shall be entitled to do so through the agency of the Executive Committee, on terms mutually agreed upon.

Art. X. No amendment shall be made in this Constitution without the concurrence of two-thirds of the members present at a regular annual meeting; nor unless the proposed amendment has been submitted to a previous meeting, or to the Executive Committee in season to be published by them (as it shall be their duty to do, if so submitted) in the regular official notification of the meeting.

*By evangelical sentiments we understand, among others, a belief in the guilty and lost condition of all men without a Saviour; the Supreme Deity, Incarnation and Atoning Sacrifice of Jesus Christ, the only Saviour of the world; the necessity of regeneration by the Holy Spirit; repentance, faith, and holy obedience, in order to [achieve] salvation; the immortality of the soul; and the retributions of the judgment, in the eternal punishment of the wicked, and salvation of the righteous.

[*Source*: *American Missionary*, inside cover of each issue]

APPENDIX B

Beliefs of the National Freedman's Relief Association, as Stated in Its First Annual Report

This Association originated at a meeting held in the hall of the Cooper Institute, on the 20th February, 1862, in response to an appeal from Gen. Sherman and Commodore DuPont, representing in a General Order, dated the 6th of that month, the helpless condition of the blacks within the vast area occupied by the forces under their command, and calling upon the benevolent and philanthropic of the land for aid.

At that meeting the following gentlemen:

Wm. C. Bryant	Wm. Allen Butler
Stephen H. Tyng	George C. Ward
Charles C. Leigh	Mansfield French
Charles Gould	Joseph B. Collins
Francis G. Shaw	Edgar Ketchum

John Edmonds,

were appointed to organize an Association, to make a special apeal to the public, to appoint suitable teachers to instruct the Freedmen in industrial and mechanical arts, in the rudiments of education, the principles of Christianity, their accountability to the laws of God and man, their relation to each other as social beings, and all that might be necessary to render them competent to sustain themselves as members of a civilized society:—

In pursuance of this appointment and of these instructions, the Committee met on the 22nd day of February, 1862, and organized the NATIONAL FREEDMAN'S RELIEF ASSOCIATION, declaring its objects to be as above stated, and requesting the co-operation and aid of Societies formed or to be formed in other cities, having the like purpose in view.

To attain the end proposed, so far as might be within the reach of the Association, the following plan, with regard to the treatment of the blacks, was adopted:

I. They must be treated as Freemen.

II. As such they must earn their livelihood as we do, and not be dependent on charity.

III. Their labor must be preformed under a well-organized superintendence.

IV. They will receive compensation for their labor, in the shape of daily wages, reserving thereout a sufficient percentage to defray the cost of superintendence.

V. As soon as their labor shall be organized, they will be required to provide their own support.

VI. In the meanwhile, and until their earnings shall provide the means of their support, they will be aided with food, clothing, and shelter, but such supplies shall be charged to them as advances, to be paid by the receiver, without interest.

VII. They may erect tenements on the land, and occupy them, free of charge, but when they occupy tenements erected or supplied by the Association, they shall pay rent.

VIII. Schools and churches shall be established among them, and the sick be cared for.

IX. No idlers will be allowed among them, but all must work who can.

X. Each one will be encouraged to raise on his own ground such articles of food as his family may require, and be so taught gardening as to raise quantities for the army and navy and other markets.

XI. To guard against imposition upon their ignorance and inexperience, no stores will be allowed among them except those licensed by the Association.

[*Source*: "First Annual Report of the National Freedman's Relief Association, New York, February 19th, 1863," American Missionary Association Archives, New York files, Amistad Research Center, Tulane University]

APPENDIX C

Horace James's Letter to the Public, 27 June 1863

New York, June 27, 1863

To the Public:

Four days ago, I was ordered by Major-General Foster, commanding the 18th army corps, to proceed northward as far as this city and Boston, TO COLLECT MATERIALS AND IMPLEMENTS FOR COLONIZING THE FAMILIES OF COLORED SOLDIERS UPON ROANOKE ISLAND.

It might have been done through other agencies, but not so quickly. Time is an object with us, that we may save a portion of the present season for crops and gardens, and gather together within a few days, the resources which might not have been secured by correspondence alone, in as many months. This is my apology to the public, if one were necessary, for being here.

The exigency now existing in the department of North Carolina, is this: We hold possession of several important places along the coast, the principal of which are *Beaufort*, *Newbern*, *Washington*, *Plymouth*, *Roanoke Island*, and *Hatteras Inlet*. At all these points we have troops, and from them our lines extend back some distance into the country. Within these lines dwell large numbers of loyal colored people, and but few whites. Eight thousand negroes reside at Newbern, and at the other points named several thousands more. It is among these people that Gen. E. A. Wild is now enlisting his African brigade. One regiment is already full, and another is well advanced. As the work goes on, it becomes a question of more and more interest what shall be done with the families of these colored soldiers? How shall we dispose of the aged and infirm, the women and the children, the youth not old enough to enlist in the regiments? In the absence of the able-bodied men to whom they would naturally look for protection and support, it is evident that the government, or benevolent individuals and agencies co-operating with the government, must make temporary provision for them, locate them in places of safety, and teach them, in their ignorance, how to live and support themselves.

The remedy proposed to meet this unique state of things, is to colonize these freed people, not by deportation out of the country, but by giving them facilities for living in it; not by removing them north, where they are not wanted, and could not be happy; nor even by transporting them beyond the limits of their own State; but by giving them land, and implements wherewith to subdue and till it, thus stimulating their exertions by making them proprietors of the soil, and by directing their labor into such channels as promise to be remunerative and self-supporting.

The location decided upon in which to commence this work, in North Carolina, is Roanoke Island. Its insular position favors this design, making it, like the islands around Hilton Head, in South Carolina, comparatively safe against attack, and free from fear of depredation. It is an island ten or twelve miles long, by four or five in breadth, well wooded, having an abundance of good water, a tolerably productive soil, a sufficient amount of cleared land for the commencement of operations, and surrounded by waters abounding in delicious fish.

The time in which to do this work, is the present. It is desirable not to lose a single day. Two months earlier, had circumstances favored, would have been better. That there may be no longer delay in setting the project on foot, and commencing to give it a practical development, an appeal is hereby made to all the friends of the NEW SOCIAL ORDER IN THE SOUTH, and in particular to those who believe that the solution of the negro question is the turning point of the war, for prompt and efficient help in the prosecution of our designs.

The materials required are the same which any colony, designed to be agricultural and mechanical, must need at the start, viz: boards and shingles, and a *steam-engine*, to saw our own lumber, and grind our own corn after the first few months, cross-cut saws and hand-saws, crow-bars, shovels, picks and spades, hoes, axes, hammers and nails, two or three sets of carpenters' tools, with extra augurs, squares, and gimlets; butt-hinges, screws, and latches; an assortment of garden seeds, padlocks, and door-locks, oil-stones and grind-stones, bush scythes, water-buckets, baking-kettles and covers, tin plates, cups, spoons, pans, and basins, knives and forks, files and rasps, coopering and soldering tools, glass and putty, fish-hooks, lines, and lead, and twine for seines, a pair of platform scales, and counter scales, and a quantity of tin and sheet iron, and tools to work it. All these we need this moment. And as the government has few supplies of this sort in the department of North Carolina, and of many of the kinds none at all, we are compelled to appeal to charitable associations, and patriotic individuals, to furnish them.

To clothe and educate these people we need quantities of clothing of all descriptions, particularly for women and children, with shoes of large sizes; primers and first reading books, primary arithmetics and geographies, with slates, pencils, and stationery of all sorts.

To present this subject personally to all interested in it, during the few days of my sojourn at the North, is simply impossible. Will not the ready good sense, and eager philanthropy of thousands of warm-hearted men and women respond to this appeal immediately, and place at my control within a few days all we need and ask for?

To fight the country's battles, is our *first* grand duty. *To lay new foundations* for a just and prosperous peace throughout the recreant South, is our *second*. For some time to come the two processes must be carried on *together*. Let us fight with our right hand, and civilize with our left, till the courage, the enterprise, and the ideas of the North have swept away the barbarism and treason of the South, and made of this country ONE GOODLY AND FREE LAND.

Send contributions in cash, clothing, shoes, instruments, and supplies of every kind needed, to the undersigned at *No. 1 Mercer street, New York*, (rooms of the National Freedman's Relief Association.)

HORACE JAMES,
Supt. of Blacks for the Dept. of N. Carolina

[*Source*: Horace James to the Public, 27 June 1863, Letters Received, Department of North Carolina, RG 393, pt. 1, ser. 3238, Box 2, National Archives]

APPENDIX D

Missionaries Who Served on Roanoke Island

Name	*Home*	*Sponsor*
David T. Bachelder	Potsdam, N.Y.	NYAFUC
Ella B. Bachelder	Potsdam, N.Y.	NYAFUC
Diana A. Belden	Eaton, N.Y.	NFRA
Elizabeth P. Bennett	Gloucester, Mass.	NFRA
Richard Boyle	Unknown	NFRA
Mary A. Burnap	Fitchburg, Mass.	AMA
Sarah A. Carr	Virginia	NFRA
Hannah W. Cole	Elizabeth City, N.J.	NFRA
Martha Culling	Unknown	NFRA
Kate S. Freeman	Maine	NFRA
Sarah P. Freeman	Maine	NFRA
Mary C. Gunn	Campville, Conn.	NFRA
Elizabeth James	Medford, Mass.	AMA
Mary R. Kimball	Salem, Mass.	NEAFUC
Helen E. Luckey	Sing Sing, N.Y.	NFRA
Robert Morrow	North Carolina	NFRA
Samuel S. Nickerson	Tamworth, N.H.	AMA & FWB
Profinda B. S. Nickerson	Tamworth, N.H.	AMA
Susan Odell	Biddeford, Maine	NFRA
Ella Roper	Templeton, Mass.	AMA & NFRA
Kate A. Shepard	Richfield, N.Y.	NFRA
Lydia G. Stinson	Barnstable, Mass.	AMA
Peter Vogelsang	Brooklyn, N.Y.	NFRA
E. A. Warner	Lowell, Mass.	NFRA
Lydia G. Warrick	Norfolk, Va.	NFRA
Esther A. Williams	Douglas, Mass.	NFRA
E. P. Worthington	Vineland, N.J.	NFRA

AMA = American Missionary Association
FWB = Free Will Baptists

NEAFUC = New England Branch of the American Freedmen's Union Commission
NFRA = New York Branch of the National Freedman's Relief Association
NYAFUC = New York Branch of the American Freedmen's Union Commission

[*Source*: This list was compiled from a variety of sources, including letters in the American Missionary Association Archives, as well as articles in *American Missionary*, the *National Freedman*, and *Freedmen's Advocate*. Spellings of names occasionally varied. This list features the most frequent spellings.]

APPENDIX E

Extant Lists of Freedmen Who Lived in the Roanoke Island Freedmen's Colony

No roster of the Roanoke Island colonists has surfaced. Given the constant change in the colony, it is not likely that one existed. The following documents do, however, include lists of some of the names of Roanoke Island colonists.

Report of Transportation Furnished to Freedmen, January 1866

Names	*Destination*	*Date*
Barbara Skinner	Edenton	January 1, 1866
M. Etheridge	Edenton	January 1, 1866
Priscilla Gordon	Edenton	January 1, 1866
Joshua Bond	Edenton	January 1, 1866
Owen Forbes	Edenton	January 1, 1866
Eda Forbes	Edenton	January 1, 1866
Owen Bartlett	Edenton	January 1, 1866
Matilda Bartlett	Edenton	January 1, 1866
Charlotte Granby	Edenton	January 1, 1866
Jane Dyer	Edenton	January 1, 1866
Nancy Sessons	Edenton	January 1, 1866
Smith Wilson	Edenton	January 1, 1866
Annie Wilson	Edenton	January 1, 1866
Jim Walker	Edenton	January 1, 1866
Betsey Walker	Edenton	January 1, 1866
Fred Granby	Edenton	January 1, 1866
Martha Granby	Edenton	January 1, 1866
Thos. White	Edenton	January 1, 1866
N. Shannonhouse	Edenton	January 1, 1866
M. Shannonhouse	Edenton	January 1, 1866
Henry White	Edenton	January 1, 1866

Names	*Destination*	*Date*
Martha White	Edenton	January 1, 1866
Ambrose Morcet	Edenton	January 1, 1866
Lydia Morcet	Edenton	January 1, 1866
Brace Bennett	Edenton	January 1, 1866
Mary Bennett	Edenton	January 10, 1866
Matilda Bennett	Edenton	January 10, 1866
Hardy Banks	Edenton	January 10, 1866
Hester Banks	Edenton	January 10, 1866
Jason Banks	Edenton	January 10, 1866
Albert Tucker	Edenton	January 10, 1866
Julia Tucker	Edenton	January 10, 1866
Ezekiel Baum	Edenton	January 10, 1866
Nancy Baum	Edenton	January 10, 1866
Sarah Baum	Edenton	January 10, 1866
Mary Etheredge	Edenton	January 10, 1866
Ogden[?] Midgett	Edenton	January 10, 1866
Sarah Midgett	Edenton	January 10, 1866
Lucy Tucker	Edenton	January 10, 1866
Mary Blane[?]	Edenton	January 10, 1866
Susan Goodrich	Edenton	January 10, 1866
Amanda Pugh	Edenton	January 10, 1866
Sampson Pugh	Edenton	January 10, 1866
Louisa Johnson	Edenton	January 10, 1866
Jack Johnson	Edenton	January 10, 1866
Jos. Wescott	Edenton	January 10, 1866
Mary Wescott	Edenton	January 10, 1866
Nancy Wescott	Edenton	January 10, 1866
Amanda Freeman	Edenton	January 10, 1866
Zack Meekins	Edenton	January 10, 1866
Nancy Meekins	Edenton	January 10, 1866
James Walker	Plymouth	January 15, 1866
Sampson Walker	Plymouth	January 15, 1866
Moses Turner	Plymouth	January 15, 1866
Nancy Turner	Plymouth	January 15, 1866
George Washington	Plymouth	January 15, 1866
John Randolph	Plymouth	January 15, 1866
Sue Randolph	Plymouth	January 15, 1866
Annie McClellan	Plymouth	January 15, 1866
James Sampson	Plymouth	January 15, 1866
Mary Sampson	Plymouth	January 15, 1866
Eva May	Plymouth	January 15, 1866
Lottie Ingalls	Plymouth	January 15, 1866
Amasa Wright	Plymouth	January 15, 1866
Nancy Wright	Plymouth	January 15, 1866

Names	*Destination*	*Date*
Alpheus Stevens	Plymouth	January 15, 1866
Pelina[?] Stevens	Plymouth	January 15, 1866
Jenny Trotman	Plymouth	January 15, 1866
Louisa Trotman	Plymouth	January 15, 1866
Jason Jones	Plymouth	January 15, 1866
Elijah Brown	Plymouth	January 15, 1866
Andy Brown	Plymouth	January 15, 1866
Nancy Brown	Plymouth	January 15, 1866
Orson Pratt	Plymouth	January 15, 1866
Jerry Eggleston	Plymouth	January 15, 1866
Henry Carson	Plymouth	January 15, 1866
Nancy Carson	Plymouth	January 15, 1866
Henry Jackson	Plymouth	January 15, 1866
Mary Jackson	Plymouth	January 15, 1866
Sam'l. Johnson	Plymouth	January 15, 1866
Chas. Loomis	Plymouth	January 15, 1866
Kate Loomis	Plymouth	January 15, 1866
Moses Manly	Plymouth	January 15, 1866
Sarah Manly	Plymouth	January 15, 1866
Hester Manly	Plymouth	January 15, 1866
Sam'l. Sutton	Plymouth	January 15, 1866
Eda Sutton	Plymouth	January 15, 1866
Amie[?] Doe	Plymouth	January 15, 1866
Henrietta Hardy	Plymouth	January 15, 1866
Penny Gordon	Plymouth	January 15, 1866
Rose Gordon	Plymouth	January 15, 1866
Ephraim Edwards	Plymouth	January 15, 1866
Hezekiah Edwards	Plymouth	January 15, 1866
Sally Edwards	Plymouth	January 15, 1866
Lacy James	Plymouth	January 15, 1866
Thos. Owens	Plymouth	January 15, 1866
Mary Owens	Plymouth	January 15, 1866
Albert Streeter	Plymouth	January 15, 1866
Mary Streeter	Plymouth	January 15, 1866
Hester Leech	Plymouth	January 15, 1866
Henry Moore	Plymouth	January 15, 1866
Thos. Anderson	Plymouth	January 15, 1866
Lovey Anderson	Plymouth	January 15, 1866
Lucy Stone	Coynjock	January 25, 1866
Sam'l. Jacobs	Coynjock	January 25, 1866
Mary Jacobs	Coynjock	January 25, 1866
Henry Chapin	Coynjock	January 25, 1866
Lydia Sprewell	Coynjock	January 25, 1866
Sampson Sprewell	Coynjock	January 25, 1866

Names	*Destination*	*Date*
Henry Proctor	Coynjock	January 25, 1866
Ellen Proctor	Coynjock	January 25, 1866
Hester Bradley	Coynjock	January 25, 1866
Mary Bradley	Coynjock	January 25, 1866
Susan Sampson	Coynjock	January 25, 1866
Enoch Small	Coynjock	January 25, 1866
Harrison Etheredge	Coynjock	January 25, 1866
James Baldwin	Plymouth	January 30, 1866
Annie Baldwin	Plymouth	January 30, 1866
Emma Ashby	Plymouth	January 30, 1866
Maria Ashby	Plymouth	January 30, 1866
Allen Bruce	Plymouth	January 30, 1866
Emona Buck	Plymouth	January 30, 1866
Henry Smart	Plymouth	January 30, 1866
Otto Smart	Plymouth	January 30, 1866
Lucinda Smart	Plymouth	January 30, 1866
Pelina Smart	Plymouth	January 30, 1866
Henry Hubbard	Plymouth	January 30, 1866
Tom. Hubbard	Plymouth	January 30, 1866
Penny Hubbard	Plymouth	January 30, 1866
Wm H. Harrison	Plymouth	January 30, 1866

[*Source*: Report of Transportation furnished to Freedmen during the month of January 1866, Cap't. Alex Goslin, A.Q.M., Roanoke Island, Records of the Assistant Commissioner for North Carolina, RG 105, ser. 2821, National Archives]

Freedmen Living on Roanoke Island Likely to Become Destitute during the Winter of 1866–1867

Names	*Children*	*Desired Destination*
Dorsey Sharp & Wife	7	Hertford County
Morning White		Perquimons County
Betsi Baxter	4	
Anis Simon	1	Hertford County
Joseph Reddick & Wife		Hyde County
Venus Banks	3	Pascotang County*
Charles Lewis & Wife	7	Hertford County
Marand Woodhouse	3	
Daniel Woodhouse & Wife	7	
Joshua Clement & Wife	4	Chowan County
Cesar Skinner & Wife	3	Perquimons County
Peter Brockett & Wife	4	

Names	*Children*	*Desired Destination*
George Neals & Wife	2	Onslow County
Bristol Fletcher & Wife	5	Perquimons County
Willis Mabin & Wife	5	Bertie County
Matilda Bastlett	2	
Lucy Small		
Judy Skinner	2	Perquimons County
Juda Hoskins		Edenton Town
Rachel Sauders		
Isaac Morner & Wife	1	Craven County
Osborn Harris & Wife		Pascotang County
Mills Cuningham & Wife		Edenton Town
Francis Wiggins	1	Martin County
Harriet Grey	1	Bertie County
Gordon Bryant & Wife	4	Bertie County
Edy Gillert	1	Bertie County
Rose Horton	4	Edenton Town
Harriet Tooler	3	
Lovey Weeks	1	Pascotang County
Daniel Pierce & Wife	3	Bertie County
George Idle & Wife		Edenton Town
Cherry Stevenson	3	Hertford County
Edward Wood & Wife	2	Loudon County, Va.**
Sauders Swan & Wife		Edenton County
Simon Cohns & Wife	6	Terrell County***
Lidy Capehart	2	Bertie County
Sam Capehart & Wife		Bertie County
Sindey Bacon	4	Hertford County
Cesar Smiddeck & Wife	1	Martin County
Nelly Williams		
Margaret Askew	1	
James Reespass & Wife	5	Washington County
Lidy Capehart	2	Bertie County
Axom Meeds & Wife	3	Edenton Town
Fred Spruel & Wife	6	
Nelly Armstead	1	Plymouth
Silas Sykes & Wife	5	Terrell County
Hester Sykes		Terrell County
Anny McCleary	1	Plymouth
Jenny Pierce		Plymouth
Caroline Griffin		Plymouth
Mary Watson		
Sam Welsh & Wife	4	Chowan County
Serena Granberry	3	Hertford County
Rhody Walker	3	Newbern

Names	*Children*	*Desired Destination*
Jenny Paxton	4	Edenton
Rachel King	4	Bertie County
Rebecca Wynne		Hyde County
Mariah Jennett	2	Hyde County
Nancy Sassons	6	Hertford County
Hester Easton		Bertie County
Edy Williams	1	Bertie County
Lucy Wilson	2	Bertie County
Esther Brown		
Mary Smith		Bertie County
Kate Reddick	1	Bertie County
Miles Baxter & Wife	2	
Sarah Bray	4	
Sarah Blont		Edenton
Annie Boston	4	Martin
David Skinner & Wife		Perquimons
July Granberry	2	Pascotang
John Rose & Wife	4	Eastern Maryland
Marianna Reddick	8	Bertie County
Mary Trotten	4	Camlin County****
Emilie Rogers		Camlin County
Esther Capehart		Bertie County
Harriet Butler		Bertie County
Rachel Small		Elizabeth City
Nelly Simpson		Terrell County
John Perkins & Wife		Elizabeth City
Ellen Perkins		Edenton City
Peter Cotton & Wife		Chowan County
Charity Reddick		Bertie County
Emma Gillem	2	Bertie County
Malvina Wood		Edenton
Jane Floyd		
Alfus Martin & Wife	6	Bertie County
Annette Soil	4	Elizabeth City
Julius Perkins & Wife		
Emma Peterson	1	
William Kelly & Wife	4	Hyde County
Marcer Jennett		Hyde County
Samson Simmons & Wife	8	
Petty Gillem	2	
John Walker & Wife	5	Perquimons County
Allen Trotter & Wife	8	
Amis Ashby		
Jasper Wilson & Wife	2	Camlin County

Names	*Children*	*Desired Destination*
Emmy Granberry	1	
Martha Cherry	1	
Mary Gaskins	1	
Lovey McKliss	1	Hyde County
Harry Bearley & Wife	4	Plymouth
Amy Bearley		Plymouth
Lewis Harrison & Wife	3	
John Cressy & Wife	2	Edenton
Tony Courtwright & Wife	4	Pascotang County
Major Trottman & Wife		Camlin County
Emilie Blont	1	
Penny Gillem	2	
Peggie Briton	3	Bertie County
David Elliot & Wife		
Lavinia Wynne	4	Edenton
Lavinia Sharp	3	Hertford County
Rachel Slide	3	Plymouth
Mike Wilder & Wife	1	Edenton
Salie Wilder		Edenton
Virgil Man & Wife	2	Edenton
Isaac Bright & Wife	4	
Harriet Whitby	3	Edenton
Harriet Skinner	4	Perquimons County
Mills Skinner & Wife	4	Perquimons County
Chadduk Newby		
Mariah Boyd		
Charlotte Chancey		
Mary Banks		
Lewis Lee & Wife	3	Perquimons County
Jack Lee & Wife	1	
Ellen Meekins	3	Elizabeth City
John Woodhouse	4	
Dolly Fereby	1	Camlin County
Lottie Skinner		
James Banks & Wife		Pascotang County
David Cherry & Wife	3	Bertie County
Gilbert Fletcher & Wife	2	
Mike Tucker		
Abby Snowden		Pascotang County
Hester Snowden	4	Pascotang County
Mariah Snowden	1	Pascotang County
Mary Dowdy		
Judy Alexander	4	
Sallie Howdley		

Names	*Children*	*Desired Destination*
Jennie Nixon	3	Wilson County
Harlow Lee & Wife	2	
Mahala Owens	3	
Jack Caps & Wife	2	
Serena Capehart		Plymouth
Stephen Hoskins & Wife	1	
Louise Tooler		
Stephen Skinner & Wife	6	Perquimons County
Emmy Boil		
Penny Spruel	4	
Millie Pool		
Elias Pool		
Sobrana Lee		
Daniel Lee	1	
Jesse Simmons & Wife	3	
Benjamin Ashby & Wife		
Edmond Morissey & Wife	1	Camlin County
Livy Gordon	1	
Ben Ryan & Wife	5	Bertie County
Royal White & Wife	3	
Sarah McPherson		
Mary Piner	2	Camlin County
Mary Harris	2	
Jonas Midgett & Wife	3	Hyde County
Maranda Simmons	3	
Mariah Long		
Mingo Spruel	1	
Jacob Whitby & Wife	4	
Franklin Lewis & Wife	5	Terrell County
Margaret Liverman	1	
Sylvia Cohon	2	Terrell County
Melinda Bowser	1	
Nancy Spillman		
Mary Brown		
Philip McDual & Wife	3	
Marianna Johnson		
David Blont		
Ida [?] Sharp & Wife	3	
Ming Wynne & Wife	3	Terrell County
Silas Wyatt & Wife	1	Plymouth
Annie Warf		Edenton
Fannie Pierce		Plymouth
Emilie Speller	1	Bertie County
Malvina Morning		Martin County

Names	*Children*	*Desired Destination*
Francis Morning		Martin County
Janie Fuller		Martin County
Alice Moore		Edenton
Hannah Downing	4	Plymouth
Peter Downing & Wife	2	Washington County
Perry Currell & Wife		Plymouth
Lirrie Garrett	2	Plymouth
Matilda Askew	1	Bertie County
Harriet Whiters		
Larey Peterson & Wife		Hyde County
Emiline Cooper		
Mike Gallup & Wife	4	
Grace Skinner & Wife	2	Perquimons County
Dina Davis	1	Pascotang County
Martha Alexander	2	Pascotang County
Abraham Gillem & Wife	1	Bertie County
Hannah White	1	Washington County
George Dough & Wife	2	
Jenny Fisher	2	Beaufort
Elizabeth Gregory	2	Bertie County
Burnette Hordley [?]		Chowan County
Margarett Ann		Martin County

* Pascotang County = Pasquotank County
** Loudon County, Va. = Loudoun County, Va.
*** Terrell County = Tyrrell County
**** Camlin County = Camden County

[*Source*: List of names of freedpeople living on Roanoke Island N.C. likely to become destitute during the ensuing Winter [1866–1867], Roanoke Island, Records of the Assistant Commissioner for North Carolina, RG 105, ser. 2821, National Archives]

APPENDIX F

Petitions from Freedmen Wishing to Stay on Roanoke Island, December 1866 and December 1867

The following letters were written by freedmen residing on Roanoke Island in December 1866 and December 1867. Both letters complain that the men and their families were being forced to leave the island, despite the freedmen's desires to pay rent or purchase lots. Since many of the correspondents' names show up on the 1870 and 1880 census reports, it is likely that many of these men and their families stayed on the island.

Old Resident Freedmen of Roanoke Island, N.C. to the Assistant Commissioner, Bureau of Refugees, Freedmen, and Abandoned Lands, December 4, 1866.

To the Assistant Commissioner,
Bureau Refugees, Freedmen
& Aband Lands, State of N.C.,
Raleigh—

Sir: The undersigned freedmen, old citizens of Currituck County, State of North Carolina, born and reared upon Roanoke Island, humbly complaining respectfully sheweth—

That there is a disposition on the part of those whose lands have been restored to them by Maj. Gen. Howard to do the undersigned and those for whom they act injustice—in that the aforesaid owners of lands refuse to allow the petitioners to remain upon the land so restored notwithstanding the fact that the undersigned offer to pay rent or express a desire to purchase lots.

As before stated, born and reared here, the undersigned know only how to make a living by fishing, fowling and "progging"—these being their means of support from their youth to the present day. They are not farmers: this is a sterile section, consequently, but little attention has been paid to agriculture. This being the case, the undersigned, if driven to the necessity of leaving their old home, around which cluster many pleasant recollections—would be able to earn but a poor living, being inexperienced laborers on a farm. The undersigned are sure that you will sympathize with them. They know not what to do in the matter, neither do they know where to go—indeed, they here ask whether they shall be made to leave their birth-place, merely to gratify the whims of men who are not well-affected towards the government of the United States.

They therefore ask that you will take such action in this matter as will insure the undersigned *justice*—protect them in everything they may do in a *lawful* manner, or rather, see to it, that, by paying reasonable rent, they will be permitted to reside where it is their wish to spend their days, and "when life's fitful fever's over," lay their bones to mingle with the dust of their childhood's home.

And your petitioners, as in duty bound, will ever pray, &c.

Joseph X Tillett	Ernest X Tillett
Jno. Franklin X Tillett	James D. X Midgett
Francis X Tillett Sr.	Sam'l X Midgett
Henry X Ashbee	Riley X Midgett
George X W. Bowzer	Edward X Wise
John X Tyler	Zachary X Taylor
George X Baum	Benjamin X Mann
James X Baum	Moses X Madre

For themselves and other old resident freedmen of Roanoke Island, N.C.
December 4th, 1866

[Marginal note: Witness to the marks of all petitioners Mr B. Gilbert]

[*Source*: Letters and Orders Received, Reports, and Supply Requests, Roanoke Island, Records of the Assistant Commissioner for North Carolina, RG 105, ser. 2821, National Archives]

Colored Citizens of Roanoke Island, North Carolina to Col. Charles Benzoni, Commanding Officer, Post of Plymouth, North Carolina [December 1867].

Col. Charles Benzoni
Comd'g Post Plymouth N.C.

The undersigned Colored Citizens of Roanoke Island N.C. having received orders to remove from the lands of I. C. Meekins and others respectfully request a short extension of time. It being midwinter and having to be thrown out without shelter, our suffering must be very great. Also the season for Shad fishing, an occupation which we nearly all follow for a living comes in direct conflict with said order we being constantly engaged in filling our nets, Boats, &c. If in your judgement you can show us a little leniency and give us till the middle of May or the first of June next, we promise faithfully and pledge ourselves to vacate every foot of said lands by that time. At a public meeting held on the 23rd Decr, 67 the following named Colored Citizens were appointed, viz.: Benjamin D. Midgett, Joseph Tillett, and Richard Davis, to wait upon you and set forth our [grievances] and pray you to consider our condition. Hoping you will show mercy towards us we do ever pray &c.

George Baum	W. F. Cobb	Leon Bembery
James Baum	Benjamin D. Midgett	Richard Davis
Richard Etheridge	John Wescott	Benjamin Mann X

Jeremiah Green X
George W. Bowzer X
Edward Baxter X
John Baum X
Dempsey Baum X
Fields Midgett X
Riley Midgett X
Jeffrey Baxter X
Henry Daniel X
Spencer Bowzer X
Benjamin Ashbee X
Stephen Mann X
Miles Tillett X
Adam Miller X
Isaac Daniel X
George Hayes X
Sampson Snowden X
Henry Martin X
Zachary Taylor X
Alanda Boyle X

Julius Perkins X
Dempsey Divers X
Samuel Midgett X
William Toodle X
Levi Tillett X
Mingo Spruill X
David Lindsey X
Luke Wise X
Pompey Woodhouse X
John Meekins X
Joseph C. Bowzer X
William Riley X
G. R. Midgett X
John Tillett X
Benjamin Midgett X
William B. Davis X
William Barnett X
Jeremiah Davis X
Edward Wise X

Joseph Tillett X
John Freeman X
James D. Midgett X
Harmon McCleese X
Francis Simmons X
Jacob Ashbee X
Henry Ashbee X
Jesse Simmons X
Frank Tillett X
Rowan White X
David Bowzer X
Robert Simmons X
Sam'l Etheridge X
Samuel Owens X
Wm Bailey Daniel X
Thomas Hill X
David Owens X
Francis Turner X
Aaron Turner X

[*Source*: Letters Received, Headquarters, Records of the Assistant Commissioner for North Carolina, RG 105, ser. 2452, National Archives]

Notes

ABBREVIATIONS

AMA	American Missionary Association
AMAA	American Missionary Association Archives, Amistad Research Center, Tulane University
DB	Deed Book
FSSP	Freedom and Southern Society Project, University of Maryland
M	Microfilm
MOLLUS	Military Order of the Loyal Legion of the United States
NA	National Archives
NFRA	New York Branch of the National Freedman's Relief Association (also known as the National Freedmen's Relief Association)
NEFAS	New England Freedmen's Aid Society
NYAFUC	New York Branch of the American Freedmen's Union Commission
OR	U.S. War Department, *The War of the Rebellion: A Compilation of the Official Records of the Union and Confederate Armies*, 128 vols. Washington: 1880–1901.
RG	Record Group
SHC-UNC	Southern Historical Collection, University of North Carolina at Chapel Hill, Wilson Library
USAMHI	United States Army Military History Institute, Carlisle Barracks, Pennsylvania
USCHA	United States Colored Heavy Artillery
USCT	United States Colored Troops
WB	Will Book

PREFACE

1. Stick, *The Outer Banks*, 161–67; Rose, *Rehearsal for Reconstruction*. Historians have not give the Roanoke Island freedmen's colony the attention it deserves. J. G. de Roulhac Hamilton's *Reconstruction in North Carolina* (New York: Columbia University Press, 1914), the classic treatment of postwar North Carolina, briefly mentions the Roanoke colony. Showing very little sympathy for the plight of the freedmen and even less for the Northern

missionary teachers and Freedmen's Bureau officers, Hamilton notes that blacks were "so well satisfied with government support" that they did not want to leave the island. Henry Lee Swint's *The Northern Teacher in the South, 1862–1870* (1941), the first study to focus exclusively on the work of Northern missionary teachers, included references to some of the Roanoke Island teachers and their work on the island. Although Swint's treatment of teachers was slightly more charitable than what is found in Hamilton's study, he blamed the Southern opposition to freedmen schools on the Northern teachers' arrogance in attempting to make a New England of the South. Swint highlighted the way the teachers tried to use their classrooms to turn their charges into Republican voters and implied that much of the work of the teachers and other agents of the missionary associations was prompted by economic or political motivations, conclusions not borne out by the evidence pertinent to the Roanoke Island teachers. The same year that Swint's book appeared, Wilbur J. Cash also castigated the Northern teachers in his book, *The Mind of the South* (1941). According to Cash, the typical teacher, "horsefaced, bespectacled and spare of frame," was a meddlesome character "playing with explosive forces she did not understand." Several years after Cash's book appeared, George Bentley, one of the first modern historians to attempt to write a comprehensive history of the Freedmen's Bureau, referred to the Roanoke colony in passing when discussing the background to the establishment of the Bureau. Bentley's *A History of the Freedmen's Bureau* (1944, 1974) was generally very critical of abolitionists and missionary teachers. His discussion of Horace James's work on Roanoke Island was sketchy and a bit muddled, and at one point he confused New Bern's Trent River camp with the colony on Roanoke Island. Nearly twenty years after Bentley's history, John G. Barrett's comprehensive study, *The Civil War in North Carolina* (1963), briefly mentioned the freedmen on Roanoke Island. Barrett stated that a number of slaves had escaped to the island after the battle there, and that by war's end, the island "was dotted with Negro settlements." Barrett focused, however, on the battles and skirmishes that took place in North Carolina, not on what happened afterward. A decade after the publication of Barrett's book, Louis Gerteis's *From Contraband to Freedman: Federal Policy Toward Southern Blacks, 1861–1865* (1973) mentioned the colony in the context of his discussion of federal policy toward the freedmen during the war. Gerteis correctly made the distinction between "a rather shabby contraband camp" on the north end of the island and the village that freedmen superintendent Horace James had laid out for the freedmen. He was mistaken, however, in stating that the village was on the south end of the island—a conclusion that is not supported by either primary sources or geography (wetlands). In *A Right to the Land: Essays on the Freedmen's Community* (1977), Edward Magdol was interested in the way the freedmen created their own communities at contraband camps in spite of great difficulties. He discussed the failure of the Roanoke Island colony's experiment in self government, which he blamed on the colony's superintendent, Horace James. More recently, Joe A. Mobley's *James City: A Black Community in North Carolina, 1863–1900* (1981) discussed the Roanoke Island colony in the context of Horace James's work in and around New Bern.

2. Jones, *Soldiers of Light and Love*, especially 14–48.

3. My model for this sort of narrative is a Civil War history that I greatly admire, James M. McPherson's *Battle Cry of Freedom* (1988).

4. Ella Roper to Rev. George Whipple, 31 May [1864], AMAA, N.C. Letters in the AMA Archives are grouped by state of origin. Then, within each state's files, the letters are

organized chronologically. To aid researchers who might be interested in finding the letters cited in this book, I have noted the state of origin for each letter cited. The letter cited in this note, for example, will be found in the North Carolina file.

INTRODUCTION

1. Elizabeth James to Mr Whipple, 19 December 1863, AMAA, N.C.

2. This summary is based on the discussion of the establishment of federal occupations in Berlin et al., *The Wartime Genesis of Free Labor: The Upper South*, 18.

3. General Benjamin Butler's policy and the precedent it set for settlements such as the one at Roanoke Island will be discussed later in this book, in Chapter 2.

4. *U.S. Statutes at Large* 12 (1859–1863): 820 and 13 (1863–1865): 375, cited in Hamilton, *Reconstruction in North Carolina*, 295.

5. Berlin et al., *The Wartime Genesis of Free Labor: The Upper South*, 31.

6. The Freedmen and Southern Society Project's work on contraband camps is documented in Berlin et al., *The Wartime Genesis of Free Labor: The Lower South* and *The Wartime Genesis of Free Labor: The Upper South*. For a brief overview of various contraband camps, see *The Wartime Genesis of Free Labor: The Upper South*, 30–32, 41–43, 62–63. Poor record keeping, coupled with the transience of the contraband/freedmen population, makes it difficult to estimate how many former slaves lived in contraband camps during the war and in the immediate postwar period.

7. See Berlin et al., *The Wartime Genesis of Free Labor: The Lower South*, 350–51.

8. The introductory essays in Berlin et al., *The Wartime Genesis of Free Labor: The Lower South*, 1–83, and *The Wartime Genesis of Free Labor: The Upper South*, 1–82, present excellent overviews of the freedpeople's situation during wartime. For a long time after Reconstruction, historians interested in the period either ignored the contraband camps completely or dismissed them as examples of Northern carpetbagging.

9. Rose, *Rehearsal for Reconstruction*, especially 63–103, 217–41. Although Rose presents an excellent introduction to the relief and educational work in the contraband camps, she focuses on the free labor experiment that took place on the plantations. See also Berlin et al., *The Wartime Genesis of Free Labor: The Upper South*, 12–13, and Berlin et al., *The Wartime Genesis of Free Labor: The Lower South*, 88–89.

10. Berlin et al., *The Wartime Genesis of Free Labor: The Lower South*, 621–27.

11. Walker, "Corinth: The Story of a Contraband Camp," 5–22. See also Berlin et al., *The Wartime Genesis of Free Labor: The Lower South*, 628.

12. Walker, "Corinth: The Story of a Contraband Camp," 22; Hermann, *Pursuit of a Dream*, 37–60. The main focus of Hermann's book is the utopian community built by Benjamin Montgomery, a former slave of Joseph Davis, on Davis lands after the war. See also Berlin et al., *The Wartime Genesis of Free Labor: The Lower South*, 647–48.

13. Engs, *Freedom's First Generation*, 25–65. See also Berlin et al., *The Wartime Genesis of Free Labor: The Upper South*, 87–97.

14. Berlin et al., *The Wartime Genesis of Free Labor: The Upper South*, 243–44.

15. Berlin et al., *The Wartime Genesis of Free Labor: The Upper South*, 244–47; Ash, *When the Yankees Came*, 155; Leech, *Reveille in Washington*, 246; Green, *Washington: Village and Capital*, 280–81.

16. Berlin et al., *The Wartime Genesis of Free Labor: The Upper South*, 248, 255; Leech, *Reveille in Washington*, 246–49. Despite the dreadful conditions in Camp Barker, most of the residents resisted the forced move across the Potomac into Virginia.

17. Berlin et al., *The Wartime Genesis of Free Labor: The Upper South*, 254–58; Reidy, " 'Coming from the Shadow of the Past,' " 411–15. Colonel Greene appointed Danforth Nichols to be superintendent of Freedmen's Village, despite his apparent inability to get along with the contrabands.

18. As noted in the Preface, Jacqueline Jones's *Soldiers of Light and Love* was one of the first of this recent crop of scholarship. Her approach to the historical records and her insights into the evangelical context of the missionary work among the Southern freedpeople of Georgia established a framework that is still emulated in current studies. In the decade following the publication of Jones's study, several scholars contributed to this growing field of scholarship in the area. Allis Wolfe focused on the Northern teachers' motivation and work, while Joe M. Richardson presented a thoughtful overview of the American Missionary Association and its work in the South from the beginning of the Civil War until the latter part of the nineteenth century, and Maxine Deloris Jones examined the life and labors of the Northern teachers who labored in North Carolina under the sponsorship of the American Missionary Association. See Wolfe, "Women Who Dared: Northern Teachers of the Southern Freedmen, 1862–1872" (Ph.D. diss., 1982); Richardson, *Christian Reconstruction: The American Missionary Association and Southern Blacks, 1861–1890* (1986); and Jones, " 'A Glorious Work': The American Missionary Association and Black North Carolinians, 1863–1880" (Ph.D. diss., 1982). Ronald E. Butchart and Robert C. Morris both focused on the intentions and limited successes of the freedmen's teachers' educational work in the South. Both also provided some insight into the backgrounds and attitudes of the missionary teachers. See Butchart, *Northern Schools, Southern Blacks, and Reconstruction: Freedmen's Education, 1862–1875* (1980); and Morris, *Reading, 'Riting, and Reconstruction: The Education of Freedmen in the South, 1861–1870* (1981). Other significant scholarly studies include Nancy Smith Linthicum, "The American Missionary Association and North Carolina Freedmen, 1863–1868" (Master's thesis, 1977); Sandra E. Small, "The Yankee Schoolmarm in Freedmen's Schools: An Analysis of Attitudes" (1979); Robert H. Bremner, *The Public Good: Philanthropy and Welfare in the Civil War Era* (1980); Sylvia D. Hoffert, "Yankee Schoolmarms and the Domestication of the South" (1985); James D. Anderson, *The Education of Blacks in the South, 1860–1935* (1988); Ronald E. Butchart, "Recruits to the 'Army of Civilization': Gender, Race, Class, and the Freedmen's Teachers, 1862–1875" (1990); and Julie Roy Jeffrey, *The Great Silent Army of Abolitionism: Ordinary Women in the Antislavery Movement* (1998).

19. Soper, *Evangelical Christianity*, 46–47; DeBoer, *Be Jubilant My Feet*, 14. Charles C. Cole Jr. was one of the first historians to focus on the ideas of Northern evangelicals as a backdrop to the Civil War. Although Cole's study is a bit dated, his discussion of the ideas of Northern evangelicals offers much that is still valuable for understanding the evangelicals and their social agenda in the antebellum period. See *The Social Ideas of the Northern Evangelists, 1826–1860* (1954), 220. In the 1960s, James M. McPherson helped to turn more attention to the role that abolitionists played in the years leading to the Civil War. More recently, Victor B. Howard and Curtis D. Johnson have provided enlightening analyses of

the relationship between Northern evangelicalism and the coming of the Civil War. See James M. McPherson, *The Struggle for Equality: Abolitionists and the Negro in the Civil War and Reconstruction* (1964); Victor B. Howard, *Religion and the Radical Republican Movement, 1860–1870* (1990); and Curtis D. Johnson, *Redeeming America: Evangelicals and the Road to Civil War* (1993).

20. Robert A. Wauzzinski presents an intriguing overview of the relationship of nineteenth-century evangelicalism, republicanism, and industrialism in *Between God and Gold: Protestant Evangelicalism and the Industrial Revolution, 1820–1914* (1993).

21. George M. Fredrickson's superb discussion of "Race and Reconstruction" is still the clearest discussion of the paradox of the humanitarians' racism that I have read. See Fredrickson, *The Black Image*, 165–97.

22. James, *Annual Report*, 3.

23. Ibid., 3–4. James indicated great concern about the small amount of land that the Union controlled in eastern North Carolina.

24. Ibid., 3–4.

25. Mobley, *James City*, 23–25; James, *Annual Report*, 6–8.

26. James, *Annual Report*, 7–8; Horace James to Lieut. Fred H. Beecher, 20 September 1865, Letters Received, Headquarters, Records of the Assistant Commissioner for North Carolina, RG 105, ser. 2453, NA (M843, reel 8); Mobley, *James City*, xii, 92–94.

27. The significance of the difference between a "camp" and a "colony," as well Horace James's ideas related to the permanence of the Roanoke Island freedmen's colony, will be discussed in detail later in the book.

28. James, *Annual Report*, 21; J. M. Tuttle to Hon. Edwin M. Stanton, 18 September 1862, and Edwin M. Stanton to Brigadier-General Tuttle, 18 September 1862, OR, ser. 3, vol. 2, 569; John A. Dix to Hon. E. M. Stanton, 12 September 1862, OR, ser. 1, vol. 18, 391; P. H. Watson to Gen. John A. Dix, 19 September 1862, OR, ser. 1, vol. 18, 395; Berlin et al., *The Wartime Genesis of Free Labor: The Upper South*, 28–29. For a concise but thorough discussion of colonization policy, see Fredrickson, "Prejudice and Reformism: The Colonization Ideal and the Abolitionist Response, 1817–1840," in *The Black Image*, 1–42.

29. Horace James to the Public, 27 June 1864, Letters Received, Department of North Carolina, RG 393, pt. 1, ser. 3238, NA; James, *Annual Report*, 7, 23–24. For the most explicit statement of Horace James's beliefs about the postwar permanence of the Roanoke Island freedmen's colony, see Horace James to Gen'l E. A. Wilde, 16 March 1864, Edward A. Wild Papers, MOLLUS-Massachusetts Collection, USAMHI. Horace James's hopes for the permanence of the colony will be discussed later in the book, especially in Chapter 7.

30. James, *Annual Report*, 33–34; Horace James to the Public, 27 June 1864, Letters Received, Department of North Carolina, RG 393, pt. 1, ser. 3238, NA.

31. For a statement of Horace James's views about equality, see "Letter from Chaplain James," 19 August 1864, *Congregationalist* 16 (2 September 1864): 142. For a brief statement of Benjamin Butler's views of equality, see "Gen. Butler at Lowell," *National Anti-Slavery Standard* 22 (24 January 1863).

32. Hale, "Some Notes on Roanoke Island and James River," 53; *Second Annual Report*, 29.

33. Gavins, "A 'Sin of Omission,'" in Crow and Hatley, *Black Americans*, 28.

1. The Bowsers were free in 1860; the 1860 census recorded that Benjamin was a mulatto, while Director was black. In 1870, Peter Gallop recorded that both Bowsers were black, that Benjamin was engaged in fishing, and that he owned real property worth $50. In 1870, the Bowsers lived across the sound from Roanoke Island, most likely on Colington Island. Burnside and the three other children in the household were probably grandchildren, since the census information indicated that both adult Bowsers were over sixty years old in 1870. Peter Gallop lived with his wife and daughter on Roanoke Island on real property worth $150; he listed his occupation as fishing. See Federal Census, Population Schedules, Free Inhabitants, North Banks, Currituck County, N.C., 1860; and Nags Head Township, Dare County, N.C., 1870. (In 1870, Dare County was formed from part of Currituck County. That year, Roanoke Island was part of the Nags Head Township.)

2. Barrett, *Civil War in North Carolina*, 15–16, 25, 64, 73.

3. Ibid., 74, 80; McConnell, *Remember Reno*, 42–55; Report of Brig. Gen. Henry A. Wise, 21 February 1862, OR, ser. 1, vol. 9, 129. For a succinct overview of the Battle of Roanoke Island, see Mallison, *The Civil War on the Outer Banks*, 63–86; Sauers, "General Ambrose E. Burnside's 1862 North Carolina Campaign," 228–58; and Luvaas, "Burnside's Roanoke Island Campaign," 4–11, 43–48. For contemporary discussions of the battle, see *Frank Leslie's Illustrated Newspaper* 13 (1 March 1862): 225–26, and 13 (8 March 1862): 251; and *Harper's Weekly* 6 (1 March 1862): 135.

4. Quoted in Emmerton, *Twenty-Third Regiment*, 60.

5. *Congregationalist* 14 (14 February 1862): 27; Burnside, *Burnside Expedition*, 25; Hawkins, "Early Coastal Operations in North Carolina," 645–54. For more recent assessments of the significance of the Union victory, see Foote, *Civil War: A Narrative*, 1:230–32; Nevins, *War for the Union*, 2:90; Elmore, "Military and Naval Operations," 1–25; Peacock, "The Roanoke Island Campaign of 1862"; and McPherson, *Battle Cry of Freedom*, 372–73.

6. Putnam, *Story of Company A*, 72.

7. Derby, *Bearing Arms*, 56; Williams, "The Surroundings and Site at Raleigh's Colony," 58; *National Anti-Slavery Standard* 24 (27 February 1864). In 1864, Edward Everett Hale, who was very interested in determining the location of Raleigh's colony, discussed the relationship of the Union camps to the lost colony. Hale concluded that maps seemed to indicate that Ralph Lane's fort was north of the Union camps. See Hale, "Some Notes on Roanoke Island and James River," 53. Today many archaeologists and historians believe that the fort purported to be the lost colony's fort was actually a fort that had been built during a seventeenth-century engagement.

8. *Frank Leslie's Illustrated Newspaper* 13 (8 February 1862): 182; Federal Census, Population Schedules, Free Inhabitants, Roanoke Island, Currituck County, N.C., 1860; Federal Census, Population Schedules, Slave Inhabitants, Roanoke Island, Currituck County, N.C., 1860. The free black heads of households were Victoria Bowser, a seine knitter; Daffany Bowser, a washerwoman; and Spencer Bowser, a fisherman. The census enumerator indicated that Victoria Bowser was a twenty-eight-year-old mulatto; three Bowser children, aged one, four, and six, lived with her. Daffany Bowser, reported as a forty-year-old mulatto, lived by herself. Spencer Bowser, classified as black, headed a household that included his wife and two children, who were all reported as mulatto.

9. Parker, *Stealing a Little Freedom*, 21; "The Emancipated North Carolinians," 1 January 1862, *National Anti-Slavery Standard* 22 (25 January 1862). The advertisement, for two slaves who had escaped from Abel Ashbee and Abraham Baum, was found in Edenton's *Star Gazette of North Carolina* in July 1791. The absence of advertisements for runaways might be interpreted as an indication that the island's slaves were content. It is also possible that the islanders did not advertise in regional or state newspapers for runaways. Since the *National Anti-Slavery Standard* was the official journal of the American Anti-Slavery Society, it is likely that the writer of the article about the runaways on Hatteras was not an unbiased observer.

10. Johnson, *The Long Roll*, 70, 100–101. Johnson recorded that Ben was owned by a North Carolinian whose sons were with the Confederate army on Roanoke Island; supposedly, Ben was one of the son's body servants. The similarities to the Ben Tillett described in the *National Anti-Slavery Standard* are, however, striking, and suggest that Johnson might have gotten the story wrong.

11. Woodbury, *Major General Ambrose E. Burnside and the Ninth Army Corps*, 33; Moore, *Rebellion Record*, 4:100; Chenery, *Reminiscences*, 24; Burnside, *Burnside Expedition*, 24; Derby, *Bearing Arms*, 52. Robinson's owner on Roanoke Island was Joseph M. Daniel[s].

12. Johnson, *The Long Roll*, 97–98; Elmore, "Military and Naval Operations," 8–9; Walcott, *History of the Twenty-first*, 27.

13. Moore, *Rebellion Record*, 4:95; Derby, *Bearing Arms*, 69; Putnam, *Story of Company A*, 94; Lind, *The Long Road for Home*, 53; Parker, *History of the 51st*, 83–86; J. W. Wright Diary, 9 February 1862, Murdock-Wright Papers, SHC-UNC, quoted in Barrett, *Civil War in North Carolina*, 91 n.

14. Parker, *History of the 51st*, 87–88; Emmerton, *Twenty-Third Regiment*, 55. See also Roe, *Twenty-Fourth Regiment*, 72; Colyer, *Report of the Christian Mission*, 13.

15. Sauers, "General Ambrose E. Burnside's 1862 North Carolina Campaign," 249; Woodbury, *Major General Ambrose E. Burnside*, 51.

16. Battery Russell honored Colonel Charles L. Russell of the 10th Connecticut regiment, while Battery Monteil paid homage to Lieutenant-Colonel Vigeur DeMonteil of the D'Epeneuil Zouaves. Graham, *Ninth Regiment New York*, 166–67.

17. Emmerton, *Twenty-Third Regiment*, 53; Putnam, *Story of Company A*, 80; Moore, *Rebellion Record*, 4:107; Redkey, *A Grand Army*, 17; Loving, "Civil War Letters of George Washington Whitman from North Carolina," 77.

18. C. Bayard Springer Diary, SHC-UNC; Johnson, *The Long Roll*, 108; Graham, *Ninth Regiment New York*, 166; Lautzenheiser and Hargrove, " 'The Bright Glittering Sand,' " 79.

19. Emmerton, *Twenty-Third Regiment*, 54; Valentine, *Story of Co. F*, 46; Roe, *Twenty-Fourth Regiment*, 63, 76–77; Denny, *Wearing the Blue*, 78; William J. Creasey Diary, SHC-UNC.

20. Roe, *Twenty-Fourth Regiment*, 412; Day, *My Diary of Rambles*, 39; Woodbury, *Major General Ambrose E. Burnside*, 51–52; Derby, *Bearing Arms*, 77; Jackman, *History of the Sixth*, 35; Emmerton, *Twenty-Third Regiment*, 112; William J. Creasey Diary, SHC-UNC; Lautzenheiser and Hargrove, " 'The Bright Glittering Sand,' " 47.

21. Graham, *Ninth Regiment New York*, 193–200; 234; Whitney, *The Hawkins Zouaves*, 110–11. According to Graham, the Ninth New York left Roanoke Island on 10 July, sailing for Norfolk.

22. Graham, *Ninth Regiment New York*, 227.

23. J. T. Galloupe to Dr. Snelling, 24 August 1862, Letters Received, Department of North Carolina, RG 393, pt. 1, ser. 3238, NA.

24. Emmerton, *Twenty-Third Regiment*, 112.

25. Deposition for Invalid Pension, 25 March 1902, William H. Overton, Pension Papers, RG 94, NA; W. Gwynn to "Citizens of Currituck County," 9 June 1861, RG 109, NA, quoted in Barrett, *Civil War in North Carolina*, 33; Walcott, *History of the Twenty-first*, 37.

26. John S. C. Abbott, "Heroic Deeds of Heroic Men," 8; Graham, *Ninth Regiment New York*, 230; Colyer, *Brief Report*, 4.

27. William J. Creasey, Diary, SHC-UNC; William H. Johnson, Letter, 9 March 1862, *Pine and Palm* (27 March 1862), quoted in Redkey, *A Grand Army*, 19; "The Refugees at Roanoke," 3 March 1862, *National Anti-Slavery Standard* 22 (22 March 1862).

28. Colyer, *Brief Report*, 42. For general information about the early days in the slave refugee camps, see Berlin et al., *The Wartime Genesis of Free Labor: The Upper South*, 29–33; Spraggins, "Mobilization of Negro Labor," 176; Alexander, *North Carolina Faces the Freedmen*, 34; Magdol, *A Right to the Land*, 93; and Swint, *Dear Ones at Home*, 139.

CHAPTER TWO

1. Colyer, *Brief Report*, 36; "North Carolina. From Mr. H. S. Beals," *American Missionary* 7 (7 October 1863): 231; and H. S. Beals to Rev. S. S. Jocelyn, 18 August 1863, AMAA, N.C. For information about the New York Christian Commission, see "Organization and Plans of the New York Christian Commission for the Army and Navy," AMAA, N.Y. Northern missionary teacher Betsey S. Canady is usually given credit for establishing the first free black school in North Carolina, on 23 July 1863 in New Bern. Although Canady's was the first missionary-sponsored school, Martha Culling's was most likely the first free black school. I have searched census reports and a variety of genealogical sources for postwar information about Martha Culling and have uncovered nothing. I suspect that she left the island and married, making it next to impossible to find her in any printed records.

2. Special Order No. 65 of Major Genl Burnside, 30 March 1862, General and Special Orders Issued, Department of North Carolina, vol. 33, RG 393, pt. 1, ser. 3239, NA [FSSP #C-3234]; Bahney, "Generals and Negroes," 109; A. E. Burnside to Hon. E. Stanton, 21 March 1862, OR, ser. 1, vol. 9, 199–201; A. E. Burnside to Hon. E. M. Stanton, 27 March 1862, OR, ser. 1, vol. 9, 373–74; A. E. Burnside to Hon. E. M. Stanton, 19 May 1862, OR, ser. 1, vol. 9, 389–90; Graham, *Ninth Regiment New York*, 229.

3. Benjamin F. Butler to Lieutenant-General Winfield Scott, 24 May 1861, OR, ser. 1, vol. 2, 648–52; [Pierce], "The Contrabands at Fortress Monroe," 627. For Butler's account of the contraband problem, see Butler, *Butler's Book*, 256–64. For more recent historical assessments see Spraggins, "Mobilization of Negro Labor," 178; and Bentley, *A History*, 3–5.

4. Benjamin F. Butler to Winfield Scott, 27 May 1861, B-99 1861, Letters Received Irregular, RG 107, NA, cited in Ira Berlin et al., *Destruction of Slavery*, 70–72. See Bremner, *The Public Good*, 100.

5. Simon Cameron to Maj. Gen. Butler, 30 May 1861, vol. 44, 205–6, Letters Sent, RG 107, NA, cited in Berlin et al., *Destruction of Slavery*, 72–73; *The Statutes at Large* 12 (1859–1863): 319; Shannon, "The Federal Government and the Negro Soldier," 567. Shannon

notes that Butler did not use the phrase "contraband of war" in his initial letters, and suggests that he was not the author of the phrase. See also Berlin et al., *Destruction of Slavery*, 62–63. For Butler's correspondence, see Butler, *Private and Official Correspondence*, 1:185–88. The former slaves at Port Royal in South Carolina were usually referred to as freedmen rather than contrabands. See Pierce, "The Freedmen at Port Royal," 292.

6. "Regulations regarding employment of the Contrabands on Roanoke Island issued by Col R. C. Hawkins," General Order No. 2, 12 March 1862, and R. C. Hawkins to Maj. Genl A. E. Burnside, 16 March 1862, Gen. A. E. Burnside Papers, Box 20, RG 94, ser. 159, NA [FSSP #V-118, #V-126]; General Orders No. 2, 12 March 1862, OR, ser. 2, vol. 1, 810. See also Colyer, *Brief Report*, 55–56; Bentley, *A History*, 13; Gerteis, *From Contraband to Freedman*, 30; and Bremner, *The Public Good*, 100.

7. Bentley, *A History*, 13; Howard, "The Freedmen During the War," 382; Stick, *The Outer Banks*, 161; and Colyer, *Brief Report*, 6, 9, 56.

8. Colyer, *Brief Report*, 6; Vincent Colyer to Hon. Rob. Dale Owen, 25 May 1865, filed with O-328 1863, Letters Received, RG 94, ser. 12, NA (M619, reels 199–201). See also Shattuck, *A Shield and Hiding Place*, 26–27, and Graham, *Ninth Regiment New York*, 230.

9. Reilly, "Reconstruction Through Regeneration," 36; "Chaplain James Means," *Congregationalist* 15 (May 1863): 71; T. W. Conway, "Marrying on Roanoke Island," *National Anti-Slavery Standard* 23 (25 October 1862).

10. McPherson, *Struggle for Equality*, 181–91; Gerteis, *From Contraband to Freedman*, 35; *Preliminary Report Touching the Condition and Management of Emancipated Refugees*; Robert Dale Owens, James McKaye, and Saml. G. Howe to Hon. E. M. Stanton, 30 June 1863, OR, ser. 3, vol. 3, 430–54; Fredrickson, *The Black Image*, 179; Bahney, "Generals and Negroes," 35–37.

11. "Chaplain James Means," *Congregationalist* 15 (1 May 1863): 71; James, *Annual Report*, 21; Maj. Gen. Foster, Special Orders No. 138, #6, 14 May 1863, Special Orders Issued, Department of North Carolina, vol. 35, RG 393, pt. 1, ser. 3242, NA [FSSP #C-3388]; Horace James to Maj. Gen'l. M. C. Meigs, 26 December 1864, RG 92, ser. 1105, NA; and Gerteis, 31. In his report to General Meigs, James noted that Foster's letter requesting that he assume "the superintendence of the Blacks in the department of North Carolina" was dated 24 April 1863.

12. Reilly, "Reconstruction Through Regeneration," 4–5.

13. Ibid.," 3–21, 37.

14. Compiled Service Records, 25th Massachusetts Infantry, Horace James, Box 13141, RG 92, NA [FSSP #N-64]; Day, *My Diary of Rambles*, 7–8; Denny, *Wearing the Blue*, 80.

15. "Letter from Captain James," 23 April 1864, *Second Annual Report*, 73; James, *Annual Report*, 21–22.

16. For a discussion of the requisites and functions of organized black communities, see Pease and Pease, *Black Utopia*.

17. Redkey, *A Grand Army*, 1–8; Glatthaar, *Forged in Battle*, 1–10; Belz, "Law, Politics, and Race," 198; Redkey, "Black Chaplains in the Union Army," 331, 342; McPherson, *Struggle for Equality*, 212; Cornish, *The Sable Arm*, 130.

18. Thomas M. Vincent to Colonel Edward A. Wild, 14 April 1863, Edward A. Wild Papers, USAMHI; [Edward A. Wild], "Military Life of General Edward A. Wild, Brigadier General of Volunteers, Norfolk, March 12th, 1864," Edward A. Wild Papers, USAMHI;

Longacre, "Brave Radical Wild," 10–11; Longacre, *Army of Amateurs*, 55–58; Edward A. Wild to Godfrey Weitzel, 8 May 1865, Edward A. Wild Papers, USAMHI.

19. Regimental and Company Descriptive Books, 35th, 36th, and 37th USCT, RG 94, NA; McPherson, *The Negro's Civil War*, 174, 216. See also Dyer, "The Treatment of Colored Union Troops by the Confederates," 273–86; Jefferson Davis, General Orders No. 111, 24 December 1862, OR, ser. 2, vol. 5, 797.

20. James, *Annual Report*, 22; Regimental Descriptive Books for 35th, 36th, and 37th USCT, RG 94, NA; E. James to Rev. G. Whipple, 13 August 1864, AMAA, N.C. Richard Reid describes the recruitment of Wild's African brigade in "Raising the African Brigade," 266–301. According to the Descriptive Book for the 35th USCT, the first recruit was Luke Measel, who enlisted in New Bern on 20 May 1863. There is no way to be absolutely sure of the total number of soldiers whose families were on Roanoke Island. Population statistics, themselves open to questions of accuracy, indicate that there were 1,086 females and 708 males who were fourteen years or older living in the freedmen's colony in late 1864. Herbert G. Gutman's analysis of the ratios of male slaves over twenty years old to female slaves over twenty in Currituck (128.2/100), Hyde (150.7/100), Pasquotank (123.6/100), and Washington (99.1/100) Counties in 1860 indicates that the average ratio of adult male to adult female slaves was 125.6/100. Applying these ratios to the population figures from the colony is problematic since the statistics from the island do not exactly match Gutman's categories. Nevertheless, aware of the limitations of the estimates, I tentatively conclude that if the ratio of males fourteen years and older to females fourteen years and older were approximately 125.6/100, there should have been approximately 1,358 males fourteen or older in the colony in late 1864. Subtracting the number present (708) from the estimate (1,358) leads to the conclusion that approximately 650 males fourteen or older were away from the island in April 1864. Many of them were soldiers, but others were probably serving as civilians in the Quartermaster's Department in New Bern or elsewhere. See Wm. T. Briggs to Rev. George Whipple, 27 April 1864, AMAA, N.C; "Roanoke Island," *National Freedman* 1 (15 November 1865): 320; James, *Annual Report*, 26; Gutman, *The Black Family*, 43.

21. James, *Annual Report*, 22; and Horace James to the Public, 27 June 1863, in Horace James to Major Gen. J. G. Foster, 1 July 1863, Letters Received, Department of North Carolina, RG 393, pt. 1, ser. 3238, NA.

22. Horace James to the Public, 27 June 1863, in Horace James to Major Gen. J. G. Foster, 1 July 1863, Letters Received, Department of North Carolina, RG 393, pt. 1, ser. 3238, NA. See also "The Freedmen of North Carolina," *Congregationalist* 15 (10 July 1863): 110; "Letter from Captain James," 23 April 1864, *Second Annual Report*, 73. Horace James's June 1863 letter is reproduced in Appendix C.

23. James, *Annual Report*, 23; "Colony at Roanoke Island, North Carolina," *The National Freedman's Relief Association Paper for July, August and September [1863]*, AMAA, N.Y.; Jones, "'A Glorious Work,'" 10; Horace James to Gen. [Edward A. Wild], 7 July 1863, Edward A. Wild Papers, USAMHI.

24. [Edward A. Wild], "Military Life of General Edward A. Wild, Brigadier General of Volunteers, Norfolk, March 12th, 1864," Edward A. Wild Papers, USAMHI; James, *Annual Report*, 23; J. G. Foster to Hon. E. M. Stanton, 20 July 1863, OR, ser. 1, vol. 27, pt. 3, 732; Maj. General Foster, General Orders 1 & 2, vol. 52, 22 July 1863, Department of Virginia and North Carolina, RG 393, pt. 1, ser. 5078, NA [FSSP #C-3295].

25. [Edward A. Wild], "Military Life of General Edward A. Wild, Brigadier General of Volunteers, Norfolk, March 12th, 1864," Edward A. Wild Papers, USAMHI; Joseph E. Williams, 23 June 1863, *Christian Recorder* (4 July 1863) cited in Redkey, *A Grand Army*, 91.

26. Horace James, "The Freedmen of North Carolina," *Congregationalist* 15 (10 July 1863): 110. To determine the rough location of the colony, I started with the deeds that were submitted by the islanders to the Freedmen's Bureau after the war. To fill out the picture, I gathered owner and acreage information from the bureau's monthly land reports. Using this information, I went to the Currituck County Governmental Center and attempted to locate deeds that corresponded to each parcel. A few of the parcels had been conveyed in wills, and thus there were no deeds for them. Generally, however, I found deeds that corresponded to the information given in the monthly land reports. I took the metes and bounds information from these deeds and, with the help of my research assistant, Mary Bess Bolin (an undergraduate student in civil engineering), I attempted to draw a map of the land that was under Union occupation. We eventually concluded that it would be impossible to create a perfect map. It was really a three-dimensional problem of sorts; since the deeds were filed at different times, the metes and bounds descriptions did not lead to pieces that fit together tightly, in the manner of a jigsaw puzzle. Nevertheless, in combination with contemporary descriptions, the deed information helped to confirm that the colony stretched from Weir's Point south to Pork Point and that it was roughly in the shape of a rectangle, two miles long by a mile wide. For deeds submitted by the natives after the war, see Sarah E. Dough to Maj. Gen. O. O. Howard, 5 November 1866; Thomas A. Dough to Maj. Gen. O. O. Howard, 4 December 1866; J. Etheridge Jr. to Maj. Gen. O. O. Howard, 3 December 1866; Nancy Gaylord to Maj. Gen. O. O. Howard, 5 November 1866; Martin Hubbard to Maj. Gen. O. O. Howard, 3 December 1866; Matilda Miller to Maj. Gen. O. O. Howard, 5 November 1866; and John Wescott to Major General O. O. Howard, 24 May 1867, Letters Received and Unregistered Letters Received, Headquarters, Records of the Assistant Commissioner for North Carolina, RG 105, ser. 2452, NA (M843, reels 9–11). For land reports, see the Monthly Land Reports, Headquarters, Records of the Assistant Commissioner for North Carolina, RG 105, ser.2470, NA (M843, reel 36). See the following deeds in the Currituck Governmental Center: Abraham Baum to Samuel Baum, DB 14: 450–51; Jacob F. Wright to Eason Berry, DB 27: 376; J. F. Wright to Esau Berry, DB 28: 363; Nancy Brickhouse to Jesse Dough, DB 28: 300; James Pugh to Benjamin Daniel, DB 14: 159–60; Daniel W. Meekins et al. to W. T. Dough, DB 28: 195–97; Esau and Fanny Berry to W. T. Dough, DB 28: 197–99; Adam Etheridge to Jesse Etheridge, DB 21: 469; Mary Stringfields to John B. Etheridge, DB 26: 423–24; Jesse Etheridge to John B. Etheridge, DB 26: 347; Abel Ashbee to John B. Etheridge, DB 28: 33; John B. Etheridge to L. J. Etheridge, DB 28: 368; William S. Etheridge to Tart Etheridge, DB 21: 109; John Dowdy to Tart Etheridge, DB 28: 250; W. A. And Abia Dough to Tart Etheridge, DB 21: 371–72; M. A. Burgess to Lewis S. Mann, DB 28: 236; Nancy Mann to Daniel Meekins, DB 17: 253–54; Edward Mann to Esther Meekins, DB 9: 373; Samuel Midgett to Martha Midgett, DB 28: 105–6; State of North Carolina to Samuel Midgett, DB 27: 67–68; William Rollins to Samuel N. Midgett, DB 25: 87. See the following wills in the Currituck Governmental Center: Esther Meekins, WB 4: 425; Joel Etheridge, WB 4:44.

27. James, *Annual Report*, 23–24; Compiled Service Records, 43rd Massachusetts Infantry, George O. Sanderson, RG 92, NA; Horace James to Major Genl. J. G. Foster, 5 Septem-

ber 1863, filed with J-34 1863, Letters Received, Department of Virginia and North Carolina and 18th Army Corps, RG 393, pt. 1, ser. 5063, NA.

28. H. E. Rockwell, "The Colony at Roanoke Island," *Freedmen's Advocate* 1 (May 1864): 18; Horace James, "A Fragment of the Plan for colonizing Roanoke Island, N.C. with the families of Colored Soldiers, and Invalid Negroes," Letters and Orders Received, Reports, and Supply Requests, Roanoke Island, N.C., Records of the Assistant Commissioner for North Carolina, RG 105, ser. 2821, NA. Horace James mentions Rockwell's assistance in laying out the village in a letter to Lt. Col. J. B. Kinsman, A.D.C., 7 April 1864, Letters, Orders, & Telegrams Received by Lt. Col. J. B. Kinsman, Department of Negro Affairs for Virginia and North Carolina, RG 105, ser. 4108, NA. See also Elizabeth James to Mr Whipple, 19 December 1863, AMAA, N.C.

29. James, *Annual Report*, 23–25; Horace James to Major Genl J. G. Foster, 5 September 1863, filed with J-34 1863, Letters Received, Department of Virginia and North Carolina and 18th Army Corps, RG 393, pt. 1, ser. 5063, NA; Rockwell, "The Colony at Roanoke Island," 18. When discussing a plan for distribution of small plots of confiscated lands to contrabands in Hampton, Virginia, General Foster emphasized that the goal was "to make the Negro self supporting and by the offer of the opportunity—for gain—to make him work—creating an ambition of some sort—also—to relieve the Government from the enormous pressure of feeding and caring for the number of Paupers." No doubt some of these motives propelled the development of the Roanoke village as well, but Horace James saw them as part of a more complex regenerative effort—not the primary aims. See [Major General John G. Foster] to Capt. C. B. Wilder, 23 August 1863, Letters Sent, Department of Virginia and North Carolina and 18th Army Corps, vol. 49, no. 53, RG 393, pt. 1, ser. 5046, NA. The lots in Trent Village were each three thousand square feet, while the lots in the Roanoke Island village were close to an acre, or forty thousand square feet.

30. Affidavit of Priscilla Davis in support of Winney Midgett, 24 November 1874, James Midgett Pension Papers, RG 94, NA; Rockwell, "The Colony at Roanoke Island," 18; James, *Annual Report*, 25.

31. Charles Tournier Diary, 8 February 1865, East Carolina University.

32. Elinathan Davis, "Freedmen," *American Missionary* 9 (February 1865): 25–26. Although Horace James misspelled his name, Obman's homesite is indicated on the plat that Horace James filed with the Freedmen's Inquiry Commission in January 1864. See Horace James, "A Fragment of the Plan for colonizing *Roanoke Island, N.C.* with the families of Colored Soldiers and Invalid Negroes," Records of the Assistant Commissioner for North Carolina, Roanoke Island, RG 105, ser. 2821, NA.

33. Gen. J. G. Foster, Special Orders Issued, vol. 53/76, 28, #3, 18 [or 17] August 1863, RG 393, pt. 1, ser. 5084, NA [FSSP #C-3389]; James, *Annual Report*, 23; and "Letter from Chaplain James," 5 September 1863, *Congregationalist* 15 (18 September 1863): 149.

34. Horace James to Major Genl. J. G. Foster, 5 September 1863, filed with J-34 1863, Letters Received, Department of Virginia and North Carolina and 18th Army Corps, RG 393, pt. 1, ser. 5063, NA.

35. Major-General John J. Peck, General Orders No. 12, 10 September 1863, OR, ser. 1, vol. 29, pt. 2, 166; Maj. Gen. Peck, General Orders No. 12, 10 September 1863, Printed Orders, vol. 920, New Berne, N.C., Headquarters Army and District of N.C., RG 94, NA [FSSP #DD43]; James, *Annual Report*, 24.

36. James, *Annual Report*, 24; and Horace James to Major Genl. John G. Foster, 5 September 1863, filed with J-34 1863, Letters Received, Department of Virginia and North Carolina and 18th Army Corps, RG 393, pt. 1, ser. 5063, NA.

37. [Major General John G. Foster] to Maj. Gen. John J. Peck, 11 September 1863, Letters Sent, Department of Virginia and North Carolina, vol. 49, no. 76, RG 393, pt. 1, ser. 5046, NA.

38. John J. Peck to Col. Southard Hoffman, 2 October 1863, OR, ser.1, vol. 29, pt. 2, 244; John Peck to Col Southard Hoffman, 2 October 1863, Department of Virginia and North Carolina and 18th Army Corps, Letters Received, RG 393, pt. 1, ser. 5063, NA.

39. Horace James to Major Genl. John G. Foster, 17 October 1863, J-34 1863, Letters Received, Department of Virginia and North Carolina and 18th Army Corps, RG 393, pt. 1, ser. 5063, NA.

40. Special Orders, No. 118, 15 November 1863, Edward A. Wild Papers, USAMHI; General Orders No. 46, 5 December 1863, OR, ser. 3, vol. 3, 1139–44; General Orders No. 46, Head Quarters Department of Virginia and North Carolina, 5 December 1863, General Orders Issued, vol. 52, Department of Virginia and North Carolina and 18th Army Corps, RG 393, pt. 1, ser. 5078, NA.

41. Bentley, *A History*, 25; Pierce, *The Freedmen's Bureau*, 12; Benjamin F. Butler to Horace James, 16 December 1863, Letters Sent, Department of Virginia and North Carolina, vol. 49, no. 404, RG 393, pt. 1, ser.5046; and Horace James to J. B. Kinsman, 23 February 1864, Letters, Orders, & Telegrams Received by Lt. Col. J. B. Kinsman, Department of Negro Affairs for Virginia and North Carolina, RG 105, ser. 4108, NA. Although Butler's general superintendent, Kinsman, reported directly to him rather than the Quartermaster's Department, in practice the district superintendents worked closely with local quartermasters. Edward G. Longacre notes that while Butler's promotion of black troops "stemmed from political expediency," his endeavors on behalf of the dependents went beyond what was necessary "to maintain his identity as a friend of the African-American." Longacre concludes that although "it is always difficult to distinguish between Butler the idealist and Butler the opportunist, the conclusion is inescapable that a humanitarian impulse animated him throughout his tenure in Virginia." See Longacre, *Army of Amateurs*, 54–55.

42. "Letter from Horace James," *Congregationalist* 15 (18 September 1863): 149.

CHAPTER THREE

1. "From Burnside's Expedition," *Congregationalist* 14 (14 February 1862): 26.

2. James, *Annual Report*,

3. The United States Senate had confirmed James's appointment as captain and assistant quartermaster on 18 February 1864. James resigned his chaplaincy on 22 April 1864. Horace James to Lt. Col. J. B. Kinsman, 23 February 1864, Records of the Department of Negro Affairs for Virginia and North Carolina, RG 105, ser. 4108, NA; Horace James to [Benjamin Butler], 22 April 1864, Register of Letters Received, vol. 4, no. 32, Department of North Carolina and Virginia, RG 393, pt. 1, ser. 5062, NA; "Letter from Chaplain James," 5 September 1863, *Congregationalist* 15 (18 September 1863): 149; "The Freedmen of North Carolina," *Congregationalist* 15 (10 July 1863): 110.

4. Nathaniel W. Taylor, "Man, a Free Agent without the Aids of Divine Grace," quoted in

Marsden, *The Evangelical Mind*, 49; McLoughlin, *The American Evangelicals*, 2; Davis, *Joshua Leavitt*, 27; Reilly, "Reconstruction Through Regeneration," 9; "Letter from Chaplain James," 17 January 1863, *Congregationalist* 15 (30 January 1863): 18. Taylor had studied with Timothy Dwight.

5. James, *Address of the Rev. Horace James*, 2.

6. James, *Two Great Wars*, 23–29. The italics were in the original.

7. *American Missionary* 8 (August 1864): 194; James, *Two Great Wars*, 23. The capital letters were in the original. Peter J. Gomes presents an enlightening discussion of how slavery prompted significant debates in the mid-nineteenth century about interpretation of the Bible. Gomes notes that since the biblical case for slavery "was both strong and consistent," those who wished to challenge slavery had to make a moral case based on biblical principles rather than biblical example. "This was a dispute about the authority and morality of the Bible itself, and about how it ought to be read, interpreted, and applied," Gomes states. See Gomes, *The Good Book*, 92.

8. Moorhead, "Between Progress and Apocalypse"; James, *The Christian Patriot*, 5–7; *Congregationalist* (3 January 1862): 2; James, *Two Great Wars*, 23–29. The italics were in the original. For a discussion of the evangelical belief that slavery would prevent the coming of the millennium, see Johnson, *Redeeming America*, 161–62. For a discussion of the relationship between industrialism and nineteenth-century evangelicalism, see Wauzzinski, *Between God and Gold*, especially 33, 159.

9. Reilly, "Reconstruction Through Regeneration," 42; "Letter from Chaplain James," 1 June 1863, *Congregationalist* 15 (12 June 1863): 94; "Letter from Horace James," 18 October 1862, *Congregationalist* 14 (31 October 1862): 175; Horace James to the Public, 27 June 1863, Letters Received, Department of North Carolina, RG 393, pt. 1, ser. 3238, NA. See also "From Burnside's Expedition," 1 February 1862, *Congregationalist* 14 (14 February 1862): 26. The capital letters were in the original.

10. James, *Annual Report*, 46; Horace James, "Letter from Chaplain James," 19 August 1864, *Congregationalist* 16 (2 September 1864): 142; Fredrickson, *The Black Image*, 180. For a discussion of some of the ironies of the antislavery viewpoint, see Mathews, "The Abolitionists on Slavery."

11. "Letter From Chaplain James," 10 October 1862, *Congregationalist* 14 (10 October 1862): 161. For a thorough discussion of James's Republican ideas and their relationship to his work among the freedpeople, see Reilly, "Reconstruction Through Regeneration." For a discussion of Republican ideas with respect to free labor, see Foner, *Free Soil* and *Politics and Ideology*.

12. "Letter from Chaplain James," 5 September 1863, *Congregationalist* 15 (18 September 1863): 149; Foner, *Politics and Ideology*, 121; James, *Annual Report*, 45; "Letter from Captain James," 23 April 1864, *Second Annual Report*, 73.

13. "Letter from Horace James," *Congregationalist* 17 (8 December 1865): 195; Horace James to Gen'l B. F. Butler, 10 February 1864, Records of the Department of Negro Affairs for Virginia and North Carolina, RG 105, ser. 4108, NA; Fredrickson, *The Black Image*, 182.

14. James, *Annual Report*, 27; "Letter from Chaplain James," 23 April 1864, *Second Annual Report*, 74.

15. Horace James to the Secretary of the AMA, 20 October 1865, AMAA, N.C.; James, *Annual Report*, 27.

16. James, *Annual Report*, 27, 33.

17. Horace James to Major Genl B. F. Butler, 9 February 1864 and Horace James to Lt. Col. J. B. Kinsman, 11 February 1864, Records of the Department of Negro Affairs for Virginia and North Carolina, RG 105, ser. 4108, NA; Horace James to [Benjamin Butler], 22 April 1864, Letters Received, Department of Virginia and North Carolina, vol. 4, no. 37, RG 393, pt. 1, ser. 5062; "Letter from Chaplain James," 27 June 1863, *Congregationalist* 15 (3 July 1863): 106. James's letter to the readers of the *Congregationalist* was substantially the same one that he had distributed throughout the North in June.

18. "Colony at Roanoke Island, North Carolina," *The National Freedman's Relief Association Paper for July, August and September [1863]*, AMAA, N.Y.; *Congregationalist* 16 (1 April 1864): 55; *Freedmen's Advocate* 1 (March 1864): 10.

19. James, *Annual Report*, 23: Major General B. F. Butler to Horace James, 2 December 1863, Letters Sent, Department of Virginia and North Carolina, vol. 49, no. 283, RG 393, pt. 1, ser. 5046, NA; and Benjamin F. Butler to Horace James, 16 December 1863, Letters Sent, Department of Virginia and North Carolina, vol. 49, no. 404, RG 393, pt. 1, ser. 5046, NA. For examples of James's discussion of the colony's need for lumber for houses, see "The Freedmen in North Carolina," *Congregationalist* 16 (12 February 1864): 25; Horace James to General B. F. Butler, 20 February 1864, Records of the Department of Negro Affairs for Virginia and North Carolina, RG 105, ser. 4108, NA; "Letter from Chaplain James," 23 April 1864, *Second Annual Report*, 74.

20. James, *Annual Report*, 22; Moore, *Rebellion Record*, 4:299–300, 303; Edward A. Wild to Brigadier-General Barnes, 21 December 1863, OR, ser. 1, vol. 29, pt. 1, 910; Edward A. Wild to Capt. George H. Johnston, 28 December 1863, OR, ser. 1, vol. 29, pt. 1, 914; Edward A. Wild to Brigadier-General Barnes, 12 December 1863, OR, ser. 1, vol. 29, pt. 2, 562; Edward A. Wild to Brig. General Barnes, 21 December 1863, Miscellaneous Letters Received, Department of Virginia and North Carolina and 18th Army Corps, RG 393, pt. 1, ser. 5076, NA; Edwd A. Wild to Capt. George H. Johnston, 28 December 1863, Edward A. Wild Papers, SHC-UNC; 33–34; Barrett, *Civil War in North Carolina*, 177–80; Edward Longacre, "Brave Radical Wild," 10–11; Trudeau, *Like Men of War*, 112–18.

21. D. W. Hand to Major B. B. Foster, 20 January 1864, Richard O'Flynn Papers, College of the Holy Cross, Worcester, Mass.

22. D. W. Hand to Major B. B. Foster, 20 January 1864; Ella Roper to S. S. Jocelyn, 30 January 1864, AMAA, N.C.; Edwd. A. Wild to Capt. George H. Johnston, 28 December 1863, Edward A. Wild Papers, SHC-UNC.

23. "Rev. W. Hamilton's Tour," *American Missionary* 8 (April 1864): 83.

24. Horace James, "The Freedmen in North Carolina," 26 January 1864, *Congregationalist* 16 (12 February 1864): 25; George Whipple to Brethren, 27 January 1864, AMAA, N.C.; *National Anti-Slavery Standard* 24 (27 February 1864).

25. Horace James to Major Genl. Benjn. F. Butler, 20 February 1864, Records of the Department of Negro Affairs for Virginia and North Carolina, RG 105, ser. 4108, NA; Horace James to E. A. Wilde, 16 March 1864, Edward A. Wild Correspondence, MOLLUS-Massachusetts Collection, USAMHI; Holland Streeter to Lt. Col. J. B. Kinsman, 15 February 1864, 20 February 1864, Records of the Department of Negro Affairs for Virginia and North Carolina, RG 105, ser. 4108, NA; *Second Annual Report*, 30. James wrote Kinsman indicating his hope that the men from Roanoke Island would start their shad fishing

once the weather improved. See Horace James to Lt. Col. Kinsman, 20 February 1864, Records of the Department of Negro Affairs for Virginia and North Carolina, RG 105, ser. 4108, NA

26. Horace James to Major Genl. Benjn. F. Butler, 20 February 1864, Records of the Department of Negro Affairs for Virginia and North Carolina, RG 105, ser. 4108, NA.

27. Horace James to Lt. Col. Kinsman, 23 February 1864, 23 March 1864, Records of the Department of Negro Affairs for Virginia and North Carolina, RG 105, entry 4108, NA; Horace James to [George Whipple], 23 February 1864, AMAA, N.C. The misspelling of "battalion" is in the original document. Although letters from Horace James indicate that the sawmill cost approximately $8,000, I have not been able to uncover the original invoice for the machinery.

28. Horace James to Major Genl. Benjm. F. Butler, 20 February 1864, Records of the Department of Negro Affairs for Virginia and North Carolina, RG 105, ser. 4108, NA; James, *Annual Report*, 28; Elizabeth James, Letter, 7 April [1864], *American Missionary* 8 (June 1864): 141; Elizabeth James to William E. Whiting, 13 May 1865, AMAA, N.C.; Ella Roper to Mr. Whipple, 17 June 1864, AMAA, N.C.; Horace James to Lt. Col. J. B. Kinsman, 20 June 1864 and 28 June 1864, Records of the Department of Negro Affairs for Virginia and North Carolina, RG 105, ser. 4108, NA; Ella Roper to ——, 5 August 1864, AMAA, N.C.; Elizabeth James to George Whipple, 5 September 1864, AMAA, N.C.

29. James, *Annual Report*, 28; Charles Tournier Diary, 15 October 1864, 18 October 1864, Joyner Library, East Carolina University.

30. "Letter from New Berne," 6 October 1864, *Congregationalist* 16 (21 October 1864): 170; Horace James to Lt. Col. J. B. Kinsman, 28 June 1864 and 7 July 1864, Records of the Department of Negro Affairs for Virginia and North Carolina, RG 105, ser. 4108, NA.

31. [Illegible] Quartermaster General to Major General J. G. Foster, 5 November 1862, Letters Received, RG 393, pt. 1, entry 3238, NA; Benjamin F. Butler to Rear Admiral S. See, 11 February 1864, Letters Sent, Department of Virginia and North Carolina, vol. 50, no. 198, RG 393, pt. 1, ser. 5046, NA; Horace James to Lt. Col. Kinsman, 28 June 1864, 7 July 1864, Records of the Department of Negro Affairs for Virginia and North Carolina, RG 105, ser. 4108, NA; "A Statement of the Stations occupied, and duties performed, by Capt. Horace James, A.Q.M. during the time he has served in the Quartermaster's Department, up to June 30th 1864," Annual Reports of Quartermasters Officers, RG 92, ser. 1105, NA.

32. "Letter from New Berne," *Congregationalist* 16 (21 October 1864): 170.

33. Horace James to Col. J. B. Kinsman, 7 November 1864, Records of the Department of Negro Affairs for Virginia and North Carolina, RG 105, ser. 4108, NA; Wm. T. Briggs to Rev. Geo. Whipple, 25 November 1864, AMAA, N.C.

34. James, *Annual Report*, 28; Horace James to the Old South Sunday School Class of Worcester, 25 May 1863, Horace James Correspondence, American Antiquarian Society, Worcester, Mass., quoted in Reilly, "Reconstruction Through Regeneration," 66.

35. Horace James to [George Whipple], 10 June 1863, AMAA, N.C.; Horace James to [George Whipple], 27 August 1863, AMAA, N.C.; H. J. to [George Whipple], 11 September 1863, AMAA, N.C.

36. James, *Annual Report*, 29; and "Freedmen," *American Missionary* 7 (November 1863): 242.

CHAPTER FOUR

1. James, *Annual Report*, 4.

2. "Brief Outline of the History of the American Missionary Association," *American Missionary* 2 (July 1858): 188–91; American Missionary Association, *History*, 3–5; Drake, "The American Missionary Association," 2: Richardson, *Christian Reconstruction*, vii; Linthicum, "The American Missionary Association and North Carolina Freedmen, 1863–1868," 20. For a brief discussion of Lewis Tappan's contributions to the AMA, see DeBoer, *Be Jubilant My Feet*, 19. The AMA's constitution was reprinted inside every issue of the *American Missionary*. The AMA constitution is reproduced in Appendix A. For a fairly complete list of the various freedmen's societies, see *Second Annual Report*, 10–11. The New York Branch of the National Freedman's Relief Association was founded at the Cooper Institute in New York on 20 February 1862. The New England Freedmen's Aid Society was an outgrowth of the Boston Educational Commission, which was founded on 7 February 1862.

3. "Anniversary Meeting in Boston," *American Missionary* 3 (July 1859): 145; "Brief Outline of the History of the American Missionary Association," 191.

4. Sorin, *Abolitionism: A New Perspective*, 67; Hardesty, *Your Daughters Shall Prophesy*, 35–36, 43, 50; Cayton, "Who Were the Evangelicals?" 86; Wauzzinski, *Between God and Gold*, 45; Levine, *Half Slave and Half Free*, 83.

5. Cayton, "Who Were the Evangelicals?" 87; Hardesty, *Women Called to Witness*, 50; Levine, *Half Slave and Half Free*, 84; Drake, "The American Missionary Association," 122; Butchart, *Northern Schools*, 6. In an early issue of the *American Missionary*, Lewis Tappan cautioned readers not to forget that the AMA was a "*Union* Missionary Society." See "Letter to Inquirers," *American Missionary* 2 (January 1858): 17.

6. Lesick, *The Lane Rebels*, 7, 85, 88, 232; Swint, *Dear Ones at Home*, 12; "Slavery and Missions," *American Missionary* 1 (May 1857): 106; "Anniversary Meeting at Boston," *American Missionary* 1 (July 1857): 145–50; Shattuck, *A Shield and Hiding Place*, 2; Foner, *Free Soil*, 109. George Whipple, an ordained minister, had been appointed professor of mathematics at Oberlin College in 1838. An ardent abolitionist, he had worked for the American Anti-Slavery Society in Ohio and New York. He edited the *American Missionary* from 1847 until 1876. Michael E. Strieby had been a Congregational minister in Syracuse, New York. He had been praised for his oratorical skills, which he had long used to oppose slavery. See Richardson, *Christian Reconstruction*, 88, 90.

7. "Anniversary Meeting at Boston," *American Missionary* 1 (July 1857): 148; "The Abolition of Slavery Necessary to Missions at the South," *American Missionary* 1 (February 1857): 29; "Letter to Inquirers," *American Missionary* 2 (January 1858): 14; "The War—Its Cause and Remedy," *American Missionary* 5 (June: 1861): 131; "The American Tract Society, and Missions in Slave States," *American Missionary* 2 (March 1858): 59.

8. "Go Forward," *American Missionary* 5 (July 1861): 155; "Mission to the Freed 'Contrabands' at Fortress Monroe, Va." *American Missionary* 5 (October 1861): 241; Morris, *Reading, 'Riting, and Reconstruction*, 1; Wolfe, "Women Who Dared," 23; "Mission to the Freed 'Contrabands,'" 241.

9. Jones, *Soldiers of Light and Love*, 18; Gerteis, *From Contraband to Freedman*, 20;

Morris, *Reading, 'Riting, and Reconstruction*, 20; "The Freedmen," *American Missionary* 7 (March 1863) 58; General Orders No. 46, Head Quarters Department of Virginia and North Carolina, 5 December 1863, General Orders Issued, vol. 52, Department of Virginia and North Carolina and 18th Army Corps, RG 393, pt. 1, ser. 5078, NA; Drake, "The American Missionary Association," 156. Charles Wilder was appointed head of the first district in General Butler's Department of Negro Affairs. Augustus Field Beard estimated that the AMA had three thousand volunteers in the South during and after the war; two-thirds were women. James M. McPherson concluded that the AMA supported over three thousand missionaries, and that 75 percent of them were women. See Beard, *A Crusade of Brotherhood*, 231; McPherson, *The Abolitionist Legacy*, 143, 165.

10. "Colored Refugees," *American Missionary* 6 (February 1862): 29; "Teachers: Their Qualifications and Support," *American Missionary* 10 (July 1866): 152.

11. Swint, *Dear Ones at Home*, 28, 36; Mary A. Collier to ——, 24 July 1863, AMAA, Mass.; Morris, *Reading, 'Riting, and Reconstruction*, 63; "Men Wanted," *American Missionary* 8 (January 1864): 11. The AMA published a circular stating the qualifications for teachers. For a reprint of this circular, see the *American Missionary* 10 (July 1866): 152–53.

12. Sorin, *Abolitionism: A New Perspective*, 156; "Appeal for the Freedmen," *American Missionary* 7 (January 1863): 14; "Freedmen," *American Missionary* 7 (February 1863): 35; "The New Field," *American Missionary* 7 (July 1863): 154.

13. "First Annual Report of the National Freedman's Relief Association, New York, February 19th, 1863," AMAA, N.Y. At its organizational meeting, the NFRA adopted a plan with respect to the treatment of the freedpeople. See Appendix B for the text of that plan.

14. James, *Annual Report*, 42. More is known about the AMA teachers than the NFRA teachers on Roanoke Island because the former's letters to the corresponding secretaries of the AMA have been preserved, while only a handful of letters from the NFRA survive in several nineteenth-century freedmen's magazines.

15. Horace James to Rev. George Whipple, 15 September 1863, AMAA, N.C. My estimate of age of the missionaries on Roanoke Island is based on an average of the ages of the teachers for which I could find information about birth dates. I was not able to find information for all the Roanoke Island teachers, but I was able to compile a sampling that was sufficient for determining a close estimate. My information was taken from William T. Briggs, "Annual Report of the Superintendent of Colored Schools in North Carolina," 1 July 1865, AMAA, N.C.; "Ancestral File" and "International Genealogical Index," *Family Search*; Federal Census, Population Schedules for York County, Maine, 1860; Barnstable, Essex, Middlesex, and Worcester Counties, Massachusetts, 1850, 1860; Carroll County, New Hampshire, 1850, 1860; Cumberland County, New Jersey, 1860; St. Lawrence and Westchester Counties, New York, 1850, 1860, NA. Maxine Jones's study of AMA teachers in North Carolina concluded that the average age of women teachers at the time of their application to the AMA was 31, their ages ranging from 19 to 50; the average age of male applicants was 31.1, their ages ranging from 21 to 53. See Jones, " 'A Glorious Work,' " 166. See also Swint, *Dear Ones at Home*, 47–49; and Richardson, *Christian Reconstruction*, 168;

16. Currie-McDaniel, "Northern Women in the South, 1860–1880," 297; and Linda M. Perkins, "The Black Female American Missionary Association Teacher in the South, 1861–1870," in Crow and Hatley, *Black Americans*, 124. Currie-McDaniel presents a clear discussion of three prevalent motives: political/philanthropic, spiritual, and personal.

17. Bremner, *American Philanthropy*, 73; Hardesty, *Your Daughters Shall Prophesy*, 45, 60. For a discussion of women's responses to the call for freedmen teachers, see Wolfe, "Women Who Dared," 6, 22; Hoffert, "Yankee Schoolmarms."

18. Wolfe, "Women Who Dared," 9, 132; Jones, "Women Who Were More Than Men," 50–51; American Missionary Association, *Woman's Work for the Lowly, as Illustrated in the Work of the American Missionary Association Among the Freedman* (Boston: South Boston Inquirer Press, 1874), 4–5, quoted in Butchart, *Northern Schools*, 124; W. T. Briggs to C. C. Leigh, 3 March 1865, in *National Freedman* 1 (1 April 1865): 91. I have chosen not to focus on sex and status in the teaching on Roanoke Island, in part because the evidence is scanty, but mostly because I think the general subject has already been covered quite well by a number of historians, including Jacqueline Jones, Maxine Jones, Allis Wolfe, Nancy Linthicum, Ruth Currie-McDaniel, and Sylvia Hoffert.

19. [Ella Roper to George Whipple], 5 August 1865, AMAA, N.C. See Ella Roper, Monthly Report of Briggs School, 4 July 1864, AMAA, N.C.; Ella Roper to S. S. Jocelyn, 30 January 1864, AMAA, N.C.; Elizabeth James to Rev. G. Whipple, 27 March 1866, AMAA, N.C.; Ella Roper to Mr. Whipple, 17 June 1865, AMAA, N.C.

20. Elizabeth James to Rev. George Whipple, 23 January 1867, AMAA, N.C.; Horace James to ——, 27 August 1863, AMAA, N.C.; Elizabeth James to Mr. Whipple, 18 September 1863, AMAA, Mass. Elizabeth James was born on 10 June 1819 in Medford, Massachusetts; she was the eldest of three daughters of John James and Sally Cole Wade James. See "International Genealogical Index," *Family Search*. Also, see Appendix D for a list of the missionaries who served on Roanoke Island.

21. Elizabeth James to Mr. Whipple, 18 September 1863, AMAA, Mass.

22. Elizabeth James to Mr Whipple, 20 May 1864, AMAA, N.C.; E. James to Brother in Christ, 29 December 1864, AMAA, N.C.; Elizabeth James to Rev. George Whipple, 4 July 1866, AMAA, N.C.; Elizabeth James to Rev. G. Whipple, 25 September 1865, AMAA, N.C.; Elizabeth James to Rev. G. Whipple, 27 March 1866, AMAA, N.C.

23. S. S. Nickerson, "Mission Schools on Roanoke Island N.C." [29 October 1864], AMAA, N.C.; James, *Annual Report*, 29; "Ancestral File" and "International Genealogical Index," *Family Search*; Swint, *Dear Ones at Home*, 191. Although Horace James reported that Nickerson arrived in February 1864, Nickerson's own account of his arrival indicates that he was on the island in December 1863. I have chosen to accept Nickerson's account. Most published lists of missionary teachers indicate that Nickerson came from Farnworth, Farnsworth, or Farnworth IronWorks, New Hampshire. (For an example, see Swint, *The Northern Teacher*, 191.) After having no success in finding a town with any of those names, I contacted the New Hampshire Historical Society and spoke with William Copeley, who pointed out that historians must have misread Nickerson's handwriting. There was no Farnworth, but there was a Tamworth, New Hampshire, which was near the center of much nineteenth-century Free Will Baptist activity. Once I discovered the Tamworth connection, I was able to uncover a lot of information about Samuel S. Nickerson and his life.

24. Ella Roper to Sir [George Whipple], November 1861, AMAA, Mass.; Ella Roper to S. S. Jocelyn, 30 January 1864, AMAA, N.C.; Ella Roper to Mr Whipple, 17 June 1864, AMAA, N.C.; Mount Holyoke College Alumnae Association, *Biographical Directory*, 101. Ella Roper was the second of two daughters of Ephraim Roper and Eunice Swan Richardson Roper of Templeton, Massachusetts. Her father was a farmer. Ella was born in Temple-

ton on 10 July 1841. For vital information about Ella Roper, see Federal Census, Population Schedules, Templeton, Worcester, Mass., 1850; and "International Genealogical Index," *Family Search.*

25. Schurz, *Intimate Letters*, 328–29; Federal Census, Population Schedules, Fitchburg, Worcester, Mass., 1850; Mary Burnap to Mr. Whipple, 13 May 1864, AMAA, N.C.; Mary A. Burnap to Mr. Whipple, 7 January 1865, AMAA, N.C.; Horace James to Dear Bro, 27 August 1863, AMAA, N.C. Burnap was born on August 22, 1838 in Fitchburg, Massachusetts, the fifth of ten children of Stillman Burnap and Melody Cousins Burnap. See "Ancestral File," *Family Search.*

26. "Ancestral File," *Family Search*; S. S. Nickerson to Rev. Whipple, 21 December 1864, AMAA, N.C.; P. B. S. Nickerson to Mr Whipple, 8 May 1865, AMAA, N.C.; E. James to Rev George Whipple, 21 February 1866, AMAA, N.C.

27. Roanoke Island N.C. to Mr. President, 9 March 1865, and Roanoke Island to [Secretary of War], 9 March 1865, both filed as B-2 1865, Letters Received, Washington Headquarters, RG 105, ser. 15, NA (M752, reel 13). Convention of the Freedmen of North Carolina, *Official Proceedings*, 2; *Freedmen's Advocate* 1 (May 1864):17; James, *Annual Report*, 11–12, 29, 43; Swint, *Dear Ones at Home*, 184, 199; "Monthly Report" of Camp Totten Freedmen's School for February 1864, AMAA, N.C.; Robert A. Morrow, Military Service Records, RG 94, NA; Regimental Descriptive Rolls, 14th USCHA, RG 94, NA; Register of Deaths, 14th USCHA, RG 94, NA.

28. "International Genealogical Index," *Family Search*; Charles A. Hill to Gentlemen of the N.F.R.A., *National Freedman* 1 (15 September 1865): 258. The description of the mother-daughter duo is quoted in Currie-McDaniel, "Northern Women in the South," 294. I have been unable to locate any biographical information about the Freemans in any reference or census materials that I have searched.

29. Redkey, *A Grand Army*, 281–83. For a list of the missionaries who served on Roanoke Island, see Appendix D.

30. E. James to Mr Whipple, 19 December 1863, AMAA, N.C.; [Lucy Chase] to Sarah [Chase], 12 January 1865, in Swint, *Dear Ones at Home*, 138; E. James to Rev. G. Whipple, 13 August 1864, AMAA, N.C.; Horace James to Dear Bro, 23 February 1864, AMAA, N.C.; Elizabeth James to Brother in Christ, 2 February 1866, AMAA, N.C.

31. Elizabeth James to Brother in Christ, 2 February 1866, AMAA, N.C.; E. James to The Rev. G. Whipple, 13 August 1864, AMAA, N.C.,; E. James to Brother in Christ, 21 December 1864, AMAA, N.C.; Elizabeth James to Rev. G. Whipple, 25 September 1865, AMAA, N.C.; Elizabeth James to Brother in Christ, 2 February 1866, AMAA, N.C.

32. Ella Roper to Rev. Geo. Whipple, 1 December [1864], AMAA, N.C.; James, *Annual Report*, 29; E. James to The Rev. G. Whipple, 13 August 1864, AMAA, N.C.; Elizabeth James to Brother in Christ [George Whipple], 2 February 1866, AMAA, N.C.; S. S. Nickerson to Bro. Whipple, 26 November 1864, AMAA, N.C.; [Lucy Chase] to Sarah, 12 January 1865, in Swint, *Dear Ones at Home*, 138. Before his marriage, Samuel Nickerson had lived on Roanoke Island in a small house by himself. Returning from his vacation with his bride, he discovered that the house was occupied by someone else.

33. S. S. Nickerson to Rev. Whipple, 21 December 1864, AMAA, N.C.; P. B. Nickerson to Mr. Whipple, 9 January 1864 [1865], AMAA, N.C.; S. S. Nickerson to Bro Whiting, 8 May

1865, AMAA, N.C. Elizabeth James describes the Nickersons' problems with unseasoned wood in a letter to George Whipple, 21 February 1866, AMAA, N.C.

34. Ella Roper to Mr Whipple, 17 June 1864, 1 December [1864], AMAA, N.C.; Mary A. Burnap to Mr. Whipple, 21 March 1865, AMAA, N.C.; Ella Roper to Rev. Geo. Whipple, 31 May [1864], AMAA, N.C.; "From Miss E. James," 7 April 1864, *American Missionary* 8 (June 1864): 141.

35. E. James to Mr. W. E. Whiting, 5 September 1864, AMAA, N.C.; E. James to Brother in Christ, 21 December 1864, AMAA, N.C.; Wm. T. Briggs to Rev. George Whipple, 10 April 1865, AMAA, N.C.; Horace James to Bro. Whipple, 6 September 1865, AMAA, N.C.; Wm. T. Briggs to Rev. Geo. Whipple, 17 December 1864, AMAA, N.C.; Wm. T. Briggs to Rev. George Whipple, 3 December 1864, AMAA, N.C. For a description of Elizabeth James's attempts to establish an orphan asylum on Roanoke Island, see especially Elizabeth James to Brother in Christ [George Whipple], 2 February 1866, AMAA, N.C.

36. P. B. Nickerson to Mr. Whipple, 9 January 1864 [1865], AMAA, N.C.; Ella Roper to Rev. Geo. Whipple, 1 December [1864], AMAA, N.C.

37. Sarah P. Freeman to Miss Luckey, 30 August 1864, *Freedmen's Advocate* 1 (October 1864): 34. My estimate of family size is based upon the ratio of houses to the population size and upon the information contained in a list of people on the island during the winter of 1866–67 who wanted to leave. See "List of names of freedpeople living on Roanoke Island N.C. likely to become destitute during the ensuing Winter," Letters and Orders Received, Reports, and Supply Requests, Roanoke Island, Records of the Assistant Commissioner for North Carolina, RG 105, ser. 2821, NA. This list is reproduced in Appendix E.

38. S. S. Nickerson, "Mission Schools on Roanoke Island N.C." [29 October 1864], AMAA, N.C.; E. James to Mr Whipple, 19 December 1863, AMAA, N.C.; E. James to Rev. G. Whipple, 6 December 1864, AMAA, N.C.

39. E. James to Mr. Whipple, 19 December 1863, 25 December 1863, AMAA, N.C.

40. E. James to Mr. Whipple, 19 December 1863, 24 December 1863, 25 December 1863, AMAA, N.C.

41. E. James to Mr. Whipple, 19 December 1863, AMAA, N.C.; Elizabeth James to Rev. George Whipple, 22 August 1864, AMAA, N.C.; Horace James to Dear Bro [George Whipple], 4 January 1864, AMAA, N.C. See also [Lucy Chase] to Sarah, 12 January 1865, in Swint, ed., *Dear Ones at Home*, 139.

42. E. James to Rev. S. S. Jocelyn, 6 February 1864, AMAA, N.C.; Benj. B. Foster to General I. N. Palmer, 28 February 1864, OR, ser. 1, vol. 33, 612; Benj. B. Foster to General H. W. Wessells, 28 February 1864, OR, ser. 1, vol. 33, 613. The *Second Annual Report of the New England Freedmen's Aid Society* (p. 29) indicates that the surname was Storer rather than Stover. A man named A. R. (Amos R.) Storer, a baker from Lowell, did serve in the First and Fourth Massachusetts Cavalry, and it is possible that he was assigned to Roanoke Island. Both Elizabeth and Horace James wrote, however, of a man named Stover from Boston who supervised construction on Roanoke Island. A. R. (Albert R.) Stover, a marble worker from Boston, served in the Forty-fourth Massachusetts Infantry; it is likely that he is the man who served as James's assistant on Roanoke Island. See Compiled Service Records, RG 92, NA; and Ancestry.com, Civil War Research Database.

43. Wm. T. Briggs to Rev. George Whipple, 18 March 1864, AMAA, N.C.; Dickey,

History of the 103d, 63; Ella Roper to Rev. Geo. Whipple, 31 May 1864, AMAA, N.C.; S. S. Nickerson to Wm. T. Briggs, 10 May 1864, AMAA, N.C.; S. S. Nickerson, "Mission Schools on Roanoke Island," [29 October 1864], AMAA, N.C.

44. "The Refugees from Plymouth," *Freedmen's Advocate* 1 (May 1864): 19; "Letter from Mrs. Freeman," 7 July 1864, *Freedmen's Advocate* 1 (August 1864): 25–26; Holland Streeter to Col. Kinsman, 13 March 1864, 29 March 1864, 10 April 1864, 4 May 1864, Records of the Department of Negro Affairs for Virginia and North Carolina, RG 105, ser. 4108, NA.

45. *Second Annual Report*, 29–30. The italics were in the original.

46. Wm. T. Briggs to Rev. George Whipple, 27 April 1864, AMAA, N.C.; *Second Annual Report*, 30. The italics are in the original.

47. Ella Roper to Rev Geo Whipple, 28 January [1865], AMAA, N.C.; "Letter from Mrs. S. P. Freeman," February 1865, *National Freedman* 1 (March 1865): 61; "Roanoke Island," *National Freedman* 1 (April 1865): 93; S. P. Freeman to Mrs. [Charles C.] Leigh, 7 July 1864, *Freedmen's Advocate* 1 (August 1864): 25; P. B. Nickerson to Mr. Whipple, 9 January [1865], AMAA, N.C.

48. Elizabeth James to Rev. G. Whipple, 25 September 1865, AMAA, N.C.; Ella Roper to Rev. Geo. Whipple, 21 September 1865, AMAA, N.C.

49. Elizabeth James to Rev. George Whipple, 29 November 1865, AMAA, N.C.; E. James to Rev. G. Whipple, 13 August 1864, AMAA, N.C.; E. James to Mr. W. E. Whiting, 5 September 1864, AMAA, N.C.; E. James to Dear brother [George Whipple], 6 December [1864], AMAA, N.C.; Elizabeth James to Mr. William E. Whiting, 13 May 1865, AMAA, N.C.; E. James to Mr. William E. Whiting, 28 January 1867, AMAA, N.C. [Ella Roper] to ——, [5 August 1865], AMAA, N.C.; E. James to Mr. George Whipple, 23 January 1867, AMAA, N.C.; Elizabeth James to Rev. G. Whipple, 27 March 1866, AMAA, N.C.

50. E. James to W. E. Whiting, 5 September 1864, AMAA, N.C.; E. James to S. S. Jocelyn, 6 February 1864, AMAA, N.C.; [Ella Roper to George Whipple], 5 August 1864, AMAA, N.C.; P. B. Nickerson to Mr. Hunt, 6 February 1866, AMAA, N.C.

51. Ella Roper to ——, [5 August 1864], AMAA, N.C.; Ella Roper to Rev. Geo. Whipple, 31 December [1864], AMAA, N.C.; Sarah P. Freeman to Mr. C. C. Leigh, 29 September 1864, in *Freedmen's Advocate* 1 (November 1864): 38.

52. Sarah P. Freeman to Mr. Leigh, 7 November 1864, *Freedmen's Advocate* 1 (December 1864): 42.

53. Mary Burnap to George Whipple, 14 January 1864, AMAA, N.C.; [Ella Roper], "Wants of the Freedmen," 5 August 1864, AMAA, N.C.; Ella Roper to Rev. Geo. Whipple, 28 January [1865], AMAA, N.C.

54. "Aiding the Freedmen," *American Missionary* 9 (December 1864): 292; Horace James, "Sales from this office, for the Month of January, 1864," Records of the Department of Negro Affairs for North Carolina and Virginia, RG 105, ser. 4109, NA.

55. "Letter from Captain James," 23 April 1864, *Second Annual Report*, 70; Ella Roper to ——, [5 August 1864], AMAA, N.C.; E. James to Brother in Christ, 29 December 1864, AMAA, N.C.; Horace James, "Sales from this Office, for the Month of January, 1864," Records of the Department of Negro Affairs for Virginia and North Carolina, RG 105, ser. 4109, NA; Sarah P. Freeman to Mr. Leigh, 7 November 1964, *Freedmen's Advocate* 1 (December 1864): 42.

56. Mary R. Kimball to J. Miller McKim, James Miller McKim Papers, Anti-Slavery Collection, Cornell University, quoted in Wolfe, "Women Who Dared," 88; E. James to Rev. George Whipple, 22 August 1864, AMAA, N.C.; Elizabeth James to Rev George Whipple, 21 February 1866, AMAA, N.C.

57. Elizabeth James to Mr Whipple, 20 May 1864, AMAA, N.C.; E. R. to Mr. Geo. Whipple 12 December [1864], AMAA, N.C.; [Ella Roper to George Whipple], *American Missionary* (July 1865): 157–58; S. P. Freeman to Mrs. [Charles C. Leigh], 7/8 July 1864, *Freedmen's Advocate* 1 (August 1864): 26. Sarah P. Freeman to Mr. C. C. Leigh, 29 September 1864, *Freedmen's Advocate* 1 (November 1864): 38; Elizabeth James to Rev. G. Whipple, 25 September 1865, AMAA, N.C.; S. S. Nickerson to Bro Whiting, 8 May 1865, AMAA, N.C.

58. P. B. Nickerson to Mr. Whipple, 9 January 1864, AMAA, N.C.; E. James to Rev. G. Whipple, 13 August 1864, AMAA, N.C.

59. E. James to Brother in Christ [George Whipple], 21 December 1864, AMAA, N.C.; Elizabeth James to Brother in Christ [George Whipple], 2 February 1866, AMAA, N.C.

60. E. James to Rev. G. Whipple, 13 August 1864, AMAA, N.C.

61. Ibid.

62. In addition to materials already cited, see Ella Roper to [George Whipple], 20 April 1865, *American Missionary* (July 1865): 157–58; PBS Nickerson to Mr. Whipple, 22 April 1865, AMAA, N.C. The strength of the familial ties in the Roanoke Island freedmen's colony is consistent with Herbert Gutman's description of the strength of the bonds of the black family during slavery. See Gutman, *The Black Family*.

63. Affidavits filed in pension petitions indicate the extent of traditional marriages among the freedpeople. A widow, of course, had to prove that she had been married to a soldier when she applied for his pension; thus, marriage status was emphasized in pension applications. See Pension Records of Frank James and William H. Overton, RG 94, NA; Federal Census, Population Schedules, Mackey's Ferry, Washington, N.C., 1860.

64. See Pension Records of Jeffrey Johnson, John Tyler, Thomas Sanders, and Albert Banks, RG 94, NA.

65. Regimental Descriptive Books, 37th USCT, RG 94, NA; Pension Records of Leon Bembury, RG 94, NA.

66. Some historians have noted that the teachers' patronizing air with respect to the former slaves' behavior and deportment had many parallels to the missionaries' behavior with respect to the white lower classes at home. See Davis, *Joshua Leavitt*, 108. At various points in *Soldiers of Light and Love*, Jacqueline Jones stresses the differences between the teachers' values and the freedpeople's values. See Jones, especially 140–66. Similarly, Allis Wolfe discusses the difference between the teachers' expectations and the reality of slave culture. See Wolfe, "Women Who Dared," 96.

CHAPTER FIVE

1. Schurz, *Intimate Letters*, 328–9; William T. Briggs to Geo. Whipple, 10 April 1865, AMAA, N.C.

2. S. S. Nickerson to ——, [29 October 1864], AMAA, N.C.

3. Benjamin F. Butler, General Orders No. 46, Head Quarters Department of Virginia and North Carolina, 5 December 1863, General Orders Issued, vol. 52, Department of Virginia and North Carolina and 18th Army Corps, RG 393, pt. I, ser.5078, NA. Jacqueline Jones presents an excellent overview of the research of historians with respect to freedpeople and missionary teachers. See *Soldiers of Light and Love*, 3–13.

4. Wm. T. Briggs to Rev. George Whipple, 4 May 1864, AMAA, N.C.

5. Ella Roper to [George Whipple], 20 April 1865, *American Missionary* 9 (July 1865): 157.

6. S. S. Nickerson, "Mission Schools on Roanoke Island N.C." [29 October 1864], AMAA, N.C.; Elizabeth James, "Teacher's Monthly Report" for Lincoln School, June 1864, AMAA, N.C.; S. S. Nickerson to Rev Samuel Hunt, 5 March 1866, AMAA, N.C.

7. E. Roper and Mary Burnap, "Teacher's Monthly Report" for Whipple School, March 1864, AMAA, N.C.; [Horace James], "Death of Miss Getchell," 16 March [1864], *American Missionary* 8 (May 1864): 129.

8. S. S. Nickerson to Rev. Wm. T. Briggs, 10 May 1864, AMAA, N.C.; Wm. T. Briggs to Rev. George Whipple, 24 April 1864, AMAA, N.C.; S. S. Nickerson, "Mission Schools on Roanoke Island N.C.," [29 October 1864], AMAA, N.C.

9. Ella Roper to Rev. Geo. Whipple, 31 May [1864], AMAA, N.C.; S. S. Nickerson to Rev. Whipple, 21 December 1864, AMAA, N.C. See also, Ella Roper to Mr. Wm T. Briggs, 28 February 1865, AMAA, N.C.; Ella Roper to Rev. Geo. Whipple, 2 March 1865, AMAA, N.C.; Ella Roper to Rev Geo Whipple, 28 January [1865], AMAA, N.C.

10. S. S. Nickerson, "Mission Schools on Roanoke Island N.C.," [29 October 1864], AMAA, N.C.; Ella Roper to Rev. Geo. Whipple, 31 May [1864], AMAA, N.C.

11. S. S. Nickerson, "Mission Schools on Roanoke Island N.C.," [29 October 1864], AMAA, N.C.; Wm. T. Briggs to Rev. George Whipple, 21 June 1864, AMAA, N.C.; Horace James, 16 September 1864, *American Missionary* 8 (November 1864): 261; Wm T. Briggs to Rev. George Whipple, 3 December 1864, AMAA, N.C.; Wm. T. Briggs to Bro. Whipple, 10 December 1864, AMAA, N.C.; Wm. T. Briggs to Rev. Geo. Whipple, 17 December 1864, AMAA, N.C.; Wm. T. Briggs to Rev. Geo. Whipple, 7 January 1865, AMAA, N.C.; Mary A. Burnap to Mr. Whipple, 21 March 1865, AMAA, N.C.

12. Ella Roper, "Teacher's Monthly Report" for Briggs School, June 1864, AMAA, N.C.: Ella Roper to Rev. Geo. Whipple, 31 May [1864], AMAA, N.C.; S. S. Nickerson, "Teacher's Monthly Report" for Cypress Chapel School, June 1864, AMAA, N.C.; Ella Roper to Rev Geo Whipple, 28 January [1865], AMAA, N.C.; Ella Roper to Rev. Geo. Whipple, 31 December [1864], AMAA, N.C.

13. *Christian Recorder*, 2 December 1865, quoted in McPherson, *Struggle for Equality*, 397; Wolfe, "Women Who Dared," 10, 68; *American Missionary* 8 (October 1863): 235; Litwack, *Been in the Storm So Long*, 478–79; Ella Roper to Mrs Lewis Tappan, 15 February [1865], AMAA, N.C.; Drake, "The American Missionary Association," 218–19.

14. *Freedmen's Journal* 10 (January 1865): 3; Litwack, *Been in the Storm So Long*, 452; Butchart, *Northern Schools*, 31; Wolfe, "Women Who Dared," 11–12, 180.

15. [Ella Roper], "Wants of the Freedmen," AMAA, N.C.; Elizabeth James to Rev. G. Whipple, 3 February 1866, AMAA, N.C..

16. *National Freedman's Relief Association Monthly Paper for May, 1863*, 4, AMAA, N.Y.; Ella Roper to Wm T. Briggs, 28 February 1865, AMAA, N.C.

17. Susan Odell to Mr. Hawkins, 29 May 1865, *National Freedman* 1 (1 June 1865): 154; Wm. T. Briggs to Rev. George Whipple, 18 March 1864, AMAA, N.C.; Ella Roper to Rev. Geo. Whipple, 26 May [1865], AMAA, N.C.; Ella Roper to Rev. Geo. Whipple, 3 June 1865, AMAA, N.C. See also Jacqueline Jones's discussion of the operations of missionary schools in Georgia in *Soldiers of Light and Love*, 109, 128–29.

18. *Second Annual Report*, 33–4, 54; Jones " 'A Glorious Work,' " 43; Richardson, *Christian Reconstruction*, 42; Ella Roper to Rev. Geo. Whipple, 2 March 1865, AMAA, N.C.; Ella Roper to ——, 20 April 1865, AMAA, N.C.; Litwack, *Been in the Storm So Long*, 403; Butchart, *Northern Schools*, 31; Wolfe, "Women Who Dared," 11–12, 180.

19. Elizabeth James to Rev. George Whipple, 6 May 1865, AMAA, N.C.

20. Ella Roper to Rev. Geo. Whipple, 31 December [1864], AMAA, N.C.; Wm T. Briggs to Rev. George Whipple, 21 June 1864, AMAA, N.C.; E. James to Brother in Christ [George Whipple], 21 December 1864, AMAA, N.C.; E. James to Rev. G. Whipple, 13 August 1864, AMAA, N.C. Although Elizabeth James does not give Richard's surname, all that is known about Boyle indicates that he was the Richard who taught in the summer school.

21. Ella E. Roper and Mary A. Burnap, "Teacher's Monthly Report" for Whipple School, April 1864, AMAA, N.C.; S. S. Nickerson, "Teacher's Monthly Report" for Cypress Chapel School, June 1864, 6 July 1864, AMAA, N.C.; Ella Roper, "Teacher's Monthly Report" for Briggs School, June 1865, 4 July 1864, AMAA, N.C.; Ella Roper to Rev. Geo. Whipple, 3 June 1865, AMAA, N.C.

22. Ella E. Roper and Mary A. Burnap, "Teacher's Monthly Report" for Whipple School, April 1864, AMAA, N.C.; S. S. Nickerson, "Teacher's Monthly Report" for Cypress Chapel School, June 1864, 6 July 1864, AMAA, N.C.; Ella Roper, "Teacher's Monthly Report" for Briggs School, June 1865, 4 July 1864, AMAA, N.C.; Ella Roper to Rev. Geo. Whipple, 3 June 1865, AMAA, N.C.; Rev. S. S. Nickerson to Bro Hunt, 23 October 1865, AMAA, N.C.; S. S. Nickerson to Rev. Samuel Hunt, 29 December 1865, AMAA, N.C.; P. B. Nickerson to Rev. Mr. Hunt, 6 February 1866, AMAA, N.C.

23. William T. Briggs, "Annual Report of the Superintendent of the Colored Schools in North Carolina" [July 1865], AMAA, N.C..

24. Ella Roper to Rev. Geo. Whipple, 16 November 1864, AMAA, N.C.; *National Freedman* 1 (15 September 1865): 261–62; S. S. Nickerson to Rev Samuel Hunt, 29 December 1865, AMAA, N.C.

25. P. B. S. Nickerson to Mr. Whipple, 22 April 1865, AMAA, N.C.

26. Ibid.; P. B. Nickerson to Rev. Hunt, 6 February 1866, AMAA, N.C.; [Ella Roper], "Wants of the Freedmen," [5 August 1864], AMAA, N.C.

27. [Ella Roper to George Whipple], 5 August 1864, AMAA, N.C.; M. A. Burnap to Mr. Whipple, 20 May 1864.

28. Elizabeth James to Rev. George Whipple, 6 May 1865, AMAA, N.C.

29. *American Missionary*, 2 (January 1858): 10; Elizabeth James to Rev. G. Whipple, 3 February 1866, AMAA, N.C.

30. Susan Odell to Mr. Hawkins, 29 May 1865, AMAA, N.C.; Ella Roper to Mr Whipple, 17 June 1864, AMAA, N.C.; Ella Roper to Rev. Geo. Whipple, 1 December 1864, AMAA, N.C.; S. S. Nickerson to Bro. Whipple, 6 June 1865, AMAA, N.C.; and Elizabeth James to Rev. G. Whipple, 27 March 1866, AMAA, N.C.; S. S. Nickerson to Rev. Wm. T. Briggs, 6 July 1864, AMAA, N.C.

31. *American Missionary* (December 1864): 285; Mary A. Burnap to Mr. Whipple, 26 August 1864, AMAA, Mass.; E. James to Rev. G. Whipple, 14 February 1865, AMAA, N.C.; E. James to Rev. George Whipple, AMAA, N.C.

32. M.A.B. to Mr. Whipple, 4 July 1864, AMAA, N.C.; E.R. to Mr. Geo. Whipple, 12 December [1864], AMAA, N.C.

33. S. S. Nickerson to Rev. Wm. T. Briggs, 10 May 1864, AMAA, N.C.; S. S. Nickerson to Rev. Whipple, 21 December 1864, AMAA, N.C.; and S. S. Nickerson, "Mission Schools on Roanoke Island N.C.," [29 October 1864], AMAA, N.C.; E. James to Rev. G. Whipple, 13 August 1864, AMAA, N.C.; Elizabeth James to Rev. G. Whipple, 27 March 1866, AMAA, N.C.

34. Elizabeth James to Rev. G. Whipple, 25 September 1865, AMAA, N.C.

35. [Lucy Chase] to Sarah, 12 January 1865, in Swint, *Dear Ones at Home*, 140; Mary A. Burnap to Mr. Whipple, 7 January 1865, AMAA, N.C.

36. P. B. S. Nickerson to Mr. Whipple, 22 April 1865, AMAA, N.C.; P. B. Nickerson to Mr. Hunt, 6 February 1866, AMAA, N.C.; Ella Roper to Rev. Geo. Whipple, 31 May [1864], AMAA, N.C. Mary Barbour, one of the former slaves interviewed for the Federal Writers' Project, recalled seeing an old witch woman on Roanoke Island. The missionaries, however, never mentioned any concerns about witchcraft on the island. See Federal Writers' Project, *Slave Narratives*, North Carolina, vol. 11, part I, 81.

37. Elizabeth James to Rev. G. Whipple, 27 March 1866, AMAA, N.C.

38. "Roanoke Island," *National Freedman* 1 (15 November 1865): 319–20; Ella Roper to Rev. Geo. Whipple, 21 September 1865, 5 October 1865, AMAA, N.C.

39. Esther A. Williams to Hon. C. C. Leigh, 17 February 1865, *National Freedman* 1 (1 April 1865): 93; S. P. Freeman, "Industrial School, Roanoke Island," *National Freedman* 1 (15 August 1866): 215; E. P. Bennett to Rev. W. G. Hawkins, 14 November 1865, *National Freedman* 1 (15 November 1865): 320; E. A. Williams, "Industrial School, Roanoke Island," *National Freedman* 1 (15 December 1865): 348. See also Alvord, *Semi-Annual Report on Schools for Freedmen*, 1:3. The location of the Industrial School was noted in various monthly reports of the Bureau of Refugees, Freedmen, and Abandoned Lands. See, for example, Monthly Report of F. A. Seely, Abandoned or Confiscated Lands in the Eastern District of North Carolina, during the month ending Sept. 30th, 1865, Monthly Land Reports, Records of the Assistant Commissioner for the State of North Carolina, RG 105, entry 2470, NA (M843, reel 36).

40. *National Freedman* 1 (15 September 1865): 262; Roanoke Island N.C. to [Secretary of War], 9 March 1865, filed as B-2 1865, Letters Received, Washington Headquarters, RG 105, ser.15, NA (M752, reel 13); E. James, "Teacher's Monthly Report" for Lincoln School, April 1865, AMAA, N.C.

41. *National Freedman* 1 (15 September 1865): 262; E. P. Bennett to Rev. W. G. Hawkins, 31 October 1865, *National Freedman* 1 (15 November 1865): 320.

42. Raleigh *Sentinel*, 12 January 1866, 2; *Norfolk Virginian*, quoted in the *American Missionary* (July 1867): 151–52.

43. Booker T. Washington, *Future of the American Negro* (Boston: 1899), 25, quoted in Pierce, *The Freedmen's Bureau*, 85.

44. S. P. Freeman, "Industrial School, Roanoke Island," *National Freedman* 1 (15 August

1866): 216. It is easy to conclude that the AMA and NFRA missionaries were merely naive, but that evokes a presentism that judges them by our very different standards.

45. A report issued on 21 April 1864 by the New England Freedmen's Aid Society indicated that the average attendance at schools in the Third District was 60 percent. See *Second Annual Report*, 33.

46. S. S. Nickerson to Samuel Hunt, 5 March 1866, AMAA, N.C.

CHAPTER SIX

1. Graham, *Ninth Regiment New York*, 198–99.

2. Ibid., 231, 234.

3. James M. McPherson analyzed diaries and letters from a large sampling of Union soldiers and concluded that during the first eighteen months of the war, 30 percent of the soldiers believed that "the abolition of slavery was inseparably linked to the goal of preserving the Union." The soldiers' attitudes toward blacks and emancipation evolved during the Civil War years, and "many more were eventually converted" to this stance. See chapter 9, "Slavery Must Be Cleaned Out," in McPherson, *For Cause and Comrades*, 117–30.

4. S. S. Nickerson to Bro. Whipple, 6 December 1864, AMAA, N.C; S. S. Nickerson to Rev. Whipple, 21 December 1864, AMAA, N.C.; Federal Census, Population Schedules, Lowell, Middlesex, Massachusetts, 1860.

5. Ella Roper to Mr Whipple, 17 June 1864, AMAA, N.C.; Ella Roper to S. S. [W. E.] Whiting, 8 July [1865]; [Lucy Chase] to Sarah, 15 January 1865, in Swint, *Dear Ones at Home*, p.139.

6. "Teacher's Monthly Report" for Whipple School, April 1864, AMAA, N.C.; Ella Roper to Rev. Geo. Whipple, 31 May [1864], AMAA, N.C.

7. "Letter from Captain James," *Second Annual Report*, 74; James, *Annual Report*, 30; Reilly, "Regeneration Through Reconstruction," 55; "Rev. W. Hamilton's Tour," *American Missionary* 8 (April 1864): 83.

8. E. James to Rev. George Whipple, 5 September 1864, AMAA, N.C.; Sarah P. Freeman to Miss Luckey, 30 August 1864, *Freedmen's Advocate* 1 (October 1864): 34; "Letter from Mrs. Freeman," 7 July 1864, *Freedmen's Advocate* 1 (August 1864): 25–26; Sarah P. Freeman to Mr. C. C. Leigh, 29 September 1864, "A Letter To be Read and Circulated, in Public and Private Meeting, in aid of the Freedmen," *Freedmen's Advocate* 1 (November 1864): 38; Elizabeth James to Brother in Christ, 2 February 1866, AMAA, N.C.; Wm. T. Briggs to Rev. George Whipple, 27 April 1864, *American Missionary* 8 (June 1864): 140; *Second Annual Report*, 29. Sarah Freeman's estimate of the number of orphans on the island, five hundred, was a great exaggeration. The true number will never be known, as no count of orphans was ever taken.

9. "Letter from Mrs. S. P. Freeman," February 1865, *National Freedman* 1 (March 1865): 61.

10. James, *Annual Report*, 26.

11. Horace James to Gen. E. A. Wilde, 16 March 1864, Edward A. Wild Papers, MOLLUS-Massachusetts Collection, USAMHI; John J. Peck to Maj. Gen. B. F. Butler, 20 April 1864, 21 April 1864, OR, ser. 1, vol. 33, 283–84; Dickey, *History of the 103d*, 65.

12. Horace James to Major Genl. B. F. Butler, 19 July 1864, Records of the Department of Negro Affairs for Virginia and North Carolina, Letters, Orders, and Telegrams Received by Lt. Col. J. B. Kinsman, General Superintendent, RG 105, ser. 4108, NA; Berlin et al., *The Wartime Genesis of Free Labor: The Upper South*, 204. The *American Missionary* had included articles complaining about impressment of the freedmen for government service and the military since the summer of 1863. See *American Missionary* 7 (August 1863): 180.

13. Ned Baxter, Saml. Owens and forty three other contrabands from Roanoke Island N.C. to Major Genl. Butler, with endorsements, September 1864, Department of Virginia and North Carolina and Army of the James, Miscellaneous Letters Received, RG 393 pt. 1, ser. 5076, NA.

14. Horace James to Major R. S. Davis, 25 September 1864, Compiled Service Records, 43rd Massachusetts Infantry, George O. Sanderson, RG 92, NA.

15. Horace James to Lt. Col. J. B. Kinsman, 23 February 1864, Letters, Orders, and Telegrams Received by Lt. Col. J. B. Kinsman, General Superintendent, Department of Negro Affairs, Departments of Virginia and North Carolina, RG 105, ser. 4108, NA; "Letter from North Carolina," 4 March 1864, *Congregationalist* 16 (18 March 1864): 47.

16. Horace James to Lt. Col. J. B. Kinsman, 23 March 1864, 5 June 1864, 20 June 1864, 7 July 1864, 7 November 1864, Letters, Orders, and Telegrams Received by Lt. Col. J. B. Kinsman, General Superintendent, Department of Negro Affairs, Departments of Virginia and North Carolina, RG 105, ser. 4108, NA; "Letter from Chaplain James," 19 August 1864, *Congregationalist* 16 (2 September 1864): 142; Horace James to My Dear Brother [George Whipple], 26 August 1864, 16 September 1864, AMAA, N.C.

17. Sarah P. Freeman to Miss Luckey, 30 August 1864, *Freedmen's Advocate* 1 (October 1864): 34; James, *Annual Report*, 32–33. One estimate is that in 1999 dollars, the amount owed to the Roanoke Island freedmen would be approximately $185,700. My thanks to Haynes Earnhardt, Library Assistant in Government Information Resources at Alderman Library of the University of Virginia, for helping me locate the conversion information on the World Wide Web. See Sahr, "Consumer Price Index (CPI) Conversion Factors to Convert to 1999 Dollars (Preliminary)."

18. Ella Roper to Rev. Geo. Whipple, 3 June 1865, AMAA, N.C.; Pierce, *The Freedmen's Bureau*, 6; Horace James to Lt. Col. J. B. Kinsman, 17 April 1864, Letters, Orders, and Telegrams Received by Lt. Col. J. B. Kinsman, General Superintendent, Department of Negro Affairs, Departments of Virginia and North Carolina, RG 105, ser. 4108, NA; "Letter from Captain James," 23 April 1864, *Second Annual Report*, 70.

19. War Department, Adjutant General's Office, General Orders No. 30, 25 January 1864, OR, ser. 3, vol. 4, 44–45; *Second Annual Report*, 27, 30.

20. Roanoke Island N.C. to Mr. President, 9 March 1865, and Roanoke Island to [Secretary of War], 9 March 1865, filed as B-2 1865, Letters Received, Washington Headquarters, RG 105, ser. 15, NA (M752, reel 13).

21. Dickey, *History of the 103d*, 65; Jack to Father, 7 May 1865, Reynolds Laughlin Correspondence, USAMHI.

22. Dickey, *History of the 103d*, 66.

23. Roanoke Island N.C. to Mr. President, 9 March 1865, and Roanoke Island to [Secretary of War], 9 March 1865, filed as B-2 1865, Letters Received, Washington Headquarters,

RG 105, ser. 15, NA (M752, reel 13); Reilly, "Reconstruction Through Regeneration," 88; Bentley, *A History*, 51–55. Bentley notes that Stanton had recommended Howard to President Lincoln, who was assassinated before he could make the appointment. Bentley also states that Stanton, who kept his Radical Republican beliefs under cover, probably felt that Howard would help the Radical cause, especially the aims of the abolitionists.

24. Frank James to Mr Genrell A. G. Draper, 4 June 1865, Unregistered Letters Received, Records of the Assistant Commissioner for North Carolina, RG 105, ser. 2453, NA (M843, reel 16). Frank James was free prior to the war; he had been a waterman in Plymouth before bringing his wife, Indianna, to Roanoke Island.

25. Sergt Richard Etheridge and Wm Benson to Genl Howard, [May or June 1865], Office of the Assistant Commissioner of North Carolina, Letters Received, RG 105, ser. 2453, NA (M843, reel 16).

26. Horace James to Lt. Fred H. Beecher, 20 September 1865, Letters Received, Records of the Assistant Commissioner for North Carolina, RG 105, ser. 2452, NA (M843, reel 8); Ella Roper to Rev. Geo. Whipple, 3 June 1865, AMAA, N.C.; S. S. Nickerson to Bro. Whipple, 6 June 1865, AMAA, N.C.

27. Wm. A. Green et al. to Maj. Genl. O. O. Howard, 5 June 1865, Office of the Assistant Commissioner of North Carolina, Unregistered Letters Received, RG 105, ser. 2453, NA (M843, reel 16); S. S. Nickerson to Bro. Whipple, 6 June 1865, AMAA, N.C.

28. Francis George Shaw to Major General O. O. Howard, 7 June 1865, and endorsement by J. S. Fullerton, 9 June 1865, Office of the Assistant Commissioner of North Carolina, Unregistered Letters Received, RG 105, ser. 2453, NA (M843, reel 16); Chas. J. Paine to Capt. McMurray, 8 June 1865, with copy of telegram from J. A. Campbell to Brig. Gen. C. J. Paine, Office of the Assistant Commissioner of North Carolina, Unregistered Letters Received, RG 105, ser. 2453, NA (M843, reel 16).

29. John McMurray to Bvt. Maj. Genl. C. J. Paine, 11 June 1865, Office of the Assistant Commissioner of North Carolina, Unregistered Letters Received, RG 105, ser. 2453, NA (M843, reel 16); Horace James to Col. Whittlesey, 15 July 1865, Office of the Assistant Commissioner of North Carolina, Letters Received, RG 105, ser. 2452, NA (M843, reel 8). Presumably the William Benson who testified to McMurray was the same William Benson who had written from his military encampment earlier that spring complaining about the treatment of the families in the Roanoke colony.

30. John H. Holman to Solon A. Carter, 14 June 1865, Office of the Assistant Commissioner of North Carolina, Unregistered Letters Received, RG 105, ser. 2453, NA (M843, reel 16). Holman was mistaken about Carter's middle initial, which was G., not A.

31. John H. Holman to Maj. Genl O. O. Howard, with endorsement by J. S. Fullerton, 15 June 1865, Office of the Assistant Commissioner of North Carolina, Unregistered Letters Received, RG 105, ser. 2453, NA (M843, reel 16).

32. Bentley, *A History*, 58; Reilly, "Reconstruction Through Regeneration," 92–93.

33. Eliphalet Whittlesey, Circular No. 1, 1 July 1865, and Circular No. 2, 15 July 1865, General Orders and Circulars Issued, RG 105, ser. 2457, NA (M843, reel 20); "Letter from the Rev. Horace James," 8 August 1865, *Congregationalist* 17 (18 August 1865): 129; Reilly, "Reconstruction Through Regeneration," 94–95.

34. I owe a great debt to Steve Reilly for a number of discussions in which he offered me

his insights into what he calls the "three-way partnership between men of similar ideas and convictions working for the same ends." For further exploration of these ideas, see Reilly, "Reconstruction Through Regeneration," 94.

35. James, *Annual Report*, 55.

36. William G. Hawkins, "Roanoke Island," *National Freedman* 1 (July 1865): 204; Wm. G. Hawkins to Sir, 19 July 1865, *National Freedman* 1 (15 August 1865): 221–22.

37. William H. Brown, 6 July 1865, *Christian Recorder* (22 July 1865) in Redkey, *A Grand Army*, 174.

38. Court Martial MM-2836, Holland Streeter, Court Martial Case Files, Office of the Judge Advocate General, Box 1238, General Orders No. 28, New Berne, 24 July 1865, Records of the Office of the Judge Advocate General, RG 153, ser. 15, NA [FSSP H-62].

39. Horace James to Col. [Whittlesey], 25 July 1865, Records of the Assistant Commissioner for North Carolina, Letters Received, RG 105, ser. 2452, NA (M843, reel 8); Horace James to Brevt. Brig. Genl. Del. Bates, 27 July 1865, enclosed with Horace James to Col. E. Whittlesey, 30 July 1865, Case Files Relating to the Administration of Justice in North Carolina, Records of the Assistant Commissioner for North Carolina, RG 105, ser. 2484, NA (M843, reel 31).

40. Horace James to Col. E. Whittlesey, 30 July 1865, Case Files Relating to the Administration of Justice in North Carolina, Records of the Assistant Commissioner for North Carolina, RG 105, ser. 2484, NA (M843, reel 31); Horace James to Col. E. Whittlesey, 12 August 1865, Records of the Assistant Commissioner for North Carolina, Letters Received, RG 105, ser. 2452, NA (M843, reel 8).

41. Horace James to Col. J. S. Fullerton, 10 July 1865, filed with B-2 1865, Letters Received, Washington Headquarters, RG 105, ser. 15, NA (M752, reel 13).

42. E. Whittlesey to General [J. S. Fullerton], 12 July 1865, filed with B-2 1865, Letters Received, Washington Headquarters, RG 105, ser. 15, NA (M752, reel 13); *National Freedman* 1 (July 1865): 204–5; James, *Annual Report*, 28, 32.

43. S. H. Birdsall to Colonel E. Whittlesey, 25 July 1865, Office of the Assistant Commissioner of North Carolina, Unregistered Letters Received, RG 105, ser. 2453, NA (M843, reel 16); E. Whittlesey to Capt. Horace James, 29 July 1865, Office of the Assistant Commissioner of North Carolina, Letters Sent, page 20, entry 45, RG 105, ser. 2446, NA (M843, reel 1); Horace James to Col. Whittlesey, 31 July 1865, Office of the Assistant Commissioner of North Carolina, Letters Received, RG 105, ser. 2452, NA (M843, reel 8).

44. S. H. Birdsall to Horace James, 3 August 1865, Statistical Reports of Operations and Conditions of Freedmen, July 1865–November 1867, Records of the Assistant Commissioner for North Carolina, RG 105, ser. 2759, NA [FSSP A-839].

CHAPTER SEVEN

1. Elizabeth James to Rev. George Whipple, 29 November 1865, AMAA, N.C.

2. The rumors about land distribution also had a strong basis in the language of the act creating the Freedmen's Bureau.

3. Horace James, Semi-Monthly Report, Operations of the Freedmen's Bureau, Eastern District, North Carolina, 31 October 1865, Statistical Reports of Operations and Conditions of Freemen, New Berne, Records of the Assistant Commissioner for North Carolina, RG

105, ser. 2759, NA [FSSP A-841]; A. B. Chapin to Doctor, 11 June 1866, Letters Received, Records of the Assistant Commissioner for North Carolina, RG 105, ser. 2452, NA (M843, reel 9); Stephen Moore, Annual Report of the Operations of the District of New Berne for the Year ending October 31st, 1866, Annual Reports of Operations, Records of the Assistant Commissioner for North Carolina, RG 105, ser. 2463, NA (M843, reel 22).

4. Major-General John J. Peck, General Orders No. 12, 10 September 1863; OR, ser. 1, vol. 29, pt. 2, 166.

5. "Letter from Chaplain James," 5 September 1863, *Congregationalist* 15 (18 September 1863): 149.

6. Horace James to ——, 23 April 1864, *Second Annual Report*, 73; James, *Annual Report*, 24. The italics and the misspelling of "privileges" are in the original documents. James employed similar language in other letters.

7. Reilly, "Reconstruction Through Regeneration," 52; Benjamin F. Butler to Horace James, 3 February 1864, Letters Sent, vol. 50, no. 147, Department of Virginia and North Carolina, RG 393, pt. 1, ser. 5046, NA.

8. Horace James to Major Genl. B. F. Butler, 8 February 1864, 20 February 1864, Letters, Orders, and Telegrams Received by Lt. Col. J. B. Kinsman, General Superintendent, Records of the Department of Negro Affairs for Virginia and North Carolina, RG 105, ser. 4108, NA.

9. Horace James to Gen. Benjamin Butler, 3 March 1864, filed with Benjamin F. Butler to E. M. Stanton, 14 March 1864, Letters Received, B-697 (123) Box 299, 1864, Secretary of War, RG 107, NA [FSSP L-33]. The words in italics were underlined in Horace James's letter.

10. Benjamin F. Butler to E. M. Stanton, 14 March 1864, Letters Received, B-697 (123) Box 299, 1864, Records of the Office of the Secretary of War, RG 107, NA [FSSP L-33]; Benjamin F. Butler to E. Stanton, 14 March 1864, Letters Sent, vol. 50, no. 324, Department of Virginia and North Carolina, RG 393, pt. 1, ser. 5046, NA; Horace James to Gen'l E. A. Wilde, 16 March 1864, Edward A. Wild Papers, MOLLUS-Massachusetts Collection, USAMHI; Ed. R. Canby (for E. M. Stanton) to Benjamin F. Butler, 17 March 1864, filed with Benjamin F. Butler to E. M. Stanton, 14 March 1864, Letters Received, B-697 (123), Box 299, 1864, Records of the Office of the Secretary of War, RG 107, NA [FSSP L-324].

11. Horace James to Major Genl. B. F. Butler, 30 June 1864, Records of the Department of Negro Affairs for Virginia and North Carolina, RG 105, ser. 4108, NA; Reilly, "Reconstruction Through Regeneration," 54.

12. Bentley, *A History*, 44; McPherson, *Struggle for Equality*, 178; Hamilton, *Reconstruction in North Carolina*, 295.

13. James, *Annual Report*, 31–32, 52. From a modern vantage point, James's comparison of the lost colony to the freedmen's colony is doubly ironic. First, historians and archaeologists are still arguing about whether the fortifications cited in various Civil War era documents were truly remnants of the "lost colony." Also, no visible physical signs of the freedmen's colony remain today.

14. Ibid., 32–33; Reilly, "Reconstruction Through Regeneration," 54.

15. McPherson, *Struggle for Equality*, 257–58; Oubre, *Forty Acres and a Mule*, 45; Westwood, *Black Troops, White Commanders*, 114–16.

16. *U.S. Statutes at Large* 13: 507–9, quoted in McPherson, *Struggle for Equality*, 257;

Bentley, *A History*, 48; Oubre, *Forty Acres and a Mule*, 21; "Letter from Rev. Horace James," 8 August 1865, *The Congregationalist* 17 (18 August 1865): 129.

17. Horace James to Andrew Johnson, 25 April 1865, Andrew Johnson Papers, Duke University, cited in Reilly, "Reconstruction Through Regeneration," 90; Letter from Horace James, 10 May 1865, *Congregationalist* 17 (26 May 1865): 82. I owe thanks to Steve Reilly, who uncovered the letter from Horace James to Andrew Johnson in the Johnson Papers at Duke University.

18. Bentley, *A History*, 89–91; McPherson, *Struggle for Equality*, 407–8; Oubre, *Forty Acres and a Mule*, 31.

19. William S. McFeeley, *Yankee Stepfather*, 133; Reilly, "Reconstruction Through Regeneration," 91–92.

20. O. O. Howard, Circular No. 3, 22 May 1865, Circulars Received, Headquarters, Records of the Assistant Commissioner for North Carolina, RG 105, ser. 2457, NA (M843, reel 20).

21. James Speed to Hon. E. M. Stanton (official copy), 22 June 1865, Letters Received, Headquarters, Records of the Assistant Commissioner for North Carolina, RG 105, ser. 2452, NA (M843, reel 9).

22. J. S. Fullerton to Lieut. Col. E. Whittlesey, 6 July 1865, Letters Received, Headquarters, Records of the Assistant Commissioner for North Carolina, RG 105, ser. 2452, NA (M843, reel 9); O. O. Howard, Circular No. 10, 11 July 1865, Circulars Received, Headquarters, Records of the Assistant Commissioner for North Carolina, RG 105, ser. 2457, NA (M843, reel 20).

23. O. O. Howard, Circular No. 13, 28 July 1865, Circulars Received, Headquarters, Records of the Assistant Commissioner for North Carolina, RG 105, ser. 2457, NA (M843, reel 20); McFeely, *Yankee Stepfather*, 103–5; Mitchell, "A History of the Black Population of New Bern," 141; E. Whittlesey to Capt. [Horace James], 16 August 1865, Letters Sent, vol. 1, 43, no. 103, Headquarters, Records of the Assistant Commissioner for North Carolina, RG 105, ser. 2446, NA (M843, reel 1).

24. E. Whittlesey to Capt. [Horace James], 16 August 1865, Letters Sent, vol. 1, 43, no. 103, Headquarters, Records of the Assistant Commissioner for North Carolina, RG 105, ser. 2446, NA (M843, reel 1).

25. Eliphalet Whittlesey, Circulars No. 1 and No. 3, 1 July 1865, 15 August 1865, General Orders and Circulars Issued, Headquarters, Records of the Assistant Commissioner for North Carolina, RG 105, ser. 2457, NA (M843, reel 20).

26. E. Whittlesey to ——, 15 August 1865, Letters Sent, vol. 7, page 40, no. 97, Records of the Assistant Commissioner for North Carolina, RG 105, ser. 2446, NA (M843, reel 1).

27. William S. McFeely notes that "the bureau men in the field saw marriage and the formation of stable family groups as the most important thing they should accomplish for the freedmen in their charge." See McFeely, *Yankee Stepfather*, 131. Apparently Whittlesey was oblivious to the irony in his statements about work.

28. Horace James to Col Whittlesey, 18 August 1865, Letters Received, Headquarters, Records of the Assistant Commissioner for North Carolina, RG 105, ser. 2452, NA (M843, reel 8).

29. See, for example, James, *Annual Report*, 24–25.

30. "Letter from Rev. Horace James," 1 December 1865, *Congregationalist* 17 (8 December 1865): 195; James, *Annual Report*, 64; "Letter from Rev. Horace James," 8 August 1865, *Congregationalist* 17 (18 August 1865): 129; "American Congregational Association: Address of Rev. Horace James," *Congregationalist* 18 (8 June 1866): 90.

31. Horace James to Col. E. Whittlesey, 17 July 1865, Unregistered Letters Received, Headquarters, Records of the Assistant Commissioner for North Carolina, RG 105, ser. 2453, NA (M843, reel 16); Horace James to Col [Whittlesey], 20 July 1865, Letters Received, Headquarters, Records of the Assistant Commissioner for North Carolina, RG 105, ser. 2452, NA (M843, reel 8).

32. Horace James to Col. E. Whittlesey, 29 August 1865, Unregistered Letters Received, Headquarters, Records of the Assistant Commissioner for North Carolina, RG 105, ser. 2453, NA (M843, reel 16); Horace James to Lieut. Fred H. Beecher, 13 September 1865, 20 September 1865, Letters Received, Headquarters, Records of the Assistant Commissioner for North Carolina, RG 105, ser. 2452, NA (M843, reel 8).

33. Horace James to Col. [Whittlesey], 20 July 1865, 7 August 1865, 27 September 1865, Letters Received, Headquarters, Records of the Assistant Commissioner for North Carolina, RG 105, ser. 2452, NA (M843, reel 8); Horace James to Col. [Whittlesey], 4 August 1865, 22 November 1865, Unregistered Letters Received, Headquarters, Records of the Assistant Commissioner for North Carolina, RG 105, ser. 2453, NA (M843, reel 16); Horace James to Lieut. Fred H. Beecher, 13 September 1865, Letters Received, Headquarters, Records of the Assistant Commissioner for North Carolina, RG 105, ser. 2452, NA (M843, reel 8); S. H. Birdsall to Horace James, 29 September 1865, Statistical Reports of Operations and Conditions of Freedmen, July 1865–November 1865, New Berne, Records of the Assistant Commissioner for North Carolina, RG 105, ser. 2759, NA [FSSP A-839].

34. Horace James to Lieut. Fred H. Beecher, 20 September 1865, Letters Received, Headquarters, Records of the Assistant Commissioner for North Carolina, RG 105, ser. 2453, NA (M843, reel 8).

35. Horace James to Col. E. Whittlesey, 29 August 1865, Unregistered Letters Received, Headquarters, Records of the Assistant Commissioner for North Carolina, RG 105, ser. 2453, NA (M843, reel 16).

36. "The Negroes on Roanoke Island," *Congregationalist* 17 (8 September 1865): 142. Although the piece was not signed, the content, reminiscent of James's *Annual Report*, and writing style definitely indicate that it was penned by Horace James.

37. Bentley, *A History*, 93–94; O. O. Howard, Circular No. 15, 12 September 1865, Circulars Received, Headquarters, Records of the Assistant Commissioner for North Carolina, RG 105, ser. 2457, NA (M843, reel 20).

38. E. Whittlesey to Capt. Horace James, 21 October 1865, Letters Sent, vol. 1, page 60, no. 139, Records of the Assistant Commissioner for North Carolina, RG 105, ser. 2446, NA (M843, reel 1).

39. Estimates of the land in possession of the Freedmen's Bureau are found in various Land Reports for Roanoke Island, August 1865–October 1868, Headquarters, Records of the Assistant Commissioner for North Carolina, RG 105, ser. 2470, NA (M843, reel 36); Monthly Land Reports for Roanoke Island, August 1866–March 1867, Roanoke Island, Records of the Assistant Commissioner for North Carolina, RG 105, ser. 2821, NA.

40. Isaac Meekins to Hon. Edwin M. Stanton, 7 July 1865, Isaac Meekins to E. Whittlesey, 1 August 1865, and Affidavit of Isaac C. Meekins, 2 August 1865, Sworn Before S. H. Birdsall, Unregistered Letters Received, Box 44, New Berne, Records of the Assistant Commissioner for North Carolina, RG 105, ser. 2755, NA [FSSP A-974]. That Meekins saw no irony in his decision to allow blacks to stay on the property at a time when he felt that it was too dangerous to remain there himself says a lot about his beliefs. Esther Meekins's will, dated 7 August 1861, is on file at the Currituck County Governmental Center, WB 4: 245.

41. Horace James to Col. [Eliphalet Whittlesey], 5 August 1865, Letters Received, Headquarters, Records of the Assistant Commissioner for North Carolina, RG 105, ser. 2452, NA (M843, reel 8); Horace James to E. Whittlesey, 12 September 1865, Unregistered Letters Received, Box 44, New Berne, RG 105, ser. 2755, NA [FSSP A-974].

42. Isaac Meekins to O. O. Howard, 29 October 1865, Unregistered Letters Received, Box 44, New Berne, RG 105, ser. 2755, NA [FSSP A-974].

43. In late August 1865, Horace James requested that he be allowed to finish his Freedmen's Bureau business and be mustered out. Horace James to O. O. Howard, 28 August 1865, Washington Headquarters, Letters Received, J #26 (1865), RG 105, ser. 15, NA (M843, reel 2). Joe A. Mobley notes that James's efforts on behalf of James City helped it become Eliphalet Whittlesey's "favorite colony." See Mobley, *James City*, 33.

44. Sarah P. Freeman to O. O. Howard, 14 November 1865 and Francis George Shaw to O. O. Howard, Letters Received, Box 10, N-38 (1865), Washington Headquarters, RG 105, ser. 15, NA [FSSP A-2968].

45. Alexander Goslin to Col. E. Whittlesey, 13 May 1866, 24 May 1866, Letters Received, Headquarters, Records of the Assistant Commissioner for North Carolina, RG 105, ser. 2452, NA (M843, reel 7).

46. Isaac C. Meekins to the Honorable Secretary of War (with enclosures), 12 August 1866, with endorsements by Alexander Goslin, 12 August 1866, and Hugo Hillebrandt, 4 September 1866, Letters Received, Headquarters, Records of the Assistant Commissioner for North Carolina, RG 105, ser. 2452, NA (M843, reel 8).

47. Special Order No. 125, 8 October 1866, Letters and Orders Received, Reports, and Supply Requests, Roanoke Island, Records of the Assistant Commissioner for North Carolina, RG 105, ser. 2821, NA; Francis Geo. Shaw to O. O. Howard, 20 September 1866, with endorsements by Thomas P. Johnston, 9 October 1866, and E. M. Stanton, 3 December 1866, Roanoke Island, NC Industrial School, Box 927, Quartermaster's Consolidated Correspondence, RG 92, NA [FSSP Y-152]. There is no indication of what happened to the two school buildings. Descendants of Esther Meekins still reside on the Meekins property in a house (circa 1805) that is called Sunnyside. Although it would seem logical to conclude that this house was the one in which the teachers resided—even some old grapevines like those that the teachers described remain in front of it—the current owner, Roger Meekins, adamantly denied that possibility when interviewed on 11 August 1995. He suggested that the house that the teachers occupied was no longer standing.

48. S. S. Nickerson to Rev. Samuel Hunt, 6 February 1866, AMAA, N.C.; Land Reports for Roanoke Island, August 1865–October 1868, Headquarters, Records of the Assistant Commissioner for North Carolina, RG 105, ser. 2470, NA (M843, reel 36); Monthly Land Reports and Special Orders for Roanoke Island, August 1866–March 1867, Roanoke Island, Records of the Assistant Commissioner for North Carolina, RG 105, ser. 2821, NA.

49. Samuel N. Midgett to Maj. Gen. O. O. Howard, 20 October 1866, Letters Received, Headquarters, Records of the Assistant Commissioner for North Carolina, RG 105, ser. 2452, NA (M843, reel 9).

50. George W. Wescott to Maj. Gen. O. O. Howard, 5 November 1866, Nancy Gaylord to Maj. Gen. O. O. Howard, 5 November 1866, Matilda Miller to Maj. Gen. O. O. Howard, 5 November 1866, Jesse E. Dough to Major General O. O. Howard, 27 November 1866, and Sarah E. Dough to Maj. Gen. O. O. Howard, 5 November 1866, Letters Received, Headquarters, Records of the Assistant Commissioner for North Carolina, RG 105, ser. 2452, NA (M843, reels 10, 11, 13).

51. John Wescott to Major General O. O. Howard, 29 May 1867, Lewis S. Mann to the Hon. Edwin M. Stanton, [July 1866], Martin Hubbard to Maj. Gen. O. O. Howard, 3 December 1866, Letters Received, Headquarters, Records of the Assistant Commissioner for North Carolina, RG 105, ser. 2452, NA (M843, reels 8, 11, 13).

52. Walter T. Dough to Maj. Gen. O. O. Howard, 26 November 1866, Esau Berry to Maj. Gen. O. O. Howard, 27 November 1866, and Thos. A. Dough to Maj. Gen. O. O. Howard, 4 December 1866, Letters Received, Headquarters, Records of the Assistant Commissioner for North Carolina, RG 105, ser. 2452, NA (M843, reel 10).

53. See various Land Reports for Roanoke Island, August 1865–October 1868, Headquarters, Records of the Assistant Commissioner for North Carolina, RG 105, ser. 2470, NA (M843, reel 36), and Monthly Land Reports for Roanoke Island, August 1866–March 1867, Roanoke Island, Records of the Assistant Commissioner for North Carolina, RG 105, ser. 2821, NA. Frequently, the Freedmen's Bureau records indicated that the Freedmen's Bureau possessed more land than the owners requested be returned. This discrepancy was due, no doubt, to the inexact Freedmen's Bureau estimates, as well as the ambiguities inherent in the metes and bounds property descriptions.

CHAPTER EIGHT

1. O. O. Howard, Circular No. 2, 19 May 1865, reprinted in *National Freedman* 1 (1 June 1865): 167–68; Reilly, "Regeneration Through Reconstruction," 98; Bahney, "Generals and Negroes," 258; Drake, "The American Missionary Association," 40, 52; W. H. Doherty, Sanitary Report No. 11, Island of Roanoke, N.C., 6 August 1866, Subordinate Officers' Monthly Reports on Sanitary Conditions in Subdistricts, Headquarters, Records of the Assistant Commissioner for North Carolina, RG 105, ser. 2466, NA (M843, reel 24); Elizabeth James to George Whipple, 1 December 1866, AMAA, N.C.

2. Prior to his arrest, Holland Streeter had issued rations to 2,000 freedpeople on the island. Horace James to Col. [Whittlesey], 20 July 1865, Letters Received, Headquarters, Office of the Assistant Commissioner for North Carolina, RG 105, ser. 2452, NA (M843, reel 8); F. A. Seely, Semi-Monthly Report of the Condition of Freedmen, and the Operations of the Freedmen's Bureau, in the Eastern District of North Carolina, 14 January 1866, Reports from Subordinate Officers Relating to the Condition of the Freedmen, Headquarters, Records of the Assistant Commissioner for North Carolina, RG 105, ser. 2467, NA (M843, reel 23).

3. For transportation orders and correspondence about transportation, see Letters Received and Unregistered Letters Received, Records of the Assistant Commissioner for North

Carolina, Headquarters, RG 105, ser. 2452 and 2453, NA (M843, reels 6–8, 11, 16); also see Letters and Orders Received, Reports, and Supply Requests, Roanoke Island, Records of the Assistant Commissioner for North Carolina, RG 105, ser. 2821, NA. For information about population statistics, see various Monthly, Semi-Monthly, and Tri-Monthly Statistical Reports from Subordinate Officers Relating to the Condition of Freedmen, Headquarters, Records of the Assistant Commissioner for North Carolina, RG 105, ser. 2467, NA (M843, reel 23).

4. Eliphalet Whittlesey, Circulars No. 1 (1 July 1865) and No. 2 (2 July 1865), General Orders and Circulars Issued, Headquarters, Records of the Assistant Commissioner for North Carolina, RG 105, ser. 2457, NA (M843, reel 20); Reilly, "Reconstruction Through Regeneration," 98.

5. Horace James to Col. [Whittlesey], 14 August 1865, Letters Received, Headquarters, Records of the Assistant Commissioner for North Carolina, RG 105, ser. 2452 (M843, reel 8); Mrs. S. P. Freeman, 3 January 1866, *National Freedman* 1 (15 January 1866): 14. For transportation orders and correspondence about transportation, see Letters Received and Unregistered Letters Received, Records of the Assistant Commissioner for North Carolina, Headquarters, RG 105, ser. 2452 and 2453, NA (M843, reels 6–8, 11, 16); also see Letters and Orders Received, Reports, and Supply Requests, Roanoke Island, Records of the Assistant Commissioner for North Carolina, RG 105, ser. 2821, NA. For information about population statistics, see various Monthly, Semi-Monthly, and Tri-Monthly Statistical Reports from Subordinate Officers Relating to the Condition of Freedmen, Headquarters, Records of the Assistant Commissioner for North Carolina, RG 105, ser. 2467, NA (M843, reel 23).

6. The full story of the contributions of the black North Carolina soldiers remains to be told. See Regimental and Company Descriptive Books for 35th, 36th, and 37th USCT, RG 94, NA. To get a sense of the experiences of particular soldiers from Roanoke Island, see the pension files of Albert Banks, Leon Bembury, Richard Etheridge, Samuel Gregory, Henry Hill, John Lee, William Overton, and Thomas Sanders, RG 94, NA. See also Trudeau, *Like Men of War*, 128, 137–51, 284–300, 304–9.

7. Elizabeth James to Rev. G. Whipple, 3 February 1866 and S. S. Nickerson to Rev. Samuel Hunt, 6 February 1866, AMAA, N.C.

8. S. S. Nickerson to Saml. Hunt, 3 January 1866, 6 February 1866, AMAA, N.C.

9. Alexander Goslin to Col. E. Whittlesey, 18 March 1866, Letters Received, Headquarters, Records of the Assistant Commissioner for North Carolina, RG 105, ser. 2452, NA (M843, reel 7); E. Whittlesey to Capt. A. Goslin, 22 March 1866, Letters Sent, vol. 7, 96, no. 219, Headquarters, Records of the Assistant Commissioner for North Carolina, RG 105, ser. 2446, NA (M843, reel 1).

10. Alexander Goslin to ——, 15 April 1866, Letters Received, Records of the Assistant Commissioner for North Carolina, RG 105, ser. 2452, NA (M843, reel 7); Transportation Order No. 1231 enclosed in E. C. Estes to the Quarter Master, 27 September 1866, Letters and Orders Received, Reports, and Supply Requests, Roanoke Island, Records of the Assistant Commissioner for North Carolina, RG 105, ser. 2821, NA; O. O. Howard to Bvt. Maj. Genl. J. C. Robinson, 22 August 1866, and Stephen Moore to Captain Hugo Hildebrandt [sic], 4 December 1866, Letters and Orders Received, Reports, and Supply Requests, Roanoke Island, Records of the Assistant Commissioner for North Carolina, RG 105, ser. 2821, NA; Stephen Moore to Bvt. Lieut. Col. J. T. Chur, 29 December 1866, Letters

Received, Headquarters, Records of the Assistant Commissioner for North Carolina, RG 105, ser. 2452, NA (M843, reel 11).

11. F. A. Seely, Semi-Monthly Report, Operations of the Freedmen's Bureau, Eastern District, North Carolina, February 28, 1866, New Berne, Records of the Assistant Commissioner for North Carolina, RG 105, ser. 2759, NA [FSSP A-841]; F. A. Seely to Colonel [E. Whittlesey], 30 March 1866, 3 April 1866, Letters Received, Headquarters, Records of the Assistant Commissioner for North Carolina, RG 105, ser. 2452, NA (M843, reel 8). Seely did not comment on the forty-five men who signed up later in April to go to Mississippi to work for John D. Hawkins and Brothers.

12. Alexander Goslin to E. Whittlesey, 24 May 1866, Letters Received, Headquarters, Records of the Assistant Commissioner for North Carolina, RG 105, ser. 2452, NA (M843, reel 7); Mrs. S. P. Freeman to Sir, 13 June 1866, *National Freedman* 1 (July 1866): 195; E. Whittlesey to Capt. A. Goslin, 23 April 1866, Letters Sent, vol. 7, 112, no. 257 and Clinton A. Cilley to Capt. Alex. Goslin, 27 June 1866, Letters Sent, vol. 7, 142, no. 328, RG 105, ser. 2446, NA (M843, reel 1).

13. Alexander Goslin to Clinton A. Cilley, 7 July 1866, Letters Received, Headquarters, Records of the Assistant Commissioner for North Carolina, RG 105, ser. 2452, NA (M843, reel 7); W. H. Doherty, Sanitary Report No. 11 Island of Roanoke, N.C., 6 August 1866, Subordinate Officers' Monthly Reports on Sanitary Conditions in Subdistricts, Headquarters, Records of the Assistant Commissioner for North Carolina, RG 105, ser. 2466, NA (M843, reel 24)

14. Mrs. S. P. Freeman, 3 January 1866, *National Freedman* 1 (15 January 1866): 14; "Letter from Horace James," 1 December 1865, *Congregationalist* 17 (8 December 1865): 195.

15. S. S. Nickerson to Rev. Samuel Hunt, 6 February 1866, AMAA, N.C.; Mrs. S. P. Freeman to Sir, 13 June 1866, "Roanoke Island," *National Freedman* 1 (July 1866): 196.

16. Stephen Moore, Annual Report of the Operations of the District of New Berne for the Year Ending October 31st, 1866, Annual Reports of Operations Received from Staff and Subordinate Officers, Headquarters, Records of the Assistant Commissioner for North Carolina, RG 105, ser. 2463, NA (M843, reel 22). See also Mandle, *Not Slave, Not Free*, 13; Wright, *Old South, New South*, 89; Sorin, *Abolitionism: A New Perspective*, 160; Litwack, *Been in the Storm So Long*, 386.

17. Mrs. S. P. Freeman to Sir, 13 June 1866, *National Freedman* 1 (July 1866): 196.

18. A. B. Chapin to Doctor, 11 June 1866, and A. B. Chapin to M. K. Hogan, 4 July 1866, Letters Received, Headquarters, Records of the Assistant Commissioner for North Carolina, RG 105, ser. 2452, NA (M843, reels 7, 9).

19. Alexander Goslin to Assistant Commissioner, 15 July 1866, Subordinate Officers' Monthly Reports on Sanitary Conditions in Subdistricts, Headquarters, Records of the Assistant Commissioner for North Carolina, RG 105, ser. 2466, NA (M843, reel 24); Alexander Goslin to Assistant Commissioner, 15 August 1866, Letters and Orders Received, Reports, and Supply Requests, Roanoke Island, Records of the Assistant Commissioner for North Carolina, RG 105, ser. 2821, NA.

20. House Reports, 39th Cong., 1st sess., H. Rept. 30, 179–80; F. A. Seely to Col. [Whittlesey], 17 February 1866, Letters Received, Headquarters, Records of the Assistant Commissioner for North Carolina, RG 105, ser. 2452, NA (M843, reel 8).

21. Hugo Hillebrandt to Col. Clinton A. Cilley, 19 August 1866, Letters Received, Headquarters, Records of the Assistant Commissioner for North Carolina, RG 105, ser. 2452, NA (M843, reel 7); O. O. Howard, Circular No. 10, 22 August 1866, General Orders and Circulars Issued, Headquarters, RG 105, ser. 2457, NA (M843, reel 20); Report of cases of Outrage reported and disposed of in the Sub. Dist. of Roanoke Island, N.C., from August 1 to August 8th, 1866, Letters and Orders Received, Reports, and Supply Requests, Roanoke Island, RG 105, ser. 2821, NA; Elizabeth James to Rev. George Whipple, 1 December 1866, AMAA, N.C.

22. Stephen Moore, Annual Report of the Operations of the District of New Berne for the Year Ending October 31st, 1866, Annual Reports of Operations Received from Staff and Subordinate Officers, Headquarters, Records of the Assistant Commissioner for North Carolina, RG 105, ser. 2463, NA (M843, reel 22); [Hugo Hillebrandt], List of names of freedpeople living on Roanoke Island N.C. likely to become destitute during the ensuing Winter [undated], Letters and Orders Received, Reports, and Supply Requests, Roanoke Island, Records of the Assistant Commissioner for North Carolina, RG 105, ser. 2821, NA; John C. Robinson, Senate Documents, 39th Cong., S. Doc. 6, 2d series, 111–12. The list of the potentially destitute is included in Appendix E.

23. O. O. Howard to Bvt. Maj. Genl. J. C. Robinson, 22 August 1866, and Stephen Moore to Captain Hugo Hildebrandt [*sic*], 4 December 1866, Letters and Orders Received, Reports, and Supply Requests, Roanoke Island, Records of the Assistant Commissioner for North Carolina, RG 105, ser. 2821, NA; Stephen Moore to Bvt. Lieut. Col. J. T. Chur, 29 December 1866, Letters Received, Headquarters, Records of the Assistant Commissioner for North Carolina, RG 105, ser. 2452, NA (M843, reel 11).

24. Joseph Tillett et al. to the Assistant Commissioner, 4 December 1866, Letters and Orders Received, Reports, and Supply Requests, Roanoke Island, Records of the Assistant Commissioner for North Carolina, RG 105, ser. 2821, NA. This letter is presented in full in Appendix F. The language in the letter suggests the influence of the missionary teachers. Whether that was because the men had picked up the teachers' expressions or because one of the teachers helped to write the letter remains a mystery.

25. Hugo Hillebrandt to Lieut. Col. Stephen Moore, Rations report for the ten days ending January 14, 1867; Stephen Moore to Bvt. Lieut. Col. C. F. Chur, 11 January 1866 [1867]; Stephen Moore to Capt. Hugo Hildebrandt [sic], 14 January 1867; and Hugo Hillebrandt to Stephen Moore, 14 March 1867, Letters and Orders Received, Reports, and Supply Requests, Roanoke Island, Records of the Assistant Commissioner for North Carolina, RG 105, ser. 2821, NA.

26. Elizabeth James to Rev. George Whipple, 1 December 1866, 3 January 1867, 23 January 1867, 28 January 1867, AMAA, N.C.

27. Elizabeth James to Rev. George Whipple, 14 January 1867, AMAA, N.C.

28. Elizabeth James to Rev. George Whipple, 1 December 1866, AMAA, N.C.; E. James to Rev. George Whipple, 23 January 1867, AMAA, N.C.; E. James to Rev. George Whipple, 5 March 1867, AMAA, N.C.

29. D. T. Bachelder to Sir [John Kimball], 15 March 1867, Superintendent of Education, Unregistered Letters Received, Box 1, B, District of Columbia, RG 105, ser. 507, NA [FSSP A-10211]; Stephen Moore to Capt. Hugo Hillebrandt, 19 March 1867, Letters and Orders Received, Reports, and Supply Requests, Roanoke Island, Records of the Assistant Com-

missioner for North Carolina, RG 105, ser. 2821, NA; Hugo Hillebrandt to Lt. Col. Stephen Moore, 4 April 1867, Letters Received, Headquarters, Records of the Assistant Commissioner for North Carolina, RG 105, ser. 2452, NA (M843, reel 11).

30. N. A. Miles to O. O. Howard, 11 May 1867, Letters Received, Register 9, no. 96, Washington Headquarters, RG 105, ser. 15, NA (M752, reel 6); Oliver Howard to Rev. F. A. Fiske, 19 June 1867, Hugo Hillebrandt to Brevet Lt. Col. Jacob F. Chur, 25 June 1867, Letters Received, Headquarters, Records of the Assistant Commissioner for North Carolina, RG 105, ser. 2452, NA (M843, reel 11).

EPILOGUE

1. Elizabeth James to Rev. George Whipple, 5 March 1867, AMAA.

2. The rate of erosion at the north end of the island has been very dramatic. Comparisons of land features from 1851 to 1970 indicate erosion ranging from 720 to 960 feet at Northwest Point. See Lautzenheiser and Hargrove, "'The Bright Glittering Sand,'" 6–7; Alexander and Lazell, *Ribbon of Sand*, 44.

3. North Carolina's Reconstruction Constitution of 1868 extended public education to black children, mandating a four-month school term. Most localities, however, did not achieve the four-month term until after the turn of the century, when they instituted school taxes. See Stephens, *History of the Public Schools*, 391; Leloudis, *Schooling the New South*, 6, 239.

4. McCaslin, *Portraits of Conflict*, 361; Sifakis, *Who Was Who in the Union*, 186.

5. Sifakis, *Who Was Who in the Union*, 141, 451–52.

6. Horace James, "Letter from North Carolina," 11 February 1866, *Congregationalist* 18 (23 February 1866): 30–31; Reilly, "Reconstruction Through Regeneration," 117–25. In the fall of 1865, Eliphalet Whittlesey had recommended that James be promoted to lieutenant colonel, but no action was taken on the request. See Col. E. Whittlesey to O. O. Howard, 29 September 1865, Letters Received, Register N #1 (1865), Washington Headquarters, RG 105, ser. 15, NA (M752, reel 3).

7. Reilly, "Reconstruction Through Regeneration," 126–34; Mobley, *James City*, 39–40.

8. Reilly, "Reconstruction Through Regeneration," 135–52; "Letter from Rev. Horace James," 15 July 1866, *Congregationalist* 18 (27 July 1866): 118; "From North Carolina," 4 February 1867, *Congregationalist* 19 (15 February 1867): 27.

9. Reilly, "Reconstruction Through Regeneration," 135–52; "From North Carolina," 4 February 1867, *Congregationalist* 19 (15 February 1867): 27; J. Holt, Report in the Case of Horace James, 7 November 1866, Court Martial 00-1788 Horace James, Box 1363, Court Martial Case Files, Records of the Office of the Judge Advocate General (Army), RG 153, ser. 15, NA [FSSP H-57]. With the exception of Steve Reilly, most historians have based their assessments of Horace James on their readings of the Steedman-Fullerton report rather than a careful reading of the court-martial case files.

10. Reilly, "Reconstruction Through Regeneration," 182–84.

11. Ibid., 187, 194; Horace James to E. D. Townsend, 9 August 1867, Letters Received, Records of the Adjutant General's Office, RG 94, NA (M619, reel 564). Exactly where the mill went remains unclear. S. S. Nickerson indicated that the mill had been moved to Beaufort, North Carolina (Carteret County), which would have been approximately forty

miles below New Bern, but Beaufort is not on the Neuse River. (See S. S. Nickerson to Rev. Geo. Whipple, 6 April 1866, AMAA, N.C.) In fact, the Neuse River does not extend forty miles below New Bern, so James's mileage estimate was probably mistaken. About the most that can be stated with some certainty is that the mill probably ended up in Carteret County, which was (and is) heavily forested, and thus a likely spot for a sawmill. In 1997 Rodney Barfield, who at that time was Director of the North Carolina Maritime Museum in Beaufort, offered to help search local records for information about the mill. Unfortunately, he uncovered nothing about the mill—a finding he reported to me in a letter of 10 April 1997.

12. Reilly, "Reconstruction Through Regeneration," 193–94.

13. Elizabeth James wrote a number of letters to AMA secretaries George Whipple and E. P. Smith from Columbia, North Carolina, and Harrisonburg, Virginia, before she returned to Massachusetts. Her death is recorded in the Commonwealth of Massachusetts Vital Records, Death Registration and Indices, vol. 504, 412 (microfilm).

14. "Letter from Miss Ella Roper," 1 January 1867, *American Freedman* 2 (May 1867): 218; Mount Holyoke College Alumnae Association, *Biographical Directory*, 101. Ella Roper wrote a number of letters from Macon, Georgia, and Wilmington, North Carolina, to the secretaries of the AMA.

15. Samuel Nickerson wrote a number of letters from Front Royal, Virginia, and Harper's Ferry, West Virginia, to the secretaries of the AMA. Much of the genealogical information about the Nickersons was gathered from the Church of Jesus Christ of Latter-Day Saints, "International Genealogical Index," and "Ancestral File."

16. Transportation Order No. 1231 enclosed in E. C. Estes to the Quarter Master, 27 September 1866, Letters and Orders Received, Reports, and Supply Requests, Roanoke Island, Records of the Assistant Commissioner for North Carolina, RG 105, ser. 2821, NA.

17. Descriptive Books for the 35th, 36th, and 37th USCT, RG 94, NA; Wright and Zoby, "Ignoring Jim Crow," 68–69.

18. Daniel Hart to the Commanding Officer, Post of Goldsboro, 28 December 1867, and George Baum et al. to Col. Charles Benzoni, [December 1867], Letters Received, Headquarters, Records of the Assistant Commissioner for North Carolina, RG 105, ser. 2452, NA (M843, reel 11). This letter is reproduced in Appendix F.

19. Daniel Hart to Isaac C. Meekins, 23 December 1867, Letters Received, Headquarters, Records of the Assistant Commissioner for North Carolina, RG 105, ser. 2452, NA (M843, reel 11); Walter T. Dough et al. to Benjamin D. Midgett et al., 9 September 1868, recorded 8 August 1871, DB A: 6–7, Dare County, N.C.; Report of the Commission to divide the lands of Daniel Hopkins and others, 26 November 1900, recorded 1 October 1904, DB K: 281–87, Dare County, N.C.; Federal Census, Population Schedules, Dare County, N.C., 1870. The men who purchased the California tract in common were Benjamin Ashbee, Henry Ashbee, George Baum, George W. Bowser, Harmon McCleese, Benjamin D. Midgett, Francis Tillett, John F. Tillett, Levi Tillett, Miles F. Tillett, and Joseph F. Tillett. The 1900 report that divided the California tract referred to a petition that had been filed by one of the claimants to the land, a black man named Daniel Hopkins, who by that time owned John F. Tillett's interest in the tract. Oral tradition on the island, passed on to me by David Wright, holds that Hopkins had immigrated to Roanoke Island from one of the Caribbean Islands. In 1870 he was a fifteen-year-old apprentice living in the home of Isaac Meekins. By 1900, Hopkins was married to Betsy Bowser, daughter of Joseph C. and Jane Bowser. In an

attempt to determine how Hopkins came to possess the John F. Tillett property, I searched Dare County's deed books and found no record of a grant from Tillett to Hopkins. Hoping to uncover the 1900 petition that led to the official division of the land, I looked for Dare County's early books of orders and decrees, but discovered that these books had been deposited with the N.C. Department of Archives and History. Archivist Kimberly A. Cumber searched for the old records and discovered that the 1900 petition had not been recorded in Dare County's Orders and Decrees or Special Proceedings.

20. In 1870 Roanoke Island was part of the Nags Head Township district, which also included the area across the sound previously known as the North Banks. The black men listed in the 1870 census of Nags Head Township as owners of real property and the values of their respective properties were Benjamin Ashbee, $50; Henry Ashbee, $50; William Bennett, $150; George Baum, $50; Benjamin Bowser, $50; George Bowser, $50; Spencer Bowser, $100; George Hayes, $50; B. D. Midgett, $50; Fields Rowlins, $50; Frank Tillett, $50; John Tillett, $50; Joseph Tillett, $50; Levi Tillett, $50. For some unknown reason, the 1870 census did not indicate that two of the owners-in-common of the California tract—Harmon McCleese and Miles F. Tillett—owned real property. The census did, however, include the names of two black landowners, William Bennett and Benjamin Bowser, who most likely lived across the sound from Roanoke Island on Colington Island. See Federal Census, Population Schedules, Nags Head Township, Dare County, N.C., 1870, 1880, and 1900. Since detailed tax records for Dare County in 1870 do not exist, it is impossible to determine if any of the men paid taxes on their real property in 1870. The population figures are approximate since Nags Head Township also included the area across the sound to the east. The 1880 census did not include an enumeration of real estate, and the 1890 census materials were burned in a fire in Washington, D.C.

21. Convention of the Freedmen of North Carolina, *Official Proceedings*, 2. For a thorough discussion of the convention, See Alexander, *North Carolina Faces the Freedmen*, 21–31. Andra Chappell, deputy clerk of elections for Currituck County, and Lynda Midgett, supervisor of elections for Dare County, verified that no voting records exist for the postwar period.

22. Convention of the Freedmen of North Carolina, *Official Proceedings*, 4–5.

23. *Minutes of the Freedmen's Convention*, 7; Federal Census, Population Schedules, Dare County, N.C., 1870; WB and DB, Dare County, N.C. There are no records detailing how the freedmen reached financial independence; no doubt some used savings from their military days to get established, while others probably borrowed from friends on the island, both black and white. The 1880 census did not ask for information about ownership of real or personal property.

24. Mobley, *Ship Ashore!*, 94–95; Wright and Zoby, "Ignoring Jim Crow," 72. David Wright and David Zoby are currently writing a book about the Pea Island Station and the black surfmen who worked there. Although Richard Etheridge was born a slave on Roanoke Island in 1842, he apparently was taught to read and write. After his death, in letters filed to support his wife's request for a widow's military pension, the daughter and son of his former owner, John B. Etheridge, indicated that Richard Etheridge was "an infant, child, boy, youth and man" on their property and raised "as a member" of the family. After he returned from his military service, Etheridge continued to live with the family until his marriage in 1867. Such evidence suggests that Richard Etheridge had an unusually close relationship to his

master's family, leading me to join with Wright and Zoby in speculating that he was, in fact, a son of John B. Etheridge. See the affidavits of Sarah [Etheridge] Ward and Jesse T. Etheridge, Richard Etheridge Pension File, RG 94, NA.

25. David Stick, *Graveyard of the Atlantic*, 155–58; Mobley, *Ship Ashore!*, 98; Wright and Zoby, "Ignoring Jim Crow," 72–73. Several witnesses indicated that white brothers Adam D. and Patrick H. Etheridge, along with William P. Clark, set the station on fire, but they were never formally charged. The motive, according to one witness, was to remove Richard Etheridge from his position as keeper so that Patrick could replace him. Whether the plan was racially motivated remains a mystery. If, as speculated in the previous note, Richard Etheridge were the son of John B. Etheridge, then Adam and Patrick would have been his first cousins.

26. Wright and Zoby, "Ignoring Jim Crow," 72; "Negro Justice Married White Couple in 1874," *Dare County Times*, 3 April 1936. The latter newspaper article indicates that Midgett, who was born about 1845, was never a slave. That statement is probably false on several counts. According to Midgett's death certificate, he was born in 1839. Also, evidence suggests that Midgett had been a slave. A deed filed in Currituck County on August 8, 1854 indicates that Mann Midgett gave his wife, Debro H. Midgett, "a negro boy, by the name of George Riley" for her lifetime. According to Vance Midgett, who has spent some time tracing the genealogy of various Midgett families, both black and white, this George Riley became George Riley Midgett. See Mann Midgett to Debro Midgett, 8 August 1854, DB 27: 152, Currituck County Governmental Center.

27. Click, "Letting In the Light," 29, 32, 41. Mary Wood Long discusses a number of the anecdotes about buildings supposedly connected to the freedmen's colony in "The Five Lost Colonies of Dare," especially 153–61.

28. Lautzenheiser and Hargrove, " 'The Bright Glittering Sand,' " 1. According to Lautzenheiser and Hargrove, in 1896 the Roanoke Colony Memorial Association, an organization formed in 1894 to purchase the land on which the purported fort of the "lost colony" was located, bought several tracts of land on the north end of the island. These properties included the Walter Dough tract (site of the fort) and the Thomas A. Dough tract (Sarah E. Dough's property). The association transferred the Walter Dough tract to the National Park Service in 1934. Today it is part of Fort Raleigh National Historic Site. In 1910 the association sold the Thomas A. Dough tract to W. J. Griffen, who sold it to Jerome Griffin in 1911. This property later became the location of the Sandpiper's Trace Campground. In the early 1990s it became the site of a residential development designed by Rial Corporation/W. M. Meekins Jr. It was the development of this site that triggered the investigation by North Carolina's Office of State Archaeology. See Lautzenheiser and Hargrove, " 'The Bright Glittering Sand,' " 55.

29. Endorsement by Hugo Hillebrandt, 15 November 1866, with Sarah E. Dough to Maj. Gen. O. O. Howard, 5 November 1866, Letters Received, Headquarters, Records of the Assistant Commissioner for North Carolina, RG 105, ser. 2452, NA (M843, reel 10).

30. The archaeologists found numerous potholes, most measuring five or six feet in diameter, with some measuring sixteen to eighteen feet in diameter; some of the potholes had even been back-filled. Because of the "almost complete destruction of the site by relic collecting activity," the archaeologists recommended no further archaeological work on the site. See Lautzenheiser and Hargrove, " 'The Bright Glittering Sand,' " ii–iv, 73–74, 86, 93–100.

31. Lautzenheiser and Eastman, "Archaeological Survey, Proposed Visitors Center," i–iii, 75–83.

32. Ibid., 82.

33. Literacy rates based on the manuscript census for Roanoke Island suggest that illiteracy remained high for both blacks and whites. In 1870, 8 percent of the blacks twenty and older and 48 percent of the whites twenty and older were literate. In 1880 the rate increased slightly for blacks, to 13 percent, and a bit more for whites, to 68 percent. When literacy rates are computed for men alone, the results are a bit higher. In 1870, 24 percent of the black men twenty and older and 76 percent of the white men twenty and older were literate. In 1880, 25 percent of the black men twenty and over were literate, while the rate for white men twenty and over had dropped to 66 percent. At best these rates are, however, merely rough indicators, for they are based on the estimation and judgments of the census enumerators. See Federal Census, Population Schedules, Nags Head Township, Dare County, N.C., 1870, 1880.

34. Dorothy Spruill Redford touches on the difficulties that freedpeople who had been slaves on Somerset Plantation faced on the mainland in Tyrrell County in the postwar period. See *Somerset Homecoming*, 123–25. A thorough study of the colonists who moved to various parts of the mainland is hampered by the lack of a complete roster of the Roanoke Island colony. Using the report of freedmen transportation for January 1866 and the list of people who wished to leave the island in the fall of 1866, it might be possible to design a study of many of these colonists and their descendants. See Capt. Alex Goslin, "Report of Transportation furnished to Freedmen during the month of January 1866," and "List of names of freed people living on Roanoke Island N.C. likely to become destitute during the ensuing Winter," Roanoke Island, Records of the Assistant Commissioner for North Carolina, RG 105, ser. 2821, NA. These documents are presented in Appendix E of this book.

35. George M. Fredrickson discusses the limitations of the evangelical approach. See Fredrickson, *The Black Image*, 179. Also see Zipf, "The WHITES Shall Rule," 534.

36. Lauranett Lee's study of the black community in Charlottesville, Virginia, suggests that the bonds that the freedpeople forged with sympathetic whites were very important in the establishment of a thriving middle class black community there in the postwar period. That was probably also true on Roanoke Island. In some cases, relationships between the island's blacks and whites were also strengthened by the actuality if not the outright admission of past acts of miscegenation. (Lee, a graduate student in history at the University of Virginia, is completing a dissertation that focuses on the work of NEFAS missionary teacher Philena Carkin in Charlottesville during and after the Civil War.)

Bibliography

MANUSCRIPTS

Carlisle Barracks, Pennsylvania

U.S. Army Military History Institute

- Reynolds Laughlin Papers
- William W. Lind Papers
- Nelson A. Miles Papers
- Massachusetts Commandery, Military Order of the Loyal Legion of the United States Photo Collection
- Herbert E. Valentine Papers
- Edward A. Wild Papers

Chapel Hill, North Carolina

Southern Historical Collection, University of North Carolina

- Battle Family Papers
- William J. Creasey Diary, 1861–62
- Henry A. Phelon Papers
- C. Bayard Springer Diary, 1862
- Edward A. Wild Papers

Currituck, North Carolina

Currituck County Governmental Center

- Deed Books
- Orders and Decrees
- Summons Book Number 1
- Will Books

Greenville, North Carolina

Joyner Library, East Carolina University

- Church Family Papers
- Gertrude Evans Fearing Collection
- Charles Tournier Diary, New Bern Historical Society Collection
- VonEberstein Papers

Manteo, North Carolina
Dare County Court House
Deed Books
Will Books
Death Certificates
Outer Banks History Center
Maps
Prints

New Orleans, Louisiana
Amistad Research Center, Tulane University
American Missionary Association Archives

Washington, D.C.
National Archives
Federal Census, Population Schedules, 1830–1900 (microfilm)
Record Group 92, Records of the Office of the Quartermaster General
Record Group 94, Records of the Adjutant General's Office, 1780s–1917
Record Group 105, Records of the Bureau of Refugees, Freedmen, and Abandoned Lands
Record Group 107, Records of the Office of the Secretary of War
Record Group 153, Records of the Office of the Judge Advocate General (Army)
Record Group 393, Records of United States Army Continental Commands, 1821–1920

Worcester, Massachusetts
College of the Holy Cross
Richard O'Flynn Papers

PUBLIC DOCUMENTS AND OTHER PUBLISHED PRIMARY SOURCES

Abbott, John S. C. "Heroic Deeds of Heroic Men: A Military Adventure." *Harper's New Monthly Magazine* 30 (December 1864): 3–20.

Alvord, John W. *Semi-Annual Report on Schools for Freedmen*, Numbers 1–10 (January 1866–July 1870). New York: AMS Press, 1980. Reprint of 1868–70 edition issued in 9 vols. by the U.S. Bureau of Refugees, Freedmen, and Abandoned Lands.

American Missionary Association. *History of the American Missionary Association with Illustrative Facts and Anecdotes*. New York: Bible House, 1891.

Bosbyshell, Oliver Christian. *The 48th in the War: Being a Narrative of the 48th Regiment, Infantry, Pennsylvania Veteran Volunteers During the War of the Rebellion*. Philadelphia: AVH Printing Company, 1895.

Brooks, Charles. *History of the Town of Medford, Middlesex County, Massachusetts, From Its First Settlement, in 1630, to the Present Time, 1855*. Boston: James M. Usher, 1855.

Burnside, Ambrose E. *The Burnside Expedition*. Soldiers and Sailors Historical Society of Rhode Island, *Personal Narratives of Events in the War of Rebellion*, 2d ser., no. 6. Providence, R.I.: N. Bangs Williams & Company, 1882.

Butler, Benjamin F. *Butler's Book: Autobiography and Personal Reminiscences of Major General Benj. F. Butler*. Boston: A. M. Thayer & Co., 1892.

——. *Private and Official Correspondence of Gen. Benjamin F. Butler during the Period of the Civil War*. 5 vols. Norwood, Mass.: The Plimpton Press, 1917.

The Century War Book: Battles and Leaders of the Civil War, vol. 1, no. 15. New York: The Century Co., 1894.

Chenery, William H. *Reminiscences of the Burnside Expedition*. Soldiers and Sailors Historical Society of Rhode Island, *Personal Narratives of Events in the War of Rebellion*, 7th ser., no. 1. Providence, R.I.: The Society, 1905.

Colyer, Vincent. *Brief Report of the Services Rendered by the Freed People in the United States Army in North Carolina in the Spring of 1862, After the Battle of NewBern*. New York: n.p., 1864.

——. *Report of the Christian Mission to the United States Army*. New York: G. A. Whitehorne, 1862.

Convention of the Freedmen of North Carolina. *Official Proceedings*. N.p.: 1865.

Day, D. L. *My Diary of Rambles with the 25th Mass. Volunteer Infantry, with Burnside's Coast Division; 18th Army Corps, and Army of the James*. Milford, Mass.: King & Billings, Printers, 1884.

Denny, J. Waldo. *Wearing the Blue in the Twenty-Fifth Mass. Volunteer Infantry, with Burnside's Coast Division, 18th Army Corps, and Army of the James*. Worcester, Mass.: Putnam & Davis, 1879.

Derby, W. P. *Bearing Arms in the Twenty-Seventh Massachusetts Regiment of Volunteer Infantry During the Civil War, 1861–1865*. Boston: Wright & Potter Printing Co., 1883.

Dickey, Luther S. *History of the 103d Regiment Pennsylvania Veteran Volunteer Infantry 1861–1865* . Chicago: L. S. Dickey, 1910.

DuBois, William Edgar Burghardt. "Reconstruction and Its Benefits." *American Historical Review* 15 (July 1910): 781–99.

Emilio, Luis F. *A Brave Black Regiment: History of the Fifty-Fourth Regiment of Massachusetts Volunteer Infantry 1863–1865*. 3d ed. Boston: Boston Book Co., 1894. Reprint, Salem, N.H.: Ayer Company Publishers, 1990.

Emmerton, James A. *A Record of the Twenty-Third Regiment Mass. Vol. Infantry in the War of the Rebellion 1861–1865 with Alphabetical Roster; Company Rolls; Portraits; Maps; etc.* Boston: William Ware & Co., 1886.

Federal Writers' Project. *Slave Narratives*. 17 vols. Washington, D.C.: Work Projects Administration, 1941. Reprint, Westport, Conn.: Greenwood Publishing Co., 1972.

First Annual Report of the Educational Commission for Freedmen. Boston: Prentiss & Deland, Book and Job Printers, 1863.

[Gannett, William Channing and Edward Everett Hale]. "The Education of the Freedmen." *North American Review* 101 (October 1865): 528–49.

Graham, Matthew J. *The Ninth Regiment New York Volunteers (Hawkins' Zouaves) Being History of the Regiment and Veteran Association from 1860 to 1900*. New York: E. P. Coby & Co., 1900.

Hale, Edward E. "Some Notes on Roanoke Island and James River." *Proceedings of the American Antiquarian Society* (October 21, 1864): 52–58.

Hawkins, Rush C. "Early Coastal Operations in North Carolina." In *Battles and Leaders of the Civil War*, edited by R. U. Johnson and C. C. Buel, vol. 1, 632–59. New York: The Century Company, 1887.

[Howard, O. O.]. *Autobiography of Oliver Otis Howard, Major General United States Army*. 2 vols. New York: Baker and Taylor Company, 1907.

Howard, O. O. "The Freedmen During the War." *New Princeton Review* 1 (1886): 373–85.

——. *Report of Brevet Major General O. O. Howard, Commissioner Bureau of Refugees, Freedmen, and Abandoned Lands, To the Secretary of War, October 20, 1869*. Washington, D.C.: Government Printing Office, 1869.

Jackmon, Lyman. *History of the Sixth New Hampshire Regiment in the War for the Union*. Concord, N.H.: Republican Press Association, 1891.

James, Horace. *Address of the Rev. Horace James of Worcester, Mass., at the Anniversary of the American Home Mission Society, New York, May 7, 1856*. N.p., n.d.

——. *Annual Report of the Superintendent of Negro Affairs in North Carolina, 1864. With an Appendix, Containing the History and Management of the Freedmen in this Department up to June 1st, 1865*. Boston: W. F. Brown & Co., 1865.

——. *The Christian Patriot: A Sermon*. Worcester, Mass.: n.p., 1861.

——. *The Two Great Wars of America. An Oration Delivered in Newbern, North Carolina, Before the Twenty-Fifth Regiment Massachusetts Volunteers, July 4, 1862. By Rev. Horace James, Chaplain*. Boston: W. F. Brown & Co., 1862.

Johnson, Charles. *The Long Roll*. East Aurora, N.Y.: The Roycrofters, 1911. Reprint, Shepherdstown, W.Va.: Carabelle Books, 1986.

Lind, Henry C., ed. *The Long Road for Home: The Civil War Experiences of Four Farmboy Soldiers of the Twenty-Seventh Massachusetts Regiment of Volunteer Infantry as Told by their Personal Correspondence, 1861–1864*. London and Toronto: Associated University Presses, 1992.

Loving, Jerome M., ed. "Civil War Letters of George Washington Whitman from North Carolina." *North Carolina Historical Review* 50 (January 1973): 73–92.

Minutes of the Freedmen's Convention, Held in the City of Raleigh, on the 2nd, 3rd, 4th, and 5th of October, 1866. Raleigh: Standard Book and Job Office, 1866.

Moore, Frank, ed. *The Rebellion Record: A Diary of American Events, with Documents, Narratives, Illustrative Incidents, Poetry, Etc.* 11 vols. New York: G. P. Putnam, 1861–68.

Mottelay, Paul F., and T. Campbell-Copeland, eds. *The Soldier in Our Civil War: A Pictorial History of the Conflict, 1861–1865*. New York and Atlanta: Stanley Bradley Publishing Company, 1893.

Parker, Thomas H. *History of the 51st Regiment of P.V. and V.V. from Its Organization, at Camp Curtin, Harrisburg, Pa., in 1861, to its being mustered out of the United States Service at Alexandria, Va., July 27th, 1865*. Philadelphia: King & Baird, 1869.

[Pierce, Edward L.]. "The Contrabands at Fortress Monroe." *Atlantic Monthly* 8 (November 1861): 626–40.

Pierce, Edward L. "The Freedmen at Port Royal." *Atlantic Monthly* 12 (September 1863): 291–315.

Preliminary Report Touching the Condition and Management of Emancipated Refugees Made to the Secretary of War by the American Freedmen's Inquiry Commission, June 31, 1863. New York: John F. Trow, Printer, 1863.

Putnam, Samuel Henry. *The Story of Company A, Twenty-fifth Regiment, Mass. Vols. in the War of the Rebellion*. Worcester, Mass.: Putnam, Davis, and Co., 1886.

Roe, Alfred S. *The Twenty-Fourth Regiment Massachusetts Volunteers 1861–1866.* Worcester, Mass.: The Blanchard Press, 1907.

Schurz, Carl. *Intimate Letters of Carl Schurz, 1841–1869.* Translated and edited by Joseph Schaefer. Publications of the State Historical Society of Wisconsin Collections, vol. 30. Madison: State Historical Society of Wisconsin, 1928.

Second Annual Report of the New England Freedmen's Aid Society, (Educational Commission) Presented to the Society, April 21, 1864. Boston: New England Freedmen's Aid Society, 1864.

The Statutes at Large, Treaties, and Proclamations of the United States of America. Vols. 12–15. Boston: Little, Brown, 1863–69.

Trowbridge, J. T. *The South: A Tour of Its Battle-fields and Ruinded Cities.* Hartford, Conn.: L. Stebbins, 1866.

U.S. Congress. Senate Documents. 39th Cong., 2d sess. S. Doc. 6.

U.S. War Department. *The War of the Rebellion: A Compilation of the Official Records of the Union and Confederate Armies.* 128 vols. Washington, D.C.: Government Printing Office, 1880–1901.

Valentine, Herbert E. *Story of Co. F, 23d Massachusetts Volunteers in the War for the Union 1861–1865.* Boston: W. B. Clarke & Co., 1896.

Walcott, Charles Folsom. *History of the Twenty-first Regiment Massachusetts Volunteers in the War for the Preservation of the Union 1861–1865.* Boston: Houghton, Mifflin and Company, 1882.

Whitney, J. H. E. *The Hawkins Zouaves (Ninth N.Y.V.) Their Battles and Marches.* New York: J. H. E. Whitney, 1866.

Williams, George W. *A History of the Negro Troops in the War of the Rebellion, 1861–1865. Preceded by a Review of the Military Service of Negroes in Ancient and Modern Times.* New York: Harper & Brothers, 1888.

Wilson, Joseph T. *The Black Phalanx; A History of the Negro Soldiers of the United States in the Wars of 1775–1812, 1861–'65.* Hartford, Conn.: American Publishing Company, 1888.

Woodbury, Augustus. *Major General Ambrose E. Burnside and the Ninth Army Corps.* Providence, R.I.: Sidney S. Rider & Brother, 1867.

PRIMARY SOURCES IN ELECTRONIC FORM

"Ancestral File." *Family Search.* CD-ROM. Salt Lake City: Church of Jesus Christ of the Latter-Day Saints, 1987, 1995, 1996.

Ancestry.com. Civil War Research Database. Kingston, Mass.: Historical Data Systems, 1997, 1998, 1999. Available from http://www.ancestry.com/ancestry/search/cwrd/cwrd—index.htm.

"International Genealogical Index." *Family Search.* CD-ROM. Salt Lake City: Church of Jesus Christ of the Latter-Day Saints, 1987, 1995, 1996.

National Park Service. Civil War Soldiers and Sailors Project. Available from http://www.itd.nps.gov/cwss/usct.html.

Sahr, Robert. "Consumer Price Index (CPI) Conversion Factors to Convert to 1999

Dollars (Preliminary)." Corvallis, Ore.: Oregon State University, 1999. Available from http://www.orst.edu/dept/pol—sci/fac/sahr/cv1999/htm.
United States Census Index for North Carolina and South Carolina, 1870. CD-ROM. Orem, Utah: Automated Archives, 1994.

NEWSPAPERS

The American Freedman, various issues
American Missionary, 1857–70
The Congregationalist, 1861–67
Dare County Times, various issues
Frank Leslie's Illustrated Newspaper, 1861–66
The Freedman, January 1864–March 1869
The Freedman's Torchlight, December 1866
The Freedmen's Advocate, January 1864–January 1865
The Freedmen's Journal, 1866
The Freedmen's Record, various issues
Harper's New Monthly Magazine, 1862–66
Harper's Weekly, 1862–66
National Anti-Slavery Standard, 1861–67
The National Freedman, 1 March 1865–15 September 1866

SECONDARY SOURCES

Alexander, John, and James Lazell. *Ribbon of Sand*. Chapel Hill: Algonquin Books, 1992.
Alexander, Roberta Sue. "North Carolina Faces the Freedmen: Race Relations during Presidential Reconstruction, 1865–1867." 2 vols. Ph.D. diss., University of Chicago, 1974.
Alexander, Roberta Sue. "Hostility and Hope: Black Education in North Carolina during Presidential Reconstruction, 1865–1867." *North Carolina Historical Review* 53 (April 1976): 113–32.
——. *North Carolina Faces the Freedmen*. Durham: Duke University Press, 1985.
Amistad Research Center. *Author and Added Entry Catalog of the American Missionary Association Archives with Reference to Schools and Mission Stations*. 3 vols. Westport, Conn.: Greenwood Publishing Corporation, n.d.
Anderson, James D. *The Education of Blacks in the South, 1860–1935*. Chapel Hill: University of North Carolina Press, 1988.
Ash, Stephen V. *When the Yankees Came: Conflict and Chaos in the Occupied South, 1861–1865*. Chapel Hill: University of North Carolina Press, 1995.
Bahney, Robert Stanley. "Generals and Negroes: Education of Negroes by the Union Army, 1861–1865." Ph.D. diss., University of Michigan, 1965.
Baldwin, Thomas W., comp. *Vital Records of Milford Massachusetts, to the Year 1850*. Boston: Wright & Potter Printing Company, 1917.
Barrett, John G. *The Civil War in North Carolina*. Chapel Hill: University of North Carolina Press, 1963.

Beard, Augustus Field. *A Crusade of Brotherhood: A History of the American Missionary Association*. Boston: The Pilgrim Press, 1907. Reprint, New York: Kraus Reprint Co., 1970.

Belz, Herman. "Law, Politics, and Race in the Struggle for Equal Pay During the Civil War." *Civil War History* 22 (September 1976): 197–213.

Bentley, George R. *A History of the Freedmen's Bureau*. Philadelphia: University of Pennsylvania Press, 1944. Reprint, New York: Octagon Books, 1974.

Berlin, Ira, Barbara J. Fields, Thavolia Glymph, Joseph P. Reidy, and Leslie S. Rowland, eds. *The Destruction of Slavery*. Ser. 1, vol. 1 of *Freedom: A Documentary History of Emancipation, 1861–1867*. Cambridge: Cambridge University Press, 1985.

Berlin, Ira, Barbara J. Fields, Steven F. Miller, Joseph P. Reidy, and Leslie S. Rowland, eds. *Free at Last: A Documentary History of Slavery, Freedom, and the Civil War*. New York: The New Press, 1992.

Berlin, Ira, Thavolia Glymph, Steven F. Miller, Joseph P. Reidy, Leslie S. Rowland, and Julie Saville, eds. *The Wartime Genesis of Free Labor: The Lower South*. Ser. 1, vol. 3 of *Freedom: A Documentary History of Emancipation, 1861–1867*. Cambridge: Cambridge University Press, 1990.

Berlin, Ira, Steven F. Miller, Joseph P. Reidy, and Leslie S. Rowland, eds. *The Wartime Genesis of Free Labor: The Upper South*. Ser. 1, vol. 2 of *Freedom: A Documentary History of Emancipation, 1861–1867*. Cambridge: Cambridge University Press, 1993.

Berlin, Ira, Joseph P. Reidy, and Leslie S. Rowland, eds. *The Black Military Experience*. Ser. 2 of *Freedom: A Documentary History of Emancipation, 1861–1867*. Cambridge: Cambridge University Press, 1982.

Berlin, Ira, and Leslie S. Rowland, eds. *Families and Freedom: A Documentary History of African-American Kinship in the Civil War Era*. New York: The New Press, 1997.

Bozeman, John. "Technological Millenarianism in the United States." In *Millennium, Messiahs, and Mayhem*, edited by Thomas Robbins and Susan J. Palmer, 139–58. New York: Routledge, 1997.

Bremner, Robert H. *American Philanthropy*. 2d ed. Chicago and London: University of Chicago Press, 1988.

——. *The Public Good: Philanthropy and Welfare in the Civil War*. New York: Alfred A. Knopf, 1980.

Buker, George E. *Blockaders, Refugees, and Contrabands: Civil War on Florida's Gulf Coast, 1861–1865*. Tuscaloosa: University of Alabama Press, 1993.

Butchart, Ronald E. *Northern Schools, Southern Blacks, and Reconstruction: Freedmen's Education, 1862–1875*. Westport, Conn.: Greenwood Press, 1980.

——. "Recruits to the 'Army of Civilization': Gender, Race, Class, and the Freedmen's Teachers, 1862–1875," *Journal of Education* 172 (1990): 76–87.

Butler, Jon. *Awash in a Sea of Faith: Christianizing the American People*. Cambridge, Mass.: Harvard University Press, 1990.

Carroll, John M., ed. *The Black Military Experience in the American West*. New York: Liveright, 1971.

Carwardine, Richard J. *Evangelicals and Politics in Antebellum America*. New Haven: Yale University Press, 1993.

Cash, Wilbur J. *The Mind of the South*. New York: Alfred A. Knopf, 1941.

Cayton, Mary Kupiec. "Who Were the Evangelicals?: Conservative and Liberal Identity in the Unitarian Controversy in Boston, 1804–1833." *Journal of Social History* 31 (Fall 1997): 85–107.

Click, Patricia C. "Letting In the Light: The Freedmen's Colony on Roanoke Island, 1862–1867." Manteo, N.C.: Town of Manteo, 1981.

Cole, Charles C., Jr. *The Social Ideas of the Northern Evangelists, 1826–1860*. New York: Columbia University Press, 1954.

Cornish, Dudley Taylor. *The Sable Arm: Negro Troops in the Union Army, 1861–1865*. New York: Longmans, Green and Co., 1956.

Couch, Danny, Noah Price, and Shawn Gray. "A History of the United States Life-Saving Service on Hatteras Island." *Sea Chest* 4 (Winter 1977): 1–62.

Coulter, E. Merton, *The South During Reconstruction, 1865–1877*. Baton Rouge: Louisiana State University Press, 1947.

Cox, LaWanda, and John H. Cox. "General O. O. Howard and the Misrepresented Bureau." *Journal of Southern History* 19 (November 1953): 426–56.

——. *Reconstruction, the Negro, and the New South*. Columbia: University of South Carolina Press, 1973.

Crow, Jeffrey J., and Flora J. Hatley. *Black Americans in North Carolina and the South*. Chapel Hill: University of North Carolina Press, 1984.

Currie-McDaniel, Ruth. "Northern Women in the South, 1860–1880." *The Georgia Historical Quarterly* 76 (Summer 1992): 284–312.

Davis, Hugh. *Joshua Leavitt: Evangelical Abolitionist*. Baton Rouge: Louisiana State University Press, 1990.

Davis, Robert Scott, Jr. "Freedmen's Bureau and Other Reconstruction Sources for Research in African-American Families, 1865–1874." *The Journal of the Afro-American Historical and Genealogical Society* 9 (Winter 1988): 171–76.

DeBoer, Clara. *Be Jubilant My Feet*. New York: Garland, 1994.

D'Entremont, John Philip. "White Officers and Black Troops, 1864–1865." Master's thesis, University of Virginia, 1974.

Drake, Richard Bryant. "The American Missionary Association and the Southern Negro, 1861–1888." Ph.D. diss., Emory University, 1957.

Dunbar, Gary S. *Historical Geography of the North Carolina Outer Banks*. Baton Rouge: Louisiana State University Press, 1958.

Dyer, Brainerd. "The Treatment of Colored Union Troops by the Confederates, 1861–1865." *Journal of Negro History* 20 (July 1935): 273–86.

Dyer, Frederick H. *A Compendium of the War of the Rebellion*. 3 vols. Dayton, Ohio: Morningside Press, 1979.

Elmore, Ashby Dunn. "Military and Naval Operations in the Region of the Albemarle Sound, 1862–1864." Master's thesis, East Carolina University, 1971.

Engs, Robert Francis. *Freedom's First Generation: Black Hampton, Virginia, 1861–1890*. Philadelphia: University of Pennsylvania Press, 1979.

Epstein, Barbara Leslie. *The Politics of Domesticity: Women, Evangelism, and Temperance in Nineteenth-century America*. Middletown, Conn.: Wesleyan University Press, 1981.

Evans, W. McKee. *Ballots and Fence Rails*. Chapel Hill: University of North Carolina Press, 1967.

Foner, Eric. *Free Soil, Free Labor, Free Men: The Ideology of the Republican Party Before the Civil War*. London: Oxford University Press, 1970.

———. *Politics and Ideology in the Age of the Civil War*. New York and Oxford: Oxford University Press, 1980.

———. *Reconstruction: America's Unfinished Revolution, 1863–1865*. New York: Harper & Row, 1988.

Foote, Shelby. *Fort Sumter to Perryville*. Vol. 1 of *The Civil War: A Narrative*. New York: Random House, 1958.

Fowler, Arlen L. *The Black Infantry in the West, 1869–1891*. Westport, Conn.: Greenwood Publishing Corporation, 1971.

Franklin, John Hope. *The Free Negro in North Carolina, 1790–1860*. Chapel Hill: University of North Carolina Press, 1943. Reprint, Chapel Hill: University of North Carolina Press, 1995.

———. *From Slavery to Freedom: A History of Negro Americans*. 3d ed. New York: Vintage Books, 1969.

———. *Reconstruction after the Civil War*. Chicago and London: University of Chicago Press, 1961. Reprint, Chicago: University of Chicago Press, 1994.

Fraser, James N. *Pedagogue for God's Kingdom: Lyman Beecher and the Second Great Awakening*. Lanham, N.Y., and London: University Press of America, 1985.

Fredrickson, George M. *The Black Image in the White Mind: The Debate on Afro-American Character and Destiny*. New York: Harper and Row, 1971. Reprint, Hanover, N.H.: Wesleyan University Press, 1987.

Gaillard, Frye, Richard Maschal, and Ed Williams. *Becoming Truly Free: 300 Years of Black History in the Carolinas*. Charlotte, N.C.: The Charlotte Observer, 1985.

Gerteis, Louis S. *From Contraband to Freedman: Federal Policy Toward Southern Blacks, 1861–1865*. Westport, Conn.: Greenwood Press, 1973.

Glatthaar, Joseph T. *Forged in Battle: The Civil War Alliance of Black Soldiers and White Officers*. New York: The Free Press, 1990.

Goen, C. C. *Broken Churches, Broken Nation: The Churches and the Civil War*. Macon, Ga.: Mercer University Press, 1986.

Goldhaber, Michael. "A Mission Unfulfilled: Freedmen's Education in North Carolina, 1865–1870." *Journal of Negro History* 77 (Fall 1992): 199–210.

Gomes, Peter J. *The Good Book: Reading the Bible with Mind and Heart*. New York: William Morrow and Company, 1996.

Green, Constance McLaughlin. *Washington: Village and Capital, 1800–1878*. Princeton, N.J.: Princeton University Press, 1962.

Gutman, Herbert G. *The Black Family in Slavery and Freedom, 1750–1925*. New York: Random House, 1976.

Hamilton, J. G. de Roulhac. *Reconstruction in North Carolina*. New York: Columbia University Press, 1914.

Hardesty, Nancy A. *Women Called to Witness: Evangelical Feminism in the 19th Century*. Nashville: Abingdon Press, 1984.

———. *Your Daughters Shall Prophesy: Revivalism and Feminism in the Age of Finney*. Brooklyn: Carlson Publishing, 1991.

Harris, William C. "Lincoln and Wartime Reconstruction in North Carolina, 1861–1863." *North Carolina Historical Review* 63 (April 1986): 149–68.

Hatch, Nathan O. *The Democratization of American Christianity*. New Haven: Yale University Press, 1989.

Hermann, Janet Sharp. *The Pursuit of a Dream*. New York and Oxford: Oxford University Press, 1981.

Hoffert, Sylvia D. "Yankee Schoolmarms and the Domestication of the South." *Southern Studies* 24 (Summer 1985): 188–201.

Howard, Victor B. *Religion and the Radical Republican Movement, 1860–1870*. Lexington: University Press of Kentucky, 1990.

Hummel, Jeffrey Rogers. *Emancipating Slaves, Enslaving Free Men*. Chicago and LaSalle: Open Court, 1996.

Jeffrey, Julie Roy. *The Great Silent Army of Abolitionism: Ordinary Women in the Antislavery Movement*. Chapel Hill and London: University of North Carolina Press, 1998.

Johnson, Clifton Herman. "The American Missionary Association, 1846–1861: A Study of Christian Abolitionism." Ph.D. diss., University of North Carolina, 1958.

Johnson, Curtis D. *Redeeming America: Evangelicals and the Road to Civil War*. Chicago: Ivan R. Dee, 1993.

Jones, Jacqueline. "Men and Women in Northern New England During the Era of the Civil War." *Maine Historical Society Quarterly* (Fall 1993): 70–87.

——. *Soldiers of Light and Love: Northern Teachers and Georgia Blacks, 1865–1873*. Chapel Hill: University of North Carolina Press, 1980.

——. "Women Who Were More Than Men: Sex and Status in Freedmen's Teaching." *History of Education Quarterly* (Spring 1979): 47–59.

Jones, Maxine Deloris. " 'A Glorious Work': The American Missionary Association and Black North Carolinians, 1863–1880." Ph.D. diss., Florida State University, 1982.

Joy, Deborah. "Archaeological Screening, Proposed US 64-264 Relocation from West of Manns Harbor to South of Manteo in Dare County, North Carolina." Raleigh: North Carolina Department of Transportation, Division of Highways, Planning and Environmental Branch, July 1994.

Kenzer, Robert C. *Enterprising Southerners: Black Economic Success in North Carolina, 1865–1915*. Charlottesville: University Press of Virginia, 1997.

Khoury, Angel Ellis. *Manteo: A Roanoke Island Town*. Virginia Beach, Va.: Donning Company Publishers, 1999.

Lader, Lawrence. *The Bold Brahmins: New England's War Against Slavery: 1831–1863*. New York: E. P. Dutton and Co., 1961.

Lautzenheiser, Loretta, and Jane M. Eastman. "Archaeological Survey, Proposed Visitors Center, Alligator River National Wildlife Refuge, Roanoke Island, Dare County, North Carolina." Tarboro, N.C.: Coastal Carolina Research, 1993.

Lautzenheiser, Loretta, and Thomas Hargrove. " '. . . The Bright Glittering Sand': Archaeological Survey and Test Excavations, Site 31DR61, Roanoke Island, Dare County, North Carolina." Tarboro and Raleigh: Coastal Carolina Research and Archaeological Research Consultants, 1991.

Leckie, William H. *The Buffalo Soldiers: A Narrative of the Negro Cavalry in the West*. Norman: University of Oklahoma Press, 1967.

Leech, Margaret. *Reveille in Washington, 1860–1865*. New York: Harper & Brothers, 1941.

Lefler, Hugh Talmage, and Albert Ray Newsome. *North Carolina: The History of a Southern State*. 3d ed. Chapel Hill: University of North Carolina Press, 1979.

Leloudis, James L. *Schooling the New South: Pedagogy, Self, and Society in North Carolina, 1880–1920*. Chapel Hill: University of North Carolina Press, 1996.

Lesick, Lawrence Thomas. *The Lane Rebels: Evangelicalism and Antislavery in Antebellum America*. Metuchen, N.J.: The Scarecrow Press, 1980.

Levine, Bruce. *Half Slave and Half Free: The Roots of the Civil War*. New York: Hill and Wang, 1992.

Linthicum, Nancy Smith. "The American Missionary Association and North Carolina Freedmen, 1863–1868." Master's thesis, North Carolina State University, 1977.

Litwack, Leon F. *Been in the Storm So Long*. New York: Alfred A. Knopf, 1980.

Long, Mary Wood. "The Five Lost Colonies of Dare." Unpublished manuscript in the collection of John F. Wilson IV, Manteo, N.C., [1968?].

Longacre, Edward C. *Army of Amateurs: General Benjamin F. Butler and the Army of the James, 1863–1865*. Mechanicsburg, Pa.: Stackpole Books, 1997.

——. "Brave Radical Wild: The Contentious Career of Brigadier General Edward A. Wild." *Civil War Times Illustrated* 19 (June 1980): 8–19.

Luvaas, Jay. "Burnside's Roanoke Island Campaign." *Civil War Times Illustrated* 7 (December 1968): 4–11, 48.

McCaslin, Richard B. *Portraits of Conflict: A Photographic History of North Carolina in the Civil War*. Fayetteville: University of Arkansas Press, 1997.

McConnell, William F. *Remember Reno: A Biography of Major General Jesse Lee Reno*. Shippensburg, Pa.: White Mane Publishing Co., 1996.

McFeely, William S. *Yankee Stepfather: General O. O. Howard and the Freedmen*. New Haven: Yale University Press, 1968.

McLoughlin, William G. *The American Evangelicals 1800–1900: An Anthology*. Gloucester, Mass.: Peter Smith, 1976.

McPherson, James M. *The Abolitionist Legacy: From Reconstruction to the NAACP*. Princeton: Princeton University Press, 1975.

——. *Battle Cry of Freedom*. New York and Oxford: Oxford University Press, 1988.

——. *For Cause and Comrades: Why Men Fought in the Civil War*. New York and Oxford: Oxford University Press, 1997.

——. *The Negro's Civil War: How American Negroes Felt and Acted During the War for the Union*. New York: Pantheon Books, 1965.

——. *The Struggle for Equality: Abolitionists and the Negro in the Civil War and Reconstruction*. Princeton: Princeton University Press, 1964.

McPherson, James M., And William J. Cooper Jr., eds. *Writing the Civil War: The Quest to Understand*. Columbia: University of South Carolina Press, 1998.

Magdol, Edward. *A Right to the Land: Essays on the Freedmen's Community*. Westport, Conn.: Greenwood Press, 1977.

Mallison, Fred M. *The Civil War on the Outer Banks*. Jefferson, N.C.: McFarland & Company, Publishers, 1998.

Mandle, Jay R. *Not Slave, Not Free*. Durham: Duke University Press, 1992.

Marsden, George M. *The Evangelical Mind and the New School Presbyterian Experience.* New Haven: Yale University Press, 1970.
Mathews, Donald G. "The Abolitionists on Slavery: The Critique Behind the Social Movement." *Journal of Southern History* 33 (May 1967): 163–82.
Mitchell, Mark S. "A History of the Black Population of New Bern, North Carolina, 1862–1872." Master's thesis, East Carolina University, 1980.
Mobley, Joe A. *James City: A Black Community in North Carolina, 1863–1900.* Raleigh: North Carolina Division of Archives and History, 1981.
——. *Ship Ashore!: The U.S. Lifesavers of Coastal North Carolina.* Raleigh: North Carolina Division of Archives and History, 1994.
Moebs, Thomas Truxtun. *Black Soldiers-Black Sailors-Black Ink: Research Guide on African-Americans in U.S. Military History, 1526–1900.* Chesapeake Bay [Va.] and Paris: Moebs Publishing Company, 1994.
Moorhead, James H. "Between Progress and Apocalypse: A Reassessment of Millennialism in American Religious Thought, 1800–1880." *Journal of American History* 71 (December 1984): 524–42.
Morris, Robert C. *Reading, 'Riting, and Reconstruction: The Education of Freedmen in the South, 1861–1870.* Chicago: University of Chicago Press, 1981.
Mount Holyoke College Alumnae Association. *One Hundred Year Biographical Directory of Mount Holyoke College 1837–1937.* South Hadley, Mass.: Alumnae Association of Mount Holyoke College, 1937.
"Names of Keepers and Surfmen 1874–1914." *Sea Chest* 4 (Winter 1977): 49–62.
Nevins, Allan. *War Becomes Revolution.* Vol. 2 of *The War for the Union.* New York: Charles Scribner's Sons, 1960.
Oubre, Claude F. *Forty Acres and a Mule: The Freedmen's Bureau and Black Land Ownership.* Baton Rouge: Louisiana State University Press, 1978.
Parker, Freddie L. *Stealing a Little Freedom: Advertisements for Slave Runaways in North Carolina, 1791–1840.* New York: Garland Publishing, 1994.
Peacock, John R. III. "The Roanoke Island Campaign of 1862." Master's thesis, Virginia Polytechnic Institute and State University, 1981.
Pease, William H., and Jane H. Pease. *Black Utopia: Negro Communal Experiments in America.* Madison: State Historical Society of Wisconsin, 1963.
Pierce, Paul Skeels. *The Freedmen's Bureau: A Chapter in the History of Reconstruction.* 1904. Reprint, New York: Haskell House, 1971.
Powell, Lawrence N. *New Masters: Northern Planters during the Civil War and Reconstruction.* New Haven: Yale University Press, 1980.
Quarles, Benjamin. *The Negro in the Civil War.* Boston: Little, Brown and Company, 1953.
Redford, Dorothy Spruill. *Somerset Homecoming: Recovering a Lost Heritage.* New York: Doubleday, 1988.
Redkey, Edwin S. "Black Chaplains in the Union Army." *Civil War History* 33 (December 1987): 331–50.
——, ed. *A Grand Army of Black Men: Letters from African-American Soldiers in the Union Army, 1861–1865.* Cambridge: Cambridge University Press, 1992.
——, ed. *Respect Black! The Writings and Speeches of Henry McNeal Turner.* New York: Arno Press, 1971.

Reid, Richard. "Raising the African Brigade: Early Black Recruitment in Civil War North Carolina." *North Carolina Historical Review* 70 (July 1993): 266–301.

Reidy, Joseph P. " 'Coming from the Shadow of the Past': The Transition from Slavery to Freedom at Freedmen's Village, 1863–1900." *Virginia Magazine of History and Biography* 95 (October 1987): 403–28.

Reilly, Stephen Edward. "Reconstruction through Regeneration: Horace James' Work with Blacks for Social Reform in North Carolina, 1862–1827." Ph.D. diss., Duke University, 1983.

Reilly, Wayne E., ed. *Sarah Jane Foster, Teacher of the Freedmen: A Diary and Letters.* Charlottesville: University Press of Virginia, 1990.

Richardson, Joe M. *Christian Reconstruction: The American Missionary Association and Southern Blacks, 1861–1890*. Athens: University of Georgia Press, 1986.

Rose, Willie Lee. *Rehearsal for Reconstruction: The Port Royal Experiment.* New York: Bobbs-Merrill Company, 1964.

Sauers, Richard Allen. "General Ambrose E. Burnside's 1862 North Carolina Campaign." Ph.D. diss., Pennsylvania State University, 1987.

Shannon, Fred A. "The Federal Government and the Negro Soldier, 1861–1865." *Journal of Negro History* 11 (October 1926): 563–83.

Shattuck, Gardiner H., Jr. *A Shield and Hiding Place: The Religious Life of Civil War Armies*. Macon, Ga.: Mercer University Press, 1987.

Sifakis, Stewart. *Who Was Who in the Union*. New York: Facts on File, 1988.

Small, Sandra E. "The Yankee Schoolmarm in Freedmen's Schools: An Analysis of Attitudes." *Journal of Southern History* 45 (August 1979): 381–402.

Smith, Timothy L. *Revivalism and Social Reform.* Baltimore: Johns Hopkins University Press, 1980.

Sommers, Richard J. "The Dutch Gap Affair: Military Atrocities and the Rights of Negro Soldiers." *Civil War History* 21: 51–64.

Soper, J. Christopher. *Evangelical Christianity in the United States and Great Britain: Religious Beliefs, Political Choices*. New York: New York University Press, 1994.

Sorin, Gerald. *Abolitionism: A New Perspective*. New York: Praeger Publishers, 1972.

Spraggins, Tinsley Lee. "Mobilization of Negro Labor for the Department of Virginia and North Carolina, 1861–1865." *North Carolina Historical Review* 24 (April 1947): 160–97.

Stephens, Marcus Cicero. *History of the Public Schools of North Carolina*. Chapel Hill: University of North Carolina Press, 1930.

Stewart, James Brewer. *Holy Warriors: The Abolitionists and American Slavery*. New York: Hill and Wang, 1976.

Stick, David. *Dare County: A History*. Raleigh: North Carolina State Department of Archives and History, 1970.

——. *Graveyard of the Atlantic: Shipwrecks of the North Carolina Coast.* Chapel Hill: University of North Carolina Press, 1952.

——. *The Outer Banks of North Carolina, 1584–1958*. Chapel Hill: University of North Carolina Press, 1958.

Swint, Henry L. *Dear Ones at Home: Letters from Contraband Camps*. Nashville: Vanderbilt University Press, 1966.

——. *The Northern Teacher in the South, 1862–1870*. Nashville: Vanderbilt University Press, 1941.

Topsfield Historical Society. *Vital Records of Gloucester Massachusetts to the End of the Year 1849*. Vol. 1, *Births*. Salem, Mass.: Newcomb and Gauss Printers, 1917.

Trotter, William R. *Ironclads and Columbiads: The Civil War in North Carolina*. Vol. 3, *The Coast*. Winston-Salem, N.C.: John F. Blair, 1989.

Trudeau, Noah Andre. *Like Men of War: Black Troops in the Civil War 1862–1865*. Boston: Little, Brown and Company, 1998.

Walker, Cam. "Corinth: The Story of a Contraband Camp." *Civil War History* 20 (March 1974): 5–22.

Wauzzinski, Robert A. *Between God and Gold: Protestant Evangelicalism and the Industrial Revolution, 1820–1914*. London: Associated University Presses, 1993.

Weisenfeld, Judith. " 'Who Is Sufficient for These Things?': Sara G. Stanley and the American Missionary Association, 1864–1868." *Church History* 60 (December 1991): 493–507.

Westwood, Howard C. *Black Troops, White Commanders, and Freedmen*. Carbondale: University of Southern Illinois Press, 1992.

White, Barnetta McGhee. *Somebody Knows My Name*. 3 vols. Athens, Ga.: Iberia Publishing Co., 1995.

White, Gwen A. "Richard Etheridge: An American Coastal Hero." *Journal of Marine Education* 1 (Summer 1980): 5–6.

Williams, Hessie Severt. "A Comparative Analysis of Ex-Slave Thoughts Concerning Their Masters, the United States Army, and Freedom." Master's thesis, University of North Carolina, 1969.

Williams, Talcott. "The Surroundings and Site at Raleigh's Colony." In *Annual Report of the American Historical Association 1895*. Washington, D.C.: Government Printing Office, 1896.

Wolfe, Allis. "Women Who Dared: Northern Teachers of the Southern Freedmen, 1862–1872." Ph.D. diss., City University of New York, 1982.

Wright, David, and David Zoby. "Ignoring Jim Crow: The Turbulent Appointment of Richard Etheridge and the Pea Island Lifesavers." *Journal of Negro History* 80 (Spring 1995): 66–80.

Wright, Gavin. *Old South, New South: Revolutions in the Southern Economy Since the Civil War*. New York: Basic Books, 1986.

Younts, Doris Ann. *Dare County Cemeteries*. [Currituck, N.C.]: Albemarle Genealogical Society, 1983.

Zipf, Karin L. " 'The WHITES Shall Rule the Land or Die': Gender, Race, and Class in North Carolina Reconstruction Politics." *Journal of Southern History* 55 (August 1999): 499–534.

Index